The Psychological Legacy of Slavery

The Psychological Legacy of Slavery

Essays on Trauma, Healing and the Living Past

Edited by
BENJAMIN P. BOWSER
and AIMÉ CHARLES-NICOLAS

Foreword *by* Ali Moussa Iye

McFarland & Company, Inc., Publishers
Jefferson, North Carolina

This book has undergone peer review.

Sponsored by The Slave Route: Resistance, Liberty, Heritage, United Nations Educational, Scientific and Cultural Organization

This collection is based on a conference held in Martinique and Guadeloupe, October 2016. Parts of this book are revised and updated from an originally published version in French as *L'esclavage: quel impact sur la psychologie des populations?* edited by Aimé Charles-Nicolas and Benjamin P. Bowser (Paris: Idem, 2018). Permission received from Natan Kellermann to reprint p. 77 of *Holocaust Trauma: Psychological Effects and Treatment* (New York: Iuniverse: 2009).

LIBRARY OF CONGRESS CATALOGUING-IN-PUBLICATION DATA

Names: Bowser, Benjamin P., editor. | Charles Nicolas, Aimé, editor. | Ali Moussa Iye, writer of foreword.
Title: The psychological legacy of slavery : essays on trauma, healing and the living past / edited by Benjamin P. Bowser and Aimé Charles-Nicolas ; foreword by Ali Moussa Iye.
Description: Jefferson, North Carolina : McFarland & Company, Inc., 2021 | Includes bibliographical references and index.
Identifiers: LCCN 2021005152 | ISBN 9781476678931 (paperback : acid free paper) ∞
ISBN 9781476642338 (ebook)
Subjects: LCSH: Slavery—Psychological aspects. | Freedmen—Psychology. | Children of freedmen—Psychology. | Slaveholders—Psychology.
Classification: LCC HT871 .P79 2021 | DDC 306.3/62—dc23
LC record available at https://lccn.loc.gov/2021005152

BRITISH LIBRARY CATALOGUING DATA ARE AVAILABLE

ISBN (print) 978-1-4766-7893-1
ISBN (ebook) 978-1-4766-4233-8

© 2021 Benjamin P. Bowser and Aimé Charles-Nicolas. All rights reserved

No part of this book may be reproduced or transmitted in any form or by any means, electronic or mechanical, including photocopying or recording, or by any information storage and retrieval system, without permission in writing from the publisher.

Front cover image © 2021 Shutterstock

Printed in the United States of America

McFarland & Company, Inc., Publishers
Box 611, Jefferson, North Carolina 28640
www.mcfarlandpub.com

To the millions of enslaved Africans
who were taken from their families
and stripped of their names, histories, identities,
and humanity for the profit and comfort of a few

A slaveholder's record from *Eighth Census of the United States 1860*, Series Number M653; Record Group: Records of the Bureau of the Census; Record Group Number 29 (National Archives).

Acknowledgments

We would like to acknowledge the tireless work and vision of Paul Lovejoy, Distinguished Research Professor, Department of History, Director, Harriet Tubman Institute for Research on the Global Migration of African Peoples, York University, and Rina Cáceres, Universidad de Costa Rica. It was their efforts that created the network of scholars and visionaries who made this work possible. Ali Moussa Iye, former director of the Slave Route Project in the History and Memory for Dialogue Section of UNESCO, asked the essential questions and provided steady leadership.

James Jackson, Daniel Katz Distinguished University Professor of Psychology, University of Michigan, and Thomas A. LaVeist, Dean of the Tulane University School of Public Health & Tropical Medicine in New Orleans, Louisiana, provided early support and encouragement for the participation of U.S. scholars and researchers. They did so when a National Institute of Health review panel would not.

L'Association First Caraïbes organized and sponsored the Colloque Scientifique International from which this work came. Their warm welcome to Martinique and Guadeloupe provided us with a home and inspired participants and conferees alike. Many thanks to Mr. Desnel for copyright release of the original chapters of this book in French, *L'Esclavage: quel impact sur la psychologie des populations?* We are appreciative of the support of the colloquium's Honorary Committee under the chairmanship of First Lady Michelle Obama as well as Nobel Prize winners in literature Wole Soyinka, J.M.G. Le Clezio, Derek Walcott, and the late Toni Morrison. We are appreciative as well for support from the Groupe Bernard Hayot and the Collectivité Territoriale de Martinique, République Française. Finally, we pay a special tribute to the late Professor François Sauvagnat.

Table of Contents

Acknowledgments   vi

Foreword: Engaging the Silence and Healing Post-Slavery Societies
    Ali Moussa Iye   1

Introduction: Psychological Legacies of Slavery
    Aimé Charles-Nicolas *and* Benjamin P. Bowser   5

Part One: Commonalities   33

1. Colorism in Belize
    Elma Whittaker-Augustine   34

2. Slavery and Psychological Trauma in the Haitian Crisis
    Judite Blanc   46

3. Afro-Brazilian Youth: Slavery's Influence on Crime
    Andréa Máris Campos Guerra
    and Ana Carolina André-Cadar   66

4. Slavery's Legacy in San Basilio Palenque, Colombia
    Alexandra Escobar Puche   80

5. Those Who Disappeared
    Bernard Dossa   89

Part Two: Concepts   97

6. A Psychiatric Look at the Legacy of Slavery
    Aimé Charles-Nicolas   98

7. Explaining Post Traumatic Slave Syndrome: Multigenerational Transmission of Trauma
    Joy A. DeGruy   117

8. An Exploration of the Psychological Legacy of Slavery
    BENJAMIN P. BOWSER   140

 9. The Psychological Legacy of Slavery in the United States:
    Trauma Derived from Centuries of Laws and Customs
    EDWIN J. NICHOLS   161

10. The Epigenetic Ramifications of the Trauma: Enslavement,
    Centuries of Chattel Slavery and Institutionalized Racism
    FATIMAH JACKSON, LATIFA JACKSON
    and ZAINAB EL RADI JACKSON   184

Part Three: Solutions   209

11. Shattering Delusions of Slavery: Psychosocial Re-Engineering
    of Postcolonial Jamaica
    FREDERICK W. HICKLING   210

12. How to Conduct a Psycho-Social History
    BENJAMIN P. BOWSER   230

13. Healing the Wounds of Slavery: Potentials and Challenges
    SCHERTO GILL   239

*Conclusion: Recommendations and Healing, Releasing
Trauma's Grip*
     AIMÉ CHARLES-NICOLAS *and* BENJAMIN P. BOWSER   257

Coda: Masters and Slaves No More
     BENJAMIN P. BOWSER *and* AIMÉ CHARLES-NICOLAS   279

About the Contributors   291

Index   297

Foreword

Engaging the Silence and Healing Post-Slavery Societies

Ali Moussa Iye

There has been surprisingly little attention and discussion of what the slave trade and slavery left for the functioning of contemporary societies with histories of slavery. The silence is deafening, indicating an unwillingness to address this issue. For so long, this tragedy has been ignored in the affected countries, especially for descendants of enslaved Africans who suffer the undefined consequences of slavery to this day.

Today, we know little about the reasons that have allowed this shame and guilt to go on for so long, turning major historical events into national secrets. The very idea that the descendants of slaves rather than of slaveholders might be due some consideration, if not compensation, has been met with denial and avoidance at all levels. Public authorities and administrations, as well as researchers, educators, health professionals, journalists, and families, for different reasons, observe silence about slavery and its potential legacy. They do not want to open Pandora's Box and the chaos that might ensue. However, as expected, efforts to obscure the legacy of slavery stand as obstacles to contemporary social justice, understanding history, national reconciliation, and an untroubled future—for a good reason.

Genetic research has shown the possibility that genetic markers have recorded the great traumas suffered by slave descendants and can be passed on to subsequent generations. For victims of the violence and cruelty of slave trafficking and slavery, forgotten traumatic events mark their whole life. They experienced capture, the march to the ocean, the hoarding, the terrible voyage at sea, sales, enslavement, cruel punishment, rape, and separation of slave families as well as resistance and their fight for freedom.

For decades now, the truth of this tragic story has been revealed to the world through the courageous actions of a few writers, researchers, educators, and civil society activists. This tragedy has become both a subject of study and a field of intervention in the social and human sciences. It has also become a source of reflection and inspiration for all those wishing to understand the roots of contemporary socio-economic inequalities, racial prejudices, and the conflicts dividing post-colonial societies.

In launching the Slave Route Project in 1994, UNESCO wanted to encourage this movement and contribute internationally to these efforts to break the silence regarding the greatest modern human tragedy. We did so because of its duration, many victims, the barbarism that accompanied it, and the monstrous beliefs that justified it. The research that we have carried out in various parts of the world has led us to this conclusion: Without studying the ongoing psychological consequences of this tragedy, we will not be able to understand the societies born of slavery.

The research and explorations in this collection are crucial in helping to understand several things. First are our perceptions of self and others. Second is the reproduction of practices born in slavery that continue to subjugate and to exploit descendants of slaves today. The third is to understand how prejudices and racism have been internalized, producing fears, resentments, and repressions. This knowledge is crucial to eventual reconciliation and resolution of the slave trade, slavery, and their continuing legacies.

Without a minimal awareness, knowledge, and exploration of trauma during and after slavery, it would not be possible to mobilize existing social interventions, educational programs, historical narratives, therapies, and medical care to address the continuing psychological legacy of slavery. At every meeting we have organized as part of the Slave Route Project throughout the Western Hemisphere, we have learned some new ways that slavery continues to influence the present, that slavery still triggers emotional responses, and how bitter are slavery's wounds.

It is important to remember that this legacy affects the psychology and social behavior of both the descendants of the enslaved and the descendants of slave owners. Recognizing this duality between the heirs of this history is essential for them to confront together this collective past and to discuss reconciliation frankly. In Toronto in 2010, we organized an exploration of the psychological consequences of slavery in a workshop titled "New Approaches to Teaching, Trafficking, and Slavery." The panels exchanged experiences, reviewed the research on this issue, and identified our gaps in knowledge.

For this reason, UNESCO joined the 2016 Martinique conference to deepen this reflection, to share the results of the latest studies, and to define the axes for future research. The conclusions of these conferences and this collection will undoubtedly make a significant contribution to the International Decade of People of African Descent (2015–2024) proclaimed by the United Nations under the theme "Recognition, Justice, and Development."

This Decade provides a framework and an operational platform between states and civil societies to combat stereotypes and racial prejudice against people of African descent. Also, public policies will be adopted to redress the social injustices inherited from our history of slavery and to promote the contribution of Afro-descendants and Africans to the progress of humanity and the construction of modern societies.

This Decade is also a continuation of the 2001 Durban World Conference against Racism, which recognized human trafficking and slavery as a crime against humanity. UNESCO has worked on these issues through its Slave Route and General History of Africa programs. We have been asked to contribute recommendations for program activities for the Decade. They include:

- To promote better knowledge, recognition of the culture, history, and heritage of people of African descent through research, education, and setting up sites and places of memory and reflection.
- To convince the Member States to revise textbooks and other educational materials to reflect appropriately the historical facts relating to the tragedies suffered by slave descendants, in particular, the slave trade, slavery, and colonialism.
- To help combat discrimination against people of African descent in access to quality education to counteract prejudice, stereotyping, stigmatization, and profiling.

The conference in Martinique from which this publication came provides insight into the lines of investigation that research institutes, universities, international and regional institutions, and civil society organizations will be able to utilize to advance their work within the framework of the International Decade of People of African Descent. We are pleased to have this contribution to such important work.

Ali Moussa Iye is the former chief of the History and Memory for Dialogue Section, Division of Social Transformation and Intercultural Dialogue, UNESCO.

Introduction

Psychological Legacies of Slavery[1]

Aimé Charles-Nicolas
and Benjamin P. Bowser

Slavery is a word with a multitude of meanings, like a Russian nesting doll, where each successive reality is smaller and smaller, but where the meanings the word implies are more significant and more substantial. Frequent anonymous comments are: "Slavery has always existed." "It's a universal practice." "Slavery fades away in the night of passing time." "Every civilization has practiced slavery." "There were traces of it in Neolithic times!" These characterizations are laden with denial and dilute the meaning of slavery in the West to the point where it is indistinguishable from every other form of human exploitation and forced dependence.

We understand very well what Camus meant when he stressed that misnaming things adds to the world's woes. This assertion has never been more valid than its reference to the transatlantic slave trade, which went on from the sixteenth through the nineteenth centuries. The ultimate objective of this book is to understand its effects. However, we do not ignore or minimize the existence of contemporary forms of slavery and trafficking. There are Arab-Muslim slavery, traffic in the Indian Ocean region, domestic slavery in Black Africa, sexual trafficking in the Slavic countries, the persecution of Christians in the Mediterranean region, and Greco-Roman slavery. In contrast, the transatlantic slave trade was the only one conducted by Europeans of Africans. It changed slavery in nature, scale, and profitability. Beginning in the fifteenth century, Europeans uniquely "racialized" the African slave trade, creating a stratified vision of humanity based upon physical differences in appearance. After the abolition of African slavery in the nineteenth century, fabricated racial theories were provided as rationales—evolutionist, craniometrics, and phrenological theories.[2] These theories also served as "scientific" justification for the hierarchy intricately interwoven into colonization that placed the Negro somewhere between the apes and man in Darwin's evolutionary system.

It is important to note that Europe and the United States formulated and fine-tuned these theories of race *after* the abolition of African slavery. It should be understood that the underlying functions of slavery were to keep the Other at a distance and to protect the integrity of beneficiaries. For example, in the United States, when there was no longer a legal foundation for slavery, it was urgent and essential to reinforce its scientific underpinnings and to have a legislative framework for racial segregation. In effect, African slavery was used to relegate Blacks to a position of inferiority, projecting racism forward in time as slavery's legacy. Where and when did the necessity for such theories, laws, and practices begin?

It all began with the Middle Passage of Africans transported to the West as slaves. The conditions imposed on slaves during the crossing of the Atlantic meet the criteria for Bruno Bettelheim's "extreme situation" (Bettelheim, 1940, 1979). Africans captured as slaves spent up to two months in ships' holes in "less space than a corpse in a coffin."[3] Any human being would be traumatized by such an experience. The necessity to ignore and deny the Middle Passage, and subsequent exploitation and mistreatment that began with the transatlantic slave trade, was the beginning of the refusal of the present to consider the past.

But Why Are We Talking About This? Why Bring Up This Old History?

This old history needs to be talked about and understood. The psychological legacy of this old history is still with us. Science has advanced and now rejects racist theories, and now it can help us to understand why the psychological legacy of this old history is still alive, and what can be done about it. The time is right because many are either talking about slavery or in denial of it. There are numerous events worldwide devoted to this question: in the media (radio and television broadcasts), and in literature and the arts (novels, plays, films, essays, and comics). There were expositions held throughout 2017, in Paris, Lisbon, Berlin, and London to provide an in-depth understanding of the transatlantic slave trade. Memorial museums, commemorations, and new monuments are ample proof (Nantes, Gorée Island, Atlanta, Liverpool, London, and Bristol). The United Nations' permanent memorial to the victims of slavery was inaugurated in 2015 in New York City, as was the ACTe Memorial Slavery Museum in Guadeloupe. At the end of September 2016, in Washington, D.C., President Barack Obama inaugurated the Smithsonian National

Museum of African American History and Culture. The museum is located on the very site where, two centuries earlier, there was a slave market. To mark the occasion, the United States Postal Service issued a commemorative stamp. President Obama advised President-Elect Donald Trump to "visit" the new edifice that tells not only the story of slavery and discrimination but also of the successes of Black Americans. He exhorted all Americans to understand "where we come from." Tickets to enter the museum are sold out months in advance.

Furthermore, one reads variations of the following headline on the front pages of major newspapers: "Brazil *dared* to recognize slavery during the opening ceremony of the 2016 Olympic Games in Rio." A troupe of dancers enacted the history of the country to stress the role of African slaves who were brought to Brazil in chains. Dancers in giant hamster treadmills were representative of the forced labor on the sugar cane plantations. The ceremony also acknowledged the *favelas* "where the liberated slaves are forced to live following the abolition of slavery...." French hip-hop dancers and Jamaican rappers who performed in the ceremony, made direct reference to the legacy of slavery and appealed to have access to their "true history." Even in France, this "need to know" is expressed in preparation classes for the competitive *Agrégation* exams in English for 2018, which included a question on slavery with reference to "the impact of slavery on the Afro-American families."

We could go on with other examples. It is not merely by chance that these events took place at a time of troubled current affairs. Today is marked by a withdrawal inward and a refusal to accept the Other in all his/her differences. Rejection is spreading, and growing stronger, is brandished, and has become polemical. It seems that worldwide, more cases of ethnic genocide are not very far off.[4] To counteract this trend is one reason why this book is so urgently needed. Perspectives disciplined by science can make factual and objective contributions to advance humanity in troubled times. Simultaneously, we do not neglect the fact that human beings must attribute meaning to their actions.

In countries where slavery was practiced, the times require a study that is at once epidemiological and etiopathogenic: find the causes of diseases and abnormal conditions. Besides the psychological, we must take into consideration other variables as well, such as "chronic hunger, under-employment, political repression, inter-ethnic conflicts, and racial discrimination" (Kleinman, 1995). At the same time, we take note of the interrelation between individual mental suffering and social suffering, between psychiatric symptoms and economic and discriminatory living conditions. Psychiatric symptoms such as drug and alcohol addiction, asocial and antisocial behavior, and violent outbursts cannot be viewed separately from the political and economic violence that produce them (Kleinman, 1995).

A Past Laden with Silence

The study of slavery should not be left just to historians; it is now part of the public discourse. Why? For a century, a profound silence concerning slavery has permeated the West. A veritable *law of silence*[5] was imposed "in the interests of all concerned," in every country that practiced slavery. That was especially true in the Caribbean and from South America to the United States. Here, Jim Crow laws succeeded in prolonging slavery even after its abolition, making it even more difficult to forget.

The silence was officially broken in 2001 with the World Conference against Racism in Durban, South Africa. There, the point was made that "in its scale and breadth and its duration, it (the transatlantic slave trade) is the greatest tragedy in the history of humankind" (Deveau, 1994).[6] Blame for the silence, to date, has been laid at the feet of Western professional historians. There was a consensus that their silence on the issue of slavery in the West was further proof that "the victors write history." This strange silence on the part of accredited historians, who formulate and teach history, goes a long way to explain the lack of importance given to the fate of millions of Black women and men. Inaction on their part begs for psychoanalytical investigation. The perpetuation of extremely violent acts is explained partly by historical, scientific, and ethical *forgetting* of great tragic events like slavery. Lynching during the American Jim Crow era and police violence against Black men today in the U.S. are examples and consequences. So again, why are we talking about this now?

> **"The executioner always kills twice, the second time through silence."**[7]

"In the history books of the vast majority of countries, the trafficking of slaves is quite simply ignored or, in the best cases, scarcely mentioned, and that is despite the duration, the extent and the inhumane aspect of the slave trade" (Diène, 2005). This oversight suited everybody because it was necessary for ex-slaves and ex-slaveholders to live together. Also, it was because slavery is tinged with shame for all who were involved. The shame over slavery is the driving force of forgetting. "The reason that shame exists is that we cannot hide that which we would like to hide (from ourselves)."[8]

However, "not to talk about a past tragedy, is to become its victim," said Boris Cyrulnik. It is to subjugate oneself to become the slave of one's past, "the slave of slavery," as Frantz Fanon has stated. Even though one might believe by talking about it, one relives the past in the present. One rekindles forgotten suffering. By resurfacing the resentment and shame of slavery, one suffers all over again. Repeat suffering is the feeling of some slave descendants who find "that we talk too much (or not at all) about slavery." They will never be able to trust White people until they can face this past suffering.[9]

We must face up to slavery, because "we have covered up the truth in vain. Sooner or later, it will be unveiled" (Pierre-Charles, 2013). Simone de Beauvoir says, "The primary scourge of humanity is not ignorance because those who are ignorant have excuses, but it is refusing to know." Underlying the refusal to know is again the fear of suffering through knowing. If today, some of us finally desire to know, it is because we fear no longer that knowledge will bring about suffering. We can henceforth revisit our past, return to the point of pain, "to only revisit the *memory* of pain and not its *bite*" (Philippe Claudel). That is precisely the object of this book: to look truth squarely in the face, without suffering, and to talk about it without pain.

To know, without being overwhelmed by suffering, reaffirms our calm, and allows us to confront the underlying problems of life. Frantz Fanon tells us that he does not want to dwell on a constant reminder of the suffering of slavery, but he says at the same time "to go beyond slavery, it is necessary to know it. It is precisely he who has no desire to know who is the slave of slavery" (Glissant, 1997). This book is also intended as a response to Elie Wiesel's warning: "The executioner always kills twice, the second time through silence."

Even Silence Has an End

This book comes when the prevailing idea is, "why dig up things that have been buried for so long, this past, this burden?" This is an expression of denial. It is understandably protective, but it is still denial. We intend *to transform denial into a determination to take responsibility for the past and to make it a point of departure to move forward*. We will do this by ending denial, and by transforming misfortune into an opportunity to rebound. We will reject denial as a refuge and accept the fact that the psychological legacy of slavery affects all of us in the West: the descendants of slaves, slave masters, and of European immigrants who never owned slaves. Blacks from the Americas have been humiliated. Brazilians, West Indians, Guineans and other inhabitants of the Caribbean, Panamanians, Americans, Colombians, Ecuadorians, Belizeans, have all felt the same anger and shame. They "discovered," after the forgetting, after the refusal of denial, that what was done to their ancestors affects their emotions and affectivity today. Not only is there a permanence that links the various transatlantic centers of slavery, but there is also "specificity of the kinds of trauma that are an integral part of slavery ... as well as a part of the various forms of segregation that followed."[10] In our opinion, *humiliation lends this particular characteristic to the trauma of slavery, and to its current continuation, which is both manifest and unconscious.* Humiliation brings about the internalization of inferiority. It also triggers a virtual infantilization, a need to feel that one is innocent and has never been affected.

Jean-Michel Djian, on France Culture Radio, interviewed Christiane Taubira (the first Black woman to serve as French Minister of Justice). The interview illustrates our thesis and that of François Sauvagnat. Taubira tells of the beginnings of her awareness:

> I discovered this history because I spend a lot of time in bookstores and libraries; quite by accident, I came across a history of trafficking and slavery.... I was not taught about it in school.... I read that it was extremely violent; it tormented me a great deal, but I didn't realize right away that this story concerned me personally. And then, through reading, I finally understood that it concerned me. It had an incredibly overwhelming impact on me. I was discovering, and then it hit me in my very soul. It was no longer only concepts, but real people going to Africa, people who were captured, their villages were set on fire; men, women and children were rounded up and put in chains and sent off to America, and all of that was at first a very remote thing for me and then one day it became relevant and personal. It was my country.
>
> Through the books I read, I discovered that the Bushinengues, my people from French Guiana, had rituals, divinities, venerations that were similar to those of African peoples. Moreover, then one day, the concept of interbreeding, of creolization, took shape in my mind and produced Creoles ... people like me! It hit me right between the eyes! Moreover, I said to myself: you bear within yourself slave trading and slavery! How could I possibly endure all of that? *I understood that I could quite possibly founder in a shipwreck of hatred, rage, and acrimony.* You carry within yourself this extremely violent past. I understood that. That is why young children should not have to find that out by themselves. That is why I have fought so hard to have it taught in schools. Education allows us to understand. Young children have to talk about it. We cannot let these feelings of hatred permeate their hearts and minds. I also understood that I did not want to lose myself in hatred and rage, and I sought out a beacon of light and found it in the form of my mother's[11] zest for life; I looked for light. Everything must not be all shadows and darkness. I looked for, and I found Champagney, the Canuts of Lyon, Schoelcher, and the Abbé Grégoire.

The young Christiane Taubira had unearthed the "hatred, rage and acrimony" that had been buried throughout that long period of denial, after the forgetting that allows us to recover and to be who we are. She went through the same phases of mental gymnastics as did those who had been enslaved, and that taught her ancestors resilience, "the art of navigating in the torrents" (Cyrulnik). She experienced emotions close to those of a slave, all things being equal.

A Word About African and Arab Slave Trade

Some readers might object and say the transatlantic slave trade and slavery in the Western Hemisphere is no different from all past histories of slavery. As initially stated, slavery has been practiced throughout human history and was dehumanizing in all cases. It is not well known that the Western slave trade is an offshoot of the older Arab-African slave trade. The slave trade in Arab-African countries has been going on longer and involved no Europeans. It began as early as the seventh century and subsequently has gone on for thirteen centuries: longer than the European transatlantic slave trade. Approximately 17 million Africans have been its victims, transported East in comparison to the 12 million carried West in the transatlantic trade.

The Durban World Conference against Racism in 2001, which recognized human trafficking and slavery as a crime against humanity, includes Arab-African slavery. All trade in human beings, past and present, are crimes against humanity. However, together, the Western and Arab-African slave trades and slavery rank as the greatest crime against humanity regarding the number of people affected (29 million) and duration (1,300 years). Neither slave trades have been acknowledged, appreciated, comprehended, and resolved. In this book, we focus on the transatlantic slave trade and its psychological effects, because it has compromised our potential and well-being in the West. The Arab-African slave trade, or any other one, has not done that. *To cite the Arab-African slave trade or any other current or past slave trade, in no way lessens the culpability of those who organized and sustain the transatlantic trade in other human beings.* Nor does it absolve the psychological damage inherited by descendants of enslaved Africans in the West. Any slave trade or genocidal crime that ends without recognition and resolution for its victims will do the following: psychological damages will be perpetuated for the descendants of those who committed the crime, as well as for the victims of the crime. The damage will go on as long as the crime goes unrecognized.

Furthermore, much less is known about the Arab-African slave trade. It is because the refusal to know applies to the descendants of both the slave owners and their victims. Moreover, we can share the surprise concerning this with the Senegalese historian and anthropologist Tidiane N'Diaye. He wrote, "there is no avoiding the facts, there is sufficient archival evidence to attest to it (the crimes of the Arab-African slave trade): it is a reality that historians, journalists, and activists have often shrouded with a veil, through intellectual cowardice or ideological opportunism."[12] In the Maghreb, Arabs systematically castrated African men. Infanticide was practiced to maintain control and to eliminate evidence of their crimes by preventing the establishment of permanent slave populations and any descendants. Well-respected Arab scholars[13] and interpretations of Muslim religious texts were supportive of slavery. They contributed to the creation of racial hierarchy in the minds of African slaves, where they were inferior to the masters. European slave masters did the same thing. What has been the impact of racial hierarchies on the psychology of slaves and their descendants in both trades? It is not our intent or ability to answer this question of both slave trades. Our challenge is to answer this question for the transatlantic trade, comprehensively, and transnationally.

Slavery as an Ongoing Psychological Trauma

Something readers need to know: the violence necessary for the successful practice of slavery could not fail to leave its mark. Then and now, psychological counseling was available daily in France for demonstrably minor psychological disturbances compared to the massive trauma caused by transatlantic slavery. Psychic trauma is a scientific reality, unanimously recognized by the international psychiatric community. *The outcome of both the implicit and explicit violence necessary to maintain* slavery *meets the criteria of the definition of psychological trauma, as defined by the (European) International Classification of Mental and Behavioural Disorders* (ICMBD) (Organisation Mondiale de la Santé, 1992). The omission of the psychological outcome of slavery as trauma from the American Diagnostic and Statistical Manual is curious, suggesting that Americans have yet to address this historic skeleton in their closet.

The *consequences of psychic trauma* are proportional to the seriousness and duration of the trauma and the psychological vulnerability of the subject. What are the symptoms? At the time of trauma, a person is subjected to an "unusually threatening or catastrophic stressful event that would cause distress to anyone" (ICMBD 92), and the symptoms are:

Fright;
A feeling of absolute helplessness, distress;
Anxiety and depression (*at the end of the traumatic event*).

Those who experience trauma now have a predisposition to the following:

Drug and alcohol abuse;
Day and nighttime recurrence of the original trauma;
Intrusive thoughts, nightmares, bouts of nighttime, and occasionally daytime, terror;
Asthenia, lethargy, indolence, drowsiness;
Depersonalization, altered states of identity and self-awareness;
Dissociative amnesia, hypervigilance, and anxiety.

These disorders constitute the condition of post-traumatic stress disorder (PTSD). PTSD is used to describe the anxiety, depression, or pathologies of temperament following a traumatic event. Joy A. DeGruy, an American specialist (who has a chapter in this book), has quite rightly used "Post Traumatic Slave Syndrome" to describe unresolved trauma passed on transgenerationally from slavery (2005).

We differentiate between stress and trauma. The mental suffering brought about by stress lasts just as long as the stressful circumstance lasts and ends when the circumstance ends. Alternatively, trauma remains in the subject's psyche, sometimes indefinitely. It is like "an internal foreign object," the effects of which will be felt following the traumatic experience, and which will prolong the suffering. Long after the event, it suddenly re-emerges; the person relives the traumatic circumstance. He or she once again experiences the anguish, or else the event resurfaces in the form of nightmares or daytime bouts of terror. These disturbances that most certainly haunted slaves have not been the subject of studies. Slaves had few means to have their feelings and emotions[14] heard. This inspired the poet and liberation writer from Martinique, Aimé Césaire, to say: "My mouth will be the mouth of the hardships that have no mouth; my voice, the liberty of those who are crouching in the dungeon of despair" (Césaire, 1956).

Whether or not slaves successfully practiced *passive resistance*, traumatic symptoms became part of the way that enslaved Africans were described during slavery. The same symptoms, derived from trauma, have paved the way for the eventual "portrait of Blacks" that we have today. Many of the prejudices about Blacks persist today, such as laziness,[15] indolence, stupidity, and credulity.[16] These characteristics were fabricated from observations of actual traumatic symptoms among slaves. They were attested to and corroborated by eighteenth- and nineteenth-century travelers, who observed slaves in the Caribbean, and in North and South America.

Post-traumatic effects are passed on to subsequent generations as memories and define both functional (resilience) and dysfunctional coping skills. Fortunately, the content of post-traumatic effects wanes in salience and power over time and generations. The necessity to react to past traumatic events and memories lessen. The will to survive compels the psyche to process (to "digest") its memories and to change itself over decades and events. Relationships with others are imbued subsequently with these changes, especially relationships with children. Still, there is a *transmission* of remaining traumatic content, and its effects, to one's descendants via socialization and, perhaps, by DNA, as well. The good news is the epigenetic imprint on the DNA can fade away with psychotherapy. This is an area where we could benefit from further research, perhaps, with geneticists collaborating with historians and psychiatrists.

Limitations: No Linear Continuity

Slaves lived under diverse conditions, as were the ways and severity of how they were treated. Some conditions and forms of control minimized psychological distress and emotional disorders; others were unmitigated in cruelty and in generating traumas. There was no predictability and linearity in the overall experience of slavery. At different times, the living conditions of the slaves were different in the Francophone, Anglophone and Hispanophone Caribbean, in the United States, and Brazil. Then, variations in the abolition of slavery, by country, diversified the experiences and conditions of ex-slaves. What we know least is the diversity of the after-effects of slavery and coping at the family level. Before and after abolition, living, eating, working, talking with, or encountering White people may or may not have been dangerous and stressful. For any specific individuals and families, we do not know if slavery left effects, traumatic or otherwise. For others, early traumatic experiences were evident from self-loathing in their own and subsequent generations.

In some cases, protective factors made it possible to prevent transgenerational transmission of trauma; here again, we have no estimates. It must be pointed out that human qualities such as courage and tenacity have always played a role at some point in the generational chain. We are dealing with a complex phenomenon where the causes of trauma do not automatically trigger predictable consequences.

An Ongoing Quest

A United Nations report on Brazil, published in September of 2014, revealed that a large portion of the Brazilian population lives in denial of racism, which is institutionalized and subtly and systematically underestimated by the media. The first Black judge to sit on the Supreme Court in Brasilia, Joaquim Barbosa, speaks of racism in Brazil as "extremely intense." The United Nations established the link with slavery, whose "presence is extremely pronounced here.... After three centuries of (the) black slave trade and under pressure from the British, Brazil eventually put an end to Slavery on May 13, 1888. It was the last western country to do so" (Dallari, 2021).

Slavery is not the sole cause of trauma after its abolishment. Natural disasters trigger psycho-traumatic stress and lead to the development of resilience as well. However, several studies have shown that trauma causes even more psychiatric disorders when it is intentional and done personally by other humans. Several studies have shown that the type of traumatic events plays a crucial role in the development of PTSD. Deliberate acts of interpersonal violence, in particular sexual assault, and combat are more likely to lead to PTSD than accidents or disasters (Kessler, Sonnega, Bromet, Hughes, & Nelson, 1995; McFarlane & de Girolamo, 1996).

Consequently, there is a fundamental difference in the PTSD generated by the eruption of Mount Pelee, slavery, or the impact Hurricane Katrina had on New Orleans. Human beings controlled the latter two events: the first human event was of direct oppression, while the second event was from neglect. Again, the trauma of slavery was unique in its human intentionality and transgenerational duration.

Another unique aspect of slavery's trauma is that its cause, racism, has gone on long after slavery ended. The Black Codes, that legally regulated relations between masters and slaves in both the French and American worlds during slavery, continued afterward. The most notable and formally organized attempt to continue slavery post-emancipation was the Jim Crow system in the American South. It went on for one hundred years after slavery's formal end. We have no idea to what extent Jim Crow reinforced and continued the traumatic outcomes of slavery in the U.S., well into the last century, and into our lifetime. There are contemporary efforts in the U.S. by political conservatives to roll back Civil Rights protections and invent a new Jim Crow system. To what extent do such efforts reinforce the psychological legacy of slavery in the U.S. today?

A Dangerous Idea?

As mentioned, this book is the product of a 2016 international scientific colloquium in Martinique. *For the very first time,* historians, psychiatrists, geneticists, sociologists, politicians, psychologists, psychoanalysts, and anthropologists were able to *cross-reference their expertise.* They considered the complex question of the psychological consequences of slavery for descendants of slaves and slave owners alike. Before this, we had only organized colloquia where historians came together to discuss among themselves the theme of slavery, or where psychiatrists met to address the problems of psychological trauma.

What are the impacts of transatlantic slavery on its descendants? This question alone, more than any other, generated immediate and large-scale interest in the colloquium among Martiniquais that made it necessary for us to close the registration a mere nine days after its initial announcement. We had 1,200 requests, many from overseas. This unprecedented interest suggested that asking this question in public *revealed* the existence of a vast need. Somehow, asking the question *permitted us to consider an idea* that had been considered previously taboo—the psychological consequences of slavery. Conference participant evaluations revealed that some attendees had an intuitive perception of the existence of the psychological effects of slavery but were unable to articulate the problem or address it. Other participants expressed their gratitude for raising the issue. The *knowledge* provided by the colloquium and the calm tone of the discussions had fulfilled a high expectation or had permitted the audience to address an inner conflict. One of them said more precisely, "It was as though we were afraid to even think about it."

Consequently, slavery is a sensitive subject that is the source of embarrassment for some and shame for others in not only France but everywhere else as well. The speakers from four continents confirmed that fact. One of the objectives of this book is to consider with calmness and serenity the many facets of the psychological consequences of transatlantic slavery.

Thus, it is necessary to have an approach that is both subjective and objective, and that has an international focus. That is because, in our times, a poly-centered focus is the only one that will allow us to cast light on the diversity of slavery, its common core, and living psychological legacy. Furthermore, all the essential points about slavery are impossible to address as domestic issues, because the phenomenon varies widely, depending on the society and the period.

As with the colloquium, this book is part of the program of the United Nations International Decade for People of African Descent (2015–2024) and enjoys the scientific patronage of the World Psychiatric Association and the World Health Organization (WHO). Written by widely renowned university scholars, it relates facts, acts, and their significance with the intention of remaining objective over and above any outdated glorification of suffering or post-positivist presumption that objectivity is impossible. We must consider the therapeutic question: how can we help "those who are inconsolable over the fact that they do not resemble God, but rather the devil" (Césaire, 1956)? It is common in countries where slavery was practiced that psychiatrists explain some of their patients' symptoms as being vestiges of slavery. These vestiges do not take away from them the considerable progress they have made in collective and individual emancipation. However, their emancipation has failed to take into account a significant proportion of those left to their resources. Also, the statistics are very revealing concerning poverty, standards of living, employment, and life expectancy. Is the existence of these individuals closer to the conditions of those who had been enslaved? What kind of psychological stigmas do they still carry with them?

The challenge is, therefore, to compile a scientific corpus of the psychological consequences of having been enslaved. This endeavor is one of high complexity. Multidisciplinary research teams have already been organized among the participants in the colloquium. On both the collective and the individual levels, conditions of slavery and emancipation have been diverse, and the situations Blacks find themselves in today are not alike. The tree of "success stories" often hides the forest of those who have been left on their own, and who are victims of the presumption that slavery has had no lasting effects. Here, the unseen is at work. The subconscious, subconscious denial, repression, and denigration are all present. However, these unconscious mechanisms are all the more part of the psychological consequences of slavery, regardless of which side one finds oneself on. This is especially the case for the successful who proclaim that they are "not at all affected by slavery."

* * * * *

We stress the role of pride in one's identity as necessary for collective resilience. Pride in identity is understood in this context to be very different from any defensiveness or identity closure. This is not about idealizing Blacks. It is restoring understanding and dignity to one's sense of history. Our objective is to elevate Blacks from debasement and inferiority to appreciate their histories and survival of enslavement. The descendants of slaves and slave owners alike can live authentically on a higher order, based on a comprehensive understanding of the past. Such an understanding requires acceptance of differences then and now in our circumstances, and the agency to act. It involves recognition of the complexity of our past, and that parts of this past still live with us. It requires a convergence of benevolence and goodwill. It paves the way forward to a peaceful resilience, the pathway toward what Edouard Glissant called "Tout-monde" (All-world) and "Global relationship."

Like many concepts, post-slavery resilience must be thought about globally and acted upon locally.[17] We reflect here on the French West Indies, where the compelling social and identity issues are like those found in other countries where slavery existed. Moreover, it is from Martinique that Edouard Glissant formulated his ideas about Creolization and "Tout-monde." Transatlantic slave trafficking and slavery forced countries in the Caribbean (where the cultural intermingling had been the most intimate) to *invent* new forms of socialization and organization. This includes a new language, Creole[18]; original music and culture; and new ways of intercultural expression. The Caribbean has thus raised questions that reach far beyond the Caribbean geographical context. Some of those questions, in Martinique, for example, involve establishing social ties in a tense contextual dynamic between what it means to be Creole, African or Indian. What is the influence of Western culture; what is the place of White Creoles; and do we fight or resist the desire to assimilate? There is a desire for national independence for those who do not have it in the Caribbean. If these issues are not enough, we have yet to deal with family memories of slavery, intermarriage, the place of the Creole language, skin-color prejudices, and the place of migrants. There are so many questions and issues with few answers. Of course, the large neighbors to the north (the U.S.) and south (Brazil) have the same problems and the same lack of solutions. Perhaps, in the Caribbean, the greater intimacy from living together on islands makes answers more urgent.

Finally, our most significant omission is that we have not imagined the future. What happens once we have succeeded in understanding and resolving the psychological legacy of slavery, whether racism is eliminated or not? Blacks will be different people. So will White people, because Black people will no longer reinforce their Whiteness. Then, we can finally experience the real freedom to dance and for music, a rejuvenation of arts, and an even more profound exploration of history, heritage, and memory. We will create a future and rethink our relationship with the past. Our creative writers and musicians will be free, as well, and can open unseen and unheard of worlds. Our visual artists can henceforth engage in a kind of dialogue with those of other post-slavery countries. Ultimate freedom from slavery and its legacies will vitalize our tangible and intangible heritage and give us "the strength to face the future."[19] We will no longer be ashamed of our history and ourselves. We can all finally discover and accept our origins.

Introduction to the Topic

The above explanation for why one should acknowledge and reflect on the psychological legacies of slavery and the benefits of doing so leads to three things readers need to know to appreciate the following chapters.

The Concept of Race in the West

First, the very idea of race was fabricated. Races are not innate to humans, cannot be proven by science, nor have they existed for all of human history. The idea of races has been propagated so well that even scientists believed it for a while, and the public cannot imagine questioning it or not having it. In antiquity, the color of one's skin did not carry the same connotation, the same force, or the mindless images that it has held since the seventeenth century (Drake, 1987). Today, skin color is "essentially the very first assessment of a person," writes Pap Ndiaye. He adds, "Was the Roman Emperor Septimius Severus 'white,' or 'mixed,' or 'black,' according to our current criteria? We are not sure, and historical texts make no mention of it: obviously, the men of antiquity paid scant attention to it" (Ndiaye, 2009). The very idea of human races began with Western slavery and, in particular, with the defense of slavery against abolitionists in the seventh century, some two hundred years after the African slave trade began (Abramova, 1979).

Today, the most prominent racial myth comes from the United States. Race, as we know it, *was invented* in colonial Virginia in the seventeenth century and fully developed by the nineteenth century affecting every European ethnic group to immigrate into the U.S. (Allen, 1994). In Noel Ignatiev's illustration of *How the Irish Americans Became White* (1995), the British Crown wanted to rid itself of the English and Irish poor and did so by sending them to North America as *indentured servants*. The often questionably signed contracts required emigrants to work without pay for four to seven years, in exchange for passage. Because the British colonized Ireland, even the British poor looked down on the Irish. Then, enslaved Africans, sold to Virginia settlers, found themselves on the same low level as the Irish and were treated initially as indentured servants. The small British property class that controlled Virginia soon realized they had a major problem. Servants and the poor vastly outnumbered them and were increasingly rebellious. It was only a matter of time before a rebellion would succeed. Their solution was to separate Africans from the Irish and other European immigrants. The Irish were allowed to advance in status and become part of newly defined "White people" (Allen, 1994). Africans were reduced in status to a permanent under-caste as "Negroes," with skin color as their marker. Tragically, many formerly oppressed Irish became defenders of white supremacy and oppressors in their own right.

In time, the newly devised racial classification incorporated all newcomers. Gradations in whiteness evolved. Descendants of the earliest British settlers were at the top; beneath them were other European ethnic groups, and at the bottom were Blacks and other non–Europeans (Horsman, 1981). It is no surprise that Eastern European Jews were considered an inferior "race," up until the middle of the twentieth century, until they Anglo-conformed and could pass for White (Goldstein, 2006). Now, skin color is laden with numerous superior-to-inferior social evaluations of beauty, intelligence, and social privilege. Different shades of white-to-black skin color are discernible only to West Indians, Americans, Brazilians, Belizeans, and other inhabitants of countries where slavery existed. *In essence, race is a social construct without precise physiological and genetic bases.* Anthropologists now call race and racial differences myths without basis in science (American Anthropological Association, 1996). However, like any purely social construct, *what was constructed can be deconstructed.*

Psychological Legacies

It would be helpful to have a clear sense of what psychological legacies are and how to understand them. As explained earlier in the introduction, the outcome of implicit and explicit violence necessary to maintain slavery in the West meets the formal criteria of psychological trauma and its lasting effects on post-traumatic stress disorders (PTSD). Enslaved Afro-Brazilians were the last emancipated in 1888. However, the end of slavery did not resolve the PTSD of survivors or Euro-Americans' belief in their racial superiority. Since slavery, PTSD and white supremacy continued unchallenged and unchanged, embedded in the culture of slaver nations, and passed on to subsequent generations (Leary, 2005).

Slavery's legacies are apparent in the more than four thousand African Americans lynched in the U.S. and today in unwarranted police violence against Blacks. Slavery's central legacy is racism—Whites' belief in their racial superiority. Unlike a personal belief, racism is cultural; it is a given, part of a worldview, and unconscious. Without reflection or perceptions that contradict the presumption of white supremacy, one cannot be without racism. Its denial is cultural as well and aligns perfectly with White denial that they racially discriminate against Blacks and other non-Whites (Barzun, 1965). Likewise, the general shame and humiliation that the descendants of enslaved Africans feel regarding slavery, as well as racial self-hatred, self-doubt, rage, and acrimony toward one another, are also psychological legacies of slavery.

What we editors and the contributors to this collection found only touches the surface of historical influences that shape contemporary thinking and behavior. The psychological legacies addressed here are selective, preliminary, and have yet to be explored fully. There are many more legacies still unidentified. Furthermore, our difficulty in connecting historical events such as slavery with the present is because our sense of time does not do justice to psychological legacies. In cultural transmission, the past, present, and future are not discrete periods, nor are they mutually exclusive. Psychological legacies exist like ocean waves flooding a beach. Not all the water (legacies) recedes into the ocean (time). The legacies that remain carry on in new generations along with new legacies. In effect, the present is never without fragments of the past. Likewise, the future does not fully happen in some time yet to come. Even the future begins in the past and becomes increasingly salient only as the present recedes into the past.

Why These Psychological Legacies?

In Brazil, Colombia, Cuba, Jamaica, Martinique, Haiti, Belize, and the United States, contributing psychologists, psychiatrists, and social workers traced the beliefs and behaviors outlined earlier that have troubled slave descendant clients and their families since slavery. These clinicians and researchers are not the first to make connections between contemporary psychology and historically traumatic events. Similar links have been made between the World War II Jewish Holocaust, lynching in the U.S., international genocides, and psychological troubles in subsequent generations of survivors (Kellermann, 2009; Rogers, Leydesdorff, & Dawson, 1999).

It was not until investigators, who have studied the transatlantic slave trade and slavery, came together at the 2016 conference, that a richer understanding of the psychological legacies of slavery became apparent. Ideas for what might be done to resolve the lasting trauma of African slavery in the West became apparent as well. In one presentation after another, listeners affirmed that the same beliefs and behaviors existed among descendants of enslaved Africans in their country. Before the conference, presenters worked independently of one another, some for decades. They did not know of each other's work nor what others would present. Simultaneous translations were necessary between English, French, Spanish, and Portuguese. Presenters were from different Western countries that practiced slavery differently. Despite these differences, several psychological legacies were found to exist in all the countries represented. Then, we focused on the findings that are international, cross-cultural and comparative. Of course, as expected, we found other psychological legacies distinct to each presenters' country and culture. However, the legacies held in common were the surprise.

Descendants of Enslaved Africans

Finally, readers need to know that the descendants of enslaved Africans in the West are not monolithic. Their fore-parents came from a diversity of cultures before their enslavement, and a difference of circumstances when enslaved. Then, there was yet a third level of diversity in the cultures and circumstances under which they were enslaved. The variety of languages they spoke and of geographies in which they live make the psychological legacies they now hold in common even more extraordinary. Consider that before 1500 CE and the Atlantic slave trade, there were well over one thousand distinct ethnic and linguistic groups in Africa, and their group boundaries overlapped and shifted for centuries (Hall, 2005). However, amidst these multiple diversities, there were bridges between peoples. Then as now, it is common for Africans from Upper Guinea to be very familiar with neighboring ethnic cultures and to speak their languages or dialects (Hawthorne, 2010, p. 10). Also, members of relatively few ethnic groups were taken into the Atlantic slave trade. Africans closest to the Atlantic and along rivers that let out to the Atlantic were the slave trade's primary targets.

The slave trade concentrated in three successive areas on the West coast of Africa (Hall, 2005). The first was north to south from present-day Senegal down to the Ivory Coast starting around 1441 CE.[20] This area was called the Senegambia and Upper Guinea and is where it is presumed members of the Igbo, Mende, Akan, and Wolof ethnic groups were enslaved. The second area ran west to east from Liberia to present-day Nigeria, Cameroon, and Equatorial Guinea (Bight of Biafra). Beginning about 1518, presumably, the Yoruba, Fon, and Chamba people were enslaved there. In the third area, Africans were captured along the coast of present-day Gabon, the Congo, and Angola, before 1580. Here, the capture of Africans ran well into the interior of Africa (via rivers) to enslave, presumably, the Mbundu and Kongo peoples. Finally, it is believed the Makua people who lived along the coast of East Africa and the Indian Ocean of present-day Tanzania and Mozambique were captured as well and taken into Western slavery as early as 1507.

The Igbo, Mende, Akan, Wolof, Yoruba, Fon, Chamba, Mbundu, Kongo, and Makua peoples varied in not only language. They ranged in family and community organization. Some had patrilineal family lineages, like the Eve. Others had matrilineal lineages, such as the Akan (Boahen, 1999). The Akan elected the head of their lineage through councils of elders while the Fon and Yoruba were ruled through hereditary succession as in Europe (Alagoa, 1999). Furthermore, there were innumerable variations in their religious rituals, gods, theologies, beliefs in creation, and worldviews. Slave-ship captains and slave masters alike used these differences to control captives (M'Bokolo, 1999, p. 529). At sea and on farms and plantations, they mixed Africans of unfamiliar languages and cultures to keep them from organizing and rebelling. Finally, captives were taken into different Western cultures, which practiced slavery differently. For example, the Portuguese baptized slaves, recognizing that they had souls; the British did not and opposed baptizing slaves (Thomas, 1997, p. 397). The French attempted to discourage the abuse of slaves with their "code noir" regulating the relations between masters and slaves; the British had no such code (Thomas, 1997, p. 474). The Spanish also had a slave code that required slave masters to care for elderly slaves and to limit the workday to ten hours except during harvest, when it was sixteen hours (Thomas, 1997, p. 669). English abolitionists used the Spanish code to argue that British slavery was crueler than the others and should be abolished (Wyman-McCarthy, 2018).

Enslaved Africans in each of the ten ethnic groups were taken in different proportions at different times into the English, Portuguese, French, and Spanish systems of slavery. In sum, captives were culturally diverse, linguistically different, treated differently as slaves, had culturally different masters, and were slaves in different geographic locations. Opportunities for differences did not stop there. The circumstances of their emancipations differ, and their post-emancipation histories are distinct as well (Hall, 2005). In total, descendants of enslaved Africans are potentially different people many times over not only in languages. They are different in beliefs, attitudes, temperament, religion, worldview, treatment as slaves, the extent to which they have retained African cultures, and in their family and community organization. Yet, psychological legacies held in common from slavery cut through all these differences. How could this happen?

Bases of Commonality

Despite all, there were circumstances where members of specific African ethnic groups, taken as captives, were clustered in the same location at the same time because some planters sought Africans with particular agricultural skills. The Mende were brought to South Carolina for their knowledge of rice farming (Littlefield, 1981). The Igbo were favored in Virginia for tobacco cultivation (Hall, 2005, p. 141), and the Kongo were brought to Cuba because of their experience with mining and copper work (Hall, 2005, p. 20). Other planters preferred tribal members with what they thought were specific temperaments and avoided others. In this way, enslaved Africans with the same language and culture were enslaved together (Herskovits, 1958). African notions of governance, economy, formal practices of religion, and martial knowledge were suppressed—knowledge essential to challenge slavery. Alternatively, expressive arts, music, dance, humor, use of language, notions of god and gods, ancestors, spirituality, food preparation, child-rearing, ecology, and family organization were cultural practices that were less threatening to slave masters. Aspects of these practices survived. By the second generation, enslaved Africans absorbed enough French, Spanish, English, and Portuguese to communicate with their masters, to do what they were told, to survive as slaves and to devise ways to resist. Where captives were together in large numbers, they could retain more of their African cultures, teach one another, and have newly enslaved Africans refresh their memories and practices.

Remarkably, there was a common core of their diverse cultural beliefs. They had a spiritual cosmology in common underlying their religions that centered them between the world of ancestor spirits and of spirits yet to come. The present and the physical world are not all there are, but are, in fact, phases in a spiritual continuum between the living and dead. There is a "fluidity between the two worlds (living and dead) that allowed ancestral spirits to remain engaged in the everyday lives of their surviving kinsmen" (Sweet, 2003, p. 97). They had multiple ancestors and spirit guides to call on, as well as the ability to communicate with them, to seek protection, and to influence others. Death is not final nor the end. It is as if a large body of water separated the two worlds, and the living had to navigate their way to the next world. Regardless of what happens to the body, the spirit could not be killed nor injured. Catholicism, Protestantism, or Islam did not wipe out this core cosmology. Africans could accept these faiths while hiding and simultaneously practicing their own. With this core cosmology and flexibility toward beliefs and culture, Africans, regardless of ethnicity and circumstances, were able to withstand the Atlantic slave trade and slavery, make sense of their experiences and survive for generations.

Ironically, in both Brazil and the United States, Whites have had multi-generational exposure to enslaved Africans and their descendants. In this exposure, they have absorbed varying amounts of African culture, which are apparent today in their speech, attitudes, religious expression, worldview, and mannerisms. For slaves, slavemasters, and non-slaves alike, the outcome of generations of exposure to each other are blends of African, European, and Indian cultures—a Creolization of descendant populations (Sweet, 2003, p. 202). Consequently, one can find today Afro-Brazilians honoring the Yoruba Orisha spirits, Afro-Haitians practicing Voodoo brought by the Fon from the Bight of Benin, and the Kongo influenced speech of South Carolina Coastal African Americans—Black English. Out of creolization came Afro-Brazilians, Afro-Cubans, Afro-Mexicans, Afro-Colombians, Afro-Peruvians, and Afro-Americans (Mintz & Price, 1976) as national subcultures. These subcultures were vital to enslaved Africans' survival and resistance and were passed on to their descendants. However, survival as slaves and descendants of slaves has come to be seen as both a blessing and a curse. The blessing is cultural resiliency; the curse is historical trauma carried over as psychological legacies. One hundred and thirty years after the last emancipation is time enough to identify, acknowledge, and work to enhance the blessings and eliminate the curses.

About This Book

Part One: Commonalities

This collection is divided into three parts. In Part One, several of the held in-common psychological legacies of slavery are presented. The mulatto children of enslaved Africans and European parents were fair-skinned compared to children of African parents. Often, they were the slave owners' children and were given less burdensome work, no work at all, or even educated and granted freedom. Whites viewed mulattos as superior to Africans but inferior to themselves—consistent with their notions of race. In time, enslaved Africans assimilated this belief as well. Based upon years of work as a counseling psychologist, Elma Whittaker-Augustine explains colorism among predominant Afro-Belizeans in Chapter 1. Fair-skinned Belizeans are privileged, and former British colonists and Belizeans alike consider them more attractive and, in general, better than black and brown-skinned Belizeans. Colorism is not just a Belizean legacy from slavery. In every Western country that practiced slavery, it is a present-day reality.

In virtually every narrative of community life among slaves, racial self-hatred, self-doubt, rage, and acrimony were common. These are consistent but ignored features of contemporary Black psychology as well. In Haiti, psychologist Judite Blanc explores the disdain that descendants of enslaved Africans often show for each other. In Chapter 2, she explains that disdain does not have origins in individual psychology and experience. It comes from the community and culture as a direct outcome of historical traumas. Like the previous chapter, her observations are based as well upon counseling and community experience. What she shows the reader is also not unique to Haiti. She identifies other debilitating legacies as well that are unique to Haiti's history as the only country in which enslaved Africans successfully rebelled against their enslavers.

In Chapter 3, two psychologists, Andréa Máris Campos Guerra and Ana Carolina André-Cadar, trace the origins of black-on-black violence and drug dealing among young Afro-Brazilian men. Slave masters were responsible for providing slaves with enough food and clothing to do their work but rarely did. Slaves had to make up the difference by stealing what they needed to survive. Ironically, their masters expected them to steal and then punished them for it. Fast forward to the present-day Brazilian favelas. Afro-Brazilian youth are without jobs and even the prospects of work. As the nation's economic outsiders confined to urban favelas, they turn to drug dealing to survive. However, this turn is not just circumstantial; it is traditional and what their fathers, grandfathers, and great grandfathers had to do as well. Alienation from society and the police have replaced the slavemasters' and overseers' search and punishment of survival crimes. Drug dealing has become a present-day behavior with roots in slave resistance and survival. This analysis just as easily describes what young people who are descendants of enslaved Africans do and why in the ghettos of Chicago, Los Angeles, Rio, or Kingston.

Alexandra Escobar Puche, a clinical psychologist, uncovers a psychological legacy of slavery based upon her and her associates' fieldwork in rural Colombia in Chapter 4. San Basilio de Palenque in the north of Colombia was founded by runaway slaves, survived intact, and may be the first free town in the Americas predating 1691. Their Africa-originated "lumbalú" funeral rite has been practiced since the beginning of the community. The ritual provides a way for individuals and the community to grieve and mourn the passing of close relatives and friends. Its significance is that it a way to acknowledge and process past and present trauma. The principal singers and drummers take on the mourning and relieve the suffering of the family and community. This same ritual and significance are apparent today in the highly emotional and personal role that Afro-Latin singers, drummers, rhythm and blues musicians, and religious ministers play for African descendant audiences and congregations. For the audience, "performances" go way beyond entertainment and preaching—they are therapeutic.

In Chapter 5, Bernard Dossa uniquely addresses the psychological legacies of slavery and its spiritual implications. He takes West Africa, specifically Dahomey, the Fon people, and the culture of the sixteenth century as a starting point. Then, he looks from West Africa through slavery forward in time to elaborate on the psychological and cultural challenges enslaved Dahomeans had to address. Based upon what captured Dahomeans were equipped with culturally, he estimates their mental losses in identity from slavery. However, loss of culture, identity, and the passing of time does not fundamentally change their fore-parents' nor children's underlying spiritual connection and obligations in the spirit world. For those who enslaved Africans and their descendants, it does not alter their culpability and responsibility to atone for the damage done.

Part Two: Concepts

In Part Two, the concept of slavery's psychological legacies is explored. Can they be defined in theory and empirically validated? The reader is reminded that the legacies elaborated on in Part One of this book are only a few held in common cross-culturally and internationally. There are many others yet to be identified and described that are unique to each national circumstance as well as held in common. In Chapter 6, Aimé Charles-Nicolas elaborates on the introduction by providing an insightful psychiatric explanation of slavery's psychological legacies. Psychiatrists, who are familiar with their patient's family history, routinely address slavery's legacies in slave descendant patients. If therapists care to look, they find attitudes, beliefs and repetitious behaviors that patients learned from parents, other relatives, and their community. In turn, patients' parents, relatives, and communities learned the issues in question from prior generations. In other words, the source of the patient's psychological issues is from the experiences of previous generations.

Joy A. DeGruy, in Chapter 7, provides a theory to address the effects of prior generational experiences. She makes the connection between the slave past and the present and describes present-day psychological legacies from slavery as a "syndrome." Enslaved Africans experienced multiple post-traumatically stressful experiences within and across generations that have become part of African American cultures, as Charles-Nicolas describes. Symposium participants from other Western countries that practiced slavery pointed out that Joy A. DeGruy's description of the syndrome applies to their countries as well. In this case, the normal expected everyday functioning of African slave descendants carries with it the burden of hidden historical traumas.

In Chapter 8, Benjamin P. Bowser takes a hard look at the psychology attributed to slavery. While the historical reality of slavery cannot be reconstructed as it was experienced, the circumstances that made slavery traumatic are still very much with us today. He asserts that aspects of the experience of slavery are lived today by descendants of enslaved Africans and others. Therefore, psychologically, aspects of the traumas derived from slavery as it was lived are still with us.

In Chapter 9, Edwin J. Nichols writes on the legacy of slavery in the United States. Americans, including the descendants of enslaved Africans, are particularly resistant to the idea that slavery left a mark. If it did, Whites believe it is Blacks' problem, and Blacks need to "get over it." Nichols traces this resistance to acknowledge slavery and its after-effects to the belief that the U.S. is unique and exceptional among nations. He reviews aspects of U.S. history that show it is, indeed, exceptional but not in the way it is thought. For the U.S., the government and laws have played a particularly potent role in maintaining slavery's ongoing psychology and racism.

Finally, in Chapter 10, Fatimah Jackson, Latifa Jackson and Zainab El Radi Jackson review the physical evidence of slavery's damaging psychological effects on slaves. There are epigenetic markers that may be potential evidence of psychological trauma among slaves. These markers can be passed to subsequent generations. The science is not conclusive and still needs years to develop before any definitive statements can be made.

Part Three: Solutions

The final part of this collection is devoted to solutions. Our initial objective is to point out the connection between slavery's historical trauma and contemporary issues in individual and community psychology. A second objective is to encourage research on slavery's contemporary legacies in all the countries that practiced slavery and have descendants of enslaved Africans. Our final goal and, perhaps, the most important, is to find solutions—ways to confront, resolve, and eliminate historical traumas in the lives of slave descendants.

In Chapter 11, Frederick W. Hickling provides a solution. Hickling et al. directly addressed past trauma in the lives and community socialization of patients at Jamaica's Bellevue Mental Hospital in the 1970s. They were so successful that the issues that brought many patients to the hospital were resolved, and most were able to return to their communities. In the decades since then, the lessons learned at Bellevue have been refined and extended first into selective Jamaican schools and are now island-wide. An essential key to their success was to "de-colonize" psychiatry and to make it a tool for directly resolving contemporary and historical trauma. The history, lessons, techniques, and evaluations of Hickling's work are shared in this chapter.

In Chapter 12, Benjamin P. Bowser describes the ways family and community social histories can be used to identify past traumatic events and their long-term effects. Scherto Gill, in Chapter 13, describes what is required to move from the very depths of trauma from slavery and racism's dehumanization to healing. Based on research from the UNESCO Slave Route Project, this journey cannot be made alone.

Then follows the conclusion, a compilation of recommendations from all the previous chapters for how the legacies of slavery may be acknowledged, identified, and resolved. The coda focuses on the necessity of reconciliation and how that might take place.

Notes

1. Translated from French by Roger Stevenson.
2. Phrenology was promulgated as a means of determining the mental and moral characteristics of an individual based on the size and shape of the skull. F.J. Gall and J.G. Spurzheim published their ideas in 1809 in *Recherches sur le Système nerveux en général et sur le cerveau en particulier* (*Research on the Nervous System in General and on the Brain in Particular*). The scientific manual, *Grundriss der menschlichen Erblichkeitslehre und Rassenhygiene*, which could be translated as *Human Heredity and Racial Hygiene*, by Erwin Baur, Eugen Fischer and Fritz Lenz, was re-edited five times between 1921 and 1940. It served as the "scientific" basis for the forced sterilization campaigns promoted by the eugenics movement.
3. Aimé Césaire.
4. To the point where the twentieth century has been called "the century of genocides": the Armenians (1915), the European Jews (1941–1945), the Cambodians (1975), the Tutsis (1994), and Bosnian Muslims (1995).
5. Myriam Cottias confirms that "the forgetting about slavery was presented as a political issue, as a founding principle of a society that had been built on servitude," because, after the abolition of slavery, former slaves and ex-slave holders had to learn how to coexist.
6. During its World Conference, held in Durban in 2001, the United Nations recognized that slavery and the slave trade "were appalling tragedies in the history of humanity."
7. A quote attributed to the Nobel Prize Laureate, Elie Wiesel.
8. Emmanuel Lévinas, *De l'évasion* (*Of Evasion*,1st edition 1935), introduction and annotation by Jacques Rolland, Fata Morgana, 1982, and Biblio Essais/Livre de Poche.
9. Certain Black intellectuals who translate the "constant attention to slavery in the media" into a battle express, through this behavior, a discomfort, the nature of which they fail

to analyze. It is really one of shame. The defense mechanisms that we employ to avoid speaking of shame are precisely those that mirror shame itself.

10. A quote from Professor François Sauvagnat of the University of Rennes.

11. Her mother is thought to have provided her with positive narcissistic foundations.

12. For example, the princes of the states bordering the sultan of Bornou (Kanem, Wadaï, Baguirmi & Sokoto), in what is today known as Nigeria, were engaged in trafficking captive slaves. Far from desiring to put an end to this trafficking that was beneficial to them, all of these princes had no other thought than to impose a transit duty. This was their concern when they were not outright and directly "extorting" the slave traders' caravans. In the land of the Fellatas, manhunts were led by Ahmadou, the son and eminent heir of El Hadji Omar Seydou Tall. The undertaking was even worse with the Dahoman monarchs in the interior of the continent, of whom the greatest of all the slave traders was Béhanzin. These bloodthirsty monarchs, concerned about maintaining their status, were primarily preoccupied with power and prestige. In order to acquire more arms and horses, symbols of their power, they were forced to sell more captive slaves. They waged wars against neighboring kingdoms, in order to ensure their supply of captives.

13. The greatest of the Arab thinkers was Ibn Khaldoun (1332–1406). He wrote: "The only people who truly accept slavery without any hope of return are the Negroes, because of a lower degree of humanity, their status being closer to that of the animals," from *Les prolégomènes. Première partie* (1863), translated and annotated by William McGuckin, Baron De Slane (1801–1878). See also manuscripts from the Bibliothèque Nationale in Paris published by the Institute of France (1863). Paris: The Paul Geuthner Orientalist Bookstore, 1934 (reprinted in 1996), CXVI plus 486 pages. *La Chronique de Guinée* by Gomes-Eanes de Zurara (1453) who writes of the beginning of slavery in Africa by the Europeans and demonstrates that the Portuguese, as early as the mid-15th century, used the hereditary curse of Ham to justify African slavery. The Curse of Ham was repeated until the 20th century, for example, in school textbooks; see Honoré Vinck (Vinck, 1999).

14. "Until the lions have their own historians, the history of the hunt will always glorify the hunter" (an African proverb).

15. "Negroes are so naturally lazy that those who are free don't do anything" (Montesquieu, "De l'esclavage des Nègres") (Miano, 2013). When he was interviewed by Elise Lucet about the creation of the perfume Samsara on the evening news on France 2, Jean-Paul Guerlain responded: "For once, I worked like a Negro. I don't know if the Negroes have always worked so hard, but, well..."

16. It is possible, even today, to see this kind of ridiculous stereotype of the Negro in the writings of Alain Finkielkraut and Pascal Bruckner.

17. This is the slogan adopted by the First Caribbean Association that organized the colloquium, and inspired this book: "Think Globally, Act Locally."

18. Creole grew out of the sudden necessity of Europeans and Africans to communicate with one another, brought about by the presence of large numbers of slaves. "It is autonomous and has an orderly structure with its own rules and all of the intellectual functions needed to transmit and receive. The geographical area where it is spoken, its features and definitive characteristics lend its development an authentic unity with respect to all the other languages of the world" (Glissant, 1997).

19. Aimé Césaire.

20. The dates when the earliest Africans were taken into slavery by location are approximations and vary by source.

References

Abramova, S.U. (1979). Ideological, Doctrinal, Philosophical, Religious, and Political Aspacts the African Slave Trade. In UNESCO (Ed.), *The African Slave Trade from the Fifteenth to the Nineteenth Century* (Vol. 2). Paris: UNESCO.

Alagoa, E.J. (1999). Fon and Yoruba: The Niger Delta and the Cameroon. In B.A. Ogot (Ed.), *The General History of Africa* (Vol. 5, pp. 434–452). Paris: UNESCO.

Allen, T.W. (1994). *The Invention of the White Race*. New York: Verso.
American Anthropological Association. (1996). AAA Statement on Race. *American Association of Physical Anthropologists, 101*, 569–570.
Barzun, J. (1965). *Race: A Study of Superstition*. New York: Harper and Row Publishers.
Bettelheim, B. (1940). Comportement individuel et de masse dans les situations extrêmes. *The Journal of Abnormal and Social Psychology, 38*(4), 417–452.
Bettelheim, B. (1979). *Survivre*. Paris: Robert Laffont.
Boahen, A.A. (1999). The States and Cultures of the Lower Guinean Coast. In B.A. Ogot (Ed.), *The General History of Africa* (Vol. 5, pp. 399–433). Paris: UNESCO.
Césaire, A. (1956). Cahier d'un retour au pays natal. *Présence Africaine*.
Dallari, M.P.B. (2021) Affirmative Action at the Federal Supreme Court: The Difficult Promotion of Racial Equity in Brazil. In R. Becak and J. Lima (Eds.) *The Unwritten Brazilian Constitution*. Lanham, MD: Lexington.
DeGruy, J. (2005). *Post Traumatic Slave Syndrome*: Milwaukie, OR: Uptone Press.
Deveau, J.-M. (1994). *La France aux temps des négriers*. Paris: Éditions France Empire.
Diène, D. (2005). *Préface à Les codes noirs hispaniques de Manuel-Lucena Salmoral*: UNESCO.
Drake, S.C. (1987). *Black Folk Here and There* (Vol. 1–2). Los Angeles: Center for Afro-Americans Studies, University of California Los Angeles.
Glissant, E. (1997). *Le Discours Antillais*. Paris: Gallimard.
Goldstein, E.L. (2006). *The Price of Whiteness: Jews, Race, and American Identity*. Princeton: Princeton University Press.
Hall, G.M. (2005). *Slavery and African Ethnicities in the Americas: Restoring the Links*. Chapel Hill: The University of North Carolina Press.
Hawthorne, W. (2010). *From Africa to Brazil: Culture, Identity and an Atlantic Slave Trade, 1600–1830*. Cambridge: Cambridge University Press.
Herskovits, M. (1958). *The Myth of the Negro Past*. Boston: Beacon Press.
Horsman, R. (1981). *Race and Manifest Destiny the Origins of American Racial Anglo-Saxonism*. Cambridge, MA: Harvard University Press.
Ignatiev, N. (1995). *How the Irish Became White*. New York: Routledge.
Kellermann, N. (2009). *Holocaust Trama: Psychological Effects and Treatment*. New York: iUniverse.
Kessler, R., Sonnega, A., Bromet, E., Hughes, M., & Nelson, C. (1995). Posttraumatic Stress Disorder in the National Comorbidity Survey. *Arch Gen Psychiatry, 52*(12), 1048–1060.
Kleinman, A. (1995). *Writing at the margin, discourse between anthropology and medicine*. Berkeley: University of California Press.
Leary, J.D. (2005). *Post Traumatic Slave Syndrome: America's Legacy of Enduring Injury and Healing*. Milwaukie, OR: Uptone Press.
Littlefield, D. (1981). *Race and Slaves: Ethnicity and the Slave Trade in Colonial South Carolina*. Urbana: University of Illinois Press.
M'Bokolo, E.M. (1999). From the Cameroon Grasslands to the Upper Nile. In B.A. Ogot (Ed.), *The General History of Africa* (pp. 515–545). Paris: UNESCO.
McFarlane, A., & de Girolamo, G. (1996). The Nature of Traumatic Stressors and the Epidemiology of Posttraumatic Reactions. In B. van der Kolk, A. McFarlane, & L. Weisaeth (Eds.), *Traumatic Stress: The Effects of Overwhelming Experience on Mind, Body, and Society* (pp. 129–154). New York: The Guilford Press.
Miano, L. (2013). *La saison de l'ombre*. Paris: Grasset.
Mintz, S., & Price, R. (1976). *The Birth of African-American Culture: An Anthropological Perspective*. Boston: Beacon Press.
Ndiaye, P. (2009). *La condition noire: essai sur une minorité française*. Paris: Calmann-Levy.
Organisation Mondiale de la Santé. (1992). *CIM-10, Classification internationale des troubles mentaux et des troubles du comportement: descriptions cliniques et directives pour le diagnostic*. Paris: Masson.
Pierre-Charles, P. (2013). *Frantz Fanon: l'héritage*. Fort-de-France: KEditions.
Rogers, K.L., Leydesdorff, S., & Dawson, G. (Eds.). (1999). *Trauma and Life Stories: International Perspectives*. London: Routledge.

Sweet, J.H. (2003). *Recreating Africa: Culture, Kinship, and Religion in the African-Portuguese World, 1441–1770*. Chapel Hill: The University of North Carolina Press.
Thomas, H. (1997). *The Slave Trade: The Story of the Atlantic Slave Trade: 1440–1870*. New York: Simon & Schuster.
Vinck, H. (1999). Le mythe de Cham dans quelques livrets scolaires du Congo belge. *Canadian Journal of African Studies/Revue canadienne des études africaines*(33), 642–647.
Wyman-McCarthy, M. (2018). Perceptions of French and Spanish Slave Law in Late Eighteenth-Century Britain. *Journal of British Studies, 57*(1), 29–52.

PART ONE

Commonalities

Part One (Chapters 1–5) illustrates psychological legacies of slavery from four Western national cultures that have African slave descendants and from Dahomey, from which enslaved Africans were brought. While each illustration is from a single country, the legacy presented is trans-cultural and transnational. Each legacy exists in all the other Western countries in which slavery was practiced and from which White racial superiority (racism) is a contemporary problem. In the next chapter, colorism is defined and explained. Anyone who questions whether colorism exists needs to observe one thing—the extent to which African descendants in the West straighten their hair so that it can look European (White) and bleach their skin to make it lighter. These practices are standard throughout the Western Hemisphere wherever there are descendants of enslaved Africans.

1

Colorism in Belize

ELMA WHITTAKER-AUGUSTINE

This first chapter consists of reflections on the issue of colorism among Afro-Belizeans. Most Belizeans are people of color. In which case, colorism is not obscured in social relations among Afro-descendants as it is countries with mixed racial and majority European descendant populations. It is more visible, talked about, and in the open. However, Elma Whittaker-Augustine's insights from counseling are not limited to Belize. Her colleagues from Haiti, Brazil, the U.S., Colombia, France, Jamaica, Martinique, and Benin all attested to having the same issues, generally buried in personal narratives, among Afro-descendants in their countries. Thus, this chapter is a highly generalizable case study.

Color Prejudice: A Brief Historical Perspective

Colorism is defined as prejudice and discrimination based on the social meaning attached to skin color. The origin of color prejudice or colorism can be traced to European beliefs and attitudes about color, slavery, and colonialism (Evan X. Hyde, 1975). Before the settlement of Belize and the introduction of slavery, Europeans held ambivalent attitudes about skin color. One origin of the White supremacy concept is rooted in European cultures (Burgest, 1981, p. 26). One perception and classification of people as superior and inferior were based on skin color and other physical characteristics, such as hair texture and the structure of the face, nose, and eyes.

English scholars, who believed in White and European supremacy, made a distinction between "white" and "black." The color "white" connoted purity, virginity, virtue, cleanliness, godliness, and beauty, whereas "black" connoted filthiness, sin, baseness, and ugliness. The devil is black, but the angels are white. Undoubtedly, language played a part in shaping attitudes toward skin color. In the English language, white lies and white magic are innocent, not intending to cause harm. However, the word black in the European worldview connotes meanings of sinister, evil, foreboding, dirty, and nasty. Terms such as blackball, blacklist, black market, black sheep, and blackmail indicate behaviors and situations that are unacceptable.

Descartes' mind-body dualism reinforced the European attitude of cultural superiority and interactions with others based on power and dominance: a conception of the human condition, which is a dualistic way of thinking, e.g., good-bad, master-slave or inferior-superior. Those who believe in cultural superiority looked to science for justification. Darwin's theory was used to justify that those in superior positions were there because they were most "fit." This theory reinforced the idea of a superior culture, created by a superior race. The writings of Francis Galton, a biologist, William Sumner, a sociologist, and G. Stanley Hall, a psychologist, were used to show that some races were more advanced than others. Others wrote of racial hierarchy that placed whites at the top, yellows in between, and blacks at the bottom.

Undoubtedly, a reason why West Africans were taken as slaves was because of their color. "By their color, Africans were so obviously of a different race; the idea of one race enslaving another became acceptable. However, when one race considered itself superior and the other inferior, the idea became more easily acceptable. Instead of color being a superficial difference between two races, it became the basis of all differences, real and imagined, and therefore the justification of African slavery" (Greenwood & Hamber, 1979, p. 94). Although slavery has existed throughout history, in almost all cases in the Americas since European colonization, the system of slavery was associated with race. In nearly all cases, the masters were white, and the slaves were black after initial experiments with Native peoples as slaves. "In the West Indies, nearly every black man was a slave so that he would be imprisoned by his color" (Greenwood & Hamber, 1979, p. 119). This fact is documented as well in a *History of Belize* (Leslie, 1996, p. 22). It is stated that Blacks were assumed to be slaves unless they could prove otherwise, and they were discriminated against by skin color.

In addition to Europeans' beliefs and attitudes about color, the Protestant Reformation in the sixteenth century spawned the outcome that man's direct accountability to God was coupled with extremism, fanaticism, and the rise of capitalism and European expansion. These developments highlighted the need to demonstrate that slaves were less than human. In other words, those who are colored differently must be fundamentally a different type of human. The Africans, who had different cultures, appearances, and religious practices, were reduced to a savage suitable for enslavement.

European politicians and religious leaders were responsible for advocating the idea that slavery was just and beneficial. They even used scriptural quotes, taken entirely out of context, to justify slavery. Black skin color was, according to one legend, God's curse on Ham, the son of Noah, who was believed to be the ancestor of only Africans.

Beyond European beliefs, attitudes, and slavery, colonialism also helped to shape and foster a stratified view of color. Colonialism was not a civilizing mission. On the contrary, it was characterized by three main components. First was the removal of wealth, such as the extraction and exportation to Europe of Belize's logwood and mahogany. The second was the belief that colonizers had the right to take anything belonging to the colonized people for their benefit. Third, colonies were external power-bases to expand the exploitation of more colonies. Indeed, the British used Belize as a stepping stone. Organized foreign domination resulted in social and economic underdevelopment and social stratification based on color. The impact of colonialism on the colonized is reflected in inequality, injustice, a fatalistic worldview, and dependency.

The process of colonialism, and consequent color prejudice in Belize, began when British pirates and buccaneers came to Belize in the seventeenth century and brought their views of color. They settled on the coast of the Bay of Honduras, which later became the settlement of Belize. Early British settlers began trading logwood, which then shifted to the exportation of mahogany. The British needed labor for their trade, and this resulted in the importation of African slaves. Most slaves were brought to Belize in the eighteenth century from the West Indies: many from Jamaica and some directly from Africa. Descendants of Africans from several tribes can be found in Belize. One area of Belize Town in the nineteenth century was called "Eboe Town."

From its roots in slavery, it was just a matter of time before Belize became a majority Black society. The introduction of slavery resulted in a mixture of European indentured laborers and Black Africans. The mixed unions between Whites and Blacks resulted in "individuals who fell on a continuum ranging from very black to very white" (Evan X. Hyde, 1975, p. 75). According to Evan X. Hyde, who described colorism in Belize more extensively than anyone else, "Matings on top of matings resulted in children being born with different fractional percentages of white and black. So, eventually, prejudice in Belize became a matter more of color than of race because race in this hodge-podge was so difficult to identify. A system of color ranking evolved based on a ten-point scale: you get 10 points if you were white, 9 for high-brown, 8 for tan, 7 for medium-tan, 6 for coffee with milk, 5 for cocoa, 4 for coffee, 3 for chocolate, 2 for black, and 1 for nigger black" (1975, p. 16).

Evan X. also wrote: "Although colonialism and institutional colorism were interwoven.... If one got rid of colonial status, (and) eradicated colonialism, one was not necessarily going to eliminate colorism at the same time." According to Hyde, the issue of colorism was prominent, and there was a fight against it in Belize in the late 1940s and early 1950s (Evan X. Hyde, 1975, p. 17). However, color prejudice continued to impact Belize's society well into the present.

Besides, colonial administrations used colorism to divide and rule Belizean society. "The colonial administration and the British settlers succeeded in dividing slaves from each other, African-born from Creole (Creole in Belize refers to a mixture; all individuals who have any African ancestry are called Creole), blacks from brown, skilled and favored from unskilled and unfavored. They also managed to divide slaves from freed Blacks and colored by giving the freemen just enough privileges and favors to make them identify with the Whites" (Leslie, 1996, p. 34). Slaves were controlled socially and psychologically.

The Impact of Color Prejudice

Social Impact

By the end of the nineteenth century, Belize had developed into a visibly racist society. The first stage of enslaving people is to make the world believe that the people enslaved are subhuman, and next is to make his fellow countrymen believe that he is inferior. Last is to make the formerly enslaved believe he/she is inferior. Discrimination in Belize based on skin color persisted in this way after slavery was abolished (end of slavery 1834, finally abolished 1838). In Belize, color prejudice and acceptance of a negative and inferior status are evidence that inner feelings and beliefs remain from slavery and colonialism. This residual indicates that our minds are not yet free. As Bolland stated, "While his powerlessness and rightlessness as a slave may be seen as related to the juridical idea of the slave as property, his continued powerlessness as a free person was related to his racial identity" (1988, p. 193).

Joy A. DeGruy's years of research captured the impact of slavery when she wrote, "The systematic dehumanization of African Slaves was the initial trauma, and the generations of their descendants have borne the scar" (Joy A. DeGruy Leary, 2005, p. 1). Colorism is one example of the traumatic effect of slavery. Being black, which implied being inferior, less than human, resulted in internalized negative beliefs and attitudes, and damage to self-esteem, which in many cases resulted in self-hatred, denial of heritage and social discrimination.

Unfortunately, color prejudice does matter in Belize society. Its social impact/damage is apparent in the preference given to light-skinned Belizean Blacks, in jobs, in social opportunities, in politics, and education. The impact of color prejudice is reflected, as well, in hiring practices in Belize, where there is a preference for lighter-skin Belizeans, particularly in the banks and civil service.

In addition to hiring practices, the influence of color prejudice is also seen in business. In an article and book, Evan X. Hyde first asked a question and then commented, "Where are the black men in business?" He responded, "The black man of African descent plays almost no role in the business life of the community of Belize City." He further stated, "Start with the banks, a black man cannot borrow $50 to open a snow cone set. However, a White boy from America can get a $50,000 loan to buy snowmaking machinery" (1975; 1995, pp. 277–278). This issue continues to hold today. Very few Belizean Blacks are owners of stores and businesses, and very few black Belizeans can readily obtain loans from banks.

Social opportunities for lighter-skinned Blacks are better than social opportunities for darker-complexion Blacks. "A light-skinned, straight-haired Mestizo child who learns English and attends the prestigious St. John's College may be more likely to rise into the elite than a Creole-speaking black child" (Bolland, 1988, p. 173). Therefore, it is easier for light-skinned Blacks to get ahead in Belize society. This is the result of color and cultural assimilation. "Those with lighter skins used their closer assimilation to the Whites as a means of their own advancement and of their right to assume ruling positions along with Whites" (Shoman, 1994, p. 173). Also, lighter complexion Blacks are more acceptable to Whites.

Color prejudice is reflected, as well, in Belize's history of limited membership in social clubs. For example, before the 1930s, Belizean Blacks were refused membership at the Pickwick Club. Although this restriction has not been enforced since the 1970s, it is understood clearly that Blacks are still not welcomed as members.

In politics, it was stated openly in 1998 that a Black man or a "Carib" (Garifuna) cannot become prime minister of Belize. An unwritten qualification for the office was that of being light-skinned, Mestizo, or White. Black political leaders and a high percentage of voters hold this view.

In education, color prejudice is reflected in schools, as well. For example, it has been known since the 1950s, but not openly stated, that St. Catherine's high school was for the light-skinned elite, and Pallotti high school was mostly for dark-skinned Blacks.

In sharing his experience of division and prejudice in the *Amandala* Newspaper (1997), Selvin Wade stated, "At the convent school for boys by the seaside, we had three classrooms—black, brown and light-skinned.

Sister always said 'my little black boys,' then 'my little brown boys,' and then 'my little angels'" (1997).

Growing up in Belize, the impact of colorism was also reflected in the language and conversations of Belizeans. Belizeans would boast about their light-skinned child or their white ancestors. Some dark-complected Belizeans would state that they did not care to go to the Cayes (islands) because the sun made them very dark. Also, comments such as nappy head, black skin, tar baby were used as derogatory terms. Young people with such hair texture and skin color were told by their parents to lift themselves by entering relationships with lighter-skinned individuals. One way for a dark-skinned male to get ahead was to uplift himself and improve his social position by marrying a light-skinned woman. In the early 1970s, most Belizean men who went abroad to study returned home with White wives. I can still remember a color incident, which occurred in my high school. My friend, a dark-complected and attractive young woman, was approached by the father of a light-complected Belize Creole. He told her to discontinue her friendship with his son because her complexion was too dark. I can also recall many Black Belizeans being offended when they were referred to as black. They would respond that they are not black, but brown.

Another social impact of slavery is the influence of diet on Belizeans. During slavery, the slave masters consumed the thin and fleshy parts of farm animals and left the scraps for slaves. This influence continues to this day. Even today, pigtail, cow foot, oxtail, tripe are stapled foods in Belizeans diets. Many Belizeans will not cook red beans without the pigtail.

Psychological Impact

The negative attitudes and beliefs about dark-skinned individuals and preferential treatment of individuals with lighter skin continue to impact the definition of beauty. Social scientists theorize that those who strive for success see this preference for lighter skin as the acceptance of standards set by the "establishment," for appearance and behavior. Consequently, conformity is one price for success. Psychoanalytic explanations, on the other hand, suggest that it is the result of identification with the aggressor: the oppressed imitating the oppressor to survive. Whether the correct theory is acceptance of established standards or identification with the aggressor, the fact is that psychological damage is the price paid for accepting this presumed inferiority.

Identifying with Whites in Belizean society entails negating and denying blackness, and more specifically, African characteristics. It negatively affects African descendants' self-concept, self-esteem, and identity.

Self-concept is many-faceted. It is fundamental to who we are: it is the mental model of our abilities and attributes. Self-concept is the foundation on which we base our actions, thoughts, and directions in life. Self-esteem is one crucial aspect of self-concept. It refers to judgments we make about our self-worth, which also influences mood, personal, and social behaviors. Self-esteem is also interwoven into group identity and group esteem.

Damage to one's self-concept and self-esteem, caused by internalizing negative beliefs and attitudes about black skin color, is reflected in low self-esteem, rejection of self, feelings of insecurity and inadequacy, depression, and anxieties. When self-acceptance does not occur, a person's low self-esteem and self-hatred are reflected in a negative self-image, an incomplete image of self, and a preference for white skin, straight hair, and European facial features. In addition to feelings of anxiety, a person feels limited in his/her sense of personal control over his/her environment. Consequently, he/she experiences a lack of personal power. Personal power is defined as "the belief or knowledge that one is at least equal to everyone else in our society" (J.L. Robinson, 1995, p. 211).

There is direct evidence of the psychological damage seen in some dark-skinned individuals who feel unattractive, and experience shame in their appearance. Some try to change themselves with hair chemicals and skin bleaching creams. Taking such actions is all about becoming more like the "ideal" European standard of beauty, having pale skin, and even blond hair. The objective is to become more worthy of acceptance by White people.

Also, the psychological damage is reflected in adaptive inferiority and inferiority complexes (Pugh, 1972, pp. 12–13). Adaptive inferiority is defined as internalizing negative beliefs about other Blacks and is a way for Blacks to manage the anxiety provoked by the behaviors of Whites towards them. Without question, such an adaptive stance affects self-concept, ideas, images, and feelings a person holds about themselves regarding self-worth, value, and esteem. In addition to adaptive inferiority, many individuals developed an inferiority complex. An inferiority complex results when one feels inferior or is made to feel inferior. Feelings of inferiority are conscious and unconscious.

However, in the case of color prejudice, a person with an inferiority complex misjudges his/her personal worth and internalizes negative attitudes and beliefs associated with being black. A person suffering from this complex may respond in various ways in their attempt to achieve acceptance. He/she may over-identify with Whites and reject or negate the self. An example from Belize society is a "high brown," a person who pretends to be White. "It means his mind has been whitewashed to almost Caucasian, Caucasian like, or lover of the said Caucasian" (Evans X. Hyde, 1995, p.

12). Others may be driven by a quest for status or may be striving for superiority to compensate. Even though this may result in social success, such a pursuit is unhealthy because one's motivation comes from a broad sense of inferiority.

Another form of ego compensation is to exaggerate or overdo things. An example is over-dressing or getting overly dressed up to seek acceptance. By doing this, one materially overcompensates for what one feels he/she lacks as a person. Overcompensating is sometimes described as a symbolic striving for status denied. Others may assume the role of the entertainer or clown, always feeling they have to perform and entertain, or play the fool, to be accepted. Unfortunately, when we see these behaviors, we dismiss them, view them as ridiculous, and miss their underlying meaning. Our liberation is enhanced when we see these behaviors for what they indeed are, reflections of psychological damage and ego defenses resulting from color prejudice.

Another consequence of the rejection of self is difficulty in forming a healthy identity. Identity is a self-image about who and what we are. It is formed by integrating what we think about ourselves and what others think of us. In other words, it combines one's personality and one's social role. One way to achieve an identity is to see oneself as part of a social group. If our social group is evaluated negatively (black meaning bad, ugly or backward), and we internalize these evaluations, we cannot form a positive identity. An additional consequence is expressed hostility towards one's group, because of shame for having the qualities of the group, and for belonging to it. Many light-skinned Belizean Blacks, for example, not only choose to identify with Whites: they discriminate against darker Blacks as well.

Ernest Vernon wrote in *The Belize Creole*, "this trend of discrimination continues to this point.... Many Creoles with fair or brown skin are sometimes abusive to their black brothers and sisters. Creoles in high positions are mostly arrogant in their association with what they term as subordinate people." This self-hatred and lack of pride and respect for self and race are reflected in the Creole proverb "...Di moos kaman mine in Belize da bad mind" (Vernon, 1994, p. 8). This proverb reflects as Ernest Vernon stated, the lack of unity amongst Belizeans, our tearing each other down, and our low rating of each other with negative criticism.

The inability to accept oneself spawns not only disrespect but also intolerance of others. Another outcome of disrespect for self and others is increased crime against each other. It also accounts for the fact that Belizeans welcome strangers, and are helpful to them, but are not helpful to each other. Furthermore, it results in the need for validation from Whites and outsiders. What is so unfortunate is that this validation rarely occurs.

As Malcolm X stated, "One thing the white man can never give the black man is self-respect" (1965, p. 275). The hefty price that has been paid is the acceptance and internalization of harmful white standards and beliefs about blackness.

Addressing Color Prejudice

Acknowledgment: The way forward requires that we independently define ourselves, assume control over our attitudes, language, behaviors, and society. The first step to make these changes is to have awareness and acknowledgment of the problem/damage. Black playwright and director of theater and film, George C. Wolfe, once stated, "wounds heal better in the open air" (1986, p. 2). To date, many Belizeans deny they are affected by colorism. Therefore, in addressing the issue of color prejudice, Belizeans first need to accept the fact that we are all affected by color prejudice. Belizeans also need to accept the fact that slavery and colonialism shaped our mentality and that we are mentally colonized people. We find it difficult to deal seriously with our self-definition and existence, because dependency, a consequence of colonialism, has restricted our ability to act independently and to determine our destiny. There has been resistance to change in this area because many would prefer to ignore this problem.

Learn Origin and Ancestry: After acknowledging the impact of colorism, the second step is to get knowledge of our origin and ancestry, which are essential to liberation. We need to know our origin and history. Black people cannot achieve emancipation from mental slavery and achieve racial and self-pride without knowledge of their origin and ancestry. As Karenga stated, "To know oneself is to grasp the essence of one's past, one's present, and especially one's future possibility..." (1982, p. 466). Therefore, education and knowledge of one's ancestry are essential to this liberation process. As stated in Belize's *Amandala* Newspaper, "the people of this society are oppressed, and they are oppressed because they are brainwashed. Before they even begin to find solutions to the problem, they must first re-educate to a true knowledge of self and kind and understand our culture, history, and experience as a Latin Caribbean people who have been enslaved, colonized and exploited..." (Evan X. Hyde, 1972).

Knowledge can provide identity, racial pride, purpose, and direction. This process calls for the inclusion of the teaching of Black history and the histories of people of color in school curriculums. The teaching of Black history will not only foster information essential to positive self-esteem and identity, but it will also combat harmful misinformation that African history is backward when compared to European history.

Active Engagement in Self-Liberation: The third step is to assume a more active role in our mental liberation, and in assuming responsibility for our lives. Bob Marley captures this task in his Redemption Song "emancipate yourself from mental slavery, none, but ourselves can free our minds...." To promote psychological well-being, Belizeans of African ancestry need to stop seeking acceptance from Whites and to stop using Whites as a reference point for what is positive and beautiful.

Watch How We Talk to and About One Another: The fourth step is to be cognizant of the integral role that language played in color prejudice. "Black" must lose its negative meaning. We need to know we have been conditioned socially to associate negative attributes and meanings to the color black, and that this has damaged our self-worth, esteem, definition, and identity. Therefore, we need to monitor language for prejudicial and stereotypical remarks and recognize and embrace the beauty of blackness.

Organizational Efforts: Efforts to promote black consciousness were introduced in Belize society in 1920 by the Belize Black Cross Nurses Association, a direct outgrowth of Marcus Garvey's Universal Negro Improvement Association (UNIA). Ideas about being Black and proud were introduced and encouraged in the late 1960s with the formation of the United Black Association for Development (UBAD). A healthy change in meaning and attitude about black skin color must continue to be advocated. Belizeans should monitor the messages given to our Black children about who they are. They need to be taught not to let others define them and not to live a script written by others. Black Belizeans also need to acknowledge the resulting damage of rejection and even hatred of one's group. Black Belizeans, unlike other ethnic groups, do not support and help each other. They continue to find it difficult to unite around common causes. Instead, the current social situation reflects a continued increase in black-on-black crime, where Black Belizean males are violently annihilating each other.

Epigenetics offers Belizeans the potential hope that negative affective and behavioral meanings attached to the color Black and passed down through generations can be better understood in terms of any health effects they may have. Belizean medical practitioner, Dr. Bernard Bulwer, captured this in Amandala Newspaper, 2016 when he wrote: "I believe that the problems caused by human behavior can also be solved by a change in human behavior" (2016). Also, the strengths, resilience, and cultural values (e.g., the importance of families and reliance on God) of Black Belizeans equip us with qualities needed to overcome social and psychological damage.

There is a long way to go in reversing the psychological trauma of colorism. However, two improvements can be noted: the election of Belize's first Black Prime Minister in 2008, and the study on the effects of skin color in the Americas on Educational Attainment (Telles & Steele, 2013, p. 4). This study examined the relationship between years of schooling and skin color and showed that color differences in Belize and Guyana affect educational outcomes.

Another positive step forward in the overall liberation of Belize was the country's independence from England in 1981. An additional positive step forward is that Belize began *celebrating Emancipation from Slavery Day* for the first time in 2015.

Inclusion of Other Ethnic Groups: The social support for Black acceptance and pride is an essential part of the healing process. Therefore, *advocating racial and ethnic pride for Black Belizeans as well as pride in other ethnic groups is essential.* Belize is a country comprised of numerous ethnic groups: Creole, Mestizo, Maya, Garifuna, and Chinese. Advocating for Black pride should **not** be viewed as a divisive attempt or threat to other ethnic groups. It should not be reduced to an "Us vs. Them" issue. Such separation is an inherent aspect of discrimination, an issue that is at the core of color prejudice. Belizeans of other ethnic groups are a part of the social healing process. They need to be aware of the damage and the danger inherent in internalizing negative attitudes and beliefs about blackness, and in ignoring the impact of denial of self and heritage. The process of nation-building in Belize requires understanding and addressing the effects of colorism. Also, more research is needed on the impacts of colorism, slavery, and colonialism.

In sum, color prejudice, which began as a set of attitudes, was rationalized during slavery to exploit Black and non–European people. The experience of colonialism fostered it. Colorism has become internalized at the level of personality and, consequently, has become a part of the social personality of Belizeans. We cannot boast of our racial harmony and continue to deny that we have color prejudice in the face of such psychological and social damage.

Although the emphasis of this chapter is to address colorism as one of the traumatic impacts of slavery, respect for and to foster racial and ethnic pride in all Belizean ethnic groups are advocated as well. Belizeans cannot ignore the fact that prejudice and racism will lead to intergroup conflict and a dysfunctional society. Belizeans should know that a person cannot be entirely secure and possess positive self-esteem if their self-worth depends on maintaining the belief that they are better than or inferior to others. Building healthy self-esteem and racial identity in all ethnic groups in Belize will contribute to a strong national identity, in which all Belizeans can take pride.

References

Bolland, O.N. (1988). *Colonialism and Resistance in Belize: Essays in Historical Sociology*. Belize: Cubola/Spear/Iser.
Bulwer, B. (2016, July 16). A Call for Belizean Self-Reflection and Unity. *Amandala*, p. 43.
Burgest, D.R. (1981). Theory on White Supremacy/Black Oppression. *Black Books Bulletin*, 7(2), 26–30.
Greenwood, R., & Hamber, S. (1979). *Arawaks to Africans*. London: Macmillan.
Hyde, E.X. (1972, Unknown). *Amandala*.
Hyde, E.X. (1975). *Feelings: Colourism: The Deeper Problem*. Belize City: Benex Press.
Hyde, E.X. (1995). *X Communication*. Belize City, Belize: The Angelus Press.
Karenga, M. (1982). *Introduction to Black Studies*. Los Angeles: Kawaida Publication.
Leary, J.D. (2005). *Post Traumatic Slave Syndrome: America's Legacy of Enduring Injury and Healing*. Milwaukie, OR: Uptone Press.
Leslie, R. (Ed.) (1996). *A History of Belize: Nation in the Making*. Benque Viejo del Carmen, Belize: Cubola Productions.
Malcolm X. (1965). *Malcolm X Speaks*. New York: Grove Press.
Pugh, R.W. (1972). *Psychology and the Black Experience*. Monterey, CA: Brooks/Cole.
Robinson, J.L. (1995). *Racism or Attitude? The Ongoing Struggle for Black Liberation and Self-Esteem*. New York: Insight Books Plenum Press.
Shoman, A. (1994). *Thirteen Chapters of A History of Belize*. Belize City, Belize: The Angelus Press.
Telles, E., & Steele, L. (2013). *Pigmentocracy in the Americas: How Educational Attainment Is Related to Skin Color*. Latin American Public Opinion Project: Americas Barometer Insights, 2012.
Vernon, E. (1994). *The Belize Creole*. Belizean Heritage Publishers Belize City: Benex Press.
Wade, S. (1997). Social Commentary Columnist. *Amandala Newspaper Article, Belize City*.
Wolfe, G. (1986, November 6). Colored Museum Is Author's Exorcism. *New York Times*.

2

Slavery and Psychological Trauma in the Haitian Crisis[1]

Judite Blanc

From the previous chapter, we learned that colorism is a cultural belief with origins in slavery that divides and stratifies descendants of enslaved Africans by skin color. Education and efforts to raise consciousness about colorism and its source are necessary steps to lessen, if not to eliminate it. In this chapter, a psychological legacy has its origins in multi-traumas. What happens when traumas have occurred not just in slavery, but also in every generation since then? There have even been multiple traumas within a generation. Such a history runs far beyond our current knowledge of symptoms and treatments. We do not know if the effects of numerous traumas negate one another, accumulate, or transform into unidentified symptoms. The next chapter presents Haiti, which has had such a history and reflects on the multiple traumatic experiences within and across generations of other African descendant populations in the West.

Located in the Caribbean Sea, Haiti shares the western part of the island of Hispaniola with the Dominican Republic. Its territory covers an area of 27,750 km², officially divided into ten departments: West, Southeast, North, Artibonite, North, Northeast, Center, South, Grand Anse, and Northwest. The most important city is the economic and political capital of Port-au-Prince (Institut Haïtien de Statistique et d'Informatique IHSI, 2003). By 2015, the total population of Haiti was estimated at 10,911,819. The two official languages are Creole and French (Institut Haïtien de Statistiques et d'Informatique IHSI, 2009; 2007). Religious affiliations occupy a prominent place in Haitian daily life. Catholicism is the largest single faith (39.1 percent), compared to a combination of Protestant/Methodist/

Adventist/Jehovah's Witnesses (53.1 percent) and one percent "declared" as Vodoun practitioners (Cayemittes et al., 2013).

In 2003, unemployment was reported at 35 percent, and more than 50 percent of the population survived on less than one U.S. dollar per day. This means that 76 percent of Haitian families were living below the international poverty line (IHSI, 2003). By 2015, the World Bank's IHSI statistics showed an unemployment rate of 60 percent. The Haitian economy is the least developed in Latin America and the Caribbean: it ranks last. It depends on outside aid for more than 50 percent of its daily consumption (Ministère de la Planification et de la Coopération Externe, 2015). On the health front, only 3.1 percent of all households are covered by health insurance (IHSI, 2003). Haiti has the highest rates of HIV infection in the Caribbean. Tuberculosis, malaria, filariasis, dengue, and anthrax are active infectious diseases. Additional mortality is due to increasing rates of cardiovascular diseases, diabetes, and neoplasias (Ministère de la Sante Publique et de la Population MSPP, 2012). The human resource density is 3.6 per 10,000 inhabitants. This is the lowest health coverage rate in the Americas, behind Guyana (11.2), Guatemala (12.5), Honduras (13.6), and Bolivia (14.1).

There are reasons for Haiti's intense and continued poverty, related to its unique history of turmoil and crisis. This chapter will break from the familiar narrative about Haiti's poverty. *The fact is that the psychological consequences of centuries of poverty and crises have never been assessed.* I will attempt to address the underlying and unaddressed psychological toll Haitians are paying for both their history and present condition.

First, we must start with the fact that the Republic of Haiti was born after the insurrection of Santo Domingo slaves. They defeated the most powerful army of the time, that of Napoleon Bonaparte, on November 18, 1803, in Vertières (Cap-Haitien, department in the North of Haiti). About 100,000 Africans and 24,000 of 40,000 White settlers lost their lives during the revolt (Brown, 2010). Independence was proclaimed on January 1, 1804, in Gonaives in the Artibonite (Madiou, 1849). Haiti became the first nation of African descendants in the world to liberate itself militarily from slavery and European political control. Haitians have paid the price for their early independence and for how they earned it.

Crisis After Crisis

Haiti is poor for several reasons. Since independence, Haiti has been continuously in political and social turmoil. In its first hundred years, the United States and Western European nations were hostile to Haiti. It was isolated diplomatically and economically. Many of these nations, along with newly independent Latin American nations, refused to trade with Haiti. This political and economic isolation impoverished the Haitian people and negated any basis for foreign trade and exchange. From 1915 to 1934, U.S. Marines occupied the young Black republic, which protected U.S. businesses' extraction of resources and labor (Corvington, 2007). Then, during the second half of the twentieth century, Haiti was ruled by bloody Duvalierist dictators for 30 years. After escaping a coup d'etat, Francois Duvalier (Papa Doc) replaced army leaders with officers loyal to him, forming his militia, the "Tontons Macoutes." According to Hurbon (1987), they were "estimated at 40,000 ... the macoutes are placed in all the country's institutions (army, university, churches, press, administration) to mount a vigilant guard around the dictatorship" (p. 21). Any real and potential opponents were executed or exiled. The Duvalier dictatorship rigidly controlled any commerce in Haiti and allowed a few families to enrich themselves by controlling virtually all business and commerce. This continued to stifle the development of Haitian education, business, and civil society.

Before dying in 1971, Papa Doc named his 19-year-old son, Jean-Claude Duvalier (Baby Doc), president for life as the head of the country. During the reign of Baby Doc, the local press seemed to have a semblance of free expression, and even human rights groups could exist, but no promised democratic reforms emerged. Meanwhile, corruption was rampant. Jean-Claude Duvalier capitulated only after economic pressure from the Reagan administration. This came after numerous human rights violations, incarcerations, assassinations and exile of regime opponents, and closure of media outlets. On February 7, 1986, under the protection of the U.S. Army, he fled with his family to France. They returned in 2011. He was prosecuted for human rights violations and crimes against humanity. However, he died suddenly from a heart attack in 2014, before his trial and possible conviction (Alphonse, 2014; Duval, 2011; Geffrard, 2013).

The U.S. has and continues to play a central role in maintaining Haiti's poverty. It does so by considering Haiti as part of its sphere of influence. Political events and development in Haiti are to be monitored carefully to prevent Cuban, Russian, or Chinese influence. U.S. geopolitical interests are maintained if Haitian governments are anti-communist even if it means repressing the Haitian people's democratic sentiment. Ironically, the U.S. has never viewed the development of the Haitian economy as in its longer-term strategic interest. Consequently, Haiti's natural resources are extracted only for U.S. corporate benefits, but the usual wide range of trade between countries has been either overlooked or discouraged. The Organization of American States (OAS), the European Union (EU), and France have all honored the U.S. political monopoly over Haiti and neglect of its economy.

Another reason for Haiti's poverty is that the island has been the target of numerous natural cataclysms: tropical storms, long-range floods, earthquakes, periodic droughts, mass deforestation, desertification, and soil erosion. From 1751 to 1842, four massive earthquakes devastated Haiti's western half of the island of Hispaniola. The history of Haitian seismicity is extensive, and the urgency to prepare the population for earthquakes has been an issue for successive governments. Many Haitians deny their risk (Prepetit, 2008). Less than two years after the publication of numerous warnings issued by Geologist Claude Prepetit, on January 12, 2010, at 4:53 p.m., earthquakes with a magnitude of 7.3 on the Richter scale struck the department of the West and part of the South of Haiti. The quakes released an amount of energy equal to a five megaton H-bomb. According to a report by the United Nations (2010), the death toll now stands at 222,000. Six thousand were injured and one million displaced. In the aftermath, 19 million cubic meters of concrete and debris covered the capital's streets. Four thousand schools were damaged, along with 60 percent of all government administrative buildings. One and a half million survivors took refuge in makeshift camps, at the mercy of storms and floods.

Then, in October 2010, Nepalese soldiers deployed as peacekeepers by the United Nations to help Haiti after the quake reintroduced cholera in the Artibonite (Piarrous, 2010; United Nations, 2016). With the health system destroyed by the earthquake, cholera became an epidemic by quickly spreading to the rest of the country. By January 7, 2014, the epidemic had killed 8,534 people. As many as 697,256 cases were reported to the Health Ministry (Orata, Keim, & Boucher, 2014). Two years following the earthquake and epidemic, four percent of national households still lived in shelters, four percent were injured in the earthquake, and three percent had at least one family member killed, especially in metropolitan areas. Sixty-four percent of families experienced a complete lack of food for at least one month, and 16 percent of households had at least one person infected with cholera.

Mental Health Crisis

Haitians and their academics have been quick to draw attention to the psychological effects on young people who experienced the earthquake and its aftermath. Scientists strongly urged that mental health services are needed to play a crucial role in the country's reconstruction efforts. Since the earthquake, efforts have been made to develop the mental health field in Haiti and to provide services. The first mental health publication described the integration of a "mental health component" into the National Health Policy 2012–2020 for Haiti (MSPP, 2014). Many welcomed the plan, but regret that it took such a disaster to call attention to this need.

However, when we look back on our history, we have been in crisis since the founding of the nation. The recent earthquake is just the latest of our traumas. It is impossible to talk about just treating the latest trauma. We have repetitive traumas, after repeated crises, occurring over generations to address in our nation's mental health needs. The following is a translation and paraphrasing of a declaration from Haitian mental health professionals:

> On the occasion of the celebration of the World Day of Mental Health on 10 October 2015, we recognize that we live in a climate of generalized crises that has spared no sector of Haitian society—not family, schools, the university, politics, economy, churches, culture, environment, and health. The time has come to dare ask aloud the thorny question that ordinary Haitians ask in a low voice. Are we in Haiti a mentally ill society in need of treatment? To this end, we would like to invite health professionals, intellectuals, academics, and all other interested parties to join us in addressing this question. A two-centuries-old public health emergency has been ignored. We aim to reflect on what we see in the mirror by facing the "psychic agony" that we see and have struggled to free ourselves from for so long [Blanc, 2015].

From our point of view, we see the Haitian crisis as primarily a mental health crisis. It is psychological before it is social, political, economic, or ecological. A mental health crisis ordinarily refers to a sudden, violent, brief, and all-consuming event such as anxiety, panic, and existential crises. In the medical world, this notion explains morbid states that occur suddenly, with intensity and temporarily, suggesting a significant positive or adverse change in the course of a disease. It should be noted, as well, that a crisis reflects an abrupt change or break in beliefs, governance, production, and environment. We intend to isolate the root of the Haitian crisis and to uncover the central psychopathology of the abrupt changes responsible for our ongoing mental health crises. This is what we need to know to envisage the conditions for healing.

Haitian Psycho-Trauma

From ancient Greek, "traumatismos" or trauma evokes the idea of an injury. Based on psycho-dynamic etiology, trauma represents a brutal intrusion into one's mind and consciousness. The intrusion is strong enough to overwhelm one's psychological defenses and to threaten one's sense of self, and the cognitive world one lives within. The psychological threat, fear, and damage can lead, in turn, to physical injury and crisis.

Some examples of the psychological disorders and behaviors attributed to traumatic events include directly experiencing or witnessing sexual abuse, violence, aggression, neglect, acts of terror and the taking of human life, invasive diseases and physically severe illnesses (American Psychiatric Association, 2013). Trauma may occur with different outcomes during childhood, adolescence, or as adults. Formally, traumatic results are classified as psychological or somatic disorders such as post-traumatic stress disorder, anxiety disorders, and depressive disorders.

Transgenerational Transmission of Trauma

There is evidence that trauma in one generation can be transmitted to the next generation. The survivors of the 2010 earthquake in Haiti are a case in point (Blanc, Rahill, Laconi, & Mouchenik, 2016). However, instead of looking at any traumatic outcomes from the 2010 Haitian earthquake as a first trauma, they should be examining re-traumatization. Haitian experience with trauma and re-trauma has gone on for generations. In each of the following high points in Haiti's history, fore-parents of the current Haitian population were injured, violated, threatened with death, or witnessed all three repeatedly.

- 1492—Arrival of the Europeans (Columbus) on the island of Hispaniola. The native population was exterminated and died from diseases.
- 16th century (the 1500s): Establishment of the slave trade. Africans were "broken in" to serve as slaves after being captured, torn from their families, and transported through the Middle Passage between Africa and the West. Beatings, torture, rape, and the threat of all three were essential to maintain order and control. Surviving native islanders were eventually integrated into the slave population.
- 1791—General Slave Uprising. Resistance and uprisings were continuous, as were beatings, torture, and executions because of their resistance. This date is significant only because of the scale of the rebellion and its near success.
- 1804—Independence is proclaimed. Finally, there was an uprising, which could not be put down. After three bloody years of war, Haitian slaves won the war and proclaimed independence, but at a hefty price. It is estimated that up to half of their number were killed.
- 1825–1893—Haiti had to pay France the equivalent of 150 million francs as a price for independence. This was the value of the slaves,

plantations, and other properties seized or destroyed in the war of independence. Payments were still being made well into the 1950s. These payments drained Haiti of its internal revenue and kept the population in extreme poverty for over one hundred years. Deaths by starvation and disease were common.
- 1844—The secession of the Dominican Republic saw another period of warfare on the island, with more injuries and loss of lives.
- 1915–1934—American occupation: more economic dislocation, imprisonment, injuries, and lives lost.
- 1957–1986—Duvalier Dictatorship (Republic of Haiti), more injuries and lives lost, along with years of torture and terror from Duvalier's Tontons Macoutes.

All these events produced experiences for Haitians that match the criteria of profoundly traumatic events. In some cases, these events overlapped and generated the circumstances for multiple traumas within a single generation. Compared to other countries that have gone through political and economic crises and war such as Germany, Turkey, Chile, and Argentina, Haiti is much smaller in population and physical size. This means that each of the above events has affected in some way every Haitian family and community. All Haitians have been impacted by these events, as they were by the recent earthquake and its aftermath.

The above historical events can not only traumatize the generation that experienced them, that trauma might be passed on epigenetically. Subtle changes in one's genes can occur and then passed across generations (Kellerman 2001). However, the content of transmissions can contribute as well to resilience in subsequent generations, but it can also be a psychopathological inheritance, increasing subsequent generations' predisposition to a future trauma. Kellerman grouped the epigenetic plus three other modes of trauma transmission into four theoretic models:

From table 3.1, intergenerational transmission of trauma is passed unconsciously from relatives with traumatic experiences (psychodynamic). This transmission includes learned behavior (sociocultural) from the community, family development (family systems), and genes (biological). All four possibilities constitute a "bio-psycho-social" context for interpersonal trauma. The literature is extensive on the transgenerational transmission of trauma. These perspectives are derived mainly from work involving victims in four traumatic situations:

1. Major historical traumas: The Holocaust, the Armenian genocide, the dictatorships in Chile and Argentina;
2. War veterans, including those from Vietnam;

Theory	Mode of Transmission	Transmission Factor
Psychodynamic	Interpersonal relations	Unconscious & displaced emotions
Sociocultural	Socialization	Parenting & role models
Family Systems	Communication	Enmeshment
Biological	Genes	Hereditary vulnerability to PTSD

Table 2.1. Models of Traumatic Transmission (Kellerman, 2009, p. 77).

3. Parental sexual and marital abuse;
4. Special events such as the September 11, 2011, attack in the U.S. (Baubet et al., 2006).

Also, there are animal studies carried out in laboratories, or with victims of natural disasters, that provide additional evidence (Kinney et al. 2008). Subjects exposed to intrauterine stress develop a considerable number of neurological and behavioral disorders. They include physiological responses to stress; attention, language and learning disorders; abnormal development of the central nervous system (CNS); hypervigilant behavior; avoidance behavior; hypothalamic-pituitary axis dysfunction; production of high levels of stress hormone; as well as psychiatric disorders such as schizophrenia, depression, autistic disorders, epilepsy or mental retardation.

Pre-, Peri- and Post-Traumatic Factors

The Haitian crisis is not about one trauma in one generation, nor is it about one trauma carried across one or two generations. It is possible to be traumatized multiple times in each generation and carry some portion of these unresolved issues forward, socially or epigenetically, as a burden for subsequent generations. The extent of the psychological burden is determined by the interaction between pre-, peri- and post-traumatic factors across four centuries in Haiti. The pre-traumatic factors are the age at which ancestors were captured, the intra-uterine exposure of slave children to trauma, and the extent to which tribal cultures equipped enslaved Africans to deal with the Middle Passage. Also, there is the geographical vulnerability of Haiti to a natural disaster. The peri-traumatic variables refer to the sum of neurobiological reactions (distress intensity, feelings of helplessness, and neuro-vegetative activation associated with depression), as well as the nature and impact of traumatic

54   Part One—Commonalities

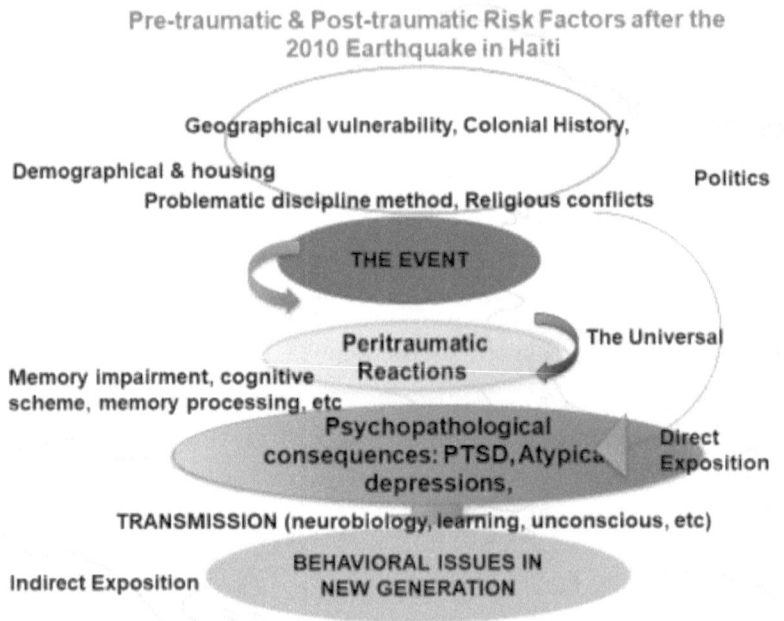

Figure 2.1. Heuristic Model of Haitian Crisis Psycho-Trauma.

events experienced by one's ascendants during slavery. Finally, there are post-traumatic factors: the imposition of poverty on Haitians by debt payment to France, of political powerlessness during successive U.S. occupations, and their support of dictators, the terror of the Tontons Macoutes, successive natural disasters and continuous dependence on foreign aid and relief.

I hypothesize that the outcomes of interactions between pre-, peri- and post-traumatic risk factors, originating in slavery, are symptoms of social trauma today in Haiti. We unconsciously live them, see them, and accept them as the norm.

Symptoms of Trauma Originating in Slavery

We have identified a set of typical behaviors among Haitians in our professional counseling and interactions and relations with each other. *We hypothesize that they are symptomatic of the lived experiences of our ancestors, yet still affect us today.* Included are our attitudes toward power, health, ecology, and our psychological coping. The following are the most obvious; there are many others yet to be identified:

1. Violence and Child Servitude

"Timoun se ti bèt" (Children are animals)
"Timoun renmen baton" (The children obey only with the whip)

In Haiti, beating a child is considered reasonable, necessary, and proper to raise them. Beating slaves was deemed to be normal, necessary, and proper to motivate slaves to work. The two beatings are related. Slavery has ended, but traditional child-rearing practices that began in slavery have not ended.

Then, there is the contemporary practice of having a young person entrusted by his parents or guardians to another family with the means to support them, providing food, clothing, shelter, access to education and care, in exchange for domestic work. These children are referred to as "restavèks." There are no official figures on the actual number of restavèk in Haiti in 2017. In 2012, UNICEF estimated that there were 225,000 of them. Frequently, these children find themselves deprived of family affection and their rights to education. They are forced to work without pay and experience various forms of physical, sexual, and psychological abuse (Kennedy, 2012). In effect, today, they spend their childhood and early adult years as slaves.

The EMMUS-V survey of Haitians showed that two-thirds of all children aged five to eleven years (65 percent) worked during the week preceding the survey. For this age group, housework took up to 28 hours or more during the week. Nearly two out of ten (18 percent) children aged twelve to fourteen years did domestic work during the week of the survey, from 14 to 28 or more hours per week. For most children aged two to fourteen (86 percent), corporal punishment was the most common form of discipline. Only eight percent of children were subjected to non-violent disciplinary sanctions, and five percent reported psychological aggression carried out against them (Cayemittes, 2013).

2. The Primacy of French Language and Culture

While Haiti may have beat the French militarily, and became politically independent, educated French Haitians did not turn away from the French language and culture. They embraced it more totally than before the Revolution. Ironically, they saw no need or value in equally embracing aspects of French commerce, science, and technology that might have advanced Haitian trade, economy, agriculture, or technology. The few schools started for Haitians focus on classical French education and language, and taught little to nothing about Haiti, or about what would be useful to Haitian advancement. Here is how their teaching has been described:

> Active learning through problem-solving or the accumulation of knowledge based on rigorous reasoning is often relegated to the background in the Haitian educational environment. Thus, students are used to memorizing in a second language if they are not obliged to summarize the texts they have learned in their own words. This can quickly give way to copy/paste. In general, what is taught to them is to memorize by repetition a faithful reproduction of texts studied in class. These children are forced to build their knowledge in a foreign language, first discovered in textbooks, which they rarely use outside the educational space. The reflex to copy/paste ... is installed commonly in the long term. In adulthood, former students may find it difficult to reconcile intellectual integrity and personal intellectual productions [Blanc, 2016].

As among ex-colonized African Francophones, original and authentic Haitian thought is forbidden, thanks to the myth of the superiority of French language propagated long ago by Haitian educational forefathers in post-colonial Haiti (Saint-Fort, 2010). Like traumatized people, they did not want to face either Haiti's historical or its contemporary traumas. Therefore, Haiti's educational leaders ignored all things Haitian, and everything about Haiti. Consequently, many contemporary Haitian intellectuals excel only in French language and literature. Haitian French-speaking literature is one of the most fecund and rewarded in the Caribbean. A total of thirteen Francophone literary prizes and honors were collected alone in 2009 (Joseph, 2009). Also, writer Dany Laferrière, who fled the Duvalier dictatorship for Quebec, was elected to the Académie Française in December 2013. Later, Michaëlle Jean, niece of the novelist René Depestre, a former presenter on Quebec television and Governor-General of Canada, won her place as Secretary-General of la Francophonie in September 2014. The roots of these achievements go back to the turn of the last century:

> Haitian writers preceded the Maghreb and Africans in their immoderate love of French language and civilization. In the Haitian literary and social magazine of February 5, 1905, a renowned Ussol (who is claimed to be Etzer Villaire himself, the famous Haitian poet of the La Ronde generation) writes: "Our language is French, French is our customs, our ideas and, whether we like it or not, French is our soul." Another great name of Haitian literature, Louis Joseph Janvier, writes in *Haiti and its Visitors*: "If for the black race, Haiti is the rising sun on the horizon, it is because France is the capital of the peoples and Haiti is black France" [Saint-Fort, 2010].

Indeed, French-speaking Haitian literature is venerated in the French-speaking world. However, when Haitian educators focus solely on French, it hides their unwillingness to face Haitian culture, history, and social needs. That would require their facing Haiti's historical and contemporary traumas. This means Haiti has never had, nor does it have now, an educational system that addresses Haitian needs from the first year of schooling through higher education. The weight of unresolved traumas prevents it from training future producers and future generators of knowledge, capable of solving concrete and urgent problems in our country.

3. "Colon" Complex

"Every Ayisyan is a leader" (Every Haitian is a leader)
"Depi nan Ginen nèg pa renmen nèg" (Since "Guinea," we detest each other)

Frantz Fanon (1983), a prominent figure in anti-colonialism, examined the troubled relationship between dark-skinned colonists and their former "white" masters. Paulo Freire reinterprets Frantz Fanon for the Haiti circumstance (Dalal, 2002) in the following way. In search of survival, the colonized acquiesces to the daily attacks and humiliations perpetrated by the colonists. The result is that the colonized are filled with anger and aggressiveness. This circumstance triggered the successful Haitian Revolution. However, Haiti's White colonists were either killed or driven off the island in the Revolution. Their social class heir-apparent is now other dark-skinned Haitians who are equally oppressive. Instead of anger and aggression being displaced on White colonists, it is displaced on one another and poor Haitians in what Freire refers to as "horizontal violence."

Freire suggests that the oppressed attack one another because it is too threatening to attack those with real power (Dalal, 2002). This horizontal violence and "settler complex" (willingness to represent oppressors) are reflected strongly in the self-selection of a growing number of political candidates. They come forward in each new Haitian presidential and legislative election. Horizontal violence is also apparent in the bloody struggles always generated by these electoral contests, followed by episodes of abuse of power by all the successive governments that come into power. Dalal (2002), restating Fanon, explains that between the colonial and post-colonial periods, intra-national racism emerged. The native bourgeoisie had enjoyed privileges while serving former colonial interests. At the same time, they adopt the colonial mode of operation, to preserve the economic exploitation that France might have put in place if Haiti had remained a French colony. They do so to exploit Haiti for their ends.

What is not explained in either Fanon or Freire is the intensity and consistency with which Haitians will turn on one another with violence, and with which individual Haitians will exploit politically and economically other Haitians if given the opportunity. I hypothesize that there are genuinely hidden traumas in the past and into the present that are unresolved in enough Haitians to account for such aggressive and conflict-filled social relations among Haitians toward one another.

4. Colorism

The European color aesthetic (White is beautiful and good; Black is ugly and bad) still shapes the Haitian imagination. In Haiti, clear skin is synonymous with beauty. However, facial features approximating the morphology of the colonizer are favored over African features and are the means of access to social and economic privileges. Micheline Labelle explored the importance of color in Haitian political life some 30 years ago in her book, *Ideologie de Couleur et Classes Sociales en Haiti* (1987). She explained that the number of traditional "mulatto bourgeois" from Haiti's original old "mulatto" families still hold higher social status and political power than dark-skinned members of the Haitian bourgeois class (more than a hundred families). Their dominance was interrupted only by the election of Dumarsais Estimé as president of Haiti, in 1946. He had no mulattos in his cabinet, and he attempted to balance power between Haiti's color divisions, referred to as the "Estimist Revolution." He was the first to do so since black governments came into being after 1915 (M.J. Smith, 2009, Chap. 3).

5. Rootless: Strangers at Home

"Sèl espwa se vwayaje" (Leaving is the only solution)

Among Haitians, collective disasters, one after the other, cause massive and forced displacements of survivors to other places. This is reasonable behavior for many people who have such experiences. However, in the Haitian context, the reaction to flee elsewhere takes on a special meaning. During the transatlantic slave trade, Africans, constrained as slaves, were displaced from one continent to another and deposited on this island in the Caribbean. Under this circumstance, Haiti is not home. One is supposed to be safe at home; here, we are not safe. One has no reason to stay and call it "home." For Haiti, there is no safety, and there are many more reasons to leave than to remain on the island. In effect, Haitians are people who do not live in their own country, even when they are on the island. Furthermore, given the continued disasters they experience in Haiti, it is unreasonable to invest emotionally in the place and be more than a perpetual stranger. The term, "Driverans," has developed among Haitians to describe this sense of existence without place and living a life of sequestered wandering ever since Haiti's independence.

Is this not what people do who have been through a traumatic experience? They are in shock and wander about to get their bearings. However, for Haitians, the traumas continue. They remain in shock, and never get their bearings. They wander as "driverans." Therefore, the willingness of Haitians to jump at any opportunity to work overseas is not merely a response to economic poverty. There is more to Haitian service as cheap laborers in Panama, Cuba, the Dominican Republic, Bahamas, United States, Canada, Guyana, and France. Today, more than one-quarter of the sons and daughters of Haiti reside abroad. More would go if they could (Madhere, 2016). It is an existential wandering through a fate of continued trauma and crisis, going back to slavery.

Depression and Suicide

"Mikwòb pa tiye Ayisyen" (Haitians are immunized against the germs)

Madhere (2016) traced a contemporary behavior among Haitians to experiences in the transatlantic slave trade. The crossing from Africa to the Caribbean took a minimum of 50 days. Kidnapped Africans were packed into tight spaces below the decks of ships pitching back and forth. A shared experience was to flounder in vomit due to "seasickness," and in one another's fecal matter. Could this and other moments like it be the time when Haitians developed their legendary insouciance: lack of concern, indifference, and contempt? An equivalent experience is to be beaten until one no longer reacts to the pain, and no longer seems to care. Louidor's (2006) thesis regarding this attitude toward health and its origin is the following. Today, the degree to which Haitians routinely disregard their health, hygiene and sanitary conditions is a thermometer to their psychological morale. When and where their morale and sense of hope are at their lowest, the people are closest to collective and personal indifference. One can ask them what they have to live for. If they have trouble answering, it speaks to their condition and closeness to suicide or murder. They "cohabitate with litter," in chaos. They have dehumanized themselves as a coping strategy, which has been reinforced by repeated trauma, since before independence.

Alternatively, when people have a reason for hope, they clean up their environment and themselves and are open to whatever is wholesome, good, and healthy. For example, during the first Aristide presidency, the people firmly believed in the possibility of a (democratic) change in the country. They cleaned up and embellished every corner of the country. This was their contribution to this change. However, once their expectations were frustrated, they returned to indifference and irresponsibility toward one another, their health, and the environment. Then, it did not matter whether the country was clean or unhealthy, beautiful, or ugly. The degradation of seeing oneself in "vomit and fecal matter in hopelessness chained below deck" still haunts the Haitian psyche and was reinforced by their treatment as slaves and in freedom. Their generational experiences in continued crises have only reinforced this original trauma and have left a finely tuned defensive insouciance.

These are only a few of the ways that contemporary Haitians have been affected psychologically by their legacy of slavery. One might argue that the above historical symptoms of trauma are something else, or have other, more recent origins. Given that this is a first effort to identify and account for the psychological legacy of slavery for Haitians, it is a beginning. I hope that others will advance what is presented here, prove it accurate, or disprove it.

Is It Resilience?

"Pito nou lèd nou la" (Better to be ugly but alive)

Most health professionals define resilience as having protection in the face of adversity. Resilience is complex, with many factors influencing it. A resilient person is one with healthy functioning after great difficulty, and who shows a conscious effort to move forward with insight and positivity (Southwick, Bonanno, Masten, Panter-Brick, & Yehuda, 2014, p. 11). After multiple disasters, humanitarian workers from abroad have come to call Haitians a "resilience people." It is now very fashionable to call Haitians "resilient." Haitians have been called "the most resilient people on earth" (Edwards, 2011). We seriously doubt that "resilient" is an accurate description of Haitians. It is hard to think of people as resilient who have a history that has knocked them unconscious, and from which they have yet to recover. "The Pearl of the Caribbean" leads the world in per capita deaths from natural disasters. One natural disaster after another has piled blow after blow on top of their historical trauma. Then, this double jeopardy is reinforced even more when one considers that Haitians have never been without poverty, nor have they ever had a functioning government that was not repressive.

Resolution and Conclusion

In this chapter, the possible links between the experience of slavery in Haiti and its contemporary psycho-traumatic outcomes are highlighted based on the biopsychosocial approach to health. These outcomes include violence and oppression of children, avoidance of thinking about anything Haitian, colorism, intra-racial conflict, social depression, and statelessness. It will require a transformation in Haitian thinking and mental health to erase these outcomes resulting from slavery and the post-slavery crises. Fortunately, the key already exists in our psyche and culture for such a transformation.

In Sterlin's (2006) view, the dominant epistemologies of sub-Saharan African societies and Amerindian societies are called cosmocentric. In contrast, the European Judeo-Christian and North American cultures have fundamentally anthropocentric epistemologies. These two types of societies are fundamentally different in their "vision of the world" or "specific knowledge of being," which fuels their understanding of health and disease. According to Sterlin, it is a mistake to think that the definition of health established by the World Health Organization (WHO) is common to all ethnic groups. In Western societies, "man" (the individual) is placed at the center of everything, and the (biological) soma and (psychological) psyche are viewed as being at man's disposal. In contrast, indigenous societies tend to focus on the preservation of human health, which is dependent on the health of their environments, and their relationships and inter-relationships.

As an illustration, the Haitian culture meets the criteria of a culture oriented towards the universe by its ancestral African and Amerindian roots. How the peasant class practices the Voodoo religion and Christianity are cosmocentric. Despite a highly westernized minority, the idea that the individual constitutes a specific combination of "the energy of the Great Cosmic All" is already evident in the worldview of most Haitians and their representations of the person, health, and disease. There is no separation between physical and mental morbidity. Disease is considered a "state of ill-being." That is a conflict between different entities of being or between one or several entities of its environment. Overall, health encompasses a "state of well-being—connection with the environment. They include the non-human environment (earth, plants, animals, air, and forces of nature); the human environment (nuclear and extended family, a network of close allies, community, and others); the ancestors and the spirits (the invisible)...."

As an illustration, three years after the 2010 earthquake, we conducted a survey examining the relationship between religious beliefs about the origin of the earthquake, post-traumatic symptomatology, and resilience among survivors of various religious denominations. Participants who perceived the earthquake as divine punishment had much less peri-traumatic distress, namely, post-traumatic stress disorder (PTSD), in comparison to others who did not associate divinity and spirituality with the earthquake (Blanc et al., 2016b).

Again, in the context of native epistemology, one recalls the story described by Plato about utopian Atlantis, destroyed by the gods in a wreck of fire. This could have referred to a volcano that partially destroyed the Greek island of Thera more than 3,500 years ago. Arnold (2017) points out that there were warning signs of imminent natural disasters in the myths of indigenous peoples around the world, a point receiving increased attention from social and earth scientists. Even if western geologists were able to predict earthquakes and volcanic eruptions, this would only be part of the holistic framework needed to remedy Haitians' mental health and ecological crises.

In our view, Haiti has sunk into the doldrums because of a rupture between Haitians' psychological condition and different environmental components. There are non-human components (land, plants, animals, air, forces of nature); and human components (families, close allies, community, and the ancestors and spirits). This society will be functional when its children become psychologically functional and can dance with the components of their living environment according to the principles of native epistemology. It is necessary to free them from the epistemic alienation and violence that has imprisoned them for four centuries. Mental slavery did not end in 1804. In practical terms, this mental liberation will have to be therapeutic and result in reconciliation and harmonization with ourselves, and our ability to manage affairs, ways of being, spirituality, language, and above all, our environment.

Nothing less than the decolonization of the Haitian mind and physical-political liberation of the Haitian body is required. We can begin this process by creating a psycho-educational and therapeutic system integrating elements of native and western knowledge and therapies. To do so requires at a minimum:

1. Work toward Haiti's *economic independence* and full participation in world markets. Economic freedom and engagement will require a democratic government that respects the Haitian people, is aware of their many needs, and works toward fulfilling them. This might begin with Haitian NGOs in and outside of Haiti lobbying the OAS and EU to develop economic trade and investments in Haiti provided appropriate government reforms are undertaken successfully. Haiti needs to seek alternate geopolitical partners to develop the Haitian economy and supersede U.S. neglect.

2. Acknowledgment and specifically study the unresolved traumas of national independence, and two centuries of external exploitation of the Haitian people.

3. We need research to understand the effects of experiencing multiple traumas. The objective of such a study is to tell us how persons who have had such experiences might be treated effectively.

4. The organization and training of nationwide mental health services with clinics systematically dispersed. These clinics will focus on community mental health with a particular focus on addressing intergenerational and historical trauma.

5. We need a nationwide educational and public health program to address family violence against children.

6. Informal child servitude should be outlawed. Child labor should be regulated by law specifying minimum age, minimum compensation to the child and family, and a guarantee of education. All children at work are to be registered, periodically interviewed, and, if they live away from their families, their work conditions should be instructed.

7. There is a need to reorient Haitian education to address the needs of the Haitian people and nation. This might begin with the reform of primary and secondary school curriculums need. These reforms would focus on integrating into Haitian education the intense and critical study of Haitian history and culture, and science and technology.

8. The colon complex, colorism, rootlessness, depression, and suicide must be address specifically as psychological issues through the Haitian educational system and community mental health campaigns. Such efforts need to be in conjunction with a nationwide radio, television, and widespread culture efforts to raise awareness and consciousness of long-term trauma symptoms and their resolution.

Note

1. Translated from the French by Benjamin P. Bowser.

References

Alphonse, R. (2014). Jean-Claude Duvalier jugeable pour crime contre l'humanité. *Le Nouvelliste*. Retrieved from http://lenouvelliste.com/lenouvelliste/article/127848/Jean.

American Psychiatric Association. (2013). *Diagnostic and Statistical Manual of Mental Disorders* (5 ed.). Washington, D.C.: American Psychiatric Association.

Blanc, J. (2015, October 6). Sommes une société de malades mentaux. *Le Nouvelliste*. Retrieved from http://lenouvelliste.com/lenouvelliste/article/150560/Sommes-nous-une-societe-de-malades-mentaux.

Blanc, J. (2016). Et si la psychologie cognitive pouvait casser le mythe que le Kreyòl n'est pas

une langue scientifique? In F. Piron, S. Regulus, & S.D. Madiba (Eds.), *Justice cognitive, libre accès et savoirs locaux*. Quebec: Editions science bien commun.
Blanc, J., Rahill, G., Laconi, S., & Mouchenik, Y. (2016). Religion, Depression and Resilience in Survivors of Earthquake in Haiti. *Journal of Affective Disorders, 190*, 697–703.
Brown, G. (2010). The Tragedy of Haïti: A Reason for Major Cultural Change. *The ABNF Journal, Fall*.
Cayemittes, M., Busangu, M.F., Bizimana, J.D., Barrère, B., Sévère, B., Cayemittes, V., & Charles, E. (2013). *Enquête Mortalité, Morbidité et Utilisation des Services, Haïti, 2012*. Maryland, USA: MSPP, IHE et ICF International.
Corvington, G. (2007). *Port-au-Prince au cours des ans. Tome III, La capitale sous l'occupation (1915-1934)*. Montreal: Les Editions CIDHICA.
Dalal, F. (2002). *Race, Color and the Process of Racialization*. London: Routledge.
Duval, F. (2011). Jean Claude Duvalier est de retour. *Le Nouvelliste*. Retrieved from http://lenouvelliste.com/lenouvelliste/article/87864/Jean-Claude-Duvalier-est-de-retour.
Edwards, B. (2011). The Most Resilient People on Earth: Haiti Still Standing After Trio of Disasters. *Frontlines*. Retrieved from https://www.usaid.gov/news-information/frontlines/haitiwomen-development/most-resilient-people-earth-haiti-still-standing.
Geffrard, R.A. (2013). Les victimes de Duvalier n'ont pas encore fait leur deuil. *Le Nouvelliste*. Retrieved from http://lenouvelliste.com/lenouvelliste/article/116154/Les-victimes-des-Duvalier-nont-pas-encore-fait-leur-deuil.
Hurbon, L. (1987). *Comprendre Haïti, Essai sur l'Etat, la Nation, la Culture*. Paris: Les Editions Karthala.
Institut Haïtien de Statistiques et d'Informatique IHSI. (2003). *Enquête sur les Conditions de Vie en Haïti (ECVH)*. Port-au-Prince, Haiti.
Institut Haïtien de Statistiques et d'Informatique IHSI. (2009). *Grandes leçons sociodémographiques tirées du 4e Recensement General de la Population Haïtienne*. Port-au-Prince.
Institut Haïtien de Statistiques et d'Informatiques IHSI. (2007). *Estimation et projection de la population totale urbaine, rurale et économiquement active*. Port-au-Prince: Bibliothèque Nationale d'Haïti.
Joseph, F. (2009, 11 decembre). Haiti-Littérature: Une abondante récolte de prix littéraires pour Haïti. *TiPiTi Biz*. Retrieved from http://tipiti.biz/site/2009/12/11/haiti-litterature-une-abondante-recolte-de-prix-litteraires-pour-haiti/.
Kennedy, C.L. (2012). Toward Effective Mental Health Intervention for Children Formerly in Restavèk. Creole Summary (Etid sou Sante Mantal Timoun ki te RestavÃ¨k.Pou rive nan entÃ¨vansyon sante mantal ki efikas.pdf). Retrieved from https://beyondborders.net/downloads/.
Labelle, M. (1987). *Idéologie de couleur et classes sociales en Haïti. Les Éditions du CIDHCA*. Montréal: Les Presses de l'Université de Montréal.
Louidor, W.E. (2006). Haïti: L'insalubrité comme thermomètre politique. *Alterpresse*. Retrieved from http://www.alterpresse.org/spip.php?article5407#.WPI8JFM1_GI.
Madhere, S. (2016). Kolonizasyon ak Ekoloji Sosyal: Konsekans Fizyolojik, Sikolojik, ak Enfliyans yo sou Lasante. In J. Blanc, S. Madhere, & S. Ulysse (Eds.), *Pensée afro-caribéenne et (psycho)traumatismes de l'esclavage et de la colonisation*. Québec: Editions science bien commun.
Madiou, T. (1849). *Histoire d'Haïti, Tome III. Les Editions Imprimerie*. Port-au-Prince, Haïti: J. H Courtois.
Ministère de la Planification et de la Coopération Externe. (2015). *Le développent social. Des Lycées construits et réhabilités dans les dix départements géographiques d'Haïti* Port-au-Prince: Gouvernement de la République d'Haïti.
Ministère de la Sante Publique et de la Population MSPP. (2012). Politique Nationale de Sante. https://mspp.gouv.ht/site/downloads/livret%20pns%20for%20web.pdf.
Orata, F.D., Keim, P.S., & Boucher, Y. (2014). The 2010 Cholera Outbreak in Haiti: How Science Solved a Controversy. *PLoS Pathog., 10*(4).
Piarrous, R. (2010). Rapport de mission sur l'épidémie de choléra en Haïti. Retrieved from http://www.ph.ucla.edu/epi/snow/piarrouxcholerareport_french.pdf.
Prepetit, C. (2008, 10–12 octobre). Tremblements de terre en Haïti: Mythes ou réalités

Le Matin. Retrieved from http://bme.gouv.ht/risques%20geologiques/LeMatin_s%C3%A9ismes.pdf.

Saint-Fort, H. (2010). Le mythe de la langue française, butin de guerre des ex colonisés francophones? Potomitan. Retrieved from http://www.potomitan.info/ayiti/langue3.php.

Smith, M.J. (2009). *Red & Black in Haiti: Radicalism, Conflict, and Political Change, 1934–1957.* Chapel Hill: University of North Carolina Press.

Southwick, S.M., Bonanno, G.A., Masten, A.S., Panter-Brick, C., & Yehuda, R. (2014). Resilience and Trauma. Resilience Definitions, Theory, and Challenges: Interdisciplinary Perspectives. *European Journal of Psychotraumatology,* 5(25338).

United Nations. (2010). Reports of the United Nations in Haïti 2010 Situation, Challenges and Outlouk. Retrieved from www.onu-haiti.org.

United Nations. (2016). Haïti: Ban Ki-moon présente les excuses de l'ONU et propose un nouveau plan de lutte contre le choléra. Centre d'Actualites de l'ONU. Retrieved from http://www.un.org/apps/newsFr/storyF.asp?NewsID=38583#.WRkVtRM18dU.

3

Afro-Brazilian Youth

Slavery's Influence on Crime[1]

ANDRÉA MÁRIS CAMPOS GUERRA *and*
ANA CAROLINA ANDRÉ-CADAR

> *Trauma after trauma, as well as political and economic oppression, has gone on for so long that the Haitian people expect them and see them as normal. Resolution of national trauma and effective treatment must include the government and entire communities—the nation, not just individuals. The issues we have looked at so far are visible in countries such as Belize and Haiti, where slave descendants are the majority. Slavery's psychological legacies are more challenging in circumstances where African descendants do not control government and the economy and are dispersed in diverse populations. Also, not all of slavery's legacies are derived from assimilating slave masters' beliefs or from trauma. In the next chapter, these legacies can be derived from long-term intergenerational poverty and neglect with an outcome one is familiar with regardless of where one lives in the West.*

This chapter discusses the repercussions of slavery in Brazil, and its effects on young Afro-Brazilians, focusing on those involved in drug trafficking. Are there adverse effects of slavery in the post-modern Afro-Brazilian communities? Are there any influences of slavery on the systemic homicide and incarceration of young Afro-Brazilians? An analysis of statistical mortality data was used as well as historical and social-psychological research to answer those questions. Furthermore, the authors conducted a psychoanalytic assessment.

It is essential to highlight the most recent work about underprivileged young people in Brazil, notably those dwelling in slums (favelas). Extensive work was done by Guerra (2008, 2010, 2011, 2014, 2016), and additional research was conducted by French investigators such as Cherki (2009) and Douville (2007). A case study of an adolescent engaged in a homicide prevention program can help us to understand the complexity of the issues these young people face, and the possible continued impact of slavery's trauma (Siqueira, 2016).

Historical Context

The chronicle of Afro-Brazilians[2] is a fundamental part of Brazil's historical and social evolution. Colonial Brazil was a country rich in natural resources, but it lacked a workforce. Its metropole, Portugal, played a leading role in the Atlantic Slave Trade. Slavery in Brazil began in the first half of the sixteenth century. Africans were brought to work on the sugar farms in the northeast of the country and lately in the southeast. Brazil received between 3.5 and 4 million Africans, the largest number of enslaved Africans in all the Americas (Saillant & Araujo, 2007). The following chart shows the number of slaves disembarked according to destination and century.

The Atlantic Slave Trade was declared illegal in 1831, and the same happened to the Brazilian slave trade in 1850 when The Eusébio De Queirós Act came into effect. It was followed by The Free Womb Act (1871) in which children of the enslaved were obliged to work until they were 21 years old, after which they were freed. Then came the Sexagenarians Act (1885) that provided freedom for the enslaved who managed to survive until they were sixty years old. They were freed subsequently after three additional years of work. These acts served to relieve slave owners from the burden of caring for invalid slaves and made it possible for the latter to be neglected and abandoned. The Golden Act promulgated on May 13, 1888, by Regent Princess Isabel, abolished slavery nationwide.

	Europe	Mainland North America	British Caribbean	French Caribbean	Dutch Americas	Danish West Indies	Spanish Americas	Brazil	Africa	Totals
1501-1600	640	0	0	0	0	0	169,370	29,275	0	199,285
1601-1700	2,981	15,147	310,477	38,685	124,158	18,146	225,504	784,457	3,122	1,522,677
1701-1800	5,240	295,482	1,813,323	995,133	295,215	68,608	145,533	1,989,017	2,317	5,609,868
1801-1900	0	78,117	194,452	86,397	25,355	22,244	752,505	2,061,625	150,130	3,370,825
Totals	8,861	388,746	2,318,252	1,120,215	444,728	108,998	1,292,912	4,864,374	155,569	10,702,655

Table 4.1. Where Slaves Were Brought in the West, 1500–1900 (slavevoyages.org).

The pre-abolitionist acts did not represent a radical change in the structure of the slavery system. They stimulated an internal slave trade and an increase in prices for slaves. Consequently, the government began replacing African slaves with the second wave of European immigrants (1877–1903). In the first wave, before 1877, European immigrants focused on becoming landowners, while in the last quarter of the nineteenth century, Europeans went to Brazil to work harvesting coffee. They could cultivate small tracts of land in exchange for their work. Just as the slave system went into disarray, European immigrants prompted the country's economic growth by bringing in different farming techniques.

Moreover, there was another use for European immigrants. The Portuguese held the belief that integrating immigrants (paid-for-labor) with Afro-Brazilian slaves and freedmen would reduce Brazil's dependence on slavery. This would also "whiten" Brazilian society, thereby reducing Brazil's likelihood of becoming a majority black-populated nation in the future.

Even though enslaved Africans were devoid of legal rights, they developed, from the beginning, many strategies of resistance, giving them access to some measure of personal freedoms. Rebellions and riots caused a decrease in agricultural production. Then, fugitive slaves, alongside army deserters, mulattos, and indigenous people, created Maroon communities called "quilombos." The quilombos facilitated the continuation of African traditions and helped create a distinct African culture in Brazil, which had up to 2,228 quilombos. The most exceptional was Palmares Quilombo, which created its monetary system, government, military, and civil codes. Their social organization followed Central African political models. People were free to speak their native language and to perform their religious ceremonies[3] (Cheney, 2014).

Brazil was the last country in the Americas to abolish slavery. The abolition addressed the discontent of slave-owners for the dismantling of the monarchy. After months of political crisis, the Emperor was removed by the military, and a Republican government was founded just one year after the abolition of slavery. The government gave no financial compensation to formerly enslaved people, did not set up any programs for land distribution, nor was there any effort made to integrate them into society and the economy. Consequently, newly freed slaves agreed to continue working for their former masters, without wages, since they were not granted the right to work in the free labor market. Consequently, the vast majority of the formerly enslaved migrated to large cities, in pursuit of economic opportunities and less hostile social environments. However, here too, they found hostility, prejudice, and a lack of opportunities.

The formerly enslaved and their descendants ended up in the slums of Brazil's cities (Joffily, 1999). Afro-Brazilians created the first urban slums in Brazil, which they shared with other racial minorities and immigrants. Today, these communities are called *favelas*, the first of which was named *bairros africanos* (African neighborhoods). Like the former quilombos, the favelas represent a significant axis of Afro-Brazilian cultural resistance to ongoing racial oppression. The number and size of the original favelas increased in the 1970s due to a new rural exodus, when many more people left the countryside, especially from the northeast of Brazil. Along with Afro-Brazilians, other rural migrants were unable to find affordable housing in the cities. Therefore, they too ended up in the favelas (Ribeiro, 1995).

The Brazilian government made several attempts in the twentieth century to reduce urban poverty. In the seventies, under the military dictatorship, the government tried to eradicate the favelas by forcibly removing over 100,000 residents and placing them in public housing projects. Others were sent back to the rural areas from which they emigrated (Perlman, 2006). Gentrification was another attempt to resolve the problem of urban poverty, by "integrating" the slums with newly urbanized middle-class residences. As "upgraded favelas" became established, they began to attract the lower-middle class. That generates the displacement of long time, low-income residents into the streets or to the suburbs, where they are further deprived of economic opportunities.

Consequences: Mortality and Homicides

In Brazil, citizens who have no legitimate way to support themselves economically have many problems in addition to housing, the most troubling of which are youth homicides. In 2002, 71.7 percent more Black than White adolescents were victims of homicides.[4] The numbers reached 108.6 percent by 2006, and 153.9 percent by 2010.

In 2010, about 50 percent of victims were between 15 and 29 years old. Of these, 75 percent were Afro-Brazilians. In other words, in 2010, 2.5 Black adolescents were murdered for each White counterpart (Waiselfisz, 2012, p. 33). The 2012 mortality rate for Afro-Brazilian men between the ages of 12 and 21 was proportionally 1.53 times higher than it was for young White men (Staff, 2014). Brazil has a juvenile mortality rate worse than countries at war, and it affects Afro-Brazilian youth more than others. Juvenile mortality rates in the country suggest a genocide of the Afro-Brazilians, especially males.

Remarkably, there are no significant differences between homicide rates among Afro-Brazilians and Whites up to age twelve. This age is of legal significance. The Brazilian Juvenile Criminal Justice system sanctions teenagers with criminal penalties from age 12 onwards. We see a steep rise in the number of homicides, both among Black and White youth, up to 20 to 21 years of age. While this increase occurs for both White and Black adolescents, the increase for Black youth is markedly higher: Between 12 and 21 years of age, the White youth homicide rate go from 1.3 to 37.3 for every 100,000 inhabitants: a 29-time increase. Disparately, Black youth homicide rate rises, in the same age range, from 2.0 to 89.6, which represents a 46-time increase (Waiselfisz, 2012, p. 26). This indicates that most homicides occur within Black communities.

Afro-Brazil homicide rates are striking, even when regional differences are considered. Although racial disparities in homicides are alarming, its cause-and-effect relation to juvenile mortality is not immediately evident. From 2003 to 2014, Brazil experienced a growth of 9.9 percent for death by gun violence among Afro-Brazilians. At the same time, it decreased by 27.1 percent for Whites (Waiselfisz, 2016). Different availability of guns may be a cause in its own right. Homicide case studies can help us understand the complexity of the role played by segregation and racial prejudice. The Brazilian government does not recognize that either exists.

The notion of racial democracy implies that Brazil has escaped racism, and racial discrimination as a barrier to social mobility is unaffected by the country's history in slavery and its consequences. Abdias do Nascimento (1978) refuted the idea of Brazil is a racial democracy by shedding light on the conditions of Afro-Brazilians during and after slavery. His critique included the particular exploitation of Black women as well as a strategic attempt at social and cultural whitening—the elimination of the African presence in Brazil. His argument includes the alarming black mortality data and various efforts to suppress African heritage, notably State policies repressing African-originated religions in Brazil. Nascimento described these efforts as genocidal attempts to exterminate Afro-Brazilians. He defined genocide as the use of deliberate and systematic measures to eradicate a racial, political or cultural group, or to destroy a group's language, religion or culture, through death, bodily and mental harm, and poor living conditions. In Brazil, the state caused and continues to create the genocide of the Afro-descendant population by practicing systemic violence. The results can be seen today in statistical data on black juvenile mortality. This violence against Afro-descendants is an update of Brazil's violence against enslaved Africans. No improvement in mortality rates has been achieved as of 2016 rates over those of 2012 (Waiselfisz, 2016).

Explanation and Hypothesis

Racial discrimination is not the only explanation for the exclusion of Afro-Brazilian youth from the economic system. Their exclusion is partly an outcome of neoliberalism. In the evolving global economy and social system, even if the present racial discrimination would no longer be a factor, Afro-Brazilians would still have disproportionately higher unemployment and mortality rates. There is no place in the evolving neoliberal world order for people who are not able to contribute significantly to the economy. In Brazil, racism is a form of *thanatopower* (Agamben, 2005) or *necropolitics* (Mbembe, 2018), a way of excluding those who cannot take part in the economy, as well as to ensure that they remain excluded. Individuals who cannot be integrated into the economy are considered expendable. They also have restricted access to cultural products, which further isolates them, and further contributes to their expendability.

Additionally, they become the object of intense police persecution. The outcome is the political practice of necropolitics—"letting them die." In this sense, Mbembe (2018) understands political sovereignty as the ultimate expression of power and decision-making power over which lives are considered redundant, and bodies are to be extinguished. Brazil is such a case for its Black population.

There is little debate about Afro-Brazilian economic marginality in Brazil. It is assumed that race "whitening" has resulted in supposedly peaceful miscegenation. The idea of a cultural and ideological Black identity is regarded as a fading notion. This is far from accurate. This desire on the part of the government and a large part of Brazilian society to see Black people disappear is the product of ignorance about racial inequality in Brazil, past and present. This disregard for the country's history and exclusion of Afro-Brazilians is remarkable. Until 1988, precisely a hundred years after the abolition of slavery, there has been no legislation to compensate descendants of enslaved Africans. The 1988 Federal Constitution, which defined Brazil's turn to democracy, was supposed to restore lands to people who could demonstrate the preservation of cultural and historical land rights—Native and African Brazilians. However, the government has yet to acknowledge the relationship between socio-economic conditions, skin color, and the heritage of enslaved people, except obliquely and indirectly. As the Palmares Foundation data demonstrates, the number of demands for the identification and demarcation of quilombos (African heritage communities) is still very high; only seven percent of the land claims have been granted (Brito, 2018).

Our first hypothesis is that *underprivileged Afro-Brazilian youngsters, especially males, continue to play out the historical trauma of slavery in*

Brazil by engaging in criminal activities. Politically and subjectively, we can see today how the traumatic experience of slavery is still strongly evident in how other Brazilians view Afro-Brazilians, and in how Afro-Brazilians view themselves. We will present some encounters with a young Afro-Brazilian named Novato to illustrate this point.

Our second hypothesis focuses on the question of whether favelas are social and geographical continuations of quilombos. We believe that, for Afro-Brazilians and especially for its youth, *the favelas are sites of continuity of Afro-Brazilians resistance culture (initiated during slavery and reinforced by a systemic social and economic exclusion) and its psychological consequences.* Could these factors incline a part of this population to engage in criminal activities? In Colonial Brazil, enslaved people had to do anything to ensure their existence and survival. Unmet socio-economic needs meant a history of fulfilling needs extra-legally. A tradition of resistance to slavery emerged that historically predisposed rejection of an economy and social system that still discriminates against descendants of enslaved Africans. This merger of culture and history in present-day favelas has influenced Afro-Brazilian youth, cut them off from the economy, and disposed them to engage in extra-mural and extra-legal means of financial support.

Clinical Evidence: The Case of Novato

The research conducted by Siqueira (2016) in Belo Horizonte, for the Federal University of Minas Gerais (UFMG), collected data from the Fica Vivo! Program.[5] This intervention is designed to monitor and prevent the occurrences of homicide in areas with high rates of violent crime in the state of Minas Gerais. The Centers for Crime Prevention runs the program. It sponsors local projects, and about 600 workshops for youngsters in social risk situations, from 12 to 24 years old. The program also offers psychological care. In the areas where it is established, the average reduction in homicides among youngsters has reached 50 percent.

The program was not conceived to operate as a type of reparation for slavery. However, it does partly address the consequences of slavery in the favelas. The program aims to improve the effectiveness of crime reduction and increase security in the territory through community interventions. It prevents crime by promoting youth workshops on soccer, rap music, capoeira, serigraphy, judo, and computer classes. Notably, the Fica Vivo! Program promotes the participation and inclusion of young people by creating a place for discussion about issues related to citizenship and human rights to resolve conflicts and group rivalries. This is where we met Novato, an Afro-Brazilian teenager. He talked about racism, police violence, drug dealing, and what it is like for him to be a young Afro-Brazilian. The following are excerpts of the meetings with him:

CHILDHOOD

> Look, I got here, to this neighborhood, when I was eight. I still remember when I entered the third grade, here, at the school, right there, in that classroom! I remember because I had a very good teacher who helped me out a lot. My family and I were totally repressed by the other boys. We came from a different, strange place; they did not even know where it was. They mocked and bullied me.... I never fought back because I was a new kid. That is how it is for a new kid, they mock you and upset you, so I never responded. When you are new, you have to go through a period of hardship in order to be accepted. I lived at Serra Pelada Street,[6] they used to yell: "Hey, Serra Pelada," and mocked me by calling me "little nigger," "little monkey." Everybody was of the same skin color, but they still bullied me. I didn't have much to wear. To tell the truth, I didn't have many clothes or sandals, I went to school and had to wear the same dirty clothes. It was total isolation.

Early on in his childhood, race emerged as an issue in the nicknames his peers gave him, even from the ones who shared his skin tone. At that moment, color became an index of difference, parallel to his origin and lack of resources. This is a consequence of the form of exclusion played out among Afro-Brazilians in the post–1888 period, immediately after the abolition of slavery. Brazilians stratified themselves by color and resources. Novato's peers unknowingly replicated their history.

ADOLESCENCE

When his teen years ended, Novato had to make a choice: in his words, either become a vagrant, a drug dealer, or maybe find work. He also questioned himself about his love and sexual life. Racial identity and history were very much a part of his life choices and reflections:

> One needs to deal with the great challenges that are imposed. My girlfriend is white. To tell the truth, being Black myself, I've never hooked up with a Black woman. My friends are just now noticing it. God forgive me for saying such a thing. It may be that I am treating as inferior my own race, but I am not attracted to Black women.
> Every woman I've hooked up with is either blond or red-haired. They say it is because of a black guy's color that he tends to hook up with White women, that it's normal. I am ashamed to talk like that about not being with Black women. I keep thinking that I don't want to have a son that has the same skin color as mine. I guess not wanting a Black child isn't discrimination towards my race. Most of the time, a Black guy says that it's because he is thinking: "I don't want to have a dark-colored child, because he will suffer too much. Black people suffer too much."

As a teenager, Novato has already endured considerable racial prejudice. However, he deals with it using the same segregationist strategy that excludes him, as revealed in the logic of his choice of partner. His apprehensions suggest an apparent form of internalized racism as he worries that his children might have the same skin color as his. As indicated, he does not have the knowledge or means to assert his racial identity. He has an ambiguous and subjective way of dealing with the consequences of his country's slave heritage.

Slums Vs. City

> I've been stopped by the police before. I hardly ever go out without ever being stopped by the police.... It seems like.... I am not sure if it is 'cause of the color of my skin, I don't know what it is. But all I know is that the cops are always harassing me, even though I don't owe them anything. They've never caught me with anything, not even when I was dealing drugs.
>
> One day, we were going to pick up some mangos, because there are no mango trees around here. We went to a place really far away, an unrestricted place, where everybody can pick up mangos. We went there, and everybody was feeling good. I climbed the mango tree. An older man from Bahia also did it. My friend and I, we are both black. On the ground, there were boys, three boys, if you look closely, blond, white and all. Then, the cops came down, putting barriers in place. I don't know the reason for that. There were five people. I was looking down from the top of the mango tree, and the cop told me: "Get down you monkeys. Get down from this fucking tree."

The police encounter lasted over half an hour. Novato and his friend asked themselves why it was that only the white kids who had been released. The issue became even more puzzling to Novato when he considered:

> ...the cop himself is black, he has the same skin color as we do, and he had the nerve to call us "monkeys." The cops, when they approach us in our community, see only the color of our skin and call us that. It's ludicrous, right?
>
> Sometimes, one forgets about one's origin. A Brazilian.... The way I think, everybody in Brazil is mulatto. I find myself thinking.... My girlfriend is white; it's complicated.... If people judge me, if they judge me because of my skin color, I try not to feel oppressed, you know? I try to go on with my life.... I take it as a joke.
>
> Until not very long ago, I was hanging out in a sort of Rock and Roll gathering. I used to go, very often, to Praça da Liberdade and Praça Sete (parks in the center of Belo Horizonte). That was cool. I used to stay until early in the morning, enjoying, chatting with a lot of people, with some rich White kids. But in this Rock and Roll life, I felt like ... as if I didn't belong there. And then you realize, being a teenager from the slums, you try to grow up and be somebody, and try not to mix yourself with who is from the outside (of the slums, meaning the city).
>
> Funk[7] is our culture. Even though I am eclectic, I enjoy funk. People tend to think: that if one is "funkeiro,"[8] he is no good. A "Funkeiro" is a drug addict, a "funkeiro" misbehaves, he steals, he kills. In order to be able to walk around well dressed like that, he must be a drug dealer. They only think about that. They don't see that people enjoy "funk" because that is the community's culture.

As a young adult, Novato experienced alternative forms of social integration, but he did not recognize them as being part of his identity. He is very much aware that his skin color and origins were always noticeable to others, yet he still wanted to know more about how people saw him. At the same time, he tried to assert his presence in the city as a Black man from the slums. He went from rock music to funk concerts and adopted a "black power" hairstyle. Although he objected to racial and social prejudice, he was still unsure of how to respond to it. He explored different social scenarios around him and was curious about them. However, he always reminded me that he is from the slums as he tried to understand the problems and complexity of his racial and social class subordination.

Discussion

The Afro-Brazilian experience illustrated by Novato is very similar to what identity must have been like during slavery. Novato was not aware of slavery and its consequences, and he had no clear cultural identification with Black people. What existed for him was an externally imposed racial identity derived from White attitudes about race and their treatment of him. Tragically, he had internalized this low regard as racial inferiority. Novato lived and illustrated the psychology of slavery, lived in the present.

Novato did not convey to us any specific traumatic experiences. He did not have to. We define trauma as a subjective experience where a foreign element (self-disdain) integrates itself into the subject's system of representations (Freud, 1996). A Freudian psychoanalytic interpretation is the following:

The original traumatic experience (generations ago) is the primary condition. It can never be "represented," meaning that it cannot be relived in its entirety. From the original traumatic experience, all that remains is affective (emotional) intensity: it is excessive, and its origin is unknown to the person expressing it. The emotional effect is now disconnected from the trauma and seems to have a life of its own. The impact and representation (trauma) remain disjointed. The person then relives the traumatic situation, repeatedly, that distresses him without intending to do so. The repetition is compulsive, and the strength of the repetition corresponds to the psychic energy that resists the process of signification— understanding what is going on. Simultaneously, the subject is trying to understand what is transpiring and attempting to control their emotions. In the case of Novato, we can see traumatic repetitions in his childhood, when he was hostilely name-called for his skin color and origin. It continued in his teenage years when he ignored his heritage and tried to identify himself as part of a group of white youngsters. It continued again as a young adult when he integrated components of the traumatic experience in the construction of a new identity, that is admittedly and proudly black.

In returning to our initial hypothesis, underprivileged Afro-Brazilian youngsters, especially males, actualize the historical trauma of slavery in Brazil by engaging in criminal activities. They do not know that their fore-parents encountered the same conditions and circumstances and responded the same way. The same response reinforced the original trauma, renewing it for yet another generation (Freud, 2003). The violence in which youth such as Novato live is a response to the continuous repetition of their former historical condition. The difference is the response is not as slaves but in the present. It was passed down to them by the prior generations that had relived the same trauma. Each generation encounters the same political powerlessness and economic poverty. Severe destitution is imprinted on them by the disconnection, repression, and disavowal of the larger society and favelas' denial of the racial issue. While living in the present, more than a century later, symbolically and psychologically, they are still slaves. A consequence is violence against one another, as illustrated in Afro-Brazilian juvenile mortality rates.

Of course, some engage in petty crime and individual anti-social acts. However, this engagement takes on a life of its own in the Brazilian racial climate. These youth realize there are higher economic gains in organized crime, in particular, drug trafficking. Their crimes might start with micro trafficking in illicit drugs (Guerra, 2011). Soon, drug gangs and imaginary rivalries arise between gangs. Accordingly, they seem to comply with a subjective response to their historical and affective trauma. Links between the slave quarters and the slums and between the conditions of slavery and the current mortality of Afro-Brazilian young adults are exposed in their criminal activities.

The trauma of slavery and its contemporary denial has produced ambivalence to the Black identity and condition of Afro-Brazilians. Again, in Brazil, many deny that racial economic and social disparities exist. An Afro-Brazilian response is to withdraw into the favelas and to (re)construct a Black identity. There is a social and subjective ambivalence in matters regarding black skin color. On the one hand, identifying as Black constitutes belonging to a specific group and community, while not identifying as Black leads to other social group identifications. A result is that Black youth such as Novato end up seeing social relationships as binary and oppositional, such as slums versus "outside," black versus white, rich versus poor, favela A vs. favela B, and so on. They are unaware that slaves had to see the world in this way: there were slaves and free men, and masters and slaves. All the historical slave codes were intended to produce binary outcomes in the same way. Penalties were dear for slaves who violated their "place." The institution of slavery is gone. However, slavery is not gone as a way of thinking for those unaware of this history and its current effects.

Today, as in the nineteenth century, to acknowledge that one is black in color (as distinct from Afro-Brazilian) still means to identify oneself with the traumatic memory of slavery, engraved in the skin of millions of Brazilians. Identification by color provides historical consistency to the current discussion about affirmative public policies in Brazil, based on a person's Black racial self-identification. In Brazil, naming a skin color still implies hierarchy, as it means breaking the pact of silence with the slavery past. More than one hundred years have passed since the abolition of slavery in Brazil. It is time to break the silence by addressing racism and racial discrimination in Brazil and to begin at last to fulfill the promise of emancipation (Mattos & Abreu, 2011, p. 19).

Conclusion

The traumatic experience of slavery remains unacknowledged or unreconciled in Brazil. The trauma continues today in the experiences of underprivileged Afro-descent youth. They replicate the trauma for themselves in each successive generation, without realizing it. They have yet to contextualize their racial experience within the Afro-Brazilian culture, which requires knowledge of their history and ethnic consciousness about which they are still ambivalent. It could be inferred that the slums have a symbiotic and historical relationship with the slave quarters. Inside that quarter, individuals traverse their varied experiences to define and redefine their identity. Some arrive at becoming Afro-Brazilians, while others do not. Novato's racial identity is still very much in the making. Finally, there is a relationship between the Afro-Brazilian youth involvement in crime today and Brazil's slave past. This relationship needs to be better understood.

Notes

1. A French version of this text was titled "Les conséquences de l'esclavage pour l'actuelle jeunesse afro-brésilienne et leurs incidence sur certains parcours délinquants dans les favelas au Brésil."

2. We prefer the term Afro-Brazilian, although there are several other denominations to refer to African ancestry, none of which reaches a consensus. The black movement, for example, normally uses the Brazilian word "Negro," which emphasizes color, and it is very different from the English language connotation, as its closest translation would be "black." The term "Afro-Brazilian" is also widely used, and it was chosen for the writing of the Statute of Racial Equality in Brazil (Estatuto da Igualdade racial: I/2e/§ III).

3. In contemporary social imaginary, the quilombos represent much more than a singular historical event. Contemporary Black political movements have renewed quilombal practices, previously illustrated negatively in history as a place of exclusion. They were able to push the production of a new juridico-political inscription of those former "Black rural communities." Starting with the 1988 Constitution, those communities were renamed quilombos. The right to the land, guaranteed to the reminiscents of the quilombos, was established in the Acts of the Transitional Constitutional Provisions. Article 68 was the first intention of reparations to African descendants one hundred years after the abolition of slavery.

4. Here we are maintaining the categories employed by the author of "Map of Violence," J.J. Waiselfisz, as its statistic data is divided between Blacks (or non–Whites) and Whites. The item "color or race" (a mixed criterion of phenotype and ancestry) of the current IBGE (Brazilian Institute of Geography and Statistics) employs the following categories: White, Brown (as in mixed), Black, Yellow and Indigenous.

5. It can be translated to "Stay Alive Program."

6. It translates to Naked Valley Street. Serra (valley) can also mean saw (tool).

7. It refers to the Funk Carioca, popularized in the 1980s in Rio de Janeiro's favelas. Funk songs discuss topics as varied as violence and social injustice, racial pride and sex life.

8. A person that enjoys funk music or is a part of the funk movement.

References

Agamben, G. (2005). *State of Exception*. Chicago: University of Chicago Press.

Brito, D. (2018). Menos de 7% das áreas quilombolas no Brasil foram tituladas. Brasília, Agência Brasil. Avaiable on: http://agenciabrasil.ebc.com.br/direitos-humanos/noticia/2018-05/menos-de-7-das-areas-quilombolas-no-brasil-foram-tituladas.

Cheney, G.A. (2014). *Quilombo dos Palmares: Brazil's Lost Nation of Fugitive Slaves*. Hanover, CT: New London Librarium.

Cherki, A. (2009). *La frontière invisible: violences de l'immigration*. Paris: Éditons Des Crépuscules.

Douville, O. (2007). *De l'adolescence errante. Variations sur les non-lieux de nos modernités*. Paris: Éditions Pleins Feux.

Freud, S. (1996). *A Project for Scientific Psychology. The Standard Edition of the Complete Psychological Works of Sigmund Freud, 1950* (Vol. 1). London: Hogarth Press.

Freud, S. (2003: 1920). *Beyond the Pleasure Principle*. London: PENG.

Guerra, A. (2008). *O laço social entre adolescentes moradores de territórios com alto índice de criminalidade violenta* Belo Horizonte: FAPEMIG.

Guerra, A. (2010). *A incidência do pai na subjetividade do jovem atravessado pela criminalidade*. Belo Horizonte: FAPEMIG.

Guerra, A. (2011). Crítica de uma morte anunciada. *Interfaces*. Belo Horizonte, Arte e Prosa, 129–145.

Guerra, A. (2014). *Adolescências em Tempos de Guerra: modos de pensar, modos de operar*. Belo Horizonte: FAPEMIG.

Guerra, A. (2016). *Adolescências e leis: impasses e soluções dos adolescentes face ao crime*. Belo Horizonte: FAPEMIG.

Joffily, B. (1999). *Isto é, Brasil 500 anos- Atlas Histórico* São Paulo: Grupo de Comunicação Três S/A.

Mattos, H., & Abreu, M. (2011). Remanescentes das Comunidades dos Quilombos: memória do cativeiro, patrimônio cultural e direito á reparação. *Iberoamericana: Madrid, 42*, 147–160.

Mbembe, Achille (2018). *Necropolítica. Biopoder, soberania, estado de exceção, política de morte*. São Paulo, N-1 edições.

Nascimento, Abdias do (1978). *O genocídio do negro brasileiro*: processo de um racismo mascarado. Rio de Janeiro: Paz e Terra.

Perlman, J. (2006). The Metamorphosis of Marginality: Four Generations in the Favelas of Rio de Janeiro. *The Annals of the American Academy of Political and Social Science*. 606 Annals 154:2, 606 Annals(154:2).

Ribeiro, D. (1995). *O Povo brasileiro: a formação e o sentido do Brasil.* São Paulo: Companhia das Letras.
Saillant, F., & Araujo, A. (2007). L'esclavage au Brésil: le travail du mouvement noir. *Ethnologie française, 37*(3), 457–466.
Siqueira, F. (2016). *Inimigo íntimo: um estudo sobre a violência e a segregaçãoo nas fronteiras entre a política e a psicanálise.* (Dissertação de metrado), Universidade Federal de Minas Gerais, Belo Horizonte.
Staff. (2014). Forum Brasileiro de Segurança Pública. *Anuário Brasileiro de Segurança Pública.*
Waiselfisz, J.J. (2012). *Mapa da violência: A Cor dos Homicídios no Brasil.* Brasília: Instituto Sangari.
Waiselfisz, J.J. (2016). *Mapa da violência: Homicídios por arma de fogo no Brasil.* Brasília: Flacso.

4

Slavery's Legacy in San Basilio Palenque, Colombia[1]

ALEXANDRA ESCOBAR PUCHE

> *In the last chapter, the young man Novato's occasional criminal activities, explorations, and girlfriends, were, in his mind, at odds with Afro-Brazilian culture and identity. However, once he engaged in Afro-Brazilian culture and community, he stopped drug dealing and participating in deadly cat-and-mouse games with the police. Afro-Brazilian culture became protective. Not all psychological legacies derived from slavery lead to dysfunctions such as colorism, trauma, and criminal activities. In the next chapter, the researcher uncovers a potentially significant and compelling way that African descendants acknowledge and address trauma and loss. This legacy has been literally in our faces.*

San Basilio de Palenque is the village center of the Mahates municipality in the north of Colombia. Historically, it is one of the runaway slave communities in the Colombian north where they built defensive walls against those intent on recapturing them. "Palenque" means walled. The significance of San Basilio de Palenque is that it survived slavery intact and is considered the first free town in the Americas, predating 1691. In the years since the emancipation of slaves in Colombia, half of the 3,000 people of San Basilio de Palenque still use the Palenquero language and maintain cultural practices dating back to slavery. Palenquero is, also, a unique synthesized Creole language derived from Spanish, the Kikongo language of the Congo and Angola, plus Portuguese, the language of their captors. In 2005, UNESCO declared the village a Masterpiece of Oral and Intangible Heritage of Humanity.

Other slave descendants, outside the Palenque, have undergone multiple cultural transformations since emancipation, and historical influences on them are far more difficult to discern. We are very much on our own in analyzing the behaviors and psychology of slave descendants in Colombia since there are only a few prior studies. In Colombian mental health practice, individual disorders and group psychosocial problems are all traced back to socio-economic and environmental factors. This way of thinking makes it difficult to factor cultural or historical influences into the analysis of Colombians. Outcomes of trauma or psychopathology are dealt with through primary care, as well as mental health care focused on immediate social causation, not on past events. More often, client behaviors are explained by forced displacement from the land, exposure to Colombia's internal violence, drug and gang wars, massacres, threats, and poverty: immediate external conditions and events (Timbert, 2010). Afro-Colombians and indigenous people are particularly vulnerable to these experiences. One does not need to look back to past slavery for traumatic experiences: the present has lots of them. For these reasons, a focus on the Palenque is essential in any search for historical influences.

My associates and I have worked with Palenquero-speakers and interviewed many in-depth. Our objective is to explore the psychological legacy of slavery that might be traced more easily through traditional speakers with direct cultural links to slavery. One area where slavery still influences Palenque speakers today is in their morning of dead relatives. The loss of a relative, whom one had a close emotional attachment to, is potentially traumatic. However, among the Palenque, mourning the passing of a current relative opens the door to the incomplete and potentially traumatic losses of relatives generations ago. The "lumbalú" funeral rite passed down for generations, serves as a script for dealing with such intergenerational trauma.

Songs and dances mask depressive feelings and other symptoms of traumatic experiences. Mourners are asked to give short testimonies revealing their sorrow for the passing (death) of a loved one. We will analyze the statements of three speakers to trace their experiences in losing loved ones and evaluate how these losses are linked to past ones. We are interested mainly in how the Palenque language and culture contextualize losses and deal with trauma, both past, and present. Their testimonies have been extracted from our anthropological field surveys. Our rapport with each person interviewed was strong enough that we believe our respondents were honest and frank about their experiences. They expressed their true feelings and provided authentic testimony.

Our central hypothesis is that deep depression derived from trauma underlies the cultural and traditional manifestation of sorrow. Undoubtedly, the Palenque are not the only ones with this underlying psychology, but they have the lumbalú ritual to contextualize it. Perhaps, we will also

82   Part One—Commonalities

come to understand, as well, how their slave forefathers dealt with depression and trauma and created the lumbalú ritual.

The Lumbalú Rite and Trauma

The way the Palenque community acknowledges and mourns death is an ancestral legacy from slavery. It begins with a premonition transmitted by the guakavó or the kajanvá birds announcing the news in their songs. Women's songs follow it called lekos, shouts, and voices that call to the deceased, as the ancestors of Luango did in the past. Here is a mourning experience reported by a Palenque woman.

First Testimony

Ana is a 50-year-old woman. She is one of the singers, or "cantaoras" of the Palenque songs in the lumbalú ritual.[2] In these songs, the spirits of the dead are called so the deceased can find their way to the afterlife. Ana's singing calls the spirits. Ana's parents were Palenque and sang the same songs Ana sings with other women of the village, continuing the lumbalú tradition. Each time Ana is called to participate in ceremonies around the dance of the dead, or lumbalú, she experiences a kind of trance and metamorphosis. In the interview with Ana by the authors, she explained that each ceremony confronts her with the pain felt by the death of her loved ones. Each ceremony also reproduces the pain of the disappearance of more distant ancestors. In particular, she often sees a single man as she says, "Hace dole mucho, hace doler mucho." Translated, that means, "It hurts very much." Ana explains, "this dance of the dead man hurts very badly." During this meeting, the author observed that, while Ana talks, her hands trembled. She seems to argue with an invisible being. When she sings, she cries at the same time:

> Chi ma Nlongo, chi ma Luango
> [Soy del Congo, soy del Luango] (I come from Congo, I come from Luango)
> Chi mar i Luango, ri Angola
> [Soy del Luango, from Angola] (I am from Luango, Angola)
> Yo me from pueblo e Palenge
> [Yo me voy del pueblo from Palenque] (I am leaving Palenque)
> Neither hermano tengo nor hijo (I do not have brothers or sons)
> [Ni hermanos tengo ni hijos] (I do not have siblings or children)

Ana experiences a kind of transformation in the ceremony, and then, she resumes her song:

Eh, poque yo no tengo a hermano
[Eh, porque yo no tengo a hermano] (Hey, why do not I have a brother?)
Ia tené vario hermano
[Yo tenía varios hermanos] (I had several brothers)
Suto of ous ia solo jui quedá
[Nosotros of ounce, sólo yo quedé] (We were together once, and there remains only me)
E the le, the le le

Ana dries her tears and says (translated from the Spanish): "I have neither brothers nor nephews. I have nothing. I had many relatives, but now I have only three. Ten of my brothers died. Also, the day before yesterday, a brother-in-law died. My race is ending."

Several elements stand out in Ana's testimony. Despite the changes they have undergone over time, Palenque members like Ana continue to maintain the tradition as a therapeutic practice when facing the effects of death. Despite the suffering she experiences, she takes on the community's loss, relieving others in the community of such intense pain. Ana's experience also shows how trauma is dealt with in the lumbalú: the practitioner experiences another's trauma and death, personally. Ana says that she "has nothing more" and that she will leave Palenque because "her race has ended." She means this figuratively from her mind and heart, not literally. We think this shows a certain melancholic feeling or depression that is clinical in-depth. It is like "withdrawing from the world of the living," the belief that life no longer makes sense. In the end, she is drained and emptied. Whatever suffering or trauma remained has been dealt with from the deceased, and among mourners.

Ana's story goes beyond mourning and the loss of a loved one. The death of each relative is experienced not only as her own. There is a sense that her social world has collapsed and been reduced in some way. In the lumbalú ritual, the songs she has interpreted from a young age do not comfort her. The opposite is the case because the burden of morning grows heavier with each passing. She mourns lost relatives and takes on whatever suffering the community has experienced, all the way back to, and during, slavery.

Second Testimony

Paulino Salgado, born in 1933, is a musician who plays the Batata (drum). He is known as the old Batata, whose mother was La Luz Valdez, a singer. She sang the bullerengue and the chalupa. As a Batata, he played only the pechiche, the drum of the dance of the dead. "We, the Salgado, we are the drum race here in Palenque." Next to Paulino stands his sister, Graciela, the only other percussionist in the village. Graciela said: "What I like in life is to drink rum! Drinking, playing, and singing—because that's what my mother, La Lu Valdez, taught me."

Paulino's father, Cho Maney, was also a drummer who played the pechiche and the drum "alegre" of the cumbia, the gaita, and the porro. He died in 1968. Paulino was able to recall his father's death: "When I got the news right away, I bought five liters of rum, and went to the village. I took my father out of his coffin and poured the five liters of rum on his body." Thirty-four years have passed since; thirty-four years that Batata has passed to mourn his father. It has been observed that on the slightest occasion when Paulino plays the drum and drinks rum, he weeps, and remembers his father's drumming. Six months after his father's death, Desiderio Valdez, his grandfather, also died. Paulino recounted, "He said to my father: If you leave before me, take me with you, for I would not want to be there." And so, it was.

During funeral vigils, Paulino drinks rum before he begins his "Rumba Palenquera." In the ceremony, he also sings: "If death knew/what it is that pains (me)/it would give even more life to my poor heart/.../heart, if you go away/never to return...." Like Ana, Paulino participates in this religious tradition which honors the deceased. He does so through the songs and dances that accompany the funeral vigil. When one sees him, it is apparent that his song turns out to be a cathartic show of sadness and pain caused by loss. It is as if he, like Ana, is being tortured to death. The deceased and the living become one in suffering. There is a mutual purging of rare emotion for everyone involved. His life is attached somehow to the one who has died. We find in this song, interpreted by Paulino, a manic-depressive dimension (extremes of happiness and sadness) where ecstasy is accompanied by a depressive state that lasts well after the ceremony.

Taking a closer look, one sees that Batata is an exceptional figure from the village of Palenque, and an extraordinary percussionist. The Salgado's family has always been the caste of drummers, the only ones who can play the sacred drums. "Cho Maney won a drum duel against the devil himself!" says Paulino. "And he won this duel ... listen well to my playing. Our Father upside down. Then the devil disappeared and never returned here. We are on a land of sorcerers." Only the Batata had the right to play the pechiche drum to send a dead man on his return trip to Africa. They were also the heads of Cabildo Lumbalú, who organized all the ceremonies of the ancestor cults. Paulino Salgado was the last descendant of this dynasty, the last of the Batatas.

In these two testimonies from Ana and Paulino, we find a melancholic dimension. The loss of a loved one is not just transitory mourning: it is long-lasting. In the analyzed testimonies, the rite of lumbalú practiced by the descendants of Blacks, maroon masks an important traumatic dimension. It can be appreciated in the case of Ana, but also for Paulino and the two generations preceding them. We see how Paulino's grandfather predestined death for him and his descendants. There is a kind of pathological morning because it is ongoing, but it appears only when a loved one is lost. In other words, one's death is perceived as the only way to join the spirits of enslaved ancestors, and thus of the African cradle.

In mourning, there is an imperfect attempt to detach from death. In the testimonies of Ana and Paulino, we see a feeling that one cannot separate the death of a relative from one's death. Henceforth, the spirits of the immediate dead and one's ancestors, accompany the living until they join them in the world of the dead. The alcohol present in the ceremony of the lumbalú allows one to experience this reality of death through euphoria, ecstasy, and the trance. Closeness to death was always present in the minds of the ancient "cimarrones" who hoped to join their African continent at the time of death. We suspect that alcohol consumption, as in the case of Graciela, Paulino's sister, may mask critical psychological disturbances such as major depressive states.

What did we learn from Batata? The funeral ceremony is not merely about the passing (death) of a single person, nor is it about his or her relationship with living friends and relatives. It is about acknowledging close and continuous relationships between those who have passed before and the living. This acknowledgment includes dealing with any pain and suffering left by those who have gone before the recently deceased. Those with an immediate role in the ceremony are empaths for those present among the living and the dead.

Third Testimony

Concepción Hernández is also a member of the community of Palenque de San Basilio. She is quoted as saying: "When the body dies, the spirit wanders until people come. Some people see the dead. I never saw a dead man, but I heard him speak, I felt him." She described a singular experience in which she heard and felt the dead. This experience is an entirely different matter from merely believing in the spirits of the dead. We see in this testimony how the experience of facing death can provoke hearing and sensory experiences. For Concepción Hernández, the spirit of the dead indeed wanders among the living. They seek resolution of whatever trauma and oppression they experienced and could not address from among the living, as the living seek help from those who have passed. In all African descendant communities, it is common for elders, especially among women, to have ongoing relationships and conversations with deceased relations: sisters, brothers, mothers, fathers, children, and even neighbors. These conversations occur in actuality and dreams.

Perhaps, Concepción and our relatives who communicate with the spirit world are not delusional and in need of psychotherapy. They might be showing us, literally in front of our noses, a psychological legacy from Africa that was a powerful survival tool during slavery and is still with us.

Finally, we propose to analyze the case of Antonio Cervantes, named Kid Pambelé, born in Palenque de San Basilio. This paradoxical case shows the difficulties of someone reared in the Palenque tradition attempting to live outside of it. From this case, one can see the very striking way the continuing influence of the culture made visible in the lumbalú ritual, affects the lives of contemporary Palenquero.

The Case of Kid Pambelé

Antonio Cervantes was born in San Basilio de Palenque. Villagers survive by selling fruits and goods on the beaches of Cartagena. Women sell sweets, and men shine boots. To keep their trade, villagers have to prevent others from selling on the beach and competing with them. They do so with the only tool they have, their fists. This is how Antonio Cervantes became known as Kid Pambelé. Alfredo Salcedo Ramos, the author of *The Golden and the Dark*, says, "Boxing is a job for desperate people, people who have no other chance in life."[3] That was the glory and tragedy of Kid Pambelé. It was his way out. He used boxing to escape Palenque and to choose his destiny.

Antonio Cervantes, Pambelé, became a junior welterweight champion. He beat Peppermint Frazer for the title, in Panama on October 28, 1972, and brought the first world boxing title to Colombia, making Palenque de San Basilio well known. The Kid became the symbol of Palenque. Locally, he provided palenqueros with a new image, one in sharp contrast with the traditional low regard the plantations owners held for non–Spanish speakers. Suddenly, "palenquero" rhymed with victory, national pride, and identification (Cunin, 2004). His successes in the boxing world recalled the warlike history of Palenque. Each of his victories was associated with palenqueros survival, and the cimarrones struggle for his or her independence.[4] The Colombian president even invited him to the palace. Beauty queens were photographed with him, and a famous singer devoted her songs to him in public. He had fame despite his inability to read.

In reality, a boxer resigns himself to being merchandise: flesh. Boxing is a sport of unlimited exploitation, where concealment and abuse are the order of things, and where physical damage and personal degradation are natural consequences of the exercise of the craft. The ring is a plantation in which managers and fighters play the roles of master and slave. This analogue can be seen in the words of Pambelé's coach: "You are a slave if you do not win this fight. You will always be an inferior race." This scenario is a cruel paradox because it recalls the worst of slavery. For example, there were small huts where slaves were confined in large numbers. The image of the ring evokes these closed spaces, this quadrilateral made for fighting, and a place of confinement and perpetual combat. Another paradox is that Black Palenqueros use boxing, like music, as a tool to obtain social recognition. Their pursuit of boxing reinforces racial stereotypes associated with "blacks" as athletes. The more athletic they are, the blacker they seem, and the more their physical capacities are associated with the animal qualities of an inferior race.

Antonio Cervantes found boxing to be a fiercely individual sport, and the opposite of the communal way he knew from San Basilio de Palenque. You cannot share defeats with anyone. When a boxer loses, he does so by himself, and when he wins, he wins on his own. However, the conflict between the real person, named Antonio Cervantes, rooted in Palenque, and Pambelé, the boxer, devoured him. He started to use drugs in a search for the communal and spiritual life he once knew. Soon, he developed an enormous appetite for alcohol and drugs that aggravated psychological disorders that might have been there already. He lost everything. When he was at the top, he did not know what to do with his life. He went crazy. In an interview during a stay in a psychiatric hospital in Havana, Cuba, Pambelé justified the words of his coach while saying that his coach "mismanaged" him. We found himself reduced to the status of merchandise, an object.

One might explain what happened to Pambelé as a classic problem of adjustment from rural folklife to the impersonal urban world that has crushed so many rural-to-urban migrants. However, what Pambelé's experience puts in relief is what happens to someone who loses a system of beliefs and rituals that were functional to them and inherited across generations. Pambelé left behind this world, and its tools for coping, and had nothing comparable with which to replace it. Here, the focus is not on Pambelé, but on the Palenque language, culture, music, and rituals he left behind. Others effectively took on the outcomes of traumas, beliefs, attitudes, and behaviors that might be diagnosed as post-traumatic stress, manic depression, and a host of other psychopathologies that accumulate over time. Then, this collective burden of the community was addressed in funerals and other rituals. Whatever they did in the community was therapeutic; it was effective in relieving individual members of their psychological burden. This sort of ritual and function was missing for Kid Pambelé outside of San Basilio de Palenque.

In the case of Pambelé, he lost touch with the culture that generations before him had devised and used to withstand slavery and oppression.

Perhaps, other migrants to cities left behind their equivalent of Palenque de San Basilio but did not lose touch with the functions that sustained them. In some way, they transformed the original culture and rituals, as did their slave forefathers and foremothers, when they found themselves in a new world. All it took was to transform the roles and rituals of Ana, Paulino, and Concepción into a new context. Then, in this skill of changing culture, they showed resilience as a feature in the psychological legacies of slavery.

Notes

1. Translated from the French by Benjamin P. Bowser.
2. *Folio Magazine*, number 8, July 2005, pp. 20–21.
3. From an interview on France Inter.
4. Op. cit, p. 204.

References

Cunin, É. (2004). *Métissage et multiculturalisme en Colombie*. Paris: IRD Éditions/L'Harmattan.

Timbert, A. (2010, Mai 3). Colombie: Le conflit armé et ses victimes « invisibles » intéressent la Croix Rouge Internationale. *Actu Latino* Retrieved from http://www.actulatino.com/2010/05/03/colombie-le-conflit-arme-et-ses-victimes-invisibles-interessent-la-croix-rouge-inter-nationale/

5

Those Who Disappeared[1]

BERNARD DOSSA

In the previous chapter, the Lumbalú is not just a funeral ritual for respecting someone's passing. It is a way to displace mourning, sorry, and pain in the loss of all those who went before. It is a community therapy for traumatic injuries. The performers take on the suffering of relatives and the community. In the next chapter, readers will get a sense of the source of such rituals among the descendants of enslaved Africans from a different vantage point. Bernard Dossa provides a window into the cultural beliefs that enslaved Dahomeans brought with them to the West. He hypothesizes on how Africans from all African ethnic backgrounds might have used their cultural tools to deal with and survive the Middle Passage and slavery. In effect, Dossa anticipates the Lumbalú ritual and its protective function.

Through the Institute of Research and Culture at the University of Benin, we are attempting to collect data on thousands of Dahomeans enslaved in the eighteenth and nineteenth centuries. By following slave trade routes to South America and the Caribbean, we are confident that we have found Dahomean descendants. However, once we found and began interviewing them, it became apparent to us that we cannot know precisely how their enslaved fore-parents reacted to their capture, deportation, and enslavement on the other side of the Atlantic. Similarly, we do not understand what aspects of their original Dahomean culture and identity they have been able to keep and pass across generations. Their beliefs, attitudes, and practices that appear to us as Dahomean could have other origins. We cannot be sure. The only thing we can be confident about is who they were and what they were like before they were captured and enslaved. Based on what we know, we can only guess what happened to them culturally and in identity between their capture and the present. For these reasons, we refer to these lost Dahomeans as "those who disappeared."

This chapter will focus on what their beliefs were about family and religion. We will describe their ways of worship, sense of profession, philosophy of life, and relations with nature. We can explain what the psychological effects might have been of their capture, their removal from their motherland, and their voyage to an unknown land. We can even estimate what their reactions were to being considered beasts, non-humans, and inferior to other human beings. The Dahomeans we use as a point of reference are the Adja-Fon peoples from present-day Togo, Benin, and western Nigeria, all of whom practiced the Vodoun tradition of worship.

Dahomean Religion and Beliefs

From the start, questions arise: who were these slaves? What were their concepts of life before they were torn away from Africa? What did they feel? What were their emotions and hopes for survival after capture and deportation to an unknown world?

It must be said that the vast majority of the Dahomean deportees were animists. They had faith that there was a living soul in all that surrounded them. Indeed, they knew how to complain to nature. They used incantations, that is, mystical words, pronounced in the language of the object, through a system of gestures and vocal signs: Irokos. If the natural object answered promptly, it distinguished itself from all else as a sacred object and was venerated as a god. Most deportees knew how to make individual pacts with nature, and how to preserve themselves rigorously from the disasters that arise because of disobedience (violations of the pact). Respect for the sacred was integral to the education of Dahomeans in the eighteenth and nineteenth centuries, even with children.

The specific animist spiritual conception or cult of the Gulf of Benin is Vodoun. There is a common expression that characterizes Vodoun: "vodoun wa ta nou min," which in the Fon language means that "the vodun has descended on the head of someone." This is a divine principle living in all things, and to which everyone is subject. For followers, its manifestations are observable. For example, Vodoun manifests itself in a dream when he wishes a sacrifice. It is a python stopped in the middle of a road in front of the person in question. Already, we can understand that nature has languages and symbolism by which the Vodoun speaks to his faithful and that the "Fâ," or geomancy (a method of divination that interprets markings on the ground) is made possible to decipher.

In other words, the Fâ is an anthropocentric conception of the universe. It is at the service of man so that he can know the will of the Vodoun: the word of the divinity. This was the cultic and sociocultural belief of captured and deported Africans who carried this knowledge with them. It is essential to know that pacts with nature, tying one to the universe through the Vodoun, are not to be betrayed. If one betrays an agreement, the consequences are severe. Above all, let us remember that at this stage, the Dahomeans being deported to an unknown world were very religious. They already knew that their lives were imbued with a sense of the divine. They were dependent on the divine, in whatever form it was manifested.

Furthermore, deportees learned of Vodoun in a social context. In Dahomean society, community, family, and clan had a "convent" run by patriarchs. They worked in close cooperation with the queen-mothers who permanently watched over the welfare of descendants, from birth to ten years of age. At this point, initiates entered the convent. They were introduced to the practices of Vodoun worship, and all the ancestral, natural, and communal rules, stemming from those practices.

Reaction to Deportation

The psychological consequences of deportation undoubtedly depend on the slaves' capacity. They had to retain enough mental and physical resources to resist physical annihilation and withstand the destruction of their culture and identity in the experiences they had after deportation. They had to deal with the erosion of memory over the years. What they retained had to sustain them in a new world governed by unjust and racist rules. Their fortitude also had to enable them to live at the bottom of a social hierarchy, and simultaneously find ways to improve their lot.

There is an essential point in diagnosing the psychological impact on Dahomeans removed, captured, and deported to a new world. Early in their deportation, Africans who had Dahomean like beliefs were likely to suffer a double penalty. First, there was an exogenous punishment. These individuals lost their freedom, their identity, and all that related to their prior lives. Second, they experienced the endogenous punishment. They had to live under the care and protection of the gods. Alternatively, one lived with what the dead say of the afterlife when one's pacts with nature, and the spirits are violated. There is a spiritual universe that binds descendants of African deportees inherited from animism. This inheritance is especially important since initiates into the faith were offered the means they needed to face the subsequent difficulties encountered as slaves in the West. Undoubtedly, those who survived capture and enslavement were traumatized. Nevertheless, we would like to think that their traumas were offset by pride and confidence in the concepts of life learned in their Vodoun convent teachings.

Significance of Facial Scars

The facial scars, seen most often on the face of a Peulh, a Bariba, or Gun, are distinctive signs of belonging to a group. These scars go back for generations, come from the ancestors, and designate clan membership within the ethnic group. They are highly symbolic in origin and connect the ancestors of a clan to an animal-divinity, a sacred object. For example, we have the scar of the Azöhouënou ethnic group recognized today in Dahomey by an arched scar on each cheek. It is the same scar on the face of the protective python of this ethnic group. Xovi-Kpö, which means "prince panther," bears two claws on each cheek that represent the look of a panther.

By looking at these clan scars, Dahomean slaves were reminded painfully of their origin. The scars took them back to the land of their forefathers where they were free, where they enjoyed relative equity, and where a little effort yielded a lot. They could smoke meat and fish, watered with palm wine. They could eat raw starchy foods (i.e., cassava and potatoes) and plow the land in cooperation with one another.

The most challenging thing deportees dealt with was being snatched from the affection of their families and communities, despite the many pacts that connected them with the supernatural. The manes of their ancestors and the protective objects of their clans failed to protect them. Nevertheless, they were to respect these pacts for their entire life. Any disobedience or betrayal of a covenant would cause psychological trauma, and even death, for them and their descendants. In short, they believe there is justice in nature. Only strict respect for these spiritual pacts can guarantee longevity on this earth.

Once cut off from the physical observation of their spiritual world, only questions remain. Can slaves burdened with servitude properly perform socio-cultic duties? Can they obey rules that govern the relationship between themselves and nature? What are the expectations of slavery? What are the geographical locations of this unknown world, and what relationship do they have with Africa? Were Dahomean slaves ingenious enough to answer these questions? How were Dahomean slaves able to maintain pride in themselves, and their self-esteem, despite being treated as beasts and objects? Also, how were deported parents able to make sense of the pain of servitude for their sons or daughters? How were Dahomean slaves ready to adopt or start new families, and pass on their knowledge of African spirituality?

The Roots of Cultural-Spiritual Continuity

By capturing Dahomeans as slaves, merchants satisfied the need of slave owners for labor. They needed farmers, artisans, blacksmiths, miners, breeders, cooks, diggers, and house servants. They had no idea that among these slaves were people with specialized knowledge, beliefs, training, and skills. Among the slaves were people with mystical or natural powers, capable of acting on beings and things to their advantage. There were warriors, herbalists, heads of worship, griots, sorcerers (one who obtains practical results through primitive endogenous knowledge), queen-mothers, kings, fetishists, trackers, and hunters. All this know-how was transmitted and practiced intergenerationally within Dahomean families.

What did Dahomeans do as slaves with their knowledge, skills, and specialized training? During days of hard work, they did whatever their masters ordered them to do. However, at night, when they were free from their master's control, they could account for nature, practice, and teach their unique skills. They could honor their pact with nature through secret rituals. For example, they could address complaints to an ant-hill, which, according to the Dahomean tradition, constitutes a return of their ancestors to life.

Communication and Pacts with Nature

It was not by chance that Dahomean slaves venerated the earth by pouring water or small drops of liquor onto it. Nor was it by chance that they hammered and kissed the ground, entrusting it with earth messages to be transmitted by telepathy, especially to their relatives in Africa. Their calls may have been answered by unforeseen interventions by the supernatural to disrupt the slave trade. These interventions may have brought misfortune to those who engaged in the slave trade and slavery in the following ways:

- Dahomean slave descendants survived slavery.
- Some slaves, referred to as Afro-Brazilians, were able to return to Africa, contradicting slavery's permanence and finality.
- The triangular slave trade was ended, and there was the eventual abolition of the African slave trade and slavery.

- The economies and the power of slave-trading nations have been in decline for some time, i.e., Portugal, Spain, France, Great Britain, and Belgium.
- The massive destruction of Europe and the millions who died in World War I and World War II were not coincidences. Both wars were fought over control of colonies (sites of slavery), which eventually gained their political independence. Failure to acknowledge and reconcile the damage done by slavery will result in future wars, more death, and more destruction.
- There are periodic curses by nature on New World communities: diseases, fires, droughts, hurricanes, floods, earthquakes, and plagues. Where and when some of these occurred may not have been coincidental.

Most African families have cult origins from which they have agreements (pacts) with nature to protect themselves against the pandemics of their time, namely measles, plagues, child deaths, death in childbirth, and crop failures. Indeed, African societies, well into the nineteenth century, were considered "primitive," meaning they were still very close to their original traditions.

In addition to these critical assets (pacts), there is also the possibility of meeting with other slaves who shared the same language and the same culture. The affinities between several slaves of the same divinity, or of the same African secret society, could bring them together and unite them to form a religious family against their masters. They could reinforce their knowledge of the different notions of sacrifices they originally learned in Africa. Slavery only reinforced the need for and ways to learn to maintain cult secrets.

The Relationship Between Land and Ancestors

Another African belief is in the immortality of ancestral souls, and the importance and necessity of acknowledging them. This is done by invoking their memory through clan panegyrics (a public speech or published text in their praise) or by other means. One of the African ways of acknowledging and praising one's ancestors is by clearing and cultivating the land. One could fulfill this requirement while working the land as a slave without one's master or overseer realizing it. We do not doubt that Dahomeans did this and might have been able to pass on ancestor veneration to their children through working the land. They were the heirs of hard work in Africa, often on the same land their ancestors worked. That is why it is likely that this tradition and belief continued in the new world. Perhaps, slaves lost this connection to the land through emancipation and urbanization. This was the beginning of the "rootedness" spoken of by Edward Glissant.

We know that African-born slaves believed they had supernatural and protective powers on the spiritual plane. Their slave masters unconsciously offended these by tearing the slaves away from their families and ancestral pacts, for an unknown world. Today, Africans believe that one effect of slavery on the descendants of slave masters is an inherited evil or curse. The diseases and misfortunes they have experienced are the consequences of their ancestors' non-respect for Africans' spiritual pacts. African slave descendants would suffer the same cursed fate if they forgot, rejected, or acted with indifference toward their ancestral pacts. It does not matter that these pacts were made generations ago, or that someone neither knew about nor was responsible for making the original pact.

Therapy: In this case, the recommended traditional treatment for the ancestors of those who engaged in slavery is an acknowledgment of the actual and spiritual damage they did and the offering of restitution to the spirits. For African slave descendants, the therapy consists of initiating rituals for permanent reconciliation between themselves and their original African spirits.

Conclusion

The mere mention of slavery among slave descendants causes a disturbance, as it does in Africa where thousands of families lost members. As Professor Charles-Nicolas pointed out, we must deal with the trauma directly and calmly. This allows us to go deeply into the trauma to understand and research its history and its psychological impacts. I also take a few words from the historian Gilbert Pago: "You are not descendants of slaves, you are descendants of people who have been enslaved" (2006). Deported Africans deserve the abandonment of the slave label to become interested in themselves as human beings: men, women, and children, whose image and culture must be revalued.

Note
1. Translated from French by Benjamin P. Bowser.

Reference
Gilbert, P. (2006). *1848: Chronique de l'abolition de l'esclavage*. Martinique: Desnel édit.

PART TWO

Concepts

Part Two: Chapters 6–10 discuss the psychological legacies of slavery. Very little is known about psychological inheritances from slavery. Can legacies be viewed and verified by science, and can they be eliminated where they are dysfunctional and reinforced when they are protective? In Chapter 6, Aimé Charles-Nicolas provides a psychiatric explanation of slavery's psychological legacies. There is a lot more to slavery's legacies than historical trauma. There are specific symptoms for slave descendants and for Whites who have inherited and assimilated a belief in racial supremacy. In Chapter 7, based on work in the U.S., Joy A. DeGruy refers to the behaviors associated with psychological legacies as syndromes and explains why. Enslaved Africans accumulated multiple PTSD experiences. Reactions to these experiences are embedded in African American culture. All of our international contributors claimed that DeGruy's explanation applied to their country as well.

Benjamin P. Bowser, in Chapter 8, asserts that compelling psychological circumstances from slavery are still with us. We have sufficient knowledge of them to recreate the slave experience conceptually. No one wants to relive slavery, but it can be estimated as a psychological experience. Edwin J. Nichols, in Chapter 9, addressed the puzzlement of our international host and partners about the U.S. How can the U.S. be the wealthiest country in the West and a scientific leader, yet be so behind in addressing issues concerning slavery and its after-effects? Finally, in Chapter 10, Fatimah Jackson, Latifah Jackson and Zainab El Radi Jackson review the physical evidence of slavery's damaging effects on slaves and assesses if epigenetic research can be used to provide tangible evidence of slavery's traumas.

6

A Psychiatric Look at the Legacy of Slavery[1]

Aimé Charles-Nicolas

> *In providing a psychiatric explanation of slavery's psychological legacies, Aimé Charles-Nicolas provides an intimate look at the social and psychological legacies that Afro-descendants must address in each generation. Descendants of slave owners and those who embrace the South's cultures and traditions have slavery legacy issues to deal with as well if they care to look. One cannot expect to be free from the traumas and appropriate guilt of slavery's legacy without looking at these issues, knowing what they are, and then dealing with them. This chapter provides a guide to take us through our suppressed past.*

Slavery and Self-Esteem

Transatlantic slavery was based on the principle of obliterating slaves' self-esteem. Indeed, for an economy and social system to work based on slavery, the Slave's self-esteem must be rendered completely nil: absolute submission to the (Slave) owner's will was a prime requisite. Self-esteem is a basic constituent of the individual, and it varies from one person to the next. A child must enjoy positive interactions early on (as soon as the first months) with its mother or a substitute parent for self-esteem to be well established. It must be sufficiently strong to enable the child, come what may, to confront the inevitable psychic trauma of life as a slave. Because self-esteem is not the willful construct of an individual, it is formed unconsciously, based on *confidence* in oneself and others. It revolves around the precocious[2] interaction with the mother (narcissistic foundations), and then through social-environmental interactions,[3] in this case, wherever slaves were tasked. Self-esteem is the value individuals place on themselves. In an environment of disdain, servitude, betrayal, and distrust, the quality of the early narcissistic relations with a child depends on the impact of slavery on the mother. It depends on the mother's moods (the baby will feel it), and on the adequacy of the messages that she transmits, and even though the way she looks at her child. It also depends on her presence and absence, on the affective quality (abundant and joyful in the best of cases) of the maternal surrogate, and duration of her relationship with the child.

It must be stressed that the development of self-esteem does not take place through imitation. It develops in a complex dialectic of reactions to the value of the self that other members of the community communicate to the child. Thus, during early childhood, the children of slaves, depending on the situation, grow up *with more or less self-esteem*. They do so as a function of the quality of their early relational interactions and the favorable, or unfavorable, aspect of events, faced as children.

The Call for Freedom, Despite Everything

Africans captured as slaves knew deep down that they were not slaves. This consciousness reduced slavery to its essential nature. The enslaved resisted. They kept alive the hope of *freedom* (even vaguely) that helped them *struggle against the loss of their self-esteem and the guilt of existing*. Resistance is in no way a case of an externally acquired taste for freedom but of an innate need for freedom. Moreover, some slaves succeeded in reaching that Holy Grail of freedom, others purchased it or acquired it through various other means. In all Western countries where slavery was practiced, the same examples of escape were prevalent and carried out at considerable risk. Also, escaped slaves knew free people of color. Throughout the four long centuries of slavery, they maintained the conviction that slavery would not last forever. This conviction grew stronger as they heard the cries of abolitionists, both White and Black. It was "as though the yearning surrounded them for freedom" (Charles-Nicolas, 2003). The dream of freedom, however slight, strengthened their self-esteem and helped them to carry on.

Today, descendants of slaves can hear the story of slavery because their slave fore-parents' embattled self-esteem developed *pride in being black*. This pride developed slowly, both before and after abolition. A great deal of our suffering over slavery stems from the way we interpret what happened to us. Some fore-parents were destroyed, others transformed the misfortune into opportunities, some revolted (the number of whom is much higher than we will ever know), while others reverted to denial. Since they had little control over events in their lives, they could only change how they confronted their circumstances. That is what they did: they gathered[4] in the evening, tried to retrace their roots and discover what they had in common. They were able to call forth and share songs, dances, rituals, and familiar divinities. Thus, they were able to recapture their humanity after long days of being slaves.

Moreover, throughout slavery in the West, the possibility of *validating one's identity as a free person*, even if an attempted revolt failed, reconfigured their relationship to one another, and the world at large. The audacity of the victorious Saint-Domingue (Haitian) insurrection is but one example.[5] We can also include the resistance of Zumbi dos Palmares (1655–1695) in Brazil, and of the Jamaican "Maroons"[6] who were the first African slaves to wrest their freedom from their European masters, around 1730. There were the brave solitude and courage of Delgrès (1766–1802) on Guadeloupe, the great historical figures of Boukman and Toussaint[7] of the Haitian revolution, the rebel Nat Turner in Virginia in 1831, the resilient Frederick Douglass (1817–1895), and the heroic Lumina Sophie (1848–1879) on Martinique. All these heroes have been the backbone of the process of validating Black identity and creating collective pride.

Surviving Destruction (Annihilation)

The Double-Edged Sword of Identity

Imagine the distress wrought on villages that saw their most vibrant members carried off. Historians describe the terrifying rounding up of Africans as slaves from coastal African communities (Hawthorne, 2010). They suggest that the slave traders killed from four to five Africans for every Slave captured. Leonora Miano's novel, *La saison de l'ombre* (Season of the Shadow) (2013), invokes the gods: "Are they dead or still alive? Why is it so difficult to establish a spiritual contact with them? If their sons are never found again, if the *ngambi* doesn't reveal what happened to them, it is impossible to relate their mothers' sorrow. They will not forget, but the community will forget the ten young initiates, the two mature men who have simply evaporated into thin air during the great fire. We won't speak again about the fire itself. Who takes pleasure in recalling defeats?"

"If you lose everything, if your very own ancestry forgets you, if, also, you are subjected to the violence of the contempt that is destructive, your inner soul is dead."[8] People forced into transatlantic slavery faced a double identity crisis. First, they lost everything that had defined them: their culture, religion, language, and past. Second, they were forced to reinvent a new culture for themselves, (Creoleness or *créolité* in this case), and even a new form of spirituality out of the circumstances in which they found themselves (where the slaveholder and the Christian church imposed new values on them). They had to draw deep from within themselves to find the motivation to go on. Their survival was dependent not only on recreating an immediate sense of self but also on having new touchstones in time, place and history, despite changes and the passage of time. Given this impossible situation, how was it possible to avoid complete annihilation or insanity?

We have sought to understand this tension between survival and annihilation. Moreover, the only way to understand it is to go to Benin, to the very place where Africans were rounded up and uprooted. We find the Voodoo religion, *Vodun,* which represents an integral part of the culture and identity, and its adherents, dignitaries, convents, and liturgies (see Dossa chapter in this volume). In Ouidah, we saw the Tree of Return, where captured Africans walked around the tree three times to ensure that their spirit would return to their homeland after their death, and which explains their suicides on the slave ships, and in the West. Voodoo was intrinsic to their real relationship to the world, and its rituals were the sole weapons at their disposal to defend themselves against the armed hordes that came in the middle of the night to carry them off. Voodoo was a weapon against slavery.[9] It was thus that spirituality, through Voodoo and during four centuries of slavery, that maintained the Slave as a human being, from Benin to the Candomblé religion in Brazil, to Cuba's Santeria, to the Voodoo in Louisiana, to the Voodoo of Haiti.

A Marvelous Misfortune?

The painful guilt of survival, together with the all-powerful sense of still being alive, posed a troublesome question: "Why me?" One need only try to imagine the determination that needed every day to affirm one's humanity. After all, the promise of transcendence was denied. All the traditionally sacred figures were discarded, or stripped of their sacred symbolism. They no longer have their protective fetishes or divinities to defend them. They no longer have access to these psychological mechanisms that can convey a sense of self-projection. Sacred elements were an integral part of their pre-slave environment, and the desecration of that former existence left them helpless in the face of violent new circumstances. However, slavery did not always succeed in its goal of dehumanizing the slaves.[10] Vodun or Voodoo is still practiced today in Brazil, and on Haiti and Cuba. Voodoo has also been supplanted by and integrated into Christianity. We know that African priests adapted Catholicism to accommodate African religious beliefs, and they formulated a one-to-one correspondence between the

Catholic saints and the voodoo *orishas* and *loas*. There was a comingling of religious practices and beliefs since slaves were able to reconcile the protection of both the saints and the *loas*.

Resistance to dehumanization meant maintaining a heartfelt urgency of becoming free human beings! Liberation from slavery was vital for everyone, and, for some, there was no price too high to pay. The film *Twelve Years a Slave* demonstrates the determination and tenacity needed to reach that goal. This determination was transmitted to the children of slaves in the form of *strength of character*. It is with this strength and determination that one moves mountains. The outstanding successes of the children of slaves can only be attributed to that. Being resilient does not mean being invulnerable. It does mean learning how to survive trauma. It is even possible that going through a particularly unjust trauma bestowed upon some individuals newfound tenacity and uncommon strength. This explains the successes of those who have risen from such depths. In these cases, traumatic experiences do not seem to have had a deleterious effect on the individual's self-esteem. They may only have produced symptoms of anxiety and depression.

Un merveilleux malheur (A marvelous misfortune) is the title of a well-known work on resilience by Boris Cyrulnik. Cyrulnik "points out the capacity to succeed, to live, to develop oneself despite adversity. Knowing that we will change how we view misfortune and, despite our suffering, we will strive toward the marvelous" (Cyrulnik, 2002).

The Racialization of Thought and Humiliation

The daily life of slaves was a litany of repetition of acute stress, and public and repetitive *humiliations*. We are familiar with the devastating impact of shame on our mental well-being. However, we know that on Martinique, and generally speaking, in those communities where there was slavery, parents, even today (sometimes publicly in the schoolyard), *use shame as a form of discipline*: a means of raising consciousness in young children and adolescents. It is said, "you have to make them feel ashamed for them to understand." The way that parents induce shame and guilt in their children has been studied (Massé, 2001). Public humiliation, as during slavery, is now a weapon of mass destruction of the self-esteem of children and adolescents. It leads directly to depression and violent delinquency (Rutter, 1985). Parents and social workers must realize that self-esteem is the most valuable asset an adolescent has!

With the racialization of thought and emotion, we find humiliation once again used in all of its manifestations. Its effects are dependent upon variations of sensitivity, of distrust, and the profound need for respect described by slaves. In the first written texts by slaves themselves, Olaudah Equiano (Charbonnier, 2000) and Mary Prince (2000) evoked this need, and Frantz Fanon recounted a similar reaction upon his arrival in France. Because of humiliation, Jorge Amado tells us that Brazilian Blacks endeavor to retain their gods. The American author Toni Morrison recounts so accurately the myriad nuances of humiliation, including that ever so paradoxical lethal violence in her novel *Beloved*.[11] While being aware that the mind is complex, and varies from person to person, and being careful not to over-generalize, it is safe to say the following. There were similarities across time and space, of elements that were indispensable in the ability of Africans to adapt to slavery then, as it is now for their descendants to adapt to a post-slavery environment. *The reaction to being humiliated is the common thread in this process of adaptation.* Coping is intrinsic to ongoing resilience and surfaces when an individual's id is threatened by the loss of self-esteem, and by survivors' guilt, particularly in the face of racial discrimination. The *racialization of thought and emotion is*, therefore, a critical psychological consequence of slavery.

Continuity of Trauma in Laws and Daily Practice

If we pursue the French psychologist, François Sauvagnat's theory, there is a continuity from slavery to the present day. The trauma of slavery is best expressed through the reciprocal equation, Slave = Black or Black = Slave. This equation persists in a more or less attenuated form in our subconscious. It is evident in hierarchical social relations based on the distinct difference in skin color. Studies in the U.S. have demonstrated how, after slavery, social policies and institutions had incorporated negative stereotypes regarding skin color, and formal laws and policies were a reflection of racist public mindsets. Raymond Massé, in studies of psychological distress on Martinique, cites Paul Ottino from La Réunion, where slavery was practiced. "The former collective memory, for example, of the violence, accompanying separation and the expulsion of populations, even though it has gradually faded into oblivion in modern memory, has, nevertheless, left a profound mark on the *social structures*, the habitus and the various ways it manifests itself."

We now know that the effects of trauma continue long after the traumatic event. Victims of violent, aggressive behavior, rape, terrorist attacks, natural catastrophes (earthquakes, hurricanes), wars, and combat veterans struggle with PTSD from trauma decades after the experience.[12] The aftermath of slavery is no different. Moreover, instead of just affecting individuals, the trauma of slavery is encoded in a racial hierarchy and continues even today. It is clearly evident in the ways judicial, political, and cultural measures were established in the West, especially in the U.S. It is also clear that even though slavery has been abolished, the question remains: what specific impacts have slavery's trauma had on slave descendants?

Laws that appear, on the surface, to be objective and independent of bias, are outcomes of racial prejudices. The entire judiciary system/framework is, in fact, responsible for shaping the national psyche, and for continuing racist beliefs long after slavery was outlawed formally. South Africa offers an eloquent example. The political and judicial changes brought about by Nelson Mandela have had little effect on the thinking and practices carried over from Apartheid, despite the progress made. Still lacking is a fundamental shift in how people think. Two elements are needed for a change in thinking: first, the purpose of the justice system needs to be reconsidered and aligned with the new South Africa.[13] Second, an absolute priority must be given to a global children's policy. Daily life in South Africa, which was not a part of the transatlantic slavery, as in the United States, demonstrates that the psychological outcome of slavery affects South Africa as well. It encompasses a psychic reality that is lasting and widespread. It is one of racialized thought, of humiliation, of hierarchy and continued white racial superiority. The heritage of slavery is still present in the continued *propagation* of a racialized collective mindset, and of the role that skin color plays in making the racial hierarchy immediately visible.

Considerations of Transgenerational Transmission

As with every living being, humans are determined by their biological heritage, but not by that alone. Also, they are influenced by the myriad environmental experiences from the very earliest moments of their development, and throughout their existence.

I will not deal with the epigenetic transmission of psychic trauma that Professor Fatimah Jackson reviews in her chapter, other than to note what a powerful psychic force the transfer of trauma to the genome is. The possibility of *transgenerational transmission* of the trauma of slavery has "shaken our thinking," to quote a journalist who attended our colloquium. What is most extraordinary about this is that, if a causal link has been established, the impact of psychological suffering on the genes might be treated successfully. In effect, epigenetics teaches us that we can change. *We are not slaves to our genes.*

We learn that a child's psychological make-up partly exists already before its birth. When a baby is born into the world, it enters a psychic universe. In the case of slavery, it is the baby's parents, who have a mental history from a life "lived" in the equivalent of concentration camps. The parents have established bonds of both ambivalence and dependency in this environment. The child's psychic development will depend on its attributes and will be infused with the psychic life of the slave system. However, the child may free itself from this psychology because the psychic state that prevails in slavery is neither monolithic nor omnipotent. It carries a powerful, albeit implicit component as well: the hope of freedom, as we have seen. His/her oppression is punctured, as well, by personal efforts toward resilience, and by a sense of belonging. These are all-important matrices of collective resilience, which are made even more effective by his/her identification with hero figures, and by the pride of identity.

Parents explicitly transmit thousands of messages to their children: they educate, they relate, they use reprimands and explanations. At the same time, the social environment also sends its message. We understand that, after the abolition of slavery, the ex-slaves tried to forget the shame associated with being a slave. They tried to *raise their children with explicit dignity*. Their children could not and did not want to hear about slavery. The silence was the price of dignity passed from generation to generation. Do not speak about it. Forget it. *Shame is a dominant attitude of post-slavery societies.*

Also, there was an *unconscious element* involved in these transmissions. The child is aware of something unspoken, something that the parents carry within themselves that they do not deliberately desire to communicate, but that they transmit anyway, unconsciously. Thus, the child intuits an unconscious shame that, from time to time, manifests itself in the parents' behavior or manner of speaking. Sometimes, the parents themselves are not aware that they bear within themselves something that we as psychiatrists have identified in our daily clinical experiences, and that also could be a feeling of guilt.[14] Through a close identification with the parent figure, the child may feel the need to atone for this feeling. Shame and guilt are, therefore, "remnants" belonging to parents, grandparents, and great-grandparents. The child unconsciously assumes the responsibility to repair the damage, for our redemption. One can understand the critical role that religion played for the enslaved, a role that was magnified because of the turmoil of the times.

We do not want to attribute greater importance to transgenerational transmission than it merits. Irrefutable scientific data substantiates the transferability of intergenerational psychic trauma caused by unthinkable concentration camp-like settings and experiences. The transatlantic slavery was the first concentration camp. The fact is, it is also true that many concentration camp survivors are silent, which is identical to the silence that followed slavery. In both cases, and all other forms of genocide, it is the feelings of shame and guilt that engender and nourish silence. It is as though the victims sought to avoid the generational transmission of shame associated with the horrible reality of what they had gone through. Everything also happens as if the underlying fantasy was the *curse* that they wanted to avoid at all costs.

The Supremacists' Psyche

The idea that the psychology of slavery[15] continues is unaddressed and is international in scope, and calls into question whether the World Court, the United Nations, and other international organizations can be called upon for redress. It also raises the question and problem of "reparations." However, the reaction to oppose reparations has also resulted in opposition to even acknowledging that slavery's psychology has continued long after the institution of slavery ended. For example, Pascal Bruckner, a French essayist, shares the same convictions as Alain Finkielkraut.[16] A large portion of the Western public believes that "the West has invented everything." They are fed up with hearing that "White men are responsible for all of the evils in the world." Bruckner came up with a statement that hit home: "The Black slave trade? We didn't do much better than the Arabs or the Africans themselves. On the other hand, we are the only ones to have invented the abolition of slavery." It is easy to understand why this statement was so pleasing to the ears of the Anglo-American critics, Brian C. Anderson, Steven Rendall, Andrew Anthony, and Eric Kaufman. To minimize the culpability of Europeans in the transatlantic slave trade, they minimize the effect of the trade on Blacks. They reject the idea that there are any lingering effects.

However, no one has pointed out that the expression "abolition of slavery" is a direct reference to the abolition of *transatlantic* slavery. Bruckner fails to mention the principle point of the *transatlantic* slave trade, and its distinction, which has nothing to do with Arab and African domestic slavery, which still prevails. The transatlantic slave trade was invented, propagated, and justified by Europeans: "white men."[17] Consequently, the institution of slavery may have ended, but White supremacy, shaped by four centuries of transatlantic slavery, did not. If it is unchanged, how has it affected the current "globalization of our values" and, particularly, the righteous advancement of "democracy"? Have not White supremacy and the arrogance that goes along with it, unleashing chaos in Iraq, Libya, Syria, and Afghanistan, and ravaged Vietnam? The same mentality that propagated slavery, and indeed denies its psychological continuity, is a major cause of the chaos in the Middle East. In other words, behind the high-minded ideology and magnanimous slogans lurk, perhaps not only economic interests but also a powerful psychic interest to dominate, exploit, and control. After slavery, how could the West impose its vision of "Good" on the rest of the world? As long as the West cannot face up to its history of complicity in slavery in the eyes of slave descendants, the trauma of slavery will continue for everyone.

Of course, there is resistance in the West to admitting and teaching about crimes committed by Europeans in the name of "civilization." This resistance enshrines, embeds, and universalizes expressions like "might makes right." Pizarro's colonization during the beginning of the sixteenth century and that of Jules Ferry at the end of the nineteenth century were driven by the same motivation, the same methods, and the same justifications. The continuity between slavery and the present is rooted in political and economic history. There is no time gap between colonization, the triangular trade of transatlantic slavery, and colonialism. They are not radically different phenomena that sprang up independently and spontaneously. Colonialism is the sequel to, and the consequence of, slavery.[18] Today's geopolitical situations do not exist in a vacuum without links to what came before. This continuity is grounded in the psychic and economic interests of those who write history, and who regularly invoke the "values" which serve to maintain their clear conscience and self-esteem. These are powerful psychic motivations.

Since the time of Pizarro, the justifications for slavery have intensified throughout the centuries. Because of the rationale provided by nineteenth-century "science," they have codified and justified racially structured hierarchies. They developed a biological basis for the inferiority of Blacks. For example, on July 28, 1885, Jules Ferry addressed the members of the French National Assembly and laid out the colonial discourse of the French left: "We must say outright that indeed the superior races enjoy rights over the inferior races.... I repeat that there is a right for the superior races because there is also a duty for them. They must civilize the inferior races.... These duties have often been ignored in the history of past centuries. When Spanish soldiers and explorers introduced slavery in Central America, they did not fulfill their duty as men of a superior race. However, in modern times, I maintain that the European nations are carrying out this higher duty of civilization with breadth, grandeur, and honesty."

Exactly two days after, on July 30, 1885, Clémenceau answered Ferry: "and you will see just how many atrocious and terrible crimes have been committed in the name of justice and civilization. Not to mention the vices that the Europeans brought with them: alcohol and opium, which he disseminates everywhere, which he imposes if he so desires. No, there are no rights of so-called superior nations over the so-called inferior nations; let us not attempt to don the cloak of violence in the name of civilization; let us not speak of right, of duty! The conquest that you are preaching is the pure and simple abuse of the power given by scientific civilization over rudimentary civilizations to enslave men, torture them and extract from them all the force that they possess solely for the benefit of the so-called civilizer. That is not a right: it is a negation. To speak of civilization in this regard is to add hypocrisy to violence...."

During this debate about French colonial policies in the Chamber of Deputies, Jules Ferry's statements scandalized several orators. Jules Maigne countered Ferry with: "You dare to say that in the very country where the Declaration of the Rights of Man was proclaimed!" Indeed, this colonial policy aroused loud protests from the radical opposition (Georges Clémenceau), as well as from conservatives such as Adolphe Thiers. This rhetorical confrontation presents an opportunity to recall that the idea of racial hierarchy is no longer "in the spirit of the times," and "accepted by all." In France, in March 2015, the hospital named after Charles Richet was renamed.[19] Likewise, controversy followed the inauguration of François Hollande as president on May 15, 2012, which he declared to be under the auspices of Jules Ferry.

The idea of slavery itself was also not "accepted by all"[20]: "a special edition of the historical revue Hérodote stressed that 'Slavery has been practiced in all sedentary and organized societies ... but it *has never been self-evident.*' Thus, Aristotle felt obliged to justify it in a famous plea." In one of his letters, Seneca (4 BCE–65 CE) was outraged. "Do you really want to say to yourself that this being whom you call your slave was born from the same seed as you, that he lives under the same sky, that he breathes the same air, that he lives and dies like you..." (Stuewig & McCloskey, 2005). Historically, there have always been intellectuals and communities who have protested against the concept and practice of slavery. In England, in America, in France, in Holland, in Portugal, during the eighteenth century, continuous petitions were calling for an end to slavery. L.G. Tin (2013) recalls that "if the Black Code introduced by Colbert remained a code and not a law, it was because the Parliament of Paris refused to register this text, which violated both natural law and Christian morality." In all of this history, the self-esteem of slave descendants and the continuing psychology of slavery were and continued to be at stake.

Slavery's Effect on Mental Health: "Not all of them died, but all of them were affected"

Slavery was not good for anyone's mental health.[21] We can surmise that the gravity of slavery's effect on mental health varied according to the severity of oppression: by environment and events. It is a taboo among historians to compare slavery's cruelty in practice between Europeans. We break this taboo. No two psychological situations were identical. At any rate, by following slavery's abolition, the outcomes were very different. For example, after the final French abolition (1848), slaves were immediately granted French citizenship and allowed to exercise their rights. However, it was almost one hundred years before France allowed its former colonies to become part of France. In the largest and most populous colonies, a strict separation was maintained until 1946, between "sujets français" (all the natives) and "citoyens français" (all males of European extraction), with different rights and duties. As was pointed out in a 1927 treatise on French colonial law, the granting of French citizenship to natives "was not a right, but rather a privilege" (Grandmaison, 2010, p. 59). In contrast, slaves in the U.S. were granted citizenship (1865), as well, but after a short attempt to integrate them, called Black Reconstruction, it was almost one hundred years (1964) before they were allowed to exercise their rights fully.

On the surface, the French and American reactions to emancipation appear alike. However, in actuality, they were not. The American Jim Crow South took white supremacy to another level; there is nothing like it in French institutional racism. Jim Crow laws negated the rights of citizenship for all Blacks, and declared, "even though you are no longer a slave, you are still inferior." The segregationist social order remained in place until the passage of the Civil Rights Act of 1964. Some Jim Crow laws are still inscribed in the constitutions of some southern states today. These laws go a long way toward explaining not only the continued white contempt for the descendants of slaves but also the extent of their hatred. Lynchings, castrations, burnings, hangings, and the Ku Klux Klan in the U.S., were unprecedented and without equivalent anywhere else in the West. The fact that the Republican Party still contests the rights of slave descendants today is a direct reflection of the depth of slavery's continuing impact in the U.S. The continued psychological damage to Blacks and Whites alike must be enormous.

The mental health of slave descendants is affected in several ways: experiencing racial discrimination has to affect one's subjective identity. Social relationships between and within the races are comprised undoubtedly with susceptibility, mistrust, social conflict, and oppositional behavior as outcomes. Perhaps, racial discrimination has the most significant impact on youngsters from 11 to 14 years old, a time when social identity and self-esteem develops, and when humiliation is felt more acutely. The distinctive nature of slavery is that *it is a totalitarian, absolute, and unrelenting system of diminishing self-esteem.* The internalization of negative stereotypes and "internalized racism" are virtually unavoidable. This sort of ongoing historical racism not only creates economic poverty but perpetuates it. On February 17, 2015, *Slate*, the American investigative magazine, ran a little-known story. Some black parents had taken their children out of school and were homeschooling them: "most chose to educate their children at home, at least in part, to avoid school-related racism."

It is no coincidence that drug addiction has been more prevalent among the descendants of slaves, and in communities where racial discrimination is ongoing. Examples are Aboriginals in Australia, Native American Indians, Afro-Brazilians, and African Americans. Studies have shown that today, feeling that one is a victim of discrimination has a strong correlation with alcohol and drug use. Perhaps, the new epidemic of heroin and opioid use among poor Whites in the U.S. is motivated partially by a diminished sense of self, relative to the rise of slave descendants, in fact, and aspirations. For reasons of race and history, now, White and Black people self-medicate embattled self-identities.

The higher incidence of high blood pressure among Blacks in the Americas has led to several explanatory hypotheses. There is the psycho-traumatic experience of the Atlantic crossing in slave ships. Then, there is Africans' ability to retain salt, which made it possible for some to survive those crossings. These advantages then have become contributing factors to high blood pressure now.

Slavery's Influence on the Expression of Emotions

A curious feature of the psychological legacy of slavery is that trauma experienced by slaves, and acts of brutality on the part of masters did not necessarily lead to mental pathology in every case. However, the psychological damage was done. The descendants of slaves and masters, like their fore-parents, cannot fully accept and live with what happened, and what was done. According to autobiographical accounts of the time, the harshness of the relations between slave masters and slaves permeated all social ties and affected even their ability to express emotions. Slavery established a climate of indifference and inhumanity for all involved. *Slavery hardened the attitudes of everyone concerned and raised mental barriers for everyone, which promoted psychological rigidity. Avoidance of history, emotional guardedness, and mental rigidity have been passed on across generations as a psychological legacy of slavery.*

Slavery perverted healthy emotional development. Everyone's mindset was affected, dependent on just how oppressive the plantation or farm was. Authors, biographers, and historians alike stress the difficulty that men had in expressing feelings of tenderness, especially in the nineteenth and early-twentieth centuries, when Blacks wrote their first autobiographies, novels, and when the psycho-sociological studies of the deep South were published. It is alleged that on some plantations, masters used male slaves as studs to impregnate slave women, thereby wiping out norms of marital stability, mutual respect, and paternal responsibility. Female slaves had no control over their bodies, nor were their preferences, desires, and emotions recognized and respected.

Ralph Ellison, in his *Invisible Man* (1952), writes that slavery wiped out individuality among slaves and imprinted a group mentality that is with us to this day. "Instead of viewing things in terms of persons, (some) descendants of slaves view social relations with respect to 'races,' of masses of people separated from other masses of people by their skin color." This is precisely how Whites saw Blacks during slavery and how many see them today. Ellison goes on to write, "He (Blacks) knows that he will never exist as a person." Social scientists have made the same observation. "We define and perceive Blacks as an undifferentiated mass without any individual variations" (Littlewood & Lipsedge, 2013, p. 372). There is a denial of emotions, feelings, and humanity when we are talking about the other side, whether we are referring to war, sports, or slavery. We do not recognize the other group as being made up of individuals. If one's humanity and individuality are denied, and one has internalized this disregard, then one's capacity to form and maintain a family, raise children, and contribute to the community is diminished for Whites and Blacks alike. These psychological legacies of slavery are with us today.

Slavery's Influence on Child Rearing and Society

Naturally, the circumstances of the parents' lives influence the way children are brought up. We have seen the role that humiliation plays in slavery, and the impact that shame has on children. Slavery has affected the way we socialize children today. Single mothers, or mothers without a supportive spouse, and in the best of conditions, both parents, have to pay more attention to a child's outward behavior than to his or her inner emotional needs. White parents cannot imagine having to do this. It is essential for Black parents and children to avoid punishment, and to observe all implicit and explicit rules. When necessary, one must act submissive and docile, regardless of one's true feelings, with White police officers, teachers, employers, and others in authority. In slavery, the price was very high and traumatic for not being able to hide one's emotions or say and act in the right way. Children were taken away and sold, and some were tortured, beaten, and raped. The more one loved one's children, the higher the trauma and pain when they were sold. To protect their children and themselves, many slaves would not allow themselves to love too much, and they avoided becoming too attached. They had to exercise ambivalence toward their children. In this context, teaching proper (survival) behavior took precedence over the development and evolution of their children's emotional needs.

Every author who has written about post-slavery societies emphasizes the continuing severity of black corporal punishment and its purpose: to train and to harden. Slave descendants continue to "love" their children by beating them to prepare them for a harsh, cruel and unforgiving world, even when it is not. They still raise them as if they risk losing them. We know, moreover, that parents who mistreat their children were subjected to violent mistreatment during their own childhood. We also know that a child who is abused is also prone to violence and delinquency, and that humiliation and shame play a role in this process (Gold, Wolan, & Lewis, 2011). The higher the incidence of community poverty and social isolation, the more prevalent is violence in child-rearing.

Conclusion: Collective Resilience

An important role was played in the psychology of slavery by the authoritative voices who condemned slavery in Europe and elsewhere. Their condemnation confirmed to slaves something they felt deep within: slavery is an abnormality and an abomination. This awareness would become a factor in the slaves' collective resilience. Many have interpreted resilience as a "way of forgetting, of turning toward the future." That is not at all the case. Resilience is not a way to whitewash history. It is not necessary to erase the past to embrace the future. Resilience is instead about overcoming and rebounding, despite the barriers.

The ways that former slaves and their descendants healed themselves have been overlooked even more so than the traumas of slavery. Their success in doing so is extraordinary and self-evident. From a psychiatric point of view, they initially used the unconscious mechanisms of forgetting, repression, and denial, to shield their own, as well as their children's self-esteem from shame. This was a vital and necessary step. However, these mechanisms were not capable of completely blocking the memory. Eventually, the collective memory gave way to doubts, signs, and allusions that contradicted the "memories," and led to a revision of the family and community narratives. The narratives on the slave experience had to be repeated, revised, and deepened as memories surfaced. Contrary to what is said about "rebounding," repetition allows for recovery from a psycho-trauma.[22] Recent studies emphasize the therapeutic value of re-recounting traumatic events. Repetition is an ancillary element in the treatment of psycho-traumatic disorders. The mere fact that "people talk a lot about it" is therapeutic.

The first and official U.S. southern histories after emancipation were tales of benevolent slavery, and that abolition was granted voluntarily. This first account was disseminated widely but found faulty. Gradually, historians, such as Herbert Aptheker, began to shed light on the events that have been obscured in the official histories (1983). Since the 1960s, two generations of historians have uncovered the variability and complexity of slavery, and its aftermath in the U.S. Computer technologies have permitted the exploration of documents, records and censuses, providing a more detailed, accurate, and nuanced history of slavery. We are no longer dependent on false and self-serving southern narratives, myths, and rumor. Facing the past, emotional healing, and rejecting denial can all be done with accurate and in-depth knowledge. The many ways that slavery was practiced and responded to are now known. It is possible to have a "true narrative" to reduce the shame and pain that is still with us. How can one have (felt) shame with the knowledge that there were Maroon Negroes who fought back and were never defeated? One cannot feel shame after reading the globally admired poetry of Aimé Césaire, the poet of anger, of symptoms and fleeting memories.

The desire to survive, to live, and to one day be vindicated was the first step in the development of collective resilience. No matter what cruelty one experienced, to resist was, first, the desire to live. Slaves' resistance proved to be extraordinary and necessary for maintaining their humanity and retaining their dignity. However, to remain human also meant to show solidarity. This was one of the first challenges of emancipation. It took an enormous degree of magnanimity for those who rebelled and suffered not to seek vengeance against those who had "collaborated." It was the slave's humanity, once damaged, and under assault, that somehow survived. This is an extraordinary heritage for their descendants. This humanity is now found in the grandchildren and great-grandchildren of slaves who continue to struggle against the continuing psychological legacy of slavery that manifests itself in white supremacy and racial discrimination throughout the West.[23] Trauma, humiliation, and shame, as well as resilience, pride, and self-vindication have been found at both ends of the slave whip.

Notes

1. Translated from French by Roger Stevenson.
2. In the limbic system in the brain, the myelin sheath forms around the nerve fibers at

between 0 and 18 months. Early relational experiences (they have an impact on the limbic and cortical zones of the right hemisphere) modulate feelings of more or less secure attachment. The security of the early attachment will, in turn, have an impact on resilience. The quality of the early environment will influence the development of a child's future self-esteem.

3. The exploitation of sugar cane, tobacco and coffee in the French Caribbean, corresponding to the cotton plantations in the United States.

4. Whenever it was not forbidden or when they were able to defy the interdiction.

5. Recent historical research highlights the important impact of the uprising of slaves, and of the loss of Saint-Domingue and its ensuing impact on the politics of France, Spain, Great Britain, Portugal and the United States. It demonstrates just how much this victorious insurrection revitalized those who were enslaved. Cf. the work of M. Cottias and also that of A. Gomez, M. Dorigny and J. Sidbury.

6. Nanny (1685–1733 or 1760) is considered to be a heroine of the slave resistance movement on Jamaica. She raised an army of mulatto slaves that carried out raids on the plantations, and is thought to have liberated between 800 and 1,000 slaves. She is on the Jamaican 500 dollar bill.

7. On the night of August 14, 1791, the slave Dutty Boukman organized the voodoo ceremony at Bois Caïman that served as a catalyst for the slave uprising. Boukman was killed in battle in 1791 while leading his troops. Toussaint, a former slave who was not yet called Louverture, was one of Boukman's lieutenants and became the leader of the Haitian revolution.

8. A comment from a member of the audience during the colloquium on the Psychological Legacy of Slavery held in Martinique, October 25–28, 2016.

9. In 1791 at Bois Caïman in Haiti, a voodoo ceremony triggered a revolt, and galvanized the slaves in an assault of the Habitations that led to the defeat of Napoleon's troops and the independence of the "First Black Republic," in 1803.

10. See Jean-Pierre Dupuy.

11. In the novel's extreme situation of slavery, dignity can be more valuable than life itself! Murder can be an act of love and the guilt experienced by the mother can be much more difficult to endure than society's sanctions.

12. Such traumatic shocks are linked to violent aggressive behavior, rape, terrorist attacks, natural catastrophes (earthquakes, hurricanes...), wars (after the Vietnam war, 40 percent of American veterans had some kind of serious mental problem ... but there are no corresponding published statistics for the Vietnamese).

13. The United States offers an additional example where White police officers who have killed unarmed young Black people are, even today, routinely acquitted of any criminal charges. It is a source of scandal for a portion of public opinion, notably abroad, but not for the American judicial system.

14. Guilt is not the same as admitting guilt (survivors have a cognitive understanding that they are not guilty) but feeling guilty, which is not at all the same thing. People who have survived can feel guilty for unconscious reasons.

15. When antiracist militants demonstrated in Charlottesville, Virginia, to have the statue of General Lee removed, a statue that conveys echoes of racism and slavery, a counter demonstration set off clashes between the two groups. A white supremacist drove his car into a group of demonstrators, killing a young woman, and injuring 19 others. For those who retain a nostalgia for the South where slavery existed, Lee is a hero of the War of Succession. Following the events in Charlottesville, several statues that were erected in honor of Confederate generals have been taken down, but numerous southern supremacist symbols remain in place. The Southern Poverty Law Center that tracks the activities of extremist movements has counted over 1,500 such symbols on American soil. Simultaneously, social media exploded with a backlash reaction, and the Facebook page, *Save the Robert E. Lee Statue*, as well as other related sites, have been filled with vehement protests.

16. Finkielkraut was behind a petition that was circulated in Paris denouncing "anti-White racism."

17. Pascal Bruchner lends a racial connotation to his statement, and uses it to signify

Western civilization. Whereas, Raoul Villetard de Laperie has written in the geographical review of the nineteenth century, *Le Tour du Monde*, "The nineteenth century was that of the conquest of the world by the white race."

18. This idea is widely accepted as fact. Strangely enough, because of various Western psychic compartmentalizations, history does not make the link between them. In his book *L'héritage de Frantz Fanon*, Philippe Pierre-Charles notes that, for Fanon, who was a major player in the criticism of colonialism, the praise of the anti-colonialist revolutionary violence was inspired by "the perception of slavery's past in his homeland."

19. Following the circulation of a petition that garnered 30,000 signatures about Richet's writings, published in a work entitled *L'Homme stupide* (*The Stupid Man*) (La Sélection Humaine): "The Blacks have been living in Africa for nearly thirty thousand years, and [...] they haven't been able to come up with anything that raises them above the monkeys." A controversy developed: some, in support of Richet, pointed out his Nobel Prize for Medicine in 1913, and argued that there was "a school of thought, unanimously shared at that time, of the superiority of the white race."

20. Regarding the events in Charlottesville in August 2017 that we have discussed above, Donald Trump, the president of the United States, tweeted a rhetorical question: "Was George Washington a slave owner?" in order to suggest that one can have been a "great" president of the United States, and be a supporter of the slave trade. This event made it possible for the whole world to witness the dominant nostalgia for slavery in the southern United States. The Civil War itself serves as a poignant reminder that slavery was not accepted by all.

21. The psyche is fundamentally associative. In short, the function of the brain consists of a constant transmission of information between different zones in the brain, which allows for the integration of current experiences with those of the past. Mental health is defined as the success of this integration process. It establishes the uninterrupted sense of existing and of remaining the same despite the diversity of life experiences.

22. An oral presentation at the colloquium by Professor Jehel. See also F. Lebigot (1998).

23. What role should an egotistical drive play in this resourcefulness and ability of people to cope? In order to preserve a moral strictness? How were they to reconcile the preservation of their personal psychological and moral sense of permanence with the fulfillment of their desire to succeed in life?

References

Aptheker, H. (1983). *American Negro Slave Revolts*. New York: International Publishers.
Charbonnier, C.-L. (Ed.) (2000). *La Véridique Histoire, par Lui-Même, d'Olaudah Equiano Africain, Esclave aux Caraïbes, Homme Libre*. Paris: Caribéennes.
Charles-Nicolas, A. (2003). La force de la magie. *Psychiatries, 140*, 31–34.
Cyrulnik, B. (2002). *Un merveilleux malheur*. Paris: Odile Jacob.
Ellison, R. (1952). *Invisible Man*. New York: Random House.
Gold, J., Wolan, S.M., & Lewis, M. (2011). The Relation Between Abuse and Violent Delinquency: The Conversion of Shame to Blame in Juvenile Offenders. *Child Abuse and Neglect, 35*, 459–467.
Grandmaison, O.L.C. (2010). *De l'Indigénat. Anatomie d'un monstre juridique: Le Droit colonial en Algérie et dans l'Empire français*. Paris: Éditions La Découverte.
Hawthorne, W. (2010). *From Africa to Brazil: Culture, Identity and an Atlantic Slave Trade, 1600–1830*. Cambridge: Cambridge University Press.
Lebigot, F. (1998). Le débriefing individuel du traumatisé psychique. *Annales Médico-Psychologiques, 156*, 417–421.
Littlewood, R., & Lipsedge, M. (2013). Aliens and Alienists. *British Journal of Psychiatry, 203*.
Massé, R. (2001). Pour une ethno-épidémiologie critique de la détresse psychologique à la Martinique. *Sciences sociales et santé, 19*(1), 45–47.
Miano, L. (2013). *La saison de l'ombre*. Paris: Grasset.
Prince, M. (2000). *La Véritable Histoire de Mary Prince: esclave antillaise*. Paris: Albin Michel.

Rutter, M. (1985). Resilience in the Face of Adversity: Protective Factors and Resilience to Psychiatric Disorder. *The British Journal of Psychiatry, 147*, 598–611.

Stuewig, J., & McCloskey, L. (2005). The Relation of Child Maltreatment to Shame and Guilt Among Adolescents: Psychological Routes to Depression and Delinquency. *Child Maltreatment, 10*(4).

Tin, L.G. (2013). *Esclavage et réparations*. Paris: Stock.

7

Explaining Post Traumatic Slave Syndrome

Multigenerational Transmission of Trauma

Joy A. DeGruy

In the previous chapter, Aimé Charles-Nicolas provides a sweeping landscape of inherited emotional and psychological damage caused by slavery and the resilience needed to resist and overcome the damage. Those who inherit this damage spend a great deal of time and psychic energy combating it. They do not know its origin or that it is not something for which they are individually responsible. In this next chapter, Joy A. DeGruy puts the pieces together and explains what is implicit in all the preceding chapters. She connects the past with the psychological present.

> I can conceive of no Negro native to this country who has not, by the age of puberty, been irreparably scarred by the conditions of his life.... The wonder is not that so many are ruined but that so many survive.—Baldwin, 1955, p. 71

Post Traumatic Slave Syndrome

Post Traumatic Slave Syndrome (PTSS) is an explanatory theory. It describes a pattern of behaviors brought on by the specific circumstances and historical traumas of American chattel slavery. PTSS is also due to continued oppression and structural inequality in existence since the official end of slavery. After 1865, where did slavery go? Since that time, Black America has labored to recover from the dehumanization of centuries of bondage, the offense of peonage, the outrage of the black codes and sundown laws, convict leasing, the indignities of Jim Crow, and the ravages of poverty. PTSS asserts that African Americans sustained a traumatic injury, starting with slavery, and they continue to be injured by traumas sustained by the larger society's ongoing racism and maintenance of inequality. There are three adverse outcomes of PTSS: ever-present anger, racist socialization, and vacant esteem.

This chapter will focus specifically on the three specific outcomes of PTSS. Ever-present anger is examined in a study of the relationship between youth violence and current and historical stressors unique to economically disadvantaged African American males. The study involved adolescents from 14 through 18 years of age who completed a written survey in Oregon. The group included 100 incarcerated youth in juvenile facilities and 100 who were members of community youth development programs. The author was interested in how these Black youths' perceptions of respect and racial socialization influenced their decisions and intentions to use or not to use violence. My interest was also to see how or if they believed that their family and community's experience with slavery and racism impacted their willingness to engage in violence.

Racist socialization will be examined through a case study of a current upper-middle-class African American family that looks at the influence of their legacy in slavery and sharecropping. The family roots are from black sharecroppers, who worked the Brooks plantation, located in Drew, Mississippi, in the Yazoo-Mississippi Delta, from 1920 through 1970. Members of the family migrated from the Mississippi Delta to St. Louis in the 1950s. The case study highlights behaviors over multiple generations associated with socialization directly related to child-rearing and discipline directly derived from slavery through 1977.

History of Multigenerational Trauma

The African Axiology

According to Nichols (1976), the primary value system that dominated the African continent was member-to-member and face-to-face social relationships. This axiology places the highest value on "relationships" between individuals, the relationship being the most critical factor in regulating human activities within the culture. The member-to-member axiology suggests that the survival of the group is primarily dependent upon the integrity of relationships among members of that group. Enslaved Africans brought to the U.S. had families torn apart. Also, members of the same cultural and linguistic groups were separated from one another. Traditional "relationships" were destroyed. Despite the loss, Africans survived the destruction of family and home by recreating what they could of their cultural customs and values. In addition to family disruption, there was forced assimilation of the oppressor's culture and racial ideology. This assimilation created "cultural dissonance," a feeling of disharmony and psychological conflict. The result is internalized racism or "racist socialization." Thus, African Americans learned to function in a system that was at variance with their traditional customs, beliefs, and values.

Racist socialization puts the psychological center of the American slavery experience for slaves and their descendants at racial inferiority. According to Thomas D. Morris in *Southern Slavery and the Law, 1619– 1860*, Africans were "presumed" to be "natural slaves," based on their skin color. Also, they were referred to as "thinking property," and inherently "right-less persons." Some English enslavers decided that a natural act of God selected Africans to a position of permanent bondage. It was this relegation to lesser humanity that allowed the institution of chattel slavery to be linked intrinsically to violence. Then, it was through violence and dehumanization that the institution of slavery was legislated, justified, and perpetuated in North America by English enslavers (J.A. DeGruy, 2017, p. 37).

Consider the cumulative and continued stressors experienced by African Americans and others of African descent who came out of chattel slavery. It is appropriate to view such stress as similar to post-traumatic stress disorders (PTSD) (American Psychiatric Association, 2013). Although the public has recognized PTSD, the condition for Post Traumatic Slave Syndrome (PTSS) does not meet the criteria of PTSD. PTSD and PTSS have different outcomes. PTSD is a clinical diagnosis. When treated with medication, counseling, and other supports, it is a resolvable problem. Alternatively, the etiology of PTSS is linked inextricably to violence, oppression, and racism. It is an outcome of social-psychological-environments created by others. Thus, PTSS cannot be remedied through clinical interventions alone. It requires correcting social environments.

Vacant Esteem, Racist Socialization and Ever-Present Anger

Vacant Esteem

Self-depreciation characterizes the first aspect of PTSS: that is vacant esteem, believing or perceiving one's self to be inferior or having minimal or no self-worth. This condition develops from the three most significant areas of influence on the individual, that is, the family, the community, and society: the "trifecta" of influences. When these three areas of importance internalize demeaning white racial perceptions about Black people, the results are catastrophic. This happens when Black people internalize white racial stereotypes about themselves. For African Americans, the outcomes are a self-denigrating sense of self-value—vacant esteem.

Vacant esteem is observed when Blacks denigrate one another. One individual verbally insults the other, calling them "black" followed by some profanity. One African American woman calls the other a "black—bit—h." The assumption here is to call her "black," adding to the insult. Both individuals tacitly accept that being "black" is offensive, and something for which one should feel shame and reflected in vacant esteem. For some, this is a daily occurrence. Another example follows: When two Black persons find themselves sparing at one another and immediately take the offensive. Bennett and Fraser elaborate on this behavior, stating, "Simply maintaining eye contact for 'too long' may be viewed as lack of respect, an insult that can escalate into a confrontation. In a similar vein, a snide remark that might otherwise be viewed as trivial may lead to an 'honor' contest where no party backs down until someone is injured" (2000, p. 97).

The following excerpt from Persaud (2004) describes a real-life example of how such face-offs play themselves out in daily encounters of Black males based upon vacant esteem. The following happens between two young Black men; it occurs as well with older Black men, though less frequently. Persaud recounts:

> On my way to school, I saw a young brother on a crowded N train eating sunflower seeds. Between his legs laid a mound of wet, disgusting sunflower shells that he kept enlarging by spitting on the floor. Though visibly frustrated and disgusted by his behavior, no one would dare correct him. An older White man motioned to him to stop spitting the seeds on the floor. In response, he spat the seeds with much more animation than before, while effortlessly trying to stare fear into the old man. I made eye contact with the young man, and he said "What?" and then I said "What?" Believe me, in the world of powerlessness this is enough for a shootout. He leered at me then said, "I thought so," and I responded with my generation's favorite confrontation closer, "Whatever!" Now, we were both staring, sneering, flexing, profiling and posturing at each other, refusing to yield the power we thought we had. We created two powerless brothers, confronting one another over bullshit. Two intellectual amputees are looking for the upper hand while mentally handcuffed [Persaud, 2004, p. 148].

Racist Socialization

The second aspect of PTSS is racist socialization. This state is often characterized by an implicit or explicit belief or perception of whiteness as the ideal. All positive attributions that pertained to skin color, hair texture, body shape, and facial characteristics were based on European and White American aesthetics. So straight hair is considered "good hair," and kinky or tightly curled hair is viewed as "bad hair." Lighter skin color is deemed more beautiful and preferred over dark skin, and European facial features are favored over African ones. Racist socialization is reflected in African American acceptance of the devaluation of their culture by Whites, and by Blacks' adoption of white superiority. At the core of this value is the deeply embedded acceptance of white dominance and black submission. Racist socialization lies in "the belief that Whites, and all things associated with whiteness are superior; and that Black people and all things associated with blackness are inferior. Through centuries of slavery and decades of institutionalized oppression that followed, many African Americans have been socialized to be something akin to white racists.... We both mold ourselves to accommodate white prejudices and endeavor to adopt their standards" (DeGruy Leary, 2009, p. 135).

Noted French Psychiatrist, Frantz Fanon identified this condition as a form of "mental colonization" in oppressed and colonized people. He wrote, "The oppressed will always believe the worst about themselves." Fanon further states:

> All colonized people—in other words, people in whom an inferiority complex has taken root, whose local cultural originality has been committed to the grave—position themselves in relation to the civilizing language: i.e., the metropolitan culture. The more the colonized has assimilated the cultural values of the metropolis, the more he will have escaped the bush. The more he rejects his blackness and the bush, the whiter he will become [F. Fanon, 1952, pp. 2–3].

Fanon further asserts that the inferiority complex can be ascribed to two influences. First is the economy. Then, there is internalization, or rather epidermalization of this inferiority. "The Negro enslaved by his inferiority, the white man enslaved by his superiority alike behaves by a neurotic orientation" (Fanon, 1952 p. xiv–xv, 41–42). This issue of racism, inferiority, and superiority are linked intimately to power and money, the control of resources, and, consequently, to the control of people's lives. The notion of "race" is not urbane, but falsely putative and misleading. It cripples the mind and corrupts the body politic by convincing the governed and the governors that race has merit beyond what is visibly perceptible.

Ta-Nehisi Coates explains:

> But race is the child of racism, not the father. And the process of naming "the people" has never been a matter of genealogy and physiognomy so much as of hierarchy. Difference in hue and hair is old. But the belief in the preeminence of hue and hair, the notion that these factors can correctly organize a society and that they signify deeper attributes, which are indelible—this is the new idea at the heart of these new people who have been brought up hopelessly, tragically, deceitfully, to believe that they are

white ... their new name has no real meaning divorced from the machinery of criminal power [Coates, 2015, p. 7].

Racist socialization is, perhaps, the most pervasive and persistent of the identified symptoms of PTSS. According to Morris (1996), the children slave masters fathered with their enslaved African mothers were born with lighter skin and referred to as "mulatto." They enjoyed more privileges than did darker-skinned siblings. Mulatto is a derogatory term. The etymology of the word describes the Mulatto as a person "of mixed breed." The Latin for "mulus" literally means "young mule." The term is used to separate "pure" White people from the "mulatto," the spurious spawn of the mixture of black and white. The lighter skin of the Mulatto proffered them more freedom and identified them as better than enslaved Blacks, but still "less" than Whites. Thomas Morris explains:

> By the end of the colonial period, Whites no longer felt comfortable with the enforced servitude of mixed-race children.... This was because of an increasing humanitarian sensibility by the end of the eighteenth century, the collapse of the institution of indentured servitude, and a "promulatto bias" emerged by the nineteenth century. Cobb provided an illustration of the latter in his Historical Sketch of Slavery when he discussed the lack of chastity in female slaves and the "corresponding immorality in the white males." An important cause, in his view, was that the "negress" knows that the offspring of such intercourse, the Mulatto, having greater intelligence, and being indeed a superior race, has a better opportunity of enjoying the privileges of domestics; in other words, is elevated by mixture of blood [Morris, 1996, p. 24].

Thomas Jefferson's intimate relationship with the adolescent Sally Hemmings demonstrated the preferential treatment of the enslaved, based on skin color. Thomas Jefferson fathered a child with the young girl, whom he favored because of her flowing hair and fair skin (Branscom, 1998). Jefferson's sexual attraction to Hemmings was in stark contrast to his opinion of dark-skinned slaves, whom he described as unattractive, and animal-like, and with monotonous skin color (Peterson, 1975).

Once again, beliefs from the slave past persist and are found among African Americans today. In 2012, African American gymnast, Gabby Douglas, was the first African American in Olympic history to become a champion, winning gold medals in both the individual all-around and team competitions. Amidst her history-making achievement, a fierce Internet backlash of criticism was launched, immediately following her win. The criticism came mainly from African Americans. They were upset that Ms. Douglas' hair was not properly straightened. The "kinky" natural texture of her hair was evident in her competition and was embarrassing to many Blacks. This obsession with the gymnast's hair took on bizarre dimensions as if there was a collective group shame among those who felt compelled to comment.

Group shame is also notable after a news announcement of a robbery, shooting or murder. Some Black people will be overly concerned about whether a Black person committed the crime. If the person accused of the crime is "black," they will view it as a mark against their race. This is an example of vacant esteem at the group level. Black people will take on the emotional burden and responsibility for the improper actions of other Black people. These actions further harm any sense of individual independence regarding the wrongdoings of others. White people could not imagine being ashamed of their race because of the criminal activities of another white person. Racist socialization is also evident at the community level, when Black people are distrustful of, or think less of, African American professionals. Some refuse to patronize black-owned establishments and businesses because they assume Blacks provide poor quality service and lack legitimacy or competence. Carter G. Woodson explained it best:

> The same educational process which inspires and stimulates the oppressor with the thought that he is everything and has accomplished everything worthwhile depresses and crushes at the same time the spark of genius in the Negro by making him feel that his race does not amount to much and never will measure up to the standards of other peoples. The Negro thus educated is a hopeless liability to the race. The difficulty is that the "educated Negro" is compelled to live and move among his own people whom he has been taught to despise. As a rule, therefore, the "educated Negro" prefers to buy his food from a white grocer because he has been taught that the Negro is not clean. It does not matter how often a Negro washes his hands, then, he cannot clean them, and no matter how often a white man uses his hands, he cannot soil them [Woodson, 1933, p. xiii].

The "educated Negro," described by Carter G. Woodson, continues to exist. However, the disdain for other Blacks described by Woodson is not limited to just educated Blacks. Today such persons are like modern-day *"overseers,"* sometimes referred to as white institutional gatekeepers. During slavery, some of the enslaved took on the characteristics of their oppressors. Black drivers (foremen of slaves) and overseers, who were assigned the duties of monitoring and disciplining enslaved Africans that worked in the fields, were often more brutal than their European counterparts. They believed they needed to prove their loyalty to the master by showing little or no mercy, and because their slave masters rewarded them for their cruelty. The historian Eugene Genovese shares this insight:

> The head driver is the most important Negro on the plantation. He is to be treated with more respect than any other Negro by both master and overseer. He is on no occasion to be treated with any indignation calculated to lose the respect of the other Negroes without breaking him. He is required to maintain proper discipline at all times, to see that no Negro idles or does bad work in the field, and to punish it with discretion on the spot. The driver is not to be flogged except by the master but in emergencies that will not admit of delay [ED. Genovese, 1976, p. 383].

The educated Negroes that Woodson wrote about went to great lengths to forget that such violence and reactions to violence ever existed. Instead, they promote the false belief that African Americans, since emancipation, have had fair and equal access to the American dream. They tend to explain the fact that African Americans are not economically and socially further along because of a lack of motivation or willingness to work hard.

Whites seeking to justify why enslaved Africans were worked excessively perpetuated this idea of African Americans not working hard or being "lazy." Misguided and racially biased seventeenth-century scientists, such as Carl Von Linnaeus, stated that Blacks, whom he referred to scientifically as "Homo Afer," were phlegmatic, cunning, lazy, lustful, careless, and governed by caprice (Haller, 1971). Additionally, physicians then concocted slave-specific disorders like Drapetomania and Dysaethesia Aethopica to describe those that tried to escape enslavement, or who resisted being forced to work. They pathologized the enslaved who sought freedom.

However, we know from modern science how hard enslaved Africans worked. In 1991, an African burial ground was discovered in New York's Lower Manhattan, where an estimated 10,000 to 20,000 enslaved Africans were buried in the seventeenth and eighteenth centuries. Most people do not think of New York as a "slave state." All the colonies had slaves, and by the late 1700s, New York had the second-largest number of slaves in the nation. Anthropologist Michael Blakey, a specialist in physical anthropology, is the scientific director for the African Burial Ground project. His analysis of the skeletal remains of the enslaved revealed just how hard they worked. Many suffered from enthesopathy, a condition resulting in the muscle detaching itself from the bone because of people being worked beyond human capacity. Those who were not worked to death died from disease, abuse, or malnutrition.

Today, a lack of motivation might be an explanation for why some individuals do not excel economically. If one is denied everyday opportunities, exploited, poorly paid, and disrespected when work is found, why should one work hard? Institutional racism bars masses of Black people from moving ahead. Individuals that endorse the "bootstrap theory" promote the myth of the "level playing field" that claims prosperity is readily available for anyone in America who is willing to work for it. Peggy McIntosh calls this the myth of meritocracy:

> The myth of meritocracy is the myth that the individual is the only unit of society, and that whatever a person ends up with must be what he or she individually wanted, worked for, earned and deserved. This myth rests on the assumption that what people experience; how they see, feel, think and behave; and what they are capable of accomplishing are not influenced by any social system or circumstance ... acknowledges no

systems of oppression or privilege that ... could make life arbitrarily more or less difficult [McIntosh, 2009, p. 2].

Ever-Present Anger

The third aspect of Post Traumatic Slave Syndrome [PTSS] is ever-present anger, the net result of cumulative oppression. Those familiar with the gruesome details of American slavery have no difficulty understanding the accretion of anger, and even rage, in African Americans. Who would not be angry after enduring centuries of torture and abuse, followed by oppressive and brutal policies during the old, and now new, Jim Crow? The end of slavery did not mean an end to the assault on black lives. It only reconfigured the old laws into newer ones with new names but ensuring the same results. When segregation was repealed legally, people found new methods to keep African Americans from enjoying the fruits of their labor and their right to life.

In May of 2015, National Public Radio (NPR) interviewed Richard Rothstein, a research associate at the Economic Policy Institute and Senior Fellow of the Chief Justice Earl Warren Institute on Law and Social Policy at the University of California, Berkeley. He was asked how and why the troubles in Ferguson, Missouri, happened. His answer must have startled some listeners. He placed the blame for the violent protests and social upheaval not on the incident that appeared to spark the conflict, the August 2014 police shooting of Michael Brown, and an unarmed 18-year-old African American youth. He attributed them to the conditions that gave rise to the civil unrest on "explicit, racially purposeful policies that were pursued at all levels of government." He stated that "federal, state, and local governments purposefully created racial boundaries in these cities ... and that it was not the unintended effect of benign policies" (Rothstein & Gross, 2015). "Without our government's purposeful imposition of racial segregation, the other causes ... still would have existed but with far less opportunity for expression" (Rothstein, 2017, p. viii). He said the U.S. government deliberately created ghettos in America. They forced people to reside in places with inadequate resources and to function in miserable living conditions. America is now reaping the consequences of these policies, expressed through angry revolts and protests from its victims.

Because of racially explicit housing policies, African Americans have suffered either racial segregation or uprooting of their communities. "Redlining," "urban renewal," curing urban blight, and, more recently, "gentrification," all describe the intentional removal of whole neighborhoods of African Americans, as well as other people of color, from their homes and communities. How can families become stable, and provide the necessary support and consistency to raise healthy and productive members, when they have no control over their environment? As a matter of policy, the Housing and Urban Development Department has sanctioned 90-day, "No-Cause Evictions," where property owners can evict families in ninety days for no stated reason. In the Pacific Northwest, there are property owners who evict entire apartment complexes of people of color. Then, the same owners replace them with white occupants that can pay higher rents. Experts call this perpetual disruption of individuals, families, and communities, "serial forced displacement" (Fullilove & Wallace, 2011, p. 381).

Given the violence committed against African Americans, together with centuries of lies about freedom and justice, it is not surprising that there is pervasive anger among Blacks. Anger is a predictable outcome. This anger, like vacant esteem and racist socialization, is a side effect of deprivation, social oppression and unjust treatment that has continued unabated from slavery (DeGruy Leary, 2009).

Transmission of Intergenerational Trauma

While PTSS provides a partial explanation of how and why African Americans have responded to intergenerational traumas, it does not reveal the whole story. Everyone exposed to one, or even a series of traumatic events is not impacted mentally or emotionally in the same way, by the same events. Some individuals' emotions might be compromised deeply, while others remain unaffected. In the case of enslaved Africans and their descendants, the extent and intensity associated with multiple traumas were excessive, profound, and practically impossible to measure over a protracted period. What we know for sure is that African Americans, during and after enslavement, developed coping and adaptive survival skills and behaviors. How did people exposed to traumas manage to survive and, in some instances, exceed White people in their success and achievements?

There is a plethora of research about the decisive role that "protective factors" can play in the prevention and alleviation of human suffering and trauma (Holden, Bradford, Hall, & Belton, 2013). As a question, who is impacted by PTSS lies in the extent and intensity of exposure that individuals, families, and groups have to trauma intergenerationally. It was also dependent on existing protective factors that were available to them at the time. They struggled to balance individual strengths with individual limitations and challenges, and social supports and reinforcements with social stressors. They had to work with environmental, material, mental, and emotional resources, despite pressures and numerous obstacles.

Today, protective factors appear to be dispersed by social class among African Americans. Many poor and low-income African Americans function daily in crisis and survival mode. Protective factors are quickly overwhelmed. They are subject to significant hardships and stressors, placing a continuous strain on their relationships. Many live under untenable conditions, and often make decisions capriciously, resulting in harm to their mental and physical wellbeing. Those with greater human and material resources do not have to operate continuously in crisis and survival mode. Their protective capacities are taxed less. They have the time, circumstance, and resources to make decisions without caprice.

Social class divisions are only one of the ways that make African Americans a diverse and multifaceted people. African Americans are depicted stereotypically as poor, living in fragmented, dysfunctional families, and lacking skills and motivation for work or achievement. This is just not the case. African Americans' social classes are divided on the same basis as other ethnic groups. Working-class African Americans are struggling to stay employed and earn living wages, as is the White working class. Both face automation of work, and globalization of jobs. Middle-class African Americans have traditional American family values, though one would never know it by the way Black people are portrayed in the media (Willie, 1981). Most wealthy Black individuals and families did not derive their wealth from rapping and entertainment. They are professionals with advanced degrees and executives in major corporations. What they all have in common, regardless of class, is that they experience structural and interpersonal racism (Bell & McBride, 2014). A 2016 *New York Times* article revealed that affluent African Americans face similar discriminatory practices as did their ancestors before them.

The choices that Black families make today are constrained inevitably by a legacy of racism. This same racism prevented their ancestors from buying quality housing. The same racism prevented them from passing down wealth that might have allowed today's generation to move into more stable communities. Moreover, even when Black households try to cross color boundaries, they are rarely welcomed. Studies have shown that White people prefer to live in communities where there are fewer black people, regardless of their income. The result: nationally, Black and White families of similar incomes still live in separate worlds.

In many of America's largest metropolitan areas, including New York, Chicago, and Los Angeles, Black families making $100,000 or more, are more likely to live in more impoverished neighborhoods than even White households making less than $25,000. This is particularly true in areas with a long history of residential segregation, like metropolitan Milwaukee (Eligon & Gebeloff, 2016).

Psychiatrist, Carl C. Bell, states, "Mental health professionals should be aware that many African Americans continue to face significant interpersonal and institutional racism. The protective factors of religion and spirituality, extended family, racial socialization, and acculturation ... when manifested in the home environment have shown to improve school performance, help adjust and control behaviors of African American youth and increase self-esteem" (Bell & McBride, 2014, p. 149). Additional epidemiological studies indicate that having "a sense of pride, belonging, and attachment to one's racial/ethnic group and participating in ethnic behaviors may protect against psychopathology. Conversely, the absence of these things may increase the likelihood of psychopathology" (Bell & McBride 2014, p. 150). According to Bell (2017), protective factors stop risk factors from becoming predictive factors. It is very plausible that individuals lacking the significant protective factors of extended family, empowerment, spirituality, and a sense of pride and belonging, as described by Milton and Bell, are at higher risk for PTSS. They are more vulnerable to racist socialization, vacant esteem, and ever-present anger. Those having significant protective factors could more effectively avoid or mitigate the adverse influence and effects of PTSS.

Trying to Kill the Part of You That Isn't Loved: The Portland Study

"Trying to kill the part of you that isn't loved" were the words uttered by a young African American male in Chicago in an interview with the author regarding his perspective on the reasons for violence in his neighborhood. In another pilot study of racist socialization, the author interviewed young African American males in inner Northeast Portland, an area that housed the largest population of African Americans in the state. The study was about their beliefs regarding violence among their peers. In nearly every interview, the issue of "respect" was brought up. Considering the frequency that the respondents spoke about respect and disrespect, it seemed an essential point to be investigated in the study. Unfortunately, there was very little information in the social science literature about the meaning and potential variations of respect. Given the paucity of research, the author developed the Adolescent African American Respect Scale (AARS), an instrument designed to measure attitudes toward respect. The AARS measured the extent to which respondents felt respected in three domains: respect about family, respect within one's peer group, and respect from society.

The scale was administered to 200 youth. The first group included 100 youth who were incarcerated in juvenile facilities, and the second group consisted of 100 who were in community youth development programs. The second group did not have records of incarceration. The results follow.

After acceptable reliability was established, and the three primary component subscales were identified. The study revealed that a history of witnessing violence strongly predicted the intensity of violent behavior for study youth. However, endorsing positive attitudes toward racial respect significantly moderated the effects of chronic exposure to violence. Additionally, racial socialization was correlated negatively with the intensity of violence. It was marginally significant in reducing the impact of witnessing violence (J. DeGruy, Kjellstrand, Briggs, & Brennan, 2011; J.D. Leary, Brennan, & Briggs, 2005, p. 466).

The author's primary interest was in the beliefs that youth held about respect and the perceived link to racism and history. The next area of interest was in the moderating effect that racial respect and racial socialization had on the youths' decision to engage in violence. Both groups of youth, those incarcerated, and those that were not, expressed beliefs that the root of the disrespect that they were experiencing was related directly to racism. They did so in response to the open-ended question, "Why do you think that people like you are disrespected?" They commented, "Because we are African Americans and society has put out a stereotype towards us.... Because it's always been that way, and it will always be because a lot of White people think that they are better than everybody..." and "Because we are Black in a White man's America." Several youths identified slavery as the reason for the disrespect (Leary, Brennan & Briggs 2005 p. 268).

The study provided a valuable glimpse into the thoughts and feelings of young African American males trying to determine their sense of "place" in a country that has historically assaulted their ancestors, and that continues to marginalize them. Lingering PTSS was reflected in the ever-present anger they continue to feel. This anger can and must be addressed as a matter of urgency if we are to eradicate the self-destructive patterns of violence that continue to plague African American communities.

> This (violence) is the experience of too many African Americans. It's no wonder we're angry. Even when we're feeling good, ever-present anger resides just below our surface: anger at the violence, degradation, and humiliation visited upon us, our ancestors, and our children; anger at being relegated to the margins of the society in which we live; anger at the misrepresentation and trivialization of our history and culture; and finally, anger at living in the wealthiest nation in the world and not having equal opportunity and access to its riches [J.A. DeGruy, 2017, p. 123].

Many of the young men in the study believed that being black is the reason for disrespect. They carried reasonable indignation for the racist systems that made it necessary to develop the protective and coping skills outlined above. From the perspective of PTSS, we might better understand Willie James Bosket, Jr., who is currently serving out three consecutive twenty-five-to-life sentences for murder. Willie is said to be the "most violent criminal in New York State history." At age fifteen, Willie shot and killed two men on the subway in Manhattan. His violent spree inspired a brand-new law, called the "Willie Bosket Law." It is a law that judged a "youth" as an adult for the first time in American history. Willie stated in court, "I am only a monster created by the system." Willie stood five feet nine inches and scored in the genius range as a young boy. This fantastic intelligence was noted in his enslaved ancestors. Willie remains in solitary confinement in a specially constructed cell at Woodbourne prison, where he continued to act out violently until 1995 when the prison psychiatrist placed Willie on Prozac. He has had no violent episodes since then (Butterfield, 1995, pp. viii-xvii, 330). Fox Butterfield investigated Willie's past and wrote a book entitled, *All God's Children: The Bosket Family and the American Tradition of Violence*. He describes an investigation into Willie's history, a history about which Willie knew nothing. This history held the answers to his violent behavior:

> Willie and I discussed each new layer of influence on him, as they were unearthed. Little did we imagine that his story could be traced back to slavery, even before the Civil War, and then eventually, back to the American Revolution. What emerged was not just a portrait of the Bosket family, but a new account of the origin and growth of violence in the United States. Violence is not, as many people today presume, a recent problem or a peculiarly urban problem. In its inception, it had little to do with race or class, with poverty or education, with television or the fractured family: in short, with most of the usual suspects. Instead, it grew out of a proud culture of self-defense that flourished in the antebellum rural South, a tradition shaped by Whites long before it was adopted and recast by some Blacks in reaction to their current plight [Butterfield, 1995, p. xvii].

Butterfield was able to trace Willie's violent behavior back to his great, great, grandfather Ruben, and his great-grandfather "Pud" Bosket. They responded with violence to violence directed at them and their loved ones. It became a family tradition to use force, if necessary, to defend members, property, and one's sense of honor. However, unlike Willie, his forefathers did not have access to their respective family histories to know and review the origin of this family tradition, nor did they know this tradition came out of slavery.

The written and verbal responses of the 200-youth revealed that they believed their "blackness" made a lifetime of slights and contempt unavoidable. What they experienced was not unlike the treatment their ancestors experienced before them. This perception alone is demoralizing and distressing for these young people. Moreover, it is encouraging that racial respect, and racial socialization can be protective factors, and show statistically significant moderating effects of witnessing violence and its intensity. However, one pilot study cannot prove that the youth's expressed belief that they are disrespected because they are Black is linked directly to slavery. Although, it is strongly suggested that family and community histories play an essential role in, not only their beliefs but in their reaction to their beliefs, as well. We need to know a lot more about the origins of the young people's ever-present anger and violence. Perhaps as we unravel the tangled web of our biological, social, and spiritual history, we can shed light on how the past shapes our future. We might learn, as well, more information about protective approaches to eliminating violence and other social problems affecting African descendant youth in the U.S. and other parts of the world.

Children Should Be Seen but Not Heard: A Final Case Study

The foundations of mental and physical health throughout the lifecycle begin in early childhood. Therefore, what we experience and learn early in life sets the stage for what the quality of our adult life will be. This was evident in sharecropping families living in the Mississippi Delta between 1920 and 1970. In most sharecropper family homes on the Brooks plantation, both the men and the women worked long hours in the fields. Women had the additional responsibility of managing the home and caring for the children. As during slavery, children were required to be obedient; as soon as they could speak, to not speak unless spoken to, and to say nothing to the White farm owner and his overseers that would jeopardize their parents' opportunity to work on the plantation. Therefore, parents often "used a strong hand in rearing them (children)"; Brooks Farm residents adopted "similar patterns of child rearing...." (1995, p. 88). The present case study investigates the child-rearing practices of one family over five generations, dating back to slavery.

This case study of racist socialization involves Stephen Gunn, (fictional name), an upper-middle class, 42-year-old African American man, married with three children: two girls, twelve and seven years old, and a boy ten years old. The family lives in a well-off suburb of Portland, Oregon. Their child-rearing practices were not created in their generation; instead, like all other families, passed along from generation-to-generation. Marital problems in the Gunn family began early in their marriage. The problems escalated when Stephen insisted on whipping their ten- and twelve-year-old daughter and son. Patricia (age 40) is Stephen's wife. In counseling, she shared that she had been "whipped" as a child, and now is opposed entirely to hitting children. She expressed concern that Stephen's severe verbal chastisement and demands that the children not speak or give him eye contact when he corrects them were excessive and inappropriate. Patricia does not approve of the way Stephen was disciplined as a child and believes Stephen is easily angered. She does not want the children to feel the brunt of his anger.

Background

Stephen is the youngest of seven siblings. He was born and raised in St. Louis and is from a family with roots in the Mississippi Delta and the Brooks Farm dating back to slavery. The author sought to determine the etiology of Stephen's beliefs and attitudes about child-rearing and child discipline practiced by four generations of his family, to determine if the practice of whipping and vilifying children, that Patricia questioned, can be traced to slavery and racist socialization. The author did one-on-one interviews with Stephen and Patricia, and telephone interviews with three of Stephen's extended family members, ranging from ages 75 to 92.

WILLIAM TATE (W.G.), STEPHEN'S MATERNAL UNCLE (AGE 92)

W.G. is retired, disabled, and lives in St. Louis. He was born on a large plantation in the Mississippi Delta, where he was the second of nineteen children born to Winnie and Samson Tate. W.G. shared that his family had lived and worked on the plantation since before the Civil war, but he was not sure how far back their presence went on the plantation. He shared that his paternal grandmother, Emma, had been a slave, and had watched her seventeen-year-old brother be sold because he "sassed" someone White. W.G. said he remembers her talking about how she was told to keep away from Whites: "don't mind them, don't looks their way, and draw no notice." He also shared that his paternal grandfather had barely escaped being lynched because he had stolen a chicken to feed his starving family.

W.G. stated that after emancipation, his family had become sharecroppers and that he started working in the fields at ten years old. I asked W.G. what his life was like as a child, and he said, "Children learned right away that you had to work hard to survive. We grew all our own food and raised our own hogs and cows. It was not like most other plantations. Our plantation owner was real, real, rich, and every sharecropper wanted to work on our plantation because most owners were mean and wouldn't let the sharecroppers have anything of their own. However, on our plantation, the owner wanted to have nothing to do with anyone that did not want to grow their own food. As kids, we stayed to ourselves. We didn't spend time with the adults, and we were not allowed to be around when grown folks were talking." He stated, "All the parents were on the same page. They could all whip you and send you home, not like now. Now, if you hit a child, they send you to jail; they have taken away the right to raise your children. That's what's wrong with these young people. They don't care about themselves or anybody else. You listened to adults, or you got whipped, it was as simple as that."

I asked W.G. what working in the fields was like, and he said, "I hated picking cotton. I just wouldn't do it! I learned to work on machines at thirteen, so I didn't have to pick cotton." W.G. left the plantation and moved to St. Louis in 1951.

Elsie Tate Gunn (E.L.) Stephen's Mother (Age 79)

E.L. is the eighth child of Millie and Samson Tate and lives in St, Louis. I asked E.L. about her childhood growing up on the plantation. She expressed fond memories of living in a community where everybody was "close." People spent time together, went to church together, kept themselves up, dressed well, and kept their hair nice. She said, "teachers whipped kids that were disobedient, but whipping other people's children wasn't no big deal. Today folks are not raised well. Kids had no choice back then. Parents were present, and kids obeyed what they said because they meant what they said. I whipped my kids." I asked E.L. why the children were so much better behaved, and she said, "You obeyed, or you got whipped, and you didn't want that!"

E.L. shared that the young people in her neighborhood in St. Louis sell drugs, and do not respect anybody. "They are standing around when they should be in school. I wanted my children to go to school and make something of themselves. I didn't care what it was they wanted to be, just that they needed to work hard and be something."

I asked her what the White people were like, and she paused and said, "The White people that lived on the plantation were nice people and wouldn't let other White people mess with us." I asked what the relationships were like between Whites and Blacks, and again she paused and said, "Everything was fine." I asked what kinds of things they did together, and she immediately responded with, "We didn't spend time around White people. They did what they did, and we did what we did." I changed the questions to how White and Black children got along, and if the White children were well behaved. She said, "The White children were nice, they played together and ate together with the Black children, but the White parents didn't believe in whipping their children for some reason." E.L. said she missed her home in Mississippi and wished that she had gone back years ago.

Candace Tate Wilson (C.T.) Stephen's Maternal Aunt (Age 75)

Candace is the youngest of nineteen children, and one of the four remaining children still alive. C.T. currently lives in Baltimore. Candace left Mississippi in 1949 after her mother died. She and her brother went to live with a maternal aunt. C.T. does not remember the exact date that her father died, but she was sure that "his heart gave out because he had worked so hard." C.T. spoke about her father, whom she said was a very generous and kind man. She stated that he had only completed the second grade before he was forced to work to help support the family. C.T. shared that she held no fondness for Mississippi and that she was whipped frequently because of her "mouth." C.T. explained, "That the fastest way to get a whipping was by talking out of order." She learned her first lesson as a young girl when an adult asked her a question, and she answered by saying "yes" instead of "yes ma'am." C.T. has two fully-grown children and four grandchildren. I asked her if she whipped her children. She paused and said, "I punished them when they did something wrong, and sometimes I whipped them if they needed it." I asked her if she whipped them as much as she was whipped, and she quickly responded, "No, I raised them different, a sign of the times you know?" C.T. said, "My mother would start working in the fields early in the morning, and by the end of the day she would have picked three to four hundred pounds of cotton, and fixed three full meals. Back then, everyone had to work hard, even the children."

I asked C.T. if her son and daughter whipped their children, and she said, "My grandchildren don't get whipped." She shared why she thinks people that grew up on the plantation were whipped. "No matter how good some of the White people were, Black folks were treated like they were less. White people talked down to grown Black people, and they had to just take it. White people had all the power when. So, they got home, the one place Black folks had power, they showed it by whipping the children. You wasn't gonna let them' disrespect you." I asked C.T. how children showed disrespect, and she explained, "not listening to an adult, talking back or too much, or moving too slowly when they were called."

Stephen's family presents a unique opportunity to look back across four generations. While the history is limited and minimal, I was able to identify some patterns about child-rearing and specifically the patterns of discipline from the interviews with Stephen and members of his extended family. Some child-rearing practices were predictable and consistent with what we know about the African American family, from the period of enslavement to the present.

During slavery, the black family and community lived under extremely harsh conditions, where the daily struggles of life included vigilance in protecting the young against the tyranny of the oppressor. Today, the African American community is made up of individuals and families who collectively share common cultural values, traditions, and habits. Some of these habits, both positive and negative, are reinforced and transmitted through the socialization process. For example, in the 1940s, according to Comer (1980), families frequently destroyed any signs of aggression in their children, particularly male children. It was an acceptable and expected practice in African American communities to beat severely unruly boys so they would never make the mistake of standing their ground with a White person in authority. Comer further states, "Given the overt suppression possible and practiced, such preparation and reaction were adaptive and necessary for Black survival. It was harmful to Black self-esteem and group esteem and social development, however" (Comer, 1980, p. 49).

Racist Socialization: Multigenerational Transmission

African Americans and other descendants of slaves have commonly viewed the practice of "whipping" children as an acceptable form of discipline. In most cases, it is not seen as violent or abusive. However, on closer investigation, the original reason for "whipping" children has its origins in slavery and Jim Crow. Whippings were to protect the child, and the rest of the family, from irreparable harm at the hands of Whites. One such harm was selling a child, as was the case in Stephen's family. Emma's brother was sold away because he disrespected a White person.

Another vital aspect of Stephen's discipline of his children involved his insistence that the children do not look at him directly while he was correcting them. This was the subservience Emma alluded to when told to avoid looking at or being near White people. She was to remain unnoticed. Isabel Wilkerson noted this carry-over behavior from slavery, in her book, *The Warmth of Other Suns: The Epic Story of America's Great Migration*. It described the hostile reception that Southern Blacks, migrating from the South, received from both Black and White northerners. She explained why they carried on their southern customs and coping strategies after leaving the South.

Wilkerson wrote:

> Unknowingly, the migrants were walking into a headwind of resentment and suspicion. They could not hide the roughcast clothes, ill-suited for northern winters or the slow, syrupy accents some Northerners could not decipher. They carried with them the scents of the South, of lye soap and earthen fields. They had emerged from a cave of restrictions into wide-open, anonymous hives that viewed them with bemusement and

contempt. They had been trained to walk humbly, look down when spoken to. It would take time to learn the ways of the North [2011, p. 260].

According to slave narratives, whippings were a common occurrence. Enslaved black children normalized the whippings that they witnessed, and even incorporated this behavior into their play. Bullwhips, Cat o' Nine Tails, even wooden boards were used as whipping devices. Genovese described how enslaved children practiced behaviors that reflected the realities of slave life. Their games reflected the pervasive violence in their condition. Julia Blanks, of Texas, remembered the children's favorite game as whipping each other with switches. "You know," she added, "after you was hit several times it didn't hurt so much." Then, there was the game of playing auction. One child would play the auctioneer and pretend to sell others to a prospective buyer (E. Genovese, 1976, p. 506).

Overseers and slave owners frequently whipped adults and children: other enslaved adults sometimes whipped children, as well. On some occasions, slaves died from severe whippings. This prompted the establishment of laws designed to protect Whites that beat enslaved Blacks to death from prosecution for murder. For example, The Casual Killing Act, Virginia Statute XXXIV of 1705, stated: "And if any slave resist his master, or owner, or other person, by his or her order, correcting such slave, and shall happen to be killed in such correction, it shall not be counted felony; but the master, owner and every other person so giving correction, shall be acquited of all punishment and accusation for the same as if such accident had never happened." Butterfield recounts the brutal beating of an enslaved pregnant woman:

> Michael DeLoache, the overseer at Cane Break, was a member of a coroner's jury that investigated the death of a slave named Dinah, a field hand who was pregnant at the time. Another overseer had stripped her and lashed her seventy times. She miscarried a few days later, and not long after she died. But no one thought the whipping caused Dinah's miscarriage or death.... Dr. Hugh Boyd testified, it was "owing to the constitution of the woman entirely," her own physical shortcomings, in other words. DeLoache, as part of the coroner's jury, found Dinah responsible for her own death [Butterfield, 1995, p. 30].

Case Study Summary

W.G. (Stephen's maternal Uncle) recollected Emma's experiences during slavery. Her seventeen-year-old brother was sold for "sassing" a White person. However, one can infer from this experience what Emma's and the rest of the family's response would be to the subsequent behavior of other children. Stephen's practice of whipping his children was associated with "racist socialization," and has roots in this family's traumatic history during slavery. Whipping children to discipline them and engender respect had been passed down through four generations. New justifications and rationalizations for the practice emerged over time until C.T. modified her method of discipline. She added "punishment" that did not involve whipping, and her decision to stop using whipping as the primary method of discipline ultimately led to the elimination of whipping altogether by some members of the family.

Conclusion

Post Traumatic Slave Syndrome (PTSS) is an explanatory theory. It describes specific social and psychological coping mechanisms that developed as survival behaviors during slavery. These behaviors have become part of family and community socialization and have passed across generations. Knowledge about the original traumatic experiences that they are in reaction to forgot was not passed on orally by elders. The racially oppressive circumstances of slave descendants in the Jim Crow South only reinforce slavery-derived whipping and other PTSS-related behaviors. Other PTSS behaviors reviewed in this chapter are the (defensive) violence of Willie James Bosket against authorities, derived from his grandfather, "Pud" Bosket, more than five generations earlier. There is the ethos of respect that drives the seemingly random black-to-black violence of Chicago and other street gangs. Then, when the need for respect combines with ever-present anger, one has the near-violent confrontation between an older and younger black man on a subway described by Peraud. These are distinctly dysfunctional behaviors in the twenty-first century and add to the already destructive burden of white racism.

It is important to note that not all coping behaviors derived from slavery were either traumatic or resulted in PTSS. Post Traumatic Slave Syndrome explicitly addresses those behaviors that can be traced back to slavery and are dysfunctional in the present. This chapter outlines a single theoretical model with a specific explanatory purpose that partly explains the complex adaptive behaviors of people of African descent with histories of colonization and chattel slavery. However, PTSS helps us to understand, and sometimes to explain both the positive and negative behaviors of contemporary people of African descent, still in recovery from slavery. We can examine which of our acquired behaviors we should keep, modify, or eliminate to ensure healthy progress. Like other groups, Black people are complex and multifaceted, with a vast repository of capabilities that have been accumulated over generations.

A fuller and a complete picture emerges of the collective experiences of the descendants of slaves, and perhaps other oppressed and marginalized people of color. These experiences are understood best by combining traditional and contemporary theories of human behavior. The results can be comprehensive explanatory frameworks that can reveal the influences of the past on the present, and the interrelationships between influences. Of course, the PTSS theory demonstrates the need for further research into how the residual effects of prolonged trauma impact African Americans today. We need to begin developing new theoretical frameworks that can help to explain and inform how we can establish protective mechanisms to reduce or eliminate trauma and mitigate harm from the past to the present for future generations.

References

American Psychiatric Association. (2013). *Diagnostic and statistical manual of mental disorders* (5 ed.). Arlington, VA: American Psychiatric Publishing.
Baldwin, J. (1955). *Notes of a Native Son.* Boston: Beacon Press.
Bell, C. (2017). Lessons Learned from 50 Years of Violence Prevention Activities in the African American Community. *Journal of the American Medical Association, 109*(4).
Bell, C., & McBride, D. (2014). Psychiatry for People of African Descent in the U.S.A.: The Massachusetts General Hospital Textbook on Diversity and Cultural Sensitivity in Mental Health. *Current Clinical Psychiatry.* doi:10.1007/978-1-4614-8918-4_6.
Bennet, D., & Fraser, M. (2000). Urban Violence Among African American Males: Integrating Family, Neighborhood, and Peer Perspectives. *Journal of Sociology and Social Welfare, 27*(3), 93–117.
Branscom, M. (1998, November 1). D.N.A. Test Finds Evidence That Thomas Jefferson and Slave Had a Child. *New York Times,* p. 20.
Butterfield, F. (1995). *All God's Children: The Bosket Family and the American Tradition of Violence.* New York: Avon Books.
Coates, T. (2015). *Between the World and Me.* New York: Random House.
Comer, J.P. (1980). *The Black Family an Adaptive Perspective.* New Haven: Yale University Child Center.
DeGruy, J., Kjellstrand, J.M., Briggs, H.E., & Brennan, E.M. (2011). Racial Respect and Racial Socialization as Protective Factors for African American Male Youth. *Journal of Black Psychology.*
DeGruy, J.A. (2017). *Post Traumatic Slave Syndrome: America's Legacy of Enduring Injury and Healing.* Portland: J.D.P. Publisher.
DeGruy, Leary, J. (2009). *Post Traumatic Slave Syndrome: America's Legacy of Enduring Injury and Healing: The Study Guide.* Portland: J.D.P. Publisher.
Eligon, J., & Gebeloff, R. (2016, August 20). Affluent and Black, and Still Trapped by Segregation: Well-Off Black Families End Up Living in Poorer Areas Than White Families with Similar or Even Lower Incomes. *New York Times.*
Fanon, F. (1952). *Black Skin White Masks.* Paris: Editions du Seuil.
Fullilove, M., & Wallace, R. (2011). Serial Forced Displacement in American Cities, 1916–2010. *Journal of Urban Health, 88*(3), 381–389.
Genovese, E. (1976). *Roll, Jordan, Roll: The World the Slaves Made.* New York: Vintage Books.
Haller, J. (1971). *Outcasts from Evolution.* Carbondale: Southern Illinois University Press.
Holden, K.B., Bradford, L.D., Hall, S.P., & Belton, A.S. (2013). Prevalence and Correlates of Depressive Symptoms and Resiliency Among African American Women in a Community-Based Primary Health Care Center. *Journal of Health Care for the Poor and Underserved, 24*(4 0), 79–93. doi:10.1353/hpu.2014.0012.

Leary, J.D., Brennan, E., & Briggs, H.E. (2005). The African American Adolescent Respect Scale: A Measure of a Prosocial Attitude. *Research on Social Work Practice, 15*, 466.
McIntosh, P. (2009). *White People Facing Race: Uncovering the Myths That Keep Racism in Place*. Wellesley, MA: The Saint Paul Foundation, Wellesley Center for Women, Wellesley College.
Morris, T. (1996). *Southern Slavery and the Law, 1619–1860*. Chapel Hill: The University of North Carolina Press.
Nichols, E.J. (1976). *Introduction to the Axiological Model*. Paper presented at the World Psychiatric Association and the Nigerian Association of Psychiatrists, University of Ibadan, Nigeria.
Persaud, R. (2004). *Why Black Men Love White Women: An Explicit Excursion in Sexual Politics*. Brooklyn, NY: D & R Publishing.
Peterson, M. (1975). *The Portable Thomas Jefferson: Notes on the State of Virginia, 1781*. New York: Viking Press.
Rothstein, R. (2017). *The Color of Law*. New York: W.W. Norton & Company.
Rothstein, R., & Gross, T. (2015). Historian Says Don't 'Sanitize' How Our Government Created Ghettos. National Public Radio. Retrieved from http://www.npr.org/2015/05/14/406699264/historian-says-dont-sanitize-how-our-government-created-the-ghettos,
Willie, C.V. (1981). *Black Families*. Bayside, NY: General Hall.
Woodson, C.G. (1933). *The Miseducation of the Negro*. Washington, D.C.: The Associated Publishers, Inc.

8

An Exploration of the Psychological Legacy of Slavery

BENJAMIN P. BOWSER

Joy A. DeGruy's previous chapter provides a theory for how past traumatic stress can be transmitted across generations and then expressed as a syndrome in present-day behaviors. In the next chapter, Benjamin P. Bowser constructs a research model that could test and, perhaps, demonstrate DeGruy's Post Traumatic Slave Syndrome. In effect, the precise lived experience of slavery with its related traumas cannot be relived as history, but they can be approximated psychologically in present-day lived experiences.

Pow! pow! pow! ... A young man is shot dead, and two bystanders are seriously injured. The police arrest the youth who did the shooting. They ask him why he did it. He answered calmly, "I do not know. He looked at me funny and needed killing." The police ask, "Did you try to avoid shooting the others?" He answers, "No, they were in the way" (private communication, police investigator).

A teacher asks an African American mother why she beat her children? The mother responds, "The only way they will know how to act right is to be beaten. Children who are not beaten are spoiled ... will say anything" (private communication, Second Grade School Teacher).

Young Black men and women are overheard talking loudly about one another on a bus, "that nigger ain't shit," ... "just another nigger" [personal observation].

From where did these attitudes come? In the United States, young Black men kill one another in black-on-black violence at a far higher rate than any other group of young men, and at a far higher rate than the police kill them (J.R. Smith, 2015). If another person, who is not their intended target, is killed or injured, they have little remorse. African American parents, even in the middle class, beat their children more often and more severely than White Americans, or any other ethnic group (Taillieu, Afifi, Mota, & et al., 2014). Black comedians get wild applause and affirmations from Black audiences when they joke about how severely their parents beat them as children. They claim that they are successful adults because of the beatings.

Regarding the young people calling themselves "niggers," members of no other ethnic group in the U.S. call one another publicly the same epithet that White racists use against them. Furthermore, when Black young people use "nigger," they mean it to be just as demeaning and degrading as racists do (B. Bowser, 2012). Why do African Americans have these attitudes and behaviors? The illustrations above are only samples.

The Legacy of Slavery?

Behavioral and social scientists have not isolated the significant causes of black-on-black violence. They have not explained the determination of Black parents to beat their children. Enough research has been done on corporal punishment to know that children who are beaten are very likely as adults to use violence against their children and other adults (Fagan, 2005). Why some African Americans feel compelled to call themselves, and others "nigger" has not been explored either. The lack of attention to these behaviors, especially among Black scholars and scientists, is as curious as to the behaviors themselves. There are certainly explanations.

Consider the following. An explanation for the three examples that began this chapter may lie in the culture of the actors, rather than in individual pathology or social-psychological circumstances. The scope of any explanation must be intergenerational, cutting across time, because the same behaviors and attitudes existed in prior generations. A consensus exists among African Americans that these attitudes and behaviors originated in slavery. I remember my parents making such attributions, as did my grandparents. Other African Americans who grew up in communities of slave descendants affirm hearing the same attributions.

Interestingly, this consensus cut two ways. Black behaviors and attitudes that were considered positive, and "credits to the race," were praised openly. People who exemplified them were celebrated. Then, there was the other side. Behaviors and attitudes considered harmful, that "held the race back," were kept better to ourselves. Examples of such behaviors were the passion with which Blacks were violent toward one another and call each other "nigger." Before the 1970s, this was "private knowledge" not intended for White people to know.

There were reasons to keep negative group behaviors to ourselves. Some Whites are intent on degrading Black people. They look for speech, mannerisms, and behaviors that distinguish Blacks from Whites. They make their living by producing vicious stereotypes, affirming beliefs in black inferiority, and white superiority. They look to affirm that Blacks are over-sexed, ignorant, dirty, thieves, violent, always laughing, lazy, superstitious, and cannot control themselves around White women. These are precisely the images used in minstrel shows, the most popular form of entertainment in the U.S. during the nineteenth century (W.T. Lhamon, 1998). Minstrel stereotypes were the content of early twentieth-century Vaudeville shows and were popular at the beginning of radio and television: most notably the Amos and Andy show (Ely, 1991). Now, these stereotypes are ingrained in American culture and get creatively updated and used in movies, advertisements, comedy, politics, on the Internet, and in sports (Sterkenburg, Knoppers, & Leeuw, 2010). Blacks have good reason to keep harmful, and negatively perceived, black behaviors hidden, and to acknowledge and talk about them only in private.

Role of Science

African Americans' unwillingness to address negatives openly in their culture is understandable. However, this reluctance has prevented exploration into the etiology of both harmful and laudatory behaviors. The central point is that historical experiences do influence contemporary behaviors. I hypothesize that specific behavior among African Americans today, either originated in or was influenced by slavery. Indeed, novelists and creative artists have drawn on the wealth of historical events and suppositions to explore this hypothesis. They have freely imagined connections between the past and present. In contrast, behavioral and social scientists are more comfortable looking at contemporary factors and influences to explain contemporary behaviors. The African American oral tradition challenges the sciences by suggesting there are influences from generations ago on contemporary behaviors.

This chapter has two purposes. The first is to identify the causes of black behaviors that might have multigenerational origins. The second is to explore the possibility of past influences on the present, opening the range of what might be possible in scientific discovery and treatment.

Evidence

Slave Narratives

Is there evidence of historical influences, such as slavery, on the present? It turns out that there is a starting point for answering this question. From 1936 to 1938, over 2,300 interviews of elderly African Americans were recorded as part of a project to put writers and artists to work during the Great Depression. The interviews took place in all the Southern states and used a life-history methodology. The people interviewed were the children of the last generation of slaves. They were asked to tell what they learned about slavery from those who lived it. The project and related materials resulted in over seventeen volumes (Work Project Administration, 1972–9). Certainly, biases limit the utility of the collection. Most of the interviewers were Whites who wanted to present slavery positively. Also, the seniors interviewed had forgotten a great deal and tended to focus on pleasant memories. However, even with these biases, some comments provide insight regarding our central question.

George Rawick, the chief editor, noted an often-repeated point in *The Slave Narratives*. Elders did not see much difference between the slavery they experienced and was described to them, and their lives in the 1930s (1972). Oppressive circumstances during slavery, seventy years earlier, had changed little from the harsh circumstances they were experiencing during the Great Depression in the Jim Crow South. The 1863 Emancipation had made little to no difference. Their day-to-day routines, their focus on hard, poorly compensated work, on family, violence, and threats of violence by Whites, and the dominance of Whites in every aspect of community life were the same in both times. A second takeaway is more intriguing than the first. Often, the elders described an event and person one way and later described another event and the same person in another way. For example, a master would first be described as cruel, and then later be described as caring. Then, a slave would be described as loyal; and later, the same person would be portrayed as plotting against their master. The few interviewers who sought to reconcile these seeming contradictions suggested something about both masters and slaves that escape us today. Both were multi-dimensional. They had different faces, played multiple roles, had shortcomings, and were sometimes consistent, inconsistent and contradictory. What they said and did depended on circumstances: they could be one person now and someone else later.

Insights from Early Studies

In addition to *The Slave Narratives*, now-classic field studies were conducted in the South during the 1930s, regarding the legacy of slavery. Investigators did in-depth interviews with a cross-section of Black residents of small Southern towns (Davis, 1941; Powdermaker, 1939). In assessing the psychological effects of Jim Crow, investigations were very much interested in any long-lasting psychological effects from slavery. In these communities, they noted that virtually every interaction between Blacks and

Whites was strictly prescribed and carefully judged by Whites for compliance with Jim Crow behavioral expectations (Chafe & et al., 2001). Whites called it "having manners ... proper upbringing." In communities where Jim Crow was enforced strictly, any non-compliance or deviation from prescribed deference was punished swiftly by humiliation, whipping, beating, tar and feathering, sexual assault, shooting, castration, and lynching. Protests, complaints, arguments, or objections from Blacks were not tolerated and were punished as well. Jim Crow community culture existed in the same way during slavery. The same expectations existed for slaves with the same outcomes for deviations.

These studies revealed a significant social context for black psychology then and, presumably, during slavery. Even in the harshest settings, white violence, and the threat of violence were not unpredictable, random, continuous, and unremitting: violence was, more often, predictable. Black people in both *The Slave Narratives* and community studies revealed that they lived in relative normality, despite their racial oppression, poverty, and physical deprivation. They could do so if they "stayed in their place" when interacting with Whites—did what was expected of them. The price they paid was occasional insult and humiliation. They had learned from an early age how to rigidly control and suppress their feelings, thoughts, and even body language in dealing with Whites. It would have been shocking and confusing for an outsider suddenly to come under such constraints and controls. However, slave descendants, who came out of multiple generations of living under such close oppression, clearly developed formidable coping skills in how to navigate within such constraints. During Jim Crow, White communities, as well as former slave masters, insisted on black powerlessness. Still, Black communities exercised agency within the limitations imposed on them, and they exploited any weaknesses in White control.

Some young people interviewed in the southern community studies displayed the kind of multiple personalities that elders described in *The Slave Narratives*. They could be remarkably subservient and overly polite in dealing with Whites and authorities. However, if you established rapport with them, or could observe them acting freely with their peers, they were articulate, lively and devastatingly perceptive about the flaws and weaknesses in the Jim Crow system, as they must have been during slavery (Davis & Dollard, 1940; Johnson, 1941). Youngsters were already expert in having multiple faces, giving limited answers, and saying what they thought Whites wanted to hear. They knew how to navigate their oppressive circumstances. They were able to describe their circumstances in detail and to reveal complex coping strategies that required becoming a different person based on various circumstances. However, young Black people did not arrive at this level of coping skillfulness overnight.

To impress upon their children the seriousness of behaving as expected, Black parents would beat them severely. Children were to speak only when spoken to, and they were never to reveal to Whites, or anyone else, anything their parents might have said or that they might have overheard. Parents, relatives, or neighbors could be punished during both slavery and Jim Crow and even lose their lives due to an innocent comment from a child. There was absolutely no room for children to make mistakes at any time and at any age.

An essential coping strategy for both Whites and Blacks was complete racial separation, even when they lived near one another. This minimized opportunities for Blacks to violate Jim Crow etiquette, and for Whites to incur the danger of having to enforce anti-black codes. Under even the most difficult circumstances, Blacks were never wholly powerless. Studies of slave revolts reveal that there was a point at which slaves would revolt if their masters oppressed them hard enough (Aptheker, 1983). There were also things slaves could do, short of open rebellion, to push back against their masters. They could break tools, burn property, kill or injure livestock, put poison in food, work slowly, injure themselves, or arrange accidents for their masters and overseers. Masters and their families were too dependent and too close to slaves in their day-to-day lives to be unremittingly cruel, violent, and punishing without regard for the unspoken pushback from slaves. Not only was one's profitability as a planter or farmer dependent on mutual working relationships with one's slaves, but one's very life was also dependent on a live-and-let-live balance with one's slaves.

Racial Identity

Something else of interest in the 1930s field studies was how Black children developed a social identity in racially segregated communities. One of the first social psychological experiments on this topic was Kenneth and Mamie Clark's doll study. Black youngsters were shown black and white dolls and asked which was the "good" doll, then which was the "bad" doll (K.B. Clark & Clark, 1940, 1947). Black children accepted the white doll and rejected the black doll. Then, they were asked which doll looked like them? With reluctance and sometimes tears, the children pointed to the black doll. The results of the Clarks' doll studies were used as evidence of the adverse effects of racial segregation in the 1954 U.S. Supreme Court case, Brown vs. Board of Education. From this case, the court outlawed racial segregation in the nation's schools, but to no avail. Schools in the U.S. are more segregated racially today than they were in 1954.

However, the Clarks left an open question. What did their study demonstrate? They claimed to have shown the damaging effects of racial segregation on Black children's social identity. The experiment has been repeated with improved methods (Porter, 1971) with much the same results (Holmes, 1995). However, in retrospect, there are several other interpretations of their findings. If the experiment was repeated with Black children reared and living in racially integrated settings, they might get the same results. This suggests that racial segregation was not the cause of the children's rejection of their blackness. It might be that the children's reactions were due to their internalizing black racial inferiority from the media, not from segregated living circumstances. Alternatively, it might be that close attention was needed to the anatomical accuracy and imaging of the dolls. Possibly, a variety of anatomically different black and white dolls would evoke opposite reactions. Finally, based on what we learned in *The Slave Narratives*, and early studies, these youngsters may have variations of their racial identity, each utilized under different circumstances. If one changed their circumstances and, perhaps, the race and gender of the interviewer, the children might switch their selection of dolls. Such an outcome would suggest that racial identity is more complicated and multi-dimensional than is currently believed.

Critical Hypotheses

Thus far, we can infer from the evidence that slavery, as a psychological experience, did not end in the U.S. in 1865, when slavery was abolished as a legal institution. Slavery as a psychological experience might have waned during Black Reconstruction (1865 to 1877). However, it was re-established with the development of Jim Crow legal and social practices in the South, after 1877. This is the testimony of elders in the 1930s. *The psychology of slavery in the U.S. was in place continuously through the end of institutional Jim Crow in 1964, up to the passage of the Civil Rights Act.* For many, freedom from slavery as a psychological state was not experienced until one hundred years after the actual emancipation. The Jim Crow experience was not psychologically distinct from slavery, nor did it complicate any long-lasting influences of slavery: it was slavery's long-lasting influence! However, one should note. Our inference of slavery's psychological continuity should not stop in 1964. If the psychology of slavery existed through 1964, a law could not have possibly ended a psychological state. Undoubtedly, for many, the psychology of slavery continued after 1965.

Some therapists have hypothesized that the psychological experience of slavery is alive and well today: consistent with our inference. They arrived at this realization based on clinical experiences with patients, and from their observations. In which case, the continuing psychology of slavery is an unassessed influence on African Americans today. It might explain some black self- and community-destructive behaviors, as well as resilience (discussed later). Some of the clinicians' and psychologists' hypotheses follow:

    1. Joy A. DeGruy has written that, in therapy, parents and children repeat self-disdaining comments about their color and physical appearance, have feelings of inadequacy as Black people, and do not see the possibility of improvement. From exploring patients' family backgrounds, she finds that these issues are intergenerational and traceable, in many cases, to repressed trauma in clients' family histories (see prior chapter). Because of the consistency, depth, and intergenerational longevity of these findings, she refers to their experiences as a "post-traumatic slave syndrome" (Joy A. DeGruy Leary, 2005).

    2. Na'im Akbar uncovered experiences in family histories that he asserts originated in slavery. A central experience is a deep distrust of other Blacks, including family. Parents pass this generalized mistrust on to their children (Akbar, 1996). This results in constant conflicts with other Blacks and the inability to develop strong personal and community ties.

    3. Jay Thomas Willis focuses on operative conditioning as the way hatred of self and others is passed along (2006). For example, children were beaten soundly from an early age during slavery. Five generations later, Black parents still beat their children at an early age, more often, and more severely than parents do in any other ethnic group (Taillieu et al., 2014). According to Willis, black-on-black violence and beatings are a direct outcome of self-disdain that originated in slavery and is still unresolved.

    4. Richardson and Wade assert that most American psychotherapists do not consider historical trauma when working with African Americans. They do not address deeply buried intergenerational issues that might date back to slavery (B.L. Richardson & Wade, 2000). There are unresolved traumas that have been accumulated during, and since slavery, that profoundly influence and distort black interpersonal relationships today.

    5. Hair straightening and skin bleaching are contemporary practices among descendants of enslaved Africans. For many, straight hair is considered beautiful, and light skin is most desirable (B.L. Richardson & Wade, 2000). The "kinkier" one's hair, and the darker one's skin, the less desirable one is (Monk, 2015). Hair straightening and

skin bleaching are virtual windows into contemporary internalized self-disdain, which started during slavery and continues to this day.

6. Some young African Americans refer to themselves casually and publicly as "niggers." They have a willingness to injure and kill each other for virtually any reason. They seem to have the mandate to use hard drugs, engage in HIV high-risk behaviors, and to go to jail (Kitwana, 1994; Perse, 2001). This social ethos has become self-perpetuating and reinforces the internalized racism for the millennial generation (Bowser, 2012). However, these behaviors are not new and have existed in every generation since slavery.

7. Ron Eyerman argues that slavery was culturally traumatic. Trauma is a defining feature of African American identity, which pervades all aspects of Black Americans' contemporary psychosocial functioning (2001). Social conditions in the South after slavery only reinforced traumas from slavery and further traumatized subsequent generations. The impacts of waves of historical trauma over generations have yet to be acknowledged, isolated, confronted, and resolved.

8. William Cross's research has shown that there are stages of black racial identity. To rise from the lowest stage of self-disdain, African Americans must successfully challenge internalized inferiority and racial stereotypes about themselves and others (W.E. Cross, 1991). At the highest stage, black racial identity is rooted in critical assessments of one's history and culture. One can acknowledge and appreciate other cultures and histories as well, without feeling that one is betraying one's own. In effect, there is a diversity of African American identities and cultural functioning based upon the extent to which historical influences and traumas have been faced and resolved.

Other authors could extend this list of propositions. Each author above has many more insights about the psychology of slavery derived from their years of clinical experiences and observations. There are four types of hypotheses here. First, there are clinical ones. Joy A. DeGruy, Na'im Akbar, and Richardson and Wade have done in-depth studies of clients in clinical practices. They found that their clients' problems were not due to individual maladjustment, personality disorders, or failure to cope. Their issues originated in family and community socialization and cut across generations. Prior generations of clients' families experienced the same issues. DSM-V diagnoses could be made, but the sources of their clients' issues are derived socially from family and community. Note that these therapists identify particular issues: disdain over color and physical appearance, distrust of other Blacks in particular, and buried trauma. For clients with knowledge and access to prior generations, they find that parents and grandparents struggled with the same issues. The consistency of these intergenerational issues is not coincidental or random.

Their clinical findings and the multigenerational nature of their clients' issues are real. The clinicians hypothesize that clients' problems date back to slavery, and do not have a more recent etiology. *The Slave Narratives* and early studies suggest that their hypotheses are valid. The grandparents of their older clients were only one generation from slavery. The conditions that created the psychology of slavery continued well into the previous century, in which case, these hypotheses provide further insights into the continuity of slave psychology today.

The second type of hypothesis is social. Clients got their psychological issues from social engagements as African Americans. Their problems are derived from social membership and experience. Dissatisfaction with one's skin color, physical appearance, and hair texture are based upon internalized aesthetic standards in which one cannot possibly be beautiful, acceptable, or attractive. Also, by referring to oneself and other Blacks with the vilest epithet in the English language, "niggers," one verbally articulates disdain for self and other Blacks. Clients could not arrive at these assessments of themselves independent of social and cultural conventions that they internalized. Of course, not all White people are happy with themselves. Some are victims of social conventions, as well. However, the issues here are specific to Black people and have little regard for individual differences among Blacks.

What these authors describe is a deeply ingrained social and cultural problem that leads to negative psychological consequences for individuals. Social and cultural problems create individual psychological maladjustment. The way to solve such an individual psychological problem is to eliminate the social and cultural norms that make Black people, by definition, defective, ugly, unattractive, and inferior.

The third type of hypothesis is cultural. Ron Eyerman asserts that individual trauma is not the only form of trauma. An entire group of people can be traumatized and carry trauma with them for generations. Their culture can respond to trauma by collective denial, very much like an individual. However, at the same time, the culture can be obsessed with the trauma. Pervasive anger, fear, anxiety, and depression among members are common outcomes of cultural trauma. The specific trauma of an entire people might occur in a single generation, but not end with that generation. It can go on in subsequent generations, even if the source of the initial trauma is forgotten. Cultural trauma ends only when it is acknowledged, and the coping behaviors and attitudes derived from it are consciously isolated and extinguished. If any people have traumatized cultures, it is the descendants of enslaved Africans in the West. They survived hundreds of years of slavery, and trauma upon trauma, none of which have been acknowledged, faced, and resolved.

Eyerman's thesis is ambitious. The psychological legacy of slavery is not an issue that can be resolved by individual efforts and therapy, nor is it an issue just for African Americans to resolve. The resolution would require Americans to acknowledge cultural racism, work to identify all its manifestations and motivations, and then spend at least a generation purging what they find. Real progress will be made when Whites no longer need to be "superior" and to use race and color as measures. Likewise, Blacks will no longer be compelled to bleach their skin, straighten their hair, and change their physical features because of a deeply ingrained sense of racial inferiority.

William Cross offers the final hypothesis. He has suggested that there are stages of racial identity. Cross does not believe that the lowest stage of black racial identity began in slavery and is skeptical of such claims. However, others may see Cross' stages of racial identity as a process by which individuals liberate themselves from a traumatized culture, and from social conventions that reinforce psychology dating back to slavery.

Other Explanations of Dysfunction

Other African American specific behaviors and health phenomena may have been affected by the psychology of slavery, as well. On measures of depression, older African American respondents have higher rates of depression than do other ethnic respondents of the same age (Ward & Mengesha, 2013). African Americans have a higher prevalence of post-traumatic stress disorder (PTSD) than Caribbean Blacks and Whites (Himle, Baser, Taylor, Campbell, & Jackson, 2009). Racial awareness and experiences of racial discrimination may partly explain these differences, but it is a mystery to health researchers, which other factors might be at work. There are explorations of possible physiological and genetic factors (Lohof, 2010). It might be that unexplained high levels of anger, anxiety, and depression are outcomes of unresolved intergenerational trauma, as well as cultural trauma, both of which are elements of the continuing psychology of slavery.

Besides, the pervasiveness of high blood pressure among African Americans may be another legacy of slavery, which is explained partly by physical and social stress with a genetic component (Hunte, Mentz, House, & et al., 2012). However, there is an unexplained variance in African American high blood pressure that might be linked to unresolved trauma, family socialization, self-disdain, and traumatic cultural influences. In the AIDS epidemic in the U.S., there was a subset of Black injection drug users and crack cocaine users with unusually high HIV risk levels (NIDA Notes, 1999). It was as if they were trying to become infected, and to infect others as a form of suicide, and black-on-black violence. These addicts were found to be identified closely in their families with troubled relatives in past generations who drank, used drugs, committed crimes, and who were violent and looked for trouble (Bowser, Word, Stanton, & Coleman, 2003). These risk-takers fulfilled some unexplained role in their family culture. Depending on how far back this pattern of designating troubled family members goes, a trauma in slavery might have triggered this multi-generational phenomenon.

Resiliency and Protective Outcomes

If the continuing psychology of slavery has an unassessed influence on African Americans today, it might also influence self and community-enhancing behaviors. It is taken for granted that the vast majority of African Americans survived, and some even thrived under American slavery and Jim Crow. Four hundred thousand Africans were brought to North America as slaves. By emancipation, there were four million descendants. Accumulated trauma, abuse, and dehumanization, over such an extended period, undoubtedly, left many insane or drove others to suicide and self-destruction, and the destruction of others. However, it is self-event that most survived, and increased ten-fold in numbers. One hypothesis is that the psychology of slavery was countered by a very effective counter-culture that negated the effects of the trauma, abuse, and dehumanization. For most, self-disdain did not overwhelm hope for self, family, and community. Ironically, a prior generation of scholars posed that the capacity of African Americans to form stable black families was undercut by slavery (Frazier, 1939). However, a more in-depth and more careful look found strengths and resilience, as well (Billingsley, 1968; Hill, 1972). The very same sources of evidence for the psychology of slavery, *The Slave Narratives*, and the early black community studies provide considerably more evidence of resilience derived from a culture that was undoubtedly protective from ongoing abuse and the accumulation of trauma.

In *The Slave Narratives*, two institutions were repeated frequently as particularly crucial to morale, to making sense of their plight, to experiencing and dealing with oppression as a community, rather than as isolated individuals. For many, the first was active engagement in religious ceremonies and enslaved Africans' spiritual beliefs. These started as secret meetings away from the plantation, at night, with recently enslaved Africans who were heads of worship, griots, and sorcerers, spiritualists (see Dossa, this volume). In time, these meetings evolved into formal churches with ministers (i.e., Baptists and Methodists), and were permitted or at least tolerated by their slave masters (Wesley, 1935). Many slaves centered their psychological world on their spiritual beliefs and the church and came to understand their lives and plight based on the Christian Gospel narrative. They survived from one Sunday worship to the next.

There was a second institution critical to slaves' psychological resilience. It was the slaves' engagement in music, dance, story-telling, and social life also at night. This second world has not been acknowledged as a vital institution, and as essential to slaves' survival. The time slaves spent together after work, at night, and on rare holidays, was the setting from which African American informal culture emerged. That culture is evident today in music, dance, food preparation, humor, story-telling, and the spoken word. By the time of Jim Crow, this informal side of African American culture was embodied in family gatherings, church picnics, and the back road "juke-joints, blues, and sugar-shacks" in the rural South that became black nightclubs and dance halls in big cities. The rise of social dance was a part of this (Hazzard-Gordon, 1990). We do not know what juke joints were called during slavery, but their equivalent existed. If one goes back far enough in the slave experience, what is now the church and social dance, music, and entertainment were parts of the same early, nighttime gatherings. One hypothesis is that these gatherings began dividing into two separate institutions in the 1800s, with formalized slave involvement in Methodism and Baptism (Wesley, 1935). Church ministers vehemently disapproved of the continuing informal slave and Black culture as worlds of sin. The worlds of churchgoers and night-lifers were supposedly mutually exclusive, but many enslaved Africans laughed at the ministers and patronized both. Somehow, both churches and "juke-joints" were instrumental not only in African American physical and psychological survival but also in their ability to thrive during slavery and Jim Crow.

Psychology of Slavery

Hypotheses regarding dysfunction and protection-resiliency call for a closer look at what constitutes the psychology of slavery. What would its essential components look like if we were able to witness slavery in the U.S. before 1865? Let us assume that the psychology of slavery continues after the Emancipation and into Jim Crow, as suggested above. Let us understand, as well, that this "psychology" can be replicated, whether we call it slavery or by some other name. There is literature on slavery in the U.S. that attempts to describe slavery as slaves might have experienced it (Blassingame, 1972; Eugene Genovese, 1972; Warren, 2016). The following figure shows the conditions that, hypothetically, produce a psychology of slavery.

8. *An Exploration* (Bowser) 153

The specifics of that psychology, as slaves might have experienced it from the above hypotheses, are detailed in the inner circle.

Figure 9.1 models the rough conditions under which slaves existed in the American South and estimates the psychological outcome of those conditions. The first pre-requisite condition is fear of violence: the constant fear of being physically whipped, beaten, and brutalized. To make this condition constant requires one to either periodically experience or witness such violence. It cannot be just a threat. The second condition heightens fear of violence, that is, one must be utterly powerless to defend one's self, or to reduce the threat of violence. Powerlessness also means that all possibilities appear closed to escape or to mitigate the threat of violence. Powerlessness is most effective when it is all-pervasive, across all aspects of one's life. In effect, all the ways to exercise individual agency over one's life are closed. The impact of powerlessness is heightened further when the third condition is met. One must be made utterly dependent upon one's oppressor. One must be entirely reliant on the person or people who control the violence, and one's powerlessness. Slaves are made to feel dependent upon their oppressors for all their needs: food, shelter, clothing, privacy, and even sleep.

The fourth condition further reinforces powerlessness and dependency—physical and mental deprivations force one to focus on immediate relief from hardship, and day-to-day survival. Closely supervised, hard work from "sun-up" to "sun-down," under the constant threat of violence,

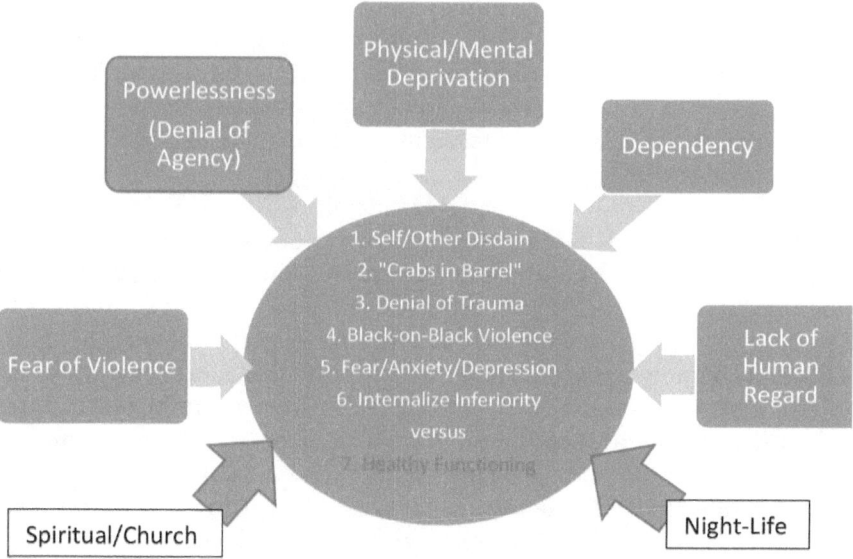

Figure 9.1. Conditions for a Psychology of Slavery.

required slaves to focus continually on the immediate moment. Being sick, diseased, injured, in pain, or physically limited, further focuses one's attention on the present moment. In chattel slavery, one can surmise, the fewer opportunities for reflection, the better. There was a fifth condition. Built into chattel slavery was a fundamental denial of slaves' humanity and spirituality. Denial of humanity made legal and normal practices of barbaric social control even for those times. They included cutting off body parts, being sold away from family and community, having one's children sold, branding with a hot iron, castration, and being stripped naked and whipped bloody in public. Also, the barbarity included powerlessness to prevent sexual assault, having one's wife and daughters raped, outright murder, and being worked to death. Also, there were being ordered by one's master to brutalize family and members of one's community, and finally, having to bear witness to all of these practices, and being unable to intervene.

Lack of human regard makes Western chattel slavery particularly criminal and reprehensible. It massively reinforced and intensified the other four conditions for the psychology of slavery. What happens to people who live under these conditions? As illustrated in the inner circle above, those who experienced all five conditions come to express disdain for self and others. The disdain developed over skin color, hair texture, physical appearance, speech, body size, weight, almost anything and everything about one's self that their masters looked down on. Next, came the "crabs in the barrel reaction." This happens if anyone finds a way around or out of any of the five conditions. The other slaves would act like "crabs in a barrel." In other words, if one crab makes progress climbing out of the barrel, the others will not try to climb out themselves or assist the first crab. They pull the first one back into the barrel. Then, the next crab that tries to escape will be pulled back in, as well. Despite having a way out of the dilemma, none of the slaves succeeds, because they do not help one another.

Every single one of the practices in condition five, denial of humanity, are traumatizing. This was not a coincidence, nor was it that people in the fifteenth through eighteenth centuries did not understand trauma. These practices were intended to be traumatic. No one who was a slave was to escape without experiencing trauma essential to maintaining them physically and mentally as slaves. Some slaves were able to address their trauma; others were not. Undoubtedly, unresolved trauma accumulated and was coped with through denial, generation after generation. An outcome of accumulated denial is intense violence, rarely directed toward the master, but more often toward other slaves. We see this today in the fierce competitiveness of black professional boxers and athletes. Blacks will make a special effort not only to beat their Black opponent but also to humiliate them as a spectacle for White audiences. The psychology of slavery produces not just fear, but anxiety and depression as well. Slaves, as a class of people, carried a seemingly inescapable emotional burden. However, anxiety and depression are viewed today as individual problems. In slavery, anxiety and depression were expected responses to powerlessness, fear of violence, dependency, and privation.

Black-on-black violence is another outcome of the five psychological conditions, as well as Blacks having a higher predisposition toward fear, anxiety, and depression. These are common outcomes of repressed traumas accumulated over generations. Then, the internalization of inferiority to Whites continues the psychology of slavery. A legacy of slavery is the presumption on the part of European Americans that they are "White" people and race and that they are superior to all other races. This is an essential part of their socialization and social identity as Americans: one that many fiercely defend today. The descendants of enslaved Africans are immersed in the same white supremacist socialization, whether they are in Brazil, the U.S., or elsewhere in the West. However, without counter socialization, the outcome for African descendants is an internalization of black inferiority. For example, until the early 1980s, the least educated Blacks whose economic dependency on Whites and circumstances were closest to slavery in the rural South, referred to one another frequently and casually as "niggers" in the same way White Southerners did. Gangster rappers with parental roots in this Southern rural inferiority popularized the use of "nigger" since the 1980s, to entertain their predominantly White audiences (B. Bowser, 2012).

Finally, this constellation of conditions and outcomes are remarkable. So many, who experienced slavery and Jim Crow, came out of both states with remarkably healthy mental and physical functioning. There was undoubtedly a continuum. Those crushed and rendered dysfunctional were at one end, and those who survived and thrived were on the other end. *The Slave Narratives* and early Southern community studies suggest the church, spirituality, and the informal culture, both expressed through slaves' nightlife, made the difference. The post-emancipation and post–Jim Crow behaviors of Black survivors suggest that most were on the well-functioning and healthy psychological end of the continuum, despite any cultural and behavioral legacies of slavery they may have inherited.

Discussion

There is no way to know precisely what the conditions were that slaves faced day-to-day. We can only approximate them from the historical record. The above model of conditions that produced a psychology of slavery is an approximation and is incomplete. Undoubtedly, there were other conditions not included in this model. Also, the model is static. We do not know the intensity of the conditions nor the full extent of interactions between conditions. The real-life conditions were dynamic. We know that slavery varied as an institution in the U.S. (Stampp, 1956). In parts of the upper South, Maryland, and Virginia, masters exercised greater flexibility in managing slaves than they did in the Deep South of Alabama and Mississippi. Paternalism toward slaves was common in the upper South, where slavery was well established.

In contrast, slavery was a death sentence early on in the Deep South, where slaves had to clear land, empty swamps, and build facilities for ambitious and less experienced masters. These masters were desperate to get established and to become rich quickly (Libby, 2004). We also know that the vast coastal plantations of Virginia and the Carolinas, with large and perhaps impersonal workforces, were not what the average slave experienced in the U.S. Typical slave owners in Virginia and North Carolina were small farmers who held nine slaves, on average (Gutman, 1976). Many of these White, small property owners and their families lived and worked side-by-side with their slaves in the fields, and their homes. Slaves debated which setting (large plantation vs. small farm) was the worst to be enslaved in (Jackson, 1976, pp. 62–65). The model above does not reflect these differences.

The psychological outcomes for someone living in slavery are also incomplete and varied. Also, there were personality differences, then as now, that varied in how individuals experienced and then coped with slavery. Some learned to cope; others did not. Malleability, flexibility, situational awareness, and the ability to selectively show and hide attitudes and feelings had to be well developed. To avoid punishment and trauma, slaves had to wear many faces. Tremendous creativity was exercised in finding and exploiting weaknesses in the circumstances in which they lived. They looked for ways to minimize violence against them and to reduce their powerlessness, deprivation, and dependency. They knew that the more they were seen as human beings, the more difficult it was for their masters to brutalize them. Also, somehow slaves were able to communicate with one another long enough and in sufficient detail to evolve a culture of resistance, despite the many variations of slavery and the restrictions imposed on them (Stuckey, 1987).

The variability of slavery suggests that the above model is undoubtedly insufficient to cover all the different ways that slavery was organized and practiced. The multiple ways that slavery was practiced calls for other models. Other forms of slavery with various pre-conditions would undoubtedly produce different psychologies. It is possible, as well, that each kind of slavery had different ways to provide the same psychological outcomes.

Finally, the psychologies of slavery need not be limited to a specific historical time and place. It is not necessary to reconstruct precisely the psychologies of slavery as slaves experienced before 1865. The challenge of reconstructing a history precisely as it was lived and experienced need not be met. That is a virtual impossibility. Enough knowledge of the conditions that perpetuated slavery is sufficient to estimate likely psychological outcomes. Therefore, the psychologies of slavery are not isolated to one time and place. My supposition is the following. If the same conditions were put in place today or tomorrow, with the same denial of humanity, the psychological outcomes would be similar to those produced during American slavery.

Conclusion

Enslaving and brutalizing a people for generations, then and now, is a crime against humanity. The crime is made worse when history leaves its victims without even a record of their existence.. Not knowing their mind, what they experienced, and what they did to survive also erases them from an unknown history. It is as if enslaved Africans in the West never existed. Suggested here is a way to understand their struggle by knowing the conditions they faced. It is a way to appreciate the miracle that they survived intact, despite what they experienced. It is not necessary to grasp their experience directly, nor for their experiences to continue to traumatize us today. However, we do have sciences and conceptual tools to approximate, estimate, and reconstruct the conditions under which they lived and to estimate the psychological outcomes of those conditions.

We have enough history of slavery to create conceptual models of it, for not only the United States but also wherever slavery was practiced. There was enough variation in the way slavery was practiced to surmise that it was experienced in different ways. Therefore, there are multiple psychologies of slavery, even in the same nation and culture. We know as well that slaves did not live slavery precisely as their masters intended. If so, they would not have survived, and we would not be here to bear witness to them. They found ways to reduce the violence, ready to fall on them at a moment's notice. They found ways to exercise agency over their lives, as well as to find some physical and mental comfort amidst deprivation. They even found ways to make their masters think twice about committing acts of brutality against them. They did so by counter threats, as already described, ultimately by running away, or by outright rebellion (Aptheker, 1983). For every set of oppressive conditions imposed on slaves, there were counter-strategies of resistance. Our models of slavery are incomplete without them.

Furthermore, there is no way for us to reach back and mitigate the horrors of slavery. However, our seemingly nameless and faceless fore-parents gave us two gifts. First, their resistance was successful enough for us to come after them, and to bear witness to them. Equally important is that their strength over more than two hundred years provides a wealth of resistance strategies, even today. The lived circumstances of many African Americans, right now, are variations of the five conditions of slavery, outlined in the model above. Institutional slavery may have ended in 1865, but the motives to exploit and abuse Black people that made slavery possible did not stop. Those motives have been re-deployed to produce today a "new Jim Crow" (Alexander, 2010). Conditions in American ghettoes are closer to slavery, then we imagine. There is a constant fear of violence (condition one), this time, from one another, and powerlessness to improve one's life (condition two). There is poverty (condition three) and dependency on often abusive social service entities (condition four). For many, the ultimate in powerlessness and dependency is incarceration. Finally, the police are only a 911 telephone call away to provide a lack of human regard. One can be stopped and frisked (humiliate), beaten, choked to death, and shot and killed while unarmed with your hands up, having committed no crime other than being black (condition five).

There is a vindication of Joy A. DeGruy, Na'im Akbar, Jay Thomas Willis, Richardson and Wade, and Ron Eyerman. They do not have to connect directly or prove that the origins of the behavior and cultural issues that plague Black people and communities today had their origins in actual historical slavery. The conditions of that slavery exist today, in part, and validate their work.

Transnational Implications

Historical experiences cannot be relived, but conditions can be reproduced. Psychological conditions defined slavery's ongoing effects today. Some specific conditions defined slavery in Brazil, Cuba, the French and English Caribbean, Columbia, Venezuela, Panama, Costa Rica, and Mexico. Those conditions that are still with us from slavery and continue to shape the contemporary experiences of the descendants of enslaved Africans in these countries. There are theoretical implications here. Slavery as conditions and responses to conditions recall the work of Frantz Fanon (Frantz Fanon, 1963, 1967). The core conditions of slavery are virtually identical to those of colonialism. In this case, the therapeutic strategies that Fanon pioneered are applicable to both.

Finally, the cultures of societies that enslaved Africans in the West have racism (the presumption of white supremacy and black inferiority) as legacies from slavery. All former slave societies in the West have living legacies of slavery that reduce the quality of life for all their citizens, not just for the descendants of enslaved Africans (Bowser & Hunt, 1996).

A psychological legacy of slavery is only one historical burden. There are economic, environmental, health, and political burdens from slavery, as well. The problem is that the sins of the past continue to live with us and to burden the present. Those sins have to be acknowledged. Whatever psychological damage was done must be understood, faced, and addressed. Reconciliation is essential within each culture and in citizens' lives to come to terms with our legacies of slavery.

References

Akbar, N. i. (1996). *Breaking the Chains of Psychological Slavery*. Tallahassee, FL: Mind Productions & Assoc.

Alexander, M. (2010). *The New Jim Crow: Mass Incarceration in the Age of Colorblindness*. New York: The New Press.

Aptheker, H. (1983). *American Negro Slave Revolts*. New York: International Publishers.

Billingsley, A. (1968). *Black Families in White America*. Englewood Cliffs, NJ: Prentice-Hall.

Blassingame, J. (1972). *The Slave Community: Plantation Life in the Antebellum South*. New York: Oxford University Press.

Bowser, B. (2012). *Gangster Rap and Its Social Cost: Exploiting Hip Hop and Using Racial Stereotypes to Entertain America*. Amherst, NY: Cambria Press.

Bowser, B., & Hunt, R. (Eds.). (1996). *Impacts of Racism on White Americans* (2nd ed.). Thousand Oaks, CA: Sage Publications.

Bowser, B., Word, C., Stanton, M.D., & Coleman, S.B. (2003). Death in the Family and HIV Risk-Taking Among Intravenous Drug Users. *Family Process, 42*(2), 291–304.

Chafe, W.H., & et al. (Eds.). (2001). *Remembering Jim Crow: African Americans Tell About Life in the Segregated South*. New York: New Press.

Clark, K.B., & Clark, M.P. (1940). Skin Color as a Factor in Racial Identification of Negro Preschool Children. *Journal of Social Psychology, 11*, 159–169.

Clark, K.B., & Clark, M.P. (1947). Racial Identification and Preference in Negro Children. In T.M. Newcomb & E.L. Hartley (Eds.), *Readings in Social Psychology* (pp. 169–178). New York: Holt.

Cross, W.E., Jr. (1991). *Shades of Black: Diversity in African-American Identity*. Philadelphia: Temple University Press.

Davis, A. (1941). *Deep South*. Chicago: University of Chicago Press.

Davis, A., & Dollard, J. (1940). *Children of Bondage*. Washington, D.C.: American Council on Education.

Ely, M.P. (1991). *The Adventures of Amos 'n' Andy: A Social History of an American Phenomenon*. New York: Free Press.

Eyerman, R. (2001). *Cultural Trauma: Slavery and the Formation of African American Identity*. New York: Cambridge University Press.

Fagan, A.A. (2005). The Relationship Between Adolescent Physical Abuse and Criminal Offending: Support for an Enduring and Generalized Cycle of Violence. *Journal of Family Violence, 20*(5), 279–290.

Fanon, F. (1963). *The Wretched of the Earth*. New York: Grove Press, Inc.

Fanon, F. (1967). *Black Skin, White Masks*. New York: Grove Press.

Frazier, E.F. (1939). *The Negro Family in the United States*. Chicago: University of Chicago Press.

Genovese, E. (1976). *Roll, Jordan, Roll: The World the Slaves Made*. New York: Vintage Books.

Gutman, H.G. (1976). *The Black Family in Slavery and Freedom 1750–1925*. New York: Pantheon Books.

Hazzard-Gordon, K. (1990). *Jookin': The Rise of Social Dance Formations in African American Culture*. Philadelphia: Temple University Press.

Hill, R. (1972). *The Strengths of Black Families*. New York: Emerson Hall.
Himle, J.A., Baser, R.E., Taylor, R.J., Campbell, R.D., & Jackson, J.S. (2009). Anxiety Disorders Among African Americans, Blacks of Caribbean descent, and Non-Hispanic Whites in the United States. *J. Anxiety Disorder, 23*(5), 578–590.
Holmes, R.M. (1995). *How Young Children Perceive Race*. Thousand Oaks, CA: Sage Publications.
Hunte, H.E., Mentz, G., House, J.S., & et al. (2012). Variations in Hypertension-Related Outcomes Among Blacks, Whites and Hispanics in Two Large Urban Areas and in the United States. *Ethn Dis, 22*(4), 391–397.
Jackson, M.Y. (1976). *The Struggle for Freedom: Phase I as Revealed in Slave Narratives of the Pre-Civil War Period*. Chicago: Adams Press.
Johnson, C. (1941). *Growing Up in the Black Belt*. Washington, D.C.: American Council on Education.
Kitwana, B. (1994). *The Rap on Gangster Rap, Who Runs It: Gangster Rap and Visions of Black Violence*. Chicago: Third World Press.
Leary, J.D. (2005). *Post Traumatic Slave Syndrome: America's Legacy of Enduring Injury and Healing*. Milwaukie, OR: Uptone Press.
Lhamon, W.T. (1998). *Raising Cain: Blackface Performance from Jim Crow to Hip Hop*. Cambridge: Harvard University Press.
Libby, D.J. (2004). *Slavery and Frontier Mississippi, 1720–1835*. Jackson: University Press of Mississippi.
Lohof, F.W. (2010). Overview of the Genetics of Major Depressive Disorder. *Curr. Psychiatry Reports, 12*(6), 539–546.
Monk, E.P. (2015). The Cost of Color: Skin Color, Discrimination, and Health Among African-Americans. *The American Journal of Sociology, 121*(2), 396–444.
NIDA Notes. (1999). *Infectious Disease and Drug Abuse*. Washington, D.C.: U.S. Department of Health and Human Services.
Perse, E.M. (2001). *Media Effects and Society*. Mahwab, NJ: Erlbaum Associates.
Porter, J. (1971). *Black Child, White Child: the Development of Racial Attitudes*. Cambridge, MA: Harvard University Press.
Powdermaker, H. (1939). *After Freedom*. New York: Viking Press.
Rawick, G. (1972). *The American Slave: A Composite Autobiography: From Sundown to Sunup. The Making of the Black Community, vol. 1*. Westport, CT: Greenwood.
Richardson, B.L., & Wade, B. (2000). *What Mama Couldn't Tell Us About Love: Healing the Emotional Legacy of Slavery by Celebrating Our Light*. New York: Perennial.
Smith, J.R. (2015). Unequal Burdens of Loss: Examining the Frequency and Timing of Homicide Deaths Experienced by Young Black Men Across the Life Course. *Am J Public Health, 105 Suppl 3*, S483–490. doi:10.2105/ajph.2014.302535.
Stampp, K.M. (1956). *The Peculiar Institution:Slavery in the Anti-Bellum South*. New York: Vintage Books.
Sterkenburg, J.V., Knoppers, A., & Leeuw, S.D. (2010). Race, Ethnicity, and Content Analysis of the Sports Media: A Critical Reflection. *Media, Culture and Society, 32*(5), 819–839.
Stuckey, S. (1987). *Slave Culture: Nationalist Theory and the Foundations of Black America*. New York: Oxford University Press.
Taillieu, T., Afifi, T., Mota, N., & et al. (2014). Age, Sex, and Racial Differences in Harsh Physical Punishment: Results from a Nationally Representative United States Sample. *Child Abuse Negl, 38*(12), 1885–1894. doi:10.1016/j.chiabu.2014.10.020.
Ward, E., & Mengesha, M. (2013). Depression in African American Men: A Review of What We Know and Where We Need to Go from Here. *Am J Orthopsychiatry, 83*(2), 386–397.
Warren, W. (2016). *New England Bound: Slavery and Colonization in Early America*. New York: Liveright Publishing Corp.
Wesley, C. (1935). *Richard Allen, Apostle of Freedom*. Washington, D.C.: Associated Publishers.
Willis, J.T. (2006). *Why Black Americans Behave as They Do: The Conditioning Process from Generation to Generation*. West Conshohocken, PA: Infinity Publishing Company.
Work Project Administration. (1972-9). *Slave Narratives: A Folk History of Slavery in the United States from Interviews with Former Slaves*. Westport, CT: Greenwood.

9

The Psychological Legacy of Slavery in the United States

Trauma Derived from Centuries of Laws and Customs

EDWIN J. NICHOLS

In the previous chapter, Benjamin P. Bowser shows that it is possible to reconstruct the psychology of slavery and that, conceptually, there are people today who are living with many of the same variables that constitute the psychology of historical slavery. The next chapter, by Edwin Nichols, addresses an issue that cast a long shadow over our international symposium and the production of this book. That is the unusually strong belief in the United States that there are no after-effects of slavery. It is believed strongly in the U.S. that whatever problems the descendants of enslaved Africans have derived from history is of their own making or is due to their weakness and inability to "get over it." Nichols addresses this belief head-on. The U.S. was the only country that did not provide support for researchers to attend the symposiums that lead up to this work. The NIH international symposium reviewers turned down our applications repeatedly with no explanation, while France, Canada, Martinique, and Brazil provided travel funds for their participants. These countries are also considering primary and secondary school curricular reforms to include the Transatlantic slave trade and slavery to address racism's effects in their countries. There are no such reforms under consideration in the U.S.

Slavery and Racism in the Western Hemisphere

In every country in the Western Hemisphere where slavery was practiced, the descendants of African slaves are at the bottom of the social hierarchy (Lovejoy & Bowser, 2012). They have the lowest incomes, highest unemployment, and most inferior education. They are segregated racially in housing, have the highest mortality and morbidity rates, and the lowest representation among leaders in business and government. It does not matter whether the history, culture, and language of the country are English, French, Spanish, or Portuguese. It does not matter that emancipation from slavery came in 1811 (Chile), 1834 (British colonies), 1865 (the United States), in 1880 (Cuba), or 1888 (Brazil). In every country, people of European ancestry are privileged, and their privilege is justified by some notion of White racial superiority (racism) over citizens of African ancestry.

Despite these striking similarities across history, cultures, and time, differences do exist. Any effort to reduce or eliminate racial inequality as a living legacy of slavery, in any of these countries, will have to work through national differences. In this chapter, the exceptionalism of slavery in the United States (U.S.) is explored with the intent of identifying barriers to slavery's acknowledgment and reconciliation. To appreciate U.S. exceptionalism, a brief comparison with other legacies in the West is in order.

The French Legacy

Slavery was introduced in France by Louis XIV's 1685 edict, Le Code Noir. The Code intended to govern the conduct of slavery in French America: in particular, Haiti, Martinique, and Guadeloupe (Buchanan, 2011). The Code Noir, and the Virginia laws defining slavery mirrored each other, to a point. The French required slaves to be baptized and instructed in Roman Catholicism. Recognizing that slaves had souls was not acknowledged in the United States. Young French slave children of intact families could not be sold away from their parents, as they could be in the United States. Also, French slaves could take their masters to court for redress of mistreatment; with a few exceptions, slaves in the United States could not. Slavery ended in France for the first time in 1794, with the French Revolution. However, slavery continued in the United States, even after the United States Revolutionary War, in 1776. However, in 1802, under Napoleon, slavery and the Code Noir were re-established. General Antoine Richepance brutally repressed recently freed slaves in the French Antilles. Hundreds were killed on Guadeloupe as they fought to retain their freedom. Slavery was finally ended in France, in 1848, a full seventeen years before it was abolished in the United States.

Unlike the British or Americans, the French were assimilationists.

They promised that after one hundred years, formerly enslaved colonies would be permitted to become part of France. Remarkably, the Third Republic (1871) allowed Black representatives from the colonies to enter the French National Assembly because they were French. In 1945, following the one-hundred-year promise, the French West Indies were designated as Departement d'Outre Mer and became a regular department of France (the equivalent of a state in the U.S.).

In contrast to the U.S., France has a highly centralized government. There are no state governments regulating education, police, and other government services, as in the U.S. For example, in France, all teachers and police officers must meet rigorous national standards before becoming civil servants. A national educational curriculum is a prerequisite to the national certification of the baccalaureate, which then qualifies students to go on to higher education. When students in the overseas department pass the examination, they may go to France to study as regular French citizens and university students.

Nevertheless, the legacy of slavery in France becomes apparent when an Antillean goes to metropolitan France. Madame Rokhaya Diallo explained, "Yes, I am French here in Martinique," however, "When I am in France, I am not French."[1] People in metropolitan France realize that Antilleans are French citizens. However, some still discriminate against them racially. Their mental image of French nationality is the textbook image of a Left Bank Parisian with a beret and a paintbrush or a girl in a traditional dress from Bourbonnais. Of course, all these time-honored images are of White people and do not include Antilleans of African descendants.

Haiti is an exception because it did not wait one hundred years to allow political assimilation into France. Haitians first defeated the famed Napoleonic Army in a successful rebellion in 1802. Haiti is the only country in the Western Hemisphere, where a slave revolt ended in independence. Haiti was considered the wealthiest island in the Caribbean. By tearing itself away from France, it threatened the practice of slavery throughout the hemisphere. For example, Haiti harbored Simon Bolivar and sent armaments and troops to aid in his fight against Spain in Bolivia (Léger, 1907). European and American banks eliminated Haiti as a threat by annually withdrawing from the Haitian treasury the amount of money the French demands for property reparations lost in the 1802 Haitian revolution (Ives, 2013). These annual payments went on for 143 years, until the end of World War II in 1945. To this day, this practice impoverished the island. Upon independence, Haiti had hundreds of sugar estates and coffee plantations, all claimed as the property of France. France also classified 465,000 former slaves as its property, as well, for whom they have been compensated many times over. The pretext for these payments was that France would defend the sovereignty of Haiti from the British and the Spanish. However, this protection did not extend to the U.S., which invaded and controlled Haiti at will.

The British Legacy

Historically, for a valid baptism, the Church of England required that an adult had to be literate to read the catechism (Bly, 2017, p. D2).[2] In the U.S., it was a crime to teach slaves to read. Any slave in the American South found capable of reading could be blinded, dismembered, or killed. Initially, in Virginia, Christian baptism of slaves was forbidden. Later, slaves in the U.S. could be baptized without being able to read. Baptism happened only after masters realized that they could use Christianity to control their slaves' behavior: e.g., the biblical passage, "*Slaves obey your master.*" Incidentally, Christian baptism did not modify the condition of slavery anywhere in the Western Hemisphere: not in the Islands of French America nor the other Caribbean colonies controlled by the British, Spanish, Danish, Dutch, or Portuguese.

Unlike the French or the Americans, the British were thoroughly pragmatic in dealing with slaves. They were equally thorough in disregarding their humanity. Slaves were to learn enough English and British customs to do whatever work was assigned to them. The British did whatever was required to maintain order and to make work efficient and effective. They did nothing more. The British maintained a definite social class hierarchy among themselves and a racial hierarchy for others. Unlike the French, for example, a British Jamaican subject had no right to enter the British Parliament, simply because he or she was British. The British colonial government kept order in the colonies and made sure that wealth continued to flow to England at all costs. The initial British attitude toward the colonies was that they were just for extracting resources, and for generating wealth for the British homeland. Colonies were also dumping grounds for criminals, prostitutes, and religious malcontents.

In 1807, the British passed a law to end the Transatlantic Slave Trade, based on abolitionist efforts (Carey, 2005). Because they dominated the seas militarily, they forced their laws on everyone else. It gave British ships the legal right to intercept and confiscate vessels of any country caught transporting slaves from Africa to the Western Hemisphere. The British gained great wealth from the confiscation of foreign ships, but there was a negative consequence for Africans. If a British man-of-war was sighted and pursued a foreign ship, the slave traders would dump their slave cargo, all chained together, into the sea (Matthews, 2007, p. 135).[3] Pushing a few slaves off the ship would cause a chain reaction, pulling all the balance of slaves into the ocean. When the British ship would finally stop them, the captain could say, "We have no slaves as cargo on this ship."

Racism is the contemporary legacy of slavery in the British Commonwealth, as it is in the U.S. White British people consider themselves racially superior to all people of color. British racism is expressed in institutional practices where British individuals of African descent, as well as those of other third world countries, are discriminated against racially (Fryer, 1984). Racial discrimination is an adjunct to the British social class hierarchy. This racism is apparent in systematic racial inequality across all aspects of British life, just as it is in the U.S.

The Portuguese Legacy

Slavery in Brazil began before it did in Britain or France. The Portuguese bought Africans and transported them to Europe from Angola, as early as the 1490s. They started the transatlantic slave trade to the Western Hemisphere, notably to Brazil (Hawthorne, 2010). As occurred in France, Africans were baptized and assigned a Christian name as they were placed on slave ships and transported to Brazil. However, the recognition that enslaved Africans had souls, and were human beings, ended there.

Early slavery in Portuguese Brazil was a death sentence. Males were enslaved, intentionally worked to death, and then replaced by others. Slaves quickly discovered their fate, and, understandably, engaged in constant and bloody rebellions. The Portuguese increased their efforts to break the will and spirit of enslaved Africans, to prevent these rebellions. In time, these efforts failed, and they began to reduce workloads, take better care of their slaves, provide incentives, import African women, and allow slaves to have families and create communities. Nonetheless, millions were lost in the almost 400 years of Portuguese slavery in Brazil.

The contemporary legacy of slavery in Brazil is apparent in the underclass status and circumstances of Afro-Brazilians and colorism (Lima, 2013). As in French and British racism, whiteness is associated automatically with high rank. One rarely sees a senior government or corporate official in Brazil who is not fair-skinned. Likewise, blackness is a mark of low status and inferiority. People of African ancestry are disproportionately poor, in the lower class, and criminalized, as they are in Britain and the U.S. Annually, Black Brazilians who practice Candomblé, the Afro-Brazilian faith, go to the ocean and offer prayers for those lost. There is no such recognition of losses during slavery in Britain or the U.S.

Slavery and "Freedom" in the United States

In 1619, a Dutch ship brought the first Africans to the British Jamestown, Virginia colony. They were pressed into indentured servitude. Like their European counterparts, the Africans were freed after seven years. Indentured servants and Africans interacted as equals and intermarried. We have known for some time that both these groups were of the same lower-social class, before slavery and before white supremacy (racism) was developed in what would become the U.S. (Bennett, 1966).

Wealthy British plantation owners were vastly outnumbered and depended upon indentured and free labor. They feared a union of ever-increasing numbers of African and European laborers would conduct progressively lethal and frequent rebellions that would eventually overthrow them i.e., Bacon's Rebellion. Only a small percentage of the adult population were landowners who could vote and serve in the colonial legislature. Planters used their status and their dominant position in government to pass laws in the colonial legislatures of Virginia and North Carolina to separate Africans from European labor. They did so by creating unequal races: one Black and another White, as a uniquely American institution (T.W. Allen, 1994; Cecil-Fronsman, 1992). They did so in the following way.

As explained in the introduction, unequal "races" were made possible by an ideology of White racial supremacy that justified the creation and expansion of a permanent slave labor workforce. Legislators redefined European ethnic and national identities (English, Irish, and German) as "white people" and declared them the superior race. Likewise, it was necessary to reduce African ethnicities (Ibo, Hausa, and Bantu) to "black people," and to declare them the inferior race. From 1620 to 1700, the House of Burgesses in the State of Virginia moved from defining and regulating inequity between Whites and Blacks to the legalization of Blacks as slaves for life.[4] From 1640 to 1705, these laws become more draconian and oppressive in legally defining and separating the races. Other colonies with the same security concerns adopted these laws and practices. By the American Revolution in 1776, slavery was well established and central to the nation's plantation economy and the basis of wealth. The American economy and the nation's initial wealth were derived from slavery (Williams, 1966). Slave labor was so central to the U.S. economy that it was maintained after the revolution and independence from Britain, and even after the British outlawed the slave trade on the high seas.

Slaves resisted. Often, slaves fled to northern free states and south to Mexico where they could escape slavery. The South moved to stop their losses. The allocation of U.S. congressional seats counted each slave as three-fifths of a person. Although slaves were not citizens and could not vote, they were counted in the apportionment of congressional seats in slave states, inflating the number of representatives from slave states in the U.S. Congress. Wealthy Southern planters used this advantage to pass the

Fugitive Slave Act of 1850. The act required Northern law enforcement officers to capture and return their property, i.e., the slaves. Many Northerners felt this was an imposition on their freedom, and they resented the law. This resentment, in turn, aided the abolitionists' cause.

In this conflict between the North and the South, slaves attempted to use the American legal system for recourse against their masters' mistreatment and to improve their conditions. A result was the U.S. Supreme Court decision, Dred Scott v. Sanford, in 1857. Dred Scott alleged that, as a slave who had been transported to a free state by his master, he was free. The court ruled that he had no rights under the law because he was not a citizen. He was returned to his master on March 16, 1857. Chief Justice Roger Taney's analysis: "[African Americans] had for more than a century before been regarded as beings of an inferior order, and altogether unfit to associate with the white race, either in social or political relations; and so far, inferior, that they had no rights which the white man was bound to respect; and that the negro might justly and lawfully be reduced to slavery for his benefit. He was bought and sold, and treated as an ordinary article of merchandise and traffic, whenever a profit could be made by it."

Ironically, slave resistance and abolition efforts did not end slavery in the U.S. as it had in France and Great Britain. By 1865, plantation economies were competing with manufacturing and industrialization for primacy in the U.S. economy (Fogel & Engerman, 1974). The U.S. fought a bloody civil war over which economic system would prevail. The slave South was crushed by the industrial might of the North and lost the war. The official abolition of slavery in the U.S. came in 1865. The Thirteenth Amendment to the Constitution abolished slavery and involuntary servitude. The Fourteenth Amendment, in 1868, granted citizenship to former slaves and granted equal protection under the law while the Fifteenth Amendment conferred voting rights on former slaves.

The period from 1865 to 1900 was transitional. The federal government, Northern churches, and civic organizations embarked on Black Reconstruction: the rebuilding of the South and the integration of former slaves into Southern civil society. However, under President Andrew Johnson, White planters re-established the "black codes," which increasingly restricted the activities of newly freed Blacks (Palmer, 2006). They could not vote, hold office, sit with Whites on public transportation, be out at night, testify against a White person in court, or go to the same schools. To be assured of a low-cost and compliant labor force, Southern property owners required Blacks to sign annual work contracts. If they refused to sign the contract, they could be arrested as vagrants. If they could not pay the fine to get out of jail, they were given lengthy jail sentences and forced into unpaid labor while incarcerated. In 1877, Congress and President

Hayes removed the federal troops who protected Black citizens and who enforced federal laws in the South.

This action removed the physical protection of Blacks had from hostile Whites and effectively eliminated Blacks' civil rights. Then, the U.S. Supreme Court made it clear what the post-slave status of Blacks was in the U.S. In Plessy v. Ferguson (1896), the court upheld state racial segregation laws for public facilities under the doctrine of "separate but equal" (Groves, 1951). Why were Southern Whites so fearful of Blacks? Major John Hammond Fordham gave the best explanation. He was a Black man who might have been the first and last Deputy Collector of the U.S. Internal Revenue for the District of South Carolina in 1889. In a speech before a White audience in 1908, Fordham is quoted as saying:

> "Forty years ago, the Negroes of the South did not own a square foot of ground nor a roof to cover them. Now, on the other hand, there are 130,000 farms owned by Negroes valued at $350 million; 150,000 homes outside farm ownership, valued at $265 million; and personal property valued at $165 million; 12 Negro banks; 3 magazines; 450 newspapers; 800 physicians in practice; 300 lawyers; 30,000 schoolteachers; 3,000 books in the home. So, starting from nothing here is an accumulation of a billion dollars.
>
> When work began, not one percent of the Negro adults of the South could read or write. Today 50 percent can do so, 55 percent of the children are attending school, and with more facilities, more would attend ... it can be said to our lasting credit that no matter what the cost, if we have to do with one meal a day and one suit a year, we are determined to educate our children" [E. Robinson, 1981].

What Whites feared most was Black economic progress, which thoroughly disproved their notions of Black inferiority and White supremacy. For the next half-century, Southern Whites evolved the most thorough and elaborate system of racial oppression ever devised: "Jim Crow" (Chafe & et al., 2001; H.C. Richardson, 2001). It regulated all interactions between Blacks and Whites, especially in the Deep South. Its purpose was to reinforce White supremacy and Black inferiority. Blacks had to sit in the back of buses and trains behind Whites, step off the sidewalk when passing Whites, and enter buildings by the back entrance. Black men were never to look directly at a White woman. Blacks were to address all White people, regardless of age, as "Mister" and "Mrs.," and were called "boy" or "gal," regardless of their status or age. It was forbidden to argue with, protest, or raise one's voice against a White person. If one worked or performed a service, one was paid whatever a White person wanted to pay. Any violation of this "etiquette" resulted in a beating. More grievous violations would lead to tar and feathering, rape, lynching, castration, dragging-to-death by rope, burning at the stake, being shot, or any combination of these punishments. Whites would come from miles around to picnic before lynchings, documented on postcards sent to friends and relatives (J. Allen, Als, Lewis, & Litwack, 2000). Whole Black communities were savagely wiped out in pogroms by nightriders who burned Black homesteads and raped and murdered Black residents. Jim Crow was such an effective system of oppression that South Africans modeled their Apartheid system after Jim Crow (Cell, 1982).

Like slavery before it, Jim Crow became an anachronism after the Second World War. The same U.S. Supreme Court that had paved the way for Jim Crow, in 1896, outlawed it in Brown v. Board of Education (1954). Like the amendments to the Constitution that followed the 1865 emancipation, the 1964 Civil Rights Act and the 1965 Voting Rights Act followed Brown V. Board of Education. These acts reinstated rights taken away by Jim Crow, which were guaranteed initially by 1865, 1868, and 1870 amendments to the Constitution.

The U.S. Legacy of Slavery

Criminal Justice: A central premise in racist ideation, dating back to colonial slavery, is that slaves and Black men, more specifically, are unable to control themselves. If left on their own, they will just run amok. As inferior beings incapable of a higher civilization, Blacks will steal, kill, suddenly fly into rages, destroy property, clown, and seek out and rape White women. As it was in the time of slavery, Black men cannot be trusted, are to be feared, must always be watched, and be physically controlled by White men. The culturally scripted role of contemporary police is precisely that of the slave overseer. It is to scrutinize Black people's day-to-day behaviors, to control them, and to confine them. Enforcing laws is just the overt expression for fulfilling a more profound and more essential mission, control of Blacks.

This is how the system works. A racist justice system will devote disproportionate numbers of police officers, courts, judges, and prosecutors to policing Black people, whether they commit crimes or not. Police will treat Blacks more harshly, will use violence against them more often, and routinely search and arrest them. The courts will prosecute them more aggressively, convict them more often, and sentence them to longer jail sentences than they do Whites. Just being in the system is enough to be convicted because of plea-bargaining (pleading guilty to a lesser charge to avoid serving a much longer jail sentence, if convicted), whether one committed a crime or not. Prosecutors and judges have no problem sending innocent Black people to jail. The presumption is that if Blacks did not commit the crime they are convicted of, they must have committed and got away with some similar crime. Therefore, any conviction is justified. In jail, they will be watched more vigilantly, treated more harshly, and released less frequently.

Blacks are more likely to be re-incarcerated repeatedly, thus remaining wards of the state for their lifetime. Laws have been passed to specifically criminalize Blacks to maintain their high numbers in the criminal justice system. Penalties for the use and possession of crack cocaine, sold mostly by Black youth, were four times those for the use and possession of powdered cocaine. The jails have been filled with Black youth for crack cocaine offenses, yet proportionately more White youth possess and use powder cocaine (Palamar, Davies, Ompad, Cleland, & Weitzman, 2015).

The criminal justice system in the U.S. is referred to cynically as "the prison industrial complex" (Alexander, 2010). One in every 15 African American men is incarcerated, as compared to one in every 106 White men. The Bureau of Justice Statistics (BJS) states that one in three Black men between 18 and 29 years old can expect to go to prison in their lifetime (NAACP, 2017). The BJS' National Prisoner Statistics reports 745,000 Black males are incarcerated in the U.S. This number is higher than the total prison populations in India, Argentina, Canada, Lebanon, Japan, Germany, Finland, Israel, and England combined.

Police racism is so prevalent in the U.S. that many young Black men accept the inevitability that jail-time is a rite of passage into manhood. Black youth see no hope for fair treatment and turn their anger upon themselves, and other young Black men. Clinically, we know that these young men are depressed. Their anger turns inward in the form of depression. They self-medicate with alcohol and drugs, leading to addiction, crime, and of course, more incarceration. Subsequently, their addiction is viewed as criminal behavior that must be punished. Their drug dependency is left untreated, both in and out of prison. Once these young men are convicted of a felony, they are unemployable and have severely limited housing opportunities. Landlords will not rent to felons. This means they are unable to support themselves or a family financially. They end up back in jail, which is the underlying goal of their involvement with criminal justice in the first place.

Education: If racism is the continued legacy of both slavery and Jim Crow, how does it affect contemporary education in the U.S.? The answer is in racism's inherited cultural script: if Blacks are to be educated at all, that education must be inferior to that of Whites. However, because of the 1964 Civil Rights Act, inferiority cannot be a direct outcome of decisions and actions by any person or organization that can be sued in court. Inferiority must be an indirect outcome of non-racially motivated behaviors and actions. In other words, inferior outcomes happen, and no one can be held directly responsible. Here is how.

State governments, rather than the federal government, fund schools in whatever way they like. The most common way to indirectly discriminate is to fund schools through local property taxes (Turner, Khrais, Lloyd, & Olgin, 2016). Each year, property owners are billed a percent of the assessed value of their property to pay for local schools. Poor (blacker) communities generate far less money than more affluent (whiter) communities. Poorer (blacker) communities have many more students, larger class sizes, and more students with a need for food, healthcare, security, and psychological help than better-off (whiter) communities. In contrast, more affluent (whiter) communities have more money to educate fewer students, and they have fewer needy students. They can maintain better facilities and pay higher salaries to hire more-experienced teachers. The outcome is better education for their students, higher graduation and college-entrance rates, than those found in more poorly funded (blacker) schools.

Even in school districts where poor (blacker) and better-off (whiter) schools pool district funding, educational outcomes are still unequal. Parent-teacher organizations in more affluent (whiter) schools can raise money to pay for academic and non-academic enhancements at their schools. The inferior schools (blacker) in the same district have no way of getting such enhancements. Their students still end up with deficient educations, lower graduation, and college-bound rates. The poorest-funded and functioning schools have all Black and Hispanic students and can be referred to as "failure factories" (Fitzpatrick, Gartner, & LaForgia, 2015). They have a high percentage of school dropouts and graduates alike who leave school illiterate. Many are attitudinally unemployable and end up going to jail and prison. Since the passage of the 1964 Civil Rights Act, the U.S. has continuously tried to improve its schools through reforms. The irony is that American schools are more segregated racially now than they were in 1954 when the Supreme Court ruled against racially segregated schools. We have known for some time precisely what improves student academic and psychosocial outcomes (R. Clark, 1983). However, schools throughout the U.S. with majority low-income students of color are still low academic performers with inferior facilities compared to higher-income White schools (Reardon, 2013). Sixty years of reforms have had no impact whatsoever.

Popular Culture: Racism in U.S. popular culture may be more toxic to Black student achievement and social development than racist school systems. Black parents, families, churches, and communities compete with corporate media, whose only interest is profits. In general, the competition is over who defines African American culture—blackness. The corporations are winning by continuously promoting sophisticated racist stereotypes of Black people (L. Lhamon, 1998). Black Hip Hop artists who are willing to act out these black racial stereotypes are rewarded with contracts, have their "art" promoted, and are well paid. Those who refuse to degrade themselves, as well as other Blacks, are ignored. The more Black youth listen to corporate Hip Hop, the lower their school performance, the more dysfunctional they become, the more common it is for them to refer to themselves and others as "niggers," and the more likely they will engage in violence (B.P. Bowser, 2012).

Other areas reaffirm the legacy of slavery and Jim Crow in the U.S. as well. There is racism in housing, employment, religion, higher education, the military, the professions, sports, and health and medicine. No institution in American life is spared. All have been impacted by racism and reinforce racial inequality. We know about racism in American institutional life, but there is another effect about which we know much less. It is the psychological legacy of slavery and Jim Crow in race-related trauma.

Psychological Legacy of Slavery: Trauma

Currently, there is increasing awareness in the U.S. that past trauma significantly affects present behavior. The most well-known example is returning military personnel suffering from Post-Traumatic Syndrome (PTS) (USDVA, 2017). To transcend PTS requires extensive psychotherapy, time, and often medication. Kellermann wrote about the Nazi-sponsored state attempt to kill all Jews in Europe during the Second World War: "Many still feel the enormous impact of Holocaust trauma upon their lives although over sixty years have passed since the Second World War" (Kellermann, 2001intro). His work extends to the grandchildren of survivors of the Holocaust trauma, who show that aspects of their grandparents' trauma can be passed on across generations.

The Trauma of Slavery and Jim Crow

The great-grandparents of living African Americans were the last generation of slaves of slaves in the 246 years of slavery in the U.S. No one is kidnapped, transported, sold to other people, against his or her will, without being forced and threatened with violence. No one is subservient to a master, does whatever he or she is told, receives no compensation whatsoever for a lifetime, without being forced and threatened with violence. No one has family members beaten, raped, and sold away, and children enslaved, as well, without force and the threat of it. Slavery was not about a single act of violence. It was about the continuous threat, swift punishment and brutality intended to make examples of violators, and to reinforce the power of their masters. Otherwise, how could a small minority of White men in Deep South counties successfully control large majority populations of slaves for generations?

Slavery was a system designed to terrorize slaves and make them internalize subservience and obedience. It was about unrelenting dehumanization and barbaric brutality, even for the times. Masters intended to traumatize their slaves with demonstrations of violence. In slavery, trauma was functional. It was designed to prevent slaves from imagining, dreaming, or even thinking about resistance, disobedience, or rebellion. It was a 246-year-long holocaust, which continued for another 100 years in the South during Jim Crow. There is a unique feature of slavery. It is possible that every slave, and every slave descendant who lived under Jim Crow, experienced multiple traumas. *There has been no acknowledgment, discussion, estimate, or assessment of the effects of multiple traumas on slaves and the descendants of slaves.* This is not about one-time trauma over 346 years (slavery and Jim Crow). It is about experiencing multiple traumas in each generation, for up to twelve generations.

The scope of trauma assessment for slavery in the U.S. is the equivalent of asking what effect twelve generations of accumulative trauma would have on any surviving descendants. What would be the Post Traumatic Syndrome (PTS) outcomes of American soldiers experiencing trauma, their children experiencing trauma, and their grandchildren experiencing trauma, and so on, for up to nine more generations? What would be the Post Traumatic Syndrome (PTS) outcomes of a 346 year long Nazi Holocaust for the descendants of Jewish slave laborers? The only way that one could deny that centuries of trauma did not leave deep psychological scars is to reject the humanity of those who experienced slavery in the West, and Jim Crow in the U.S. Any human being and their descendants who went through such an experience would be affected in some way. The psychological legacy of slavery has been left with the descendants of people who sang the Negro spiritual, "Oh, Lord How Come Me Here?": "Lord, how come me here? I wish I never was born. There ain't no freedom here, Lord. They treat me so mean here, Lord. They sold my chillen away, Lord, I wish I never was born. Lord, how come me here?" (Simpson-Curenton, 2002). The singers could not get answers to their questions during slavery. It is not clear whether their descendants can get any better answers today.

Contemporary Racial Trauma

Two Black psychiatrists, William Grier and Price Cobbs wrote a book entitled *Black Rage* years ago (1968). The book examined dimensions of the inner conflicts, desperation, and despair of black life in the United States, mirrored in the lyrics above. Grier and Cobbs may have tapped into something much more profound than black anger against modern white racism and discrimination. Others have speculated more deeply about the psychological legacy of slavery, and Jim Crow ignored by Whites and Blacks alike (Akbar, 1996; Eyerman, 2001; Willis, 2006). Joy A. DeGruy's book, *The Post Traumatic Slave Syndrome* (2005), is an example. It bridges the slave past with the present, best articulating the psychological legacy of slavery as a syndrome:

> PTSS is a condition that exists as a consequence of multigenerational oppression of Africans and their descendants resulting from centuries of chattel slavery—a form of slavery predicated on the belief that African Americans/Blacks were inherently/genetically inferior to Whites. This was then followed by institutionalized racism, which continues to perpetuate injury. Thus, multigenerational trauma together with continued oppression, the absence of opportunity to heal or access the benefits available in the society leads to Post Traumatic Slave Syndrome [Joy A. DeGruy Leary, 2005, p. 121].

DeGruy's PTSS hypothesis is a challenge to explore in-depth what might be the consequences of generations of unresolved traumas as a psychological legacy dating back to slavery. There is an illustration of criminal justice racism. Crime data show that young Black and Latino men commit most drug-related and violent crimes with weapons. The logic follows that the police should stop and frisk anyone suspected of carrying a weapon or possessing drugs. This is legally justified under "probable cause" and can be reasoned further as a preventive measure. When young men realize they may be stopped and frisked, they might stop carrying drugs and weapons, reducing spontaneous gun violence. The problem is that most White police cannot distinguish a Black or Latino crime suspect from most Blacks or Latinos who commit no crimes. They cannot distinguish most Black persons from another. As Whites, they have never had to learn how to distinguish one Black person from another. Add to this a deep-seated belief that all Blacks and Latinos are inferior, criminally prone, and must be controlled. The outcomes are arbitrary and capricious stops based upon nothing more than race: a clear civil rights violation.

Arbitrary police stops are potentially traumatic because they can compound unresolved past trauma. The young men who are stopped and frisked are reduced immediately to a slave-like condition. They are powerless not to be stopped and frisked. The young men are fearful because they know they can be shot dead if they try to run. The police can frame them for a crime they did not commit, abuse them, take away their freedom, and get away with it. Imagine, "I am in my neighborhood in front of my neighbors being forced to lean against a wall. I am bent over with my legs spread apart, and cops are feeling all over me." This is humiliating and a form of public rape. Just as during slavery, "everyone around me is also powerless to interfere and do anything." If by-standers say anything or ask questions about their legal rights, they too become victims. They get arrested and charged with interfering with the police, for insubordination, or for threatening police authority. The young men are angry because they know that what is happening to them is abusive and unjust. Some may be traumatized by this experience, along with their families. Depending upon their personal and family histories, this may be another unresolved trauma on top of many other unresolved traumas: a psychological legacy dating back to slavery.

How do the victims of police abuse cope? The answer is the same ways that slaves had to cope. They swallow their anger and displace it on family, friends, and neighbors, and sometimes in domestic violence. They turn anger inward on themselves, become depressed. They self-medicate with alcohol and drugs, and addiction is the outcome. They turn outward with suicide ideation and rage, only to risk a violent confrontation with the police: suicide by police. Finally, they can disassociate. They can deny that they were stopped and frisked ever. They might become the police and to identify with them, following the Stockholm syndrome.

Conclusion

Some White Americans respond to any reference to African slavery, and any past or present trauma, hurt, or humiliation experienced by African Americans, with the declaration to "get over it." This is precisely what we want to do, but not in the way these Whites want us to do it. The way to get over unresolved trauma accumulated in the past and present is not to ignore it and forget it, as Whites would like us to do. We will get over the psychological legacy of slavery by learning as much as possible about it. We must break our silence and denial. We must confront what happened to us and understand how the past affects us in the present. The ways we learned to cope may have been functional at the time, but now limit our lives, consciously, or unconsciously. This is how we will get over it.

Resolving past trauma and the psychological legacy of slavery is not work that we can do alone. It requires a collective effort and may take generations. "Getting over it" is also about serving as witnesses for acknowledging what we forgot and deny. A collective reconciliation with the past, as well as the effects it had, is essential to "getting over it." There are potentially exciting new tools from genetics that may help us to understand the long-term impact of trauma across generations (Kellermann, 2001). This and subsequent chapters in this book comprise the first step in this essential exploration toward understanding our psychological legacy from slavery and toward resolution of whatever burdens we carry from the past.

Notes

1. Ted Talk and personal communications, 2016.
2. Many slaveholders viewed Christian teaching as their duty and converts to the Church of England were required to be literate enough to read a catechism.
3. See You Tube: Dumping Slaves at Sea Is Wrong—https://www.youtube.com/watch?v=tF1Kj2hhXsE
4. General Assembly of VA: Slavery Law 1662.

References

Abramova, S.U. (1979). Ideological, Doctrinal, Philosophical, Religious, and Political Aspacts the African Slave Trade. In UNESCO (Ed.), *The African Slave Trade from the Fifteenth to the Nineteenth Century* (Vol. 2). Paris: UNESCO.
Akbar, N. (1996). *Breaking the Chains of Psychological Slavery*. Tallahassee, FL: Mind Productions & Assoc.
Alagoa, E.J. (1999). Fon and Yoruba: The Niger Delta and the Cameroon. In B.A. Ogot (Ed.), *The General History of Africa* (Vol. 5, pp. 434–452). Paris: UNESCO.
Alexander, M. (2010). *The New Jim Crow: Mass Incarceration in the Age of Colorblindness*. New York: The New Press.
Allen, J., Als, H., Lewis, J., & Litwack, L. (2000). *Without Sanctuary: Lynching Photography in America*. Santa Fe: Twin Palms Publishing.
Allen, T.W. (1994). *The Invention of the White Race*. New York: Verso.
Alphonse, R. (2014). Jean-Claude Duvalier jugeable pour crime contre l'humanité. *Le Nouvelliste*. Retrieved from http://lenouvelliste.com/lenouvelliste/article/127848/Jean.
American Anthropological Association. (1996). AAA Statement on Race. *American Association of Physical Anthropologists, 101*, 569–570.
American Psychiatric Association. (2013). *Diagnostic and Statistical Manual of Mental Disorders* (5 ed.). Arlington, VA: American Psychiatric Publishing.
Aptheker, H. (1983). *American Negro Slave Revolts*. New York: International Publishers.
Baldwin, J. (1955). *Notes of a Native Son*. Boston: Beacon Press.
Barzun, J. (1965). *Race: A Study of Superstition*. New York: Harper and Row Publishers.
Bell, C. (2017). Lessons Learned from 50 Years of Violence Prevention Activities in the African American Community. *Journal of the American Medical Association, 109*(4).
Bell, C., & McBride, D. (2014). Psychiatry for People of African Descent in the USA: The Massachusetts General Hospital Textbook on Diversity and Cultural Sensitivity in Mental Health. *Current Clinical Psychiatry*. doi:10.1007/978-1-4614-8918-4_6.
Bennet, D., & Fraser, M. (2000). Urban Violence Among African American Males: Integrating Family, Neighborhood, and Peer Perspectives. *Journal of Sociology and Social Welfare, 27*(3), 93–117.
Bennett, L. (1966). *Before the Mayflower, 1619–1964*. Baltimore: Penguin Books.
Bettelheim, B. (1940). Comportement individuel et de masse dans les situations extrêmes. *The Journal of Abnormal and Social Psychology, 38*(4), 417–452.
Bettelheim, B. (1979). *Survivre*. Paris: Robert Laffont.
Billingsley, A. (1968). *Black Families in White America*. Englewood Cliffs: Prentice-Hall.
Blanc, J. (2015, October 6). Sommes une société de malades mentaux. *Le Nouvelliste*. Retrieved from http://lenouvelliste.com/lenouvelliste/article/150560/Sommes-nous-une-societe-de-malades-mentaux.
Blanc, J. (2016). Et si la psychologie cognitive pouvait casser le mythe que le Kreyòl n'est pas une langue scientifique? In F. Piron, S. Regulus, & S.D. Madiba (Eds.), *Justice cognitive, libre accès et savoirs locaux*. Quebec: Editions science bien commun.
Blanc, J., Rahill, G., Laconi, S., & Mouchenik, Y. (2016). Religion, Depression and Resilience in Survivors of Earthquake in Haiti. *Journal of Affective Disorders, 190*, 697–703.
Blassingame, J. (1972). *The Slave Community: Plantation Life in the Antebellum South*. New York: Oxford University Press.

Bly, A.T. (2017). Encyclopedia Virginia. Retrieved from https://www.encyclopediavirginia.org/about.
Boahen, A.A. (1999). The States and Cultures of the Lower Guinean Coast. In B.A. Ogot (Ed.), *The General History of Africa* (Vol. 5, pp. 399–433). Paris: UNESCO.
Bolland, O.N. (1988). *Colonialism and Resistance in Belize: Essays in Historical Sociology*. Belize: Cubola/Spear/Iser.
Bowser, B. (2012). *Gangster Rap and Its Social Cost: Exploiting Hip Hop and Using Racial Stereotypes to Entertain America*. Amherst, NY: Cambria Press.
Bowser, B., & Hunt, R. (Eds.). (1996). *Impacts of Racism on White Americans* (2nd ed.). Thousand Oaks, CA: Sage Publications.
Bowser, B., Word, C., Stanton, M.D., & Coleman, S.B. (2003). Death in the Family and HIV Risk-Taking Among Intravenous Drug Users. *Family Process, 42*(2), 291–304.
Bowser, B.P. (2012). *Gangster Rap and Its Social Cost: Exploiting Hip Hop and Using Racial Stereotypes to Entertain America*. Amhurst, NY: Cambria Press.
Branscom, M. (1998, November 1). DNA Test Finds Evidence That Thomas Jefferson and Slave Had a Child. *New York Times*, p. 20.
Brown, G. (2010). The Tragedy of Haïti: A Reason for Major Cultural Change. *The ABNF Journal, Fall*.
Buchanan, K. (2011). Slavery in the French Colonies: Le Code Noir (the Black Code) of 1685. Retrieved from https://blogs.loc.gov/law/2011/01/slavery-in-the-french-colonies/
Bulwer, B. (2016, July 16). A Call for Belizean Self-Reflection and Unity. *Amandala*, p. 43.
Burgest, D.R. (1981). Theory on White Supremacy/Black Oppression. *Black Books Bulletin, 7*(2), XXXX.
Butterfield, F. (1995). *All God's Children: The Bosket Family and the American Tradition of Violence*. New York: Avon Books.
Carey, B. (2005). *British Abolitionism and the Rhetoric of Sensibility: Writing, Sentiment, and Slavery, 1760–1807*. Basingstoke: Palgrave Macmillan.
Cayemittes, M., Busangu, M.F., Bizimana, J.D., Barrère, B., Sévère, B., Cayemittes, V., & Charles, E. (2013). *Enquête Mortalité, Morbidité et Utilisation des Services, Haïti, 2012*. Maryland, USA: MSPP, IHE et ICF International.
Cecil-Fronsman, B. (1992). *Common Whites: Class and Culture in Antebellum North Carolina*. Lexington: University Press of Kentucky.
Cell, J.W. (1982). *The Highest Stage of White Supremacy: The Origins of Segregation in South Africa and the American South*. New York: Oxford University Press.
Césaire, A. (1956). Cahier d'un retour au pays natal. *Présence Africaine*.
Chafe, W.H., & et al. (Eds.). (2001). *Remembering Jim Crow: African Americans Tell About Life in the Segregated South*. New York: New Press.
Charbonnier, C.-L. (Ed.) (2000). *La Véridique Histoire, Par Lui-Même, d'Olaudah Equiano Africain, Esclave Aux Caraïbes, Homme Libre*. Paris: Caribéennes.
Charles-Nicolas, A. (2003). La force de la magie. *Psychiatries, 140*, 31–34.
Clark, K.B., & Clark, M.P. (1940). Skin Color as a Factor in Racial Identification of Negro Preschool children. *Journal of Social Psychology, 11*, 159–169.
Clark, K.B., & Clark, M.P. (1947). Racial Identification and Preference in Negro Children. In T.M. Newcomb & E.L. Hartley (Eds.), *Readings in Social Psychology* (pp. 169–178). New York: Holt.
Clark, R. (1983). *Family Life and School Achievement: Why Poor Black Children Succeed or Fail*. Chicago: The University of Chicago Press.
Coates, T. (2015). *Between the World and Me*. New York: Random House.
Comer, J.P. (1980). *The Black Family an Adaptive Perspective*. New Haven: Yale University Child Center.
Corvington, G. (2007). *Port-au-Prince au cours des ans. Tome III, La capitale sous l'occupation (1915–1934)*. Montreal: Les Editions CIDHICA.
Cross, W.E., Jr. (1991). *Shades of Black: Diversity in African-American Identity*. Philadelphia: Temple University Press.
Cunin, É. (2004). *Métissage et multiculturalisme en Colombie*. Paris: IRD Éditions/L'Harmattan.

Cyrulnik, B. (2002). *Un merveilleux malheur*. Paris: Odile Jacob.
Dalal, F. (2002). *Race, Color and the Process of Racialization*. London: Routledge.
Davis, A. (1941). *Deep South*. Chicago: The University of Chicago Press.
Davis, A., & Dollard, J. (1940). *Children of Bondage*. Washington, D.C.: American Council on Education.
DeGruy, J. (2005). *Post Traumatic Slave Syndrome*: Milwaukie, OR: Uptone Press.
DeGruy, J., Kjellstrand, J.M., Briggs, H.E., & Brennan, E.M. (2011). Racial Respect and Racial Socialization as Protective Factors for African American Male Youth. *Journal of Black Psychology*.
DeGruy, J.A. (2017). *Post Traumatic Slave Syndrome: America's Legacy of Enduring Injury and Healing*. Portland: J.D.P. Publisher.
DeGruy Leary, J. (2009). *Post Traumatic Slave Syndrome: America's Legacy of Enduring Injury and Healing: The Study Guide*. Portland: J.D.P. Publisher.
Deveau, J.-M. (1994). *La France aux temps des négriers*. Paris: Éditions France Empire.
Diène, D. (2005). *Préface à Les codes noirs hispaniques de Manuel-Lucena Salmoral*: UNESCO.
Drake, S.C. (1987). *Black Folk Here and There* (Vol. 1–2). Los Angeles: Center for Afro-Americans Studies, University of California Los Angeles.
Duval, F. (2011). Jean Claude Duvalier est de retour. *Le Nouvelliste*. Retrieved from http://lenouvelliste.com/lenouvelliste/article/87864/Jean-Claude-Duvalier-est-de-retour.
Edwards, B. (2011). The Most Resilient People on Earth: Haiti Still Standing After Trio of Disasters. *Frontlines*. Retrieved from https://www.usaid.gov/news-information/frontlines/haitiwomen-development/most-resilient-people-earth-haiti-still-standing.
Eligon, J., & Gebeloff, R. (2016, August 20). Affluent and Black, and Still Trapped by Segregation: Well-Off Black Families End Up Living in Poorer Areas Than White Families with Similar or Even Lower Incomes. *New York Times*.
Ellison, R. (1952). *Invisible Man*. New York: Random House.
Ely, M.P. (1991). *The Adventures of Amos 'n' Andy: A Social History of an American Phenomenon*. New York: Free Press.
Eyerman, R. (2001). *Cultural Trauma: Slavery and the Formation of African American Identity*. New York: Cambridge University Press.
Fagan, A.A. (2005). The Relationship Between Adolescent Physical Abuse and Criminal Offending: Support for an Enduring and Generalized Cycle of Violence. *Journal of Family Violence, 20*(5), 279–290.
Fanon, F. (1952). *Black Skin White Masks*. Paris: Editions du Seuil.
Fanon, F. (1963). *The Wretched of the Earth*. New York: Grove Press, Inc.
Fanon, F. (1967). *Black Skin, White Masks*. New York: Grove Press.
Fitzpatrick, C., Gartner, L., & LaForgia, M. (2015). *Failure Factories: The Story of How One School Board Turned Five Average Schools Into Some of the Worst in Florida*. The Tampa Bay Times.
Fogel, R.W., & Engerman, S.L. (1974). *Time on the Cross: The Economics of American Negro Slavery*. Boston: Little, Brown and Company.
Frazier, E.F. (1939). *The Negro Family in the United States*. Chicago: University of Chicago Press.
Freud, S. (1996). *A Project for Scientific Psychology. The Standard Edition of the Complete Psychological Works of Sigmund Freud, 1950* (Vol. 1). London: Hogarth Press.
Freud, S. (2003). *Beyond the Pleasure Principle*. London: PENG.
Fryer, P. (1984). *Staying Power: The History of Black People in Britain*. London: Pluto Press.
Fullilove, M., & Wallace, R. (2011). Serial Forced Displacement in American Cities, 1916–2010. *Journal of Urban Health, 88*(3), 381–389.
Geffrard, R.A. (2013). Les victimes de Duvalier n'ont pas encore fait leur deuil. *Le Nouvelliste*. Retrieved from http://lenouvelliste.com/lenouvelliste/article/116154/Les-victimes-des-Duvalier-nont-pas-encore-fait-leur-deuil.
Genovese, E. (1976). *Roll, Jordan, Roll: The World the Slaves Made*. New York: Vintage Books.
Gilbert, P. (2006). *1848: Chronique de l'abolition de l'esclavage*. Martinique: Desnel édit.
Glissant, E. (1997). *Le Discours Antillais*. Paris: Gallimard.
Gold, J., Wolan, S.M., & Lewis, M. (2011). The Relation Between Abuse and Violent

Delinquency: The Conversion of Shame to Blame in Juvenile Offenders. *Child Abuse and Neglect, 35*, 459–467.
Goldstein, E.L. (2006). *The Price of Whiteness: Jews, Race, and American Identity.* Princeton: Princeton University Press.
Grandmaison, O.L.C. (2010). *De l'Indigénat. Anatomie d'un monstre juridique: Le Droit colonial en Algérie et dans l'Empire français.* Paris: Éditions La Découverte.
Greenwood, R., & Hamber, S. (1979). *Arawaks to Africans.* London: Macmillan.
Grier, W.H., & Cobbs, P.M. (1968). *Black Rage.* New York: Basic Books.
Groves, H. (1951). Separate but Equal—The Doctrine of Plessy v. Ferguson. *Phylon, 12*(1), 66–72.
Guerra, A. (2011). Crítica de uma morte anunciada. *Interfaces. Belo Horizonte, Arte e Prosa,* 129–145.
Gutman, H.G. (1976). *The Black Family in Slavery and Freedom 1750–1925.* New York: Pantheon Books.
Hall, G.M. (2005). *Slavery and African Ethnicities in the Americas: Restoring the Links.* Chapel Hill: The University of North Carolina Press.
Haller, J. (1971). *Outcasts from Evolution.* Carbondale: Southern Illinios University Press.
Hawthorne, W. (2010). *From Africa to Brazil: Culture, Identity and an Atlantic Slave Trade, 1600–1830.* Cambridge: Cambridge University Press.
Hazzard-Gordon, K. (1990). *Jookin': The Rise of Social Dance Formations in African American Culture.* Philadelphia: Temple University Press.
Herskovits, M. (1958). *The Myth of the Negro Past.* Boston: Beacon Press.
Hill, R. (1972). *The Strengths of Black Families.* New York: Emerson Hall.
Himle, J.A., Baser, R.E., Taylor, R.J., Campbell, R.D., & Jackson, J.S. (2009). Anxiety Disorders Among African Americans, Blacks of Caribbean Descent, and Non-Hispanic Whites in the United States. *J. Anxiety Disorder, 23*(5), 578–590.
Holden, K.B., Bradford, L.D., Hall, S.P., & Belton, A.S. (2013). Prevalence and Correlates of Depressive Symptoms and Resiliency Among African American Women in a Community-Based Primary Health Care Center. *Journal of health care for the poor and underserved, 24*(4 0), 79–93. doi:10.1353/hpu.2014.0012.
Holmes, R.M. (1995). *How Young Children Perceive Race.* Thousand Oaks, CA: Sage Publications.
Horsman, R. (1981). *Race and Manifest Destiny the Origins of American Racial Anglo-Saxonism.* Cambridge, MA: Harvard University Press.
Hunte, H.E., Mentz, G., House, J.S., & et al. (2012). Variations in Hypertension-Related Outcomes Among Blacks, Whites and Hispanics in Two Large Urban Areas and in the United States. *Ethn Dis, 22*(4), 391–397.
Hurbon, L. (1987). *Comprendre Haïti, Essai sur l'Etat, la Nation, la Culture.* Paris: Les Editions Karthala.
Hyde, E.X. (1972, Unknown). *Amandala.*
Hyde, E.X. (1975). *Feelings: Colourism: The Deeper Problem.* Belize City: Benex Press.
Hyde, E.X. (1995). *X Communication.* Belize City, Belize: The Angelus Press Ltd.
Ignatiev, N. (1995). *How the Irish Became White.* New York: Routledge.
Institut Haïtien de Statistique et d'Informatique IHSI. (2003). *Enquête sur les Conditions de Vie en Haïti (ECVH).* Port-au-Prince, Haiti.
Institut Haïtien de Statistiques et d'Informatique IHSI. (2009). *Grandes leçons sociodémographiques tirées du 4e Recensement General de la Population Haïtienne.* Port-au-Prince.
Institut Haïtien de Statistiques et d'Informatiques IHSI. (2007). *Estimation et projection de la population totale urbaine, rurale et économiquement active.* Port-au-Prince: Bibliothèque Nationale d'Haïti.
Ives, K. (2013, May 10). HAITI: Independence Debt, Reparations for Slavery and Colonialism and International Aid. *Global Research.*
Jackson, M.Y. (1976). *The Struggle for Freedom: Phase I as Revealed in Slave Narratives of the Pre–Civil War Period.* Chicago: Adams Press.
Johnson, C. (1941). *Growing Up in the Black Belt.* Washington, D.C.: American Council on Education.
Joseph, F. (2009, 11 decembre). Haiti-Littérature: Une abondante récolte de prix littéraires

pour Haïti. *TiPiTi Biz*. Retrieved from http://tipiti.biz/site/2009/12/11/haiti-litterature-une-abondante-recolte-de-prix-litteraires-pour-haiti/.
Karenga, M. (1982). *Introduction to Black Studies*. Los Angeles: Kawaida Publication.
Kellerman, N. (209). *Holocaust Trama: Psychological Effects and Treatment*. New York: iUniverse.
Kellermann, N.P. (2001). Transmission of Holocaust Trauma—An Integrative View. *Psychiatry, 64*(3), 256–267.
Kennedy, C.L. (2012). Toward Effective Mental Health Intervention for Children Formerly in Restavèk. Creole Summary (Etid sou Sante Mantal Timoun ki te RestavÃ¨k.Pou rive nan entÃ¨vansyon sante mantal ki efikas.pdf). Retrieved from https://beyondborders.net/downloads/.
Kessler, R., Sonnega, A., Bromet, E., Hughes, M., & Nelson, C. (1995). Posttraumatic Stress Disorder in the National Comorbidity Survey. *Arch Gen Psychiatry, 52*(12), 1048–1060.
Kitwana, B. (1994). *The Rap on Gangster Rap, Who Runs It: Gangster Rap and Visions of Black Violence*. Chicago: Third World Press.
Kleinman, A. (1995). *Writing at the Margin, Discourse Between Anthropology and Medicine*. Berkeley: University of California Press.
Labelle, M. (1987). *Idéologie de couleur et classes sociales en Haïti. Les Éditions du CIDIHCA*. Montréal: Les Presses de l'Université de Montréal.
Leary, J.D. (2005). *Post Traumatic Slave Syndrome: America's Legacy of Enduring Injury and Healing*. Milwaukie, OR: Uptone Press.
Leary, J.D., Brennan, E., & Briggs, H.E. (2005). The African American Adolescent Respect Scale: A Measure of a Prosocial Attitude. *Research on Social Work Practice, 15*, 466.
Lebigot, F. (1998). Le débriefing individuel du traumatisé psychique. *Annales Médico-Psychologiques, 156*, 417–421.
Léger, J.N. (1907). *Haiti, Her History and Her Detractors*. New York: Neale Publishing Company.
Leslie, R. (Ed.) (1996). *A History of Belize: Nation in the Making*. Benque Viejo del Carmen, Belize: Cubola Productions.
Lhamon, W.T. (1998). *Raising Cain: Blackface Performance from Jim Crow to Hip Hop*. Cambridge: Harvard University Press.
Libby, D.J. (2004). *Slavery and Frontier Mississippi, 1720–1835*. Jackson: University Press of Mississippi.
Lima, M. (2013). The Sound of the Drum: Teaching and Learning African History and the History of Africans in Brazil. In P. Lovejoy & B. Bowser (Eds.), *The Transatlantic Slave Trade and Slavery: New Directions in Teaching and Learning* (pp. 13–28). Trenton: Africa World Press.
Littlefield, D. (1981). *Race and Slaves: Ethnicity and the Slave Trade in Colonial South Carolina*. Urbana: University of Illinois Press.
Littlewood, R., & Lipsedge, M. (2013). Aliens and Alienists. *British Journal of Psychiatry, 203*.
Lohof, F.W. (2010). Overview of the Genetics of Major Depressive Disorder. *Curr. Psychiatry Reports, 12*(6), 539–546.
Louidor, W.E. (2006). Haïti: L'insalubrité comme thermomètre politique. *Alterpresse*. Retrieved from http://www.alterpresse.org/spip.php?article5407#.WPI8JFM1_GI.
Lovejoy, P., & Bowser, B. (Eds.). (2012). *The Transatlantic Salve Trade and Slavery: New Directions in Teaching and Learning*. Trenton, NJ: Africa World Press.
Madhere, S. (2016). Kolonizasyon ak Ekoloji Sosyal: Konsekans Fizyolojik, Sikolojik, ak Enfliyans yo sou Lasante. In J. Blanc, S. Madhere, & S. Ulysse (Eds.), *Pensée afro-caribéenne et (psycho)traumatismes de l'esclavage et de la colonisation*. Québec: Editions science bien commun.
Madiou, T. (1849). *Histoire d'Haïti, Tome III. Les Editions Imprimerie*. Port-au-Prince, Haïti: J. H Courtois.
Malcolm X. (1965). *Malcolm X Speaks*. New York: Grove Press.
Massé, R. (2001). Pour une ethno-épidémiologie critique de la détresse psychologique à la Martinique. *Sciences sociales et santé, 19*(1), 45–47.
Matthews, E. (2007). *HMS Resolute and How She Prevented a War* United Kingdom: Auxilium ab Alto Press (online).

Mattos, H., & Abreu, M. (2011). Remanescentes das Comunidades dos Quilombos: memória do cativeiro, patrimônio cultural e direito á reparação. *Iberoamericana: Madrid, 42,* 147–160.
M'Bokolo, E.M. (1999). From the Cameroon Grasslands to the Upper Nile. In B.A. Ogot (Ed.), *The General History of Africa* (pp. 515–545). Paris: UNESCO.
McFarlane, A., & de Girolamo, G. (1996). The Nature of Traumatic Stressors and the Epidemiology of Posttraumatic Reactions. In B. van der Kolk, A. McFarlane, & L. Weisaeth (Eds.), *Traumatic Stress: The Effects of Overwhelming Experience on Mind, Body, and Society* (pp. 129–154). New York: The Guilford Press.
McIntosh, P. (2009). *White People Facing Race: Uncovering the Myths That Keep Racism in Place.* Wellesley, MA: The Saint Paul Foundation, Wellesley Center for Women, Wellesley College.
Miano, L. (2013). *La saison de l'ombre.* Paris: Grasset.
Miller, G.E., Chen, E., & Zhou, E.S. (2007). If It Goes Up, Must It Come Down? Chronic Stress and the Hypothalamic-Pituitary-Adrenocortical Axis in Humans. *Psychological Bulletin, 133*(1), 25–45.
Ministère de la Planification et de la Coopération Externe. (2015). *Le développent social. Des Lycées construits et réhabilités dans les dix départements géographiques d'Haïti* Port-au-Prince: Gouvernement de la République d'Haïti.
Ministère de la Sante Publique et de la Population MSPP. (2012). Politique Nationale de Sante. https://mspp.gouv.ht/site/downloads/livret%20pns%20for%20web.pdf.
Mintz, S., & Price, R. (1976). *The Birth of African-American Culture: An Anthropological Perspective.* Boston: Beacon Press.
Monk, E.P. (2015). The Cost of Color: Skin Color, Discrimination, and Health among African-Americans. *The American Journal of Sociology, 121*(2), 396–444.
Morris, T. (1996). *Southern slavery and the law, 1619–1860.* Chapel Hill: The University of North Carolina Press.
NAACP. (2017). Criminal Justice Fact Sheet. Retrieved from http://www.naacp.org/criminal-justice-fact-sheet/.
Ndiaye, P. (2009). *La condition noire: essai sur une minorité française.* Paris: Calmann-Levy.
Nichols, E.J. (1976). Introduction to the Axiological Model. Paper presented at the World Psychiatric Association and the Nigerian Association of Psychiatrists, University of Ibadan, Nigeria.
NIDA Notes. (1999). *Infectious Disease and Drug Abuse.* Washington, D.C.: U.S. Department of Health and Human Services.
Orata, F.D., Keim, P.S., & Boucher, Y. (2014). The 2010 Cholera Outbreak in Haiti: How Science Solved a Controversy. *PLoS Pathog., 10*(4).
Organisation Mondiale de la Santé. (1992). *CIM-10, Classification internationale des troubles mentaux et des troubles du comportement: descriptions cliniques et directives pour le diagnostic.* Paris: Masson.
Palamar, J.J., Davies, S., Ompad, D.C., Cleland, C.M., & Weitzman, M. (2015). Powder Cocaine and Crack Use in the United States: An Examination of Risk for Arrest and Socioeconomic Disparities in Use. *Drug and Alcohol Dependence, 149,* 108–116.
Palmer, V.V. (2006). The Customs of Slavery: The War Without Arms. *American Journal of Legal History, 2*(48), 177.
Persaud, R. (2004). *Why Black Men Love White Women: An Explicit Excursion in Sexual Politics.* Brooklyn, NY: D & R Publishing.
Perse, E.M. (2001). *Media Effects and Society.* Mahwab, NJ: Erlbaum Associates.
Peterson, M. (1975). *The Portable Thomas Jefferson: Notes on the State of Virginia, 1781.* New York: Viking Press.
Piarrous, R. (2010). Rapport de mission sur l'épidémie de choléra en Haïti. Retrieved from http://www.ph.ucla.edu/epi/snow/piarrouxcholerareport_french.pdf.
Pierre-Charles, P. (2013). *Frantz Fanon: L'héritage.* Fort-de-France: KEditions.
Porter, J. (1971). *Black Child, White Child: The Development of Racial Attitudes.* Cambridge, MA: Harvard University Press.
Powdermaker, H. (1939). *After Freedom.* New York: Viking Press.
Prepetit, C. (2008, 10–12 octobre). Tremblements de terre en Haïti: Mythes ou réalités *Le Matin.*

Retrieved from http://bme.gouv.ht/risques%20geologiques/LeMatin_s%C3%A9ismes.pdf.
Prince, M. (2000). *La Véritable Histoire de Mary Prince: Esclave antillaise*. Paris: Albin Michel.
Pugh, R.W. (1972). *Psychology and the Black Experience*. Monterey, CA: Brooks/Cole.
Puttagunta, R., Tedeschi, A., Sória, M.G., Hervera, A., Lindner, R., Rathore, K.I., ... Di Giovanni, S. (2014). PCAF-Dependent Epigenetic Changes Promote Axonal Regeneration in the Central Nervous System. *Nature Communications*, 5, 3527.
Rawick, G. (1972). *The American Slave: A Composite Autobiography: From Sundown to Sunup. The Making of the Black Community*, vol. 1. Westport, CT: Greenwood Publishing Company.
Reardon, S.F. (2013). The Widening Income Achievement Gap. *Educational Leadership*, 70(8), 10–16.
Richardson, B.L., & Wade, B. (2000). *What Mama Couldn't Tell Us About Love: Healing the Emotional Legacy of Slavery by Celebrating Our Light*. New York: Perennial.
Richardson, H.C. (2001). *The Death of Reconstruction: Race, Labor and Politics in the Post-Civil War North, 1865–1901*. Cambridge: Harvard University Press.
Robinson, E. (1981, December 13). Looking Homeward at Four Generations. *The Washington Post*.
Robinson, J.L. (1995). *Racism or Attitude? The Ongoing Struggle for Black Liberation and Self-Esteem*. New York: Insight Books Plenum Press.
Rogers, K.L., Leydesdorff, S., & Dawson, G. (Eds.). (1999). *Trauma and Life Stories: International Perspectives*. London: Routledge.
Rothstein, R. (2017). *The Color of Law*. New York: W.W. Norton & Company.
Rothstein, R., & Gross, T. (2015). Historian Says Don't 'Sanitize' How Our Government Created Ghettos. National Public Radio. Retrieved from http://www.npr.org/2015/05/14/406699264/historian-says-dont-sanitize-how-our-government-created-the-ghettos.
Rutter, M. (1985). Resilience in the Face of Adversity: Protective Factors and Resilience to Psychiatric Disorder. *The British Journal of Psychiatry*, 147, 598–611.
Saint-Fort, H. (2010). Le mythe de la langue française, butin de guerre des ex colonisés francophones? Potomitan. Retrieved from http://www.potomitan.info/ayiti/langue3.php.
Shoman, A. (1994). *Thirteen Chapters of A History of Belize*. Belize City, Belize: The Angelus Press.
Simpson-Curenton. (2002). Lord, How Come Me Here? In M. Hogan (Ed.), *The Oxford Book of Spirituals* (pp. 232). New York: Oxford University Press.
Smith, J.R. (2015). Unequal Burdens of Loss: Examining the Frequency and Timing of Homicide Deaths Experienced by Young Black Men Across the Life Course. *Am J Public Health*, 105 Suppl 3, S483–490. doi:10.2105/ajph.2014.302535.
Smith, M.J. (2009). *Red & Black in Haiti: Radicalism, Conflict, and Political Change, 1934–1957*. Chapel Hill: University of North Carolina Press.
Southwick, S.M., Bonanno, G.A., Masten, A.S., Panter-Brick, C., & Yehuda, R. (2014). Resilience and Trauma. Resilience Definitions, Theory, and Challenges: Interdisciplinary Perspectives. *European Journal of Psychotraumatology*, 5(25338).
Stampp, K.M. (1956). *The Peculiar Institution: Slavery in the Anti-Bellum South*. New York: Vintage Books.
Sterkenburg, J.V., Knoppers, A., & Leeuw, S.D. (2010). Race, Ethnicity, and Content Analysis of the Sports Media: A Critical Reflection. *Media, Culture and Society*, 32(5), 819–839.
Stuckey, S. (1987). *Slave Culture: Nationalist Theory and the Foundations of Black America*. New York: Oxford University Press.
Stuewig, J., & McCloskey, L. (2005). The Relation of Child Maltreatment to Shame and Guilt Among Adolescents: Psychological Routes to Depression and Delinquency. *Child Maltreatment*, 10(4).
Sweet, J.H. (2003). *Recreating Africa: Culture, Kinship, and Religion in the African-Portuguese World, 1441–1770*. Chapel Hill: The University of North Carolina Press.
Taillieu, T., Afifi, T., Mota, N., & et al. (2014). Age, Sex, and Racial Differences in Harsh Physical Punishment: Results from a Nationally Representative United States Sample. *Child Abuse Negl*, 38(12), 1885–1894. doi:10.1016/j.chiabu.2014.10.020.

Telles, E., & Steele, L. (2013). *Pigmentocracy in the Americas: How Educational Attainment is Related to Skin Color.* Latin American Public Opinion Project: Americas Barometer Insights, 2012.
Thomas, H. (1997). *The Slave Trade: The Story of the Atlantic Slave Trade: 1440–1870.* New York: Simon & Schuster.
Timbert, A. (2010, Mai 3). Colombie: Le conflit armé et ses victimes « invisibles » intéressent la Croix Rouge Internationale. *Actu Latino.* Retrieved from http://www.actulatino.com/2010/05/03/colombie-le-conflit-arme-et-ses-victimes-invisibles-interessent-la-croix-rouge-internationale/.
Tin, L.G. (2013). *Esclavage et réparations.* Paris: Stock.
Turner, C., Khrais, R., Lloyd, T., & Olgin, A. (2016). Why America's Schools Have a Money Problem. Retrieved from http://www.npr.org/2016/04/18/474256366/why-americas-schools-have-a-money-problem.
United Nations. (2010). Reports of the United Nations in Haïti 2010 Situation, Challenges and Outlouk. Retrieved from www.onu-haiti.org.
United Nations. (2016). Haïti: Ban Ki-moon présente les excuses de l'ONU et propose un nouveau plan de lutte contre le choléra. Centre d'Actualites de l'ONU. Retrieved from http://www.un.org/apps/newsFr/storyF.asp?NewsID=38583#.WRkVtRM18dU.
USDVA. (2017). PTSD: National Center for PTSD. Retrieved from https://www.ptsd.va.gov/.
Vernon, E. (1994). *The Belize Creole.* Belizean Heritage Publishers Belize City: Benex Press.
Vinck, H. (1999). Le mythe de Cham dans quelques livrets scolaires du Congo belge. *Canadian Journal of African Studies/Revue canadienne des études africaines*(33), 642–647.
Wade, S. (1997). Social Commentary Columnist. *Amandala Newspaper Article, Belize City.*
Ward, E., & Mengesha, M. (2013). Depression in African American Men: A Review of What We Know and Where We Need to Go from Here. *Am J Orthopsychiatry,* 83(2), 386–397.
Warren, W. (2016). *New England Bound: Slavery and Colonization in Early America.* New York: Liveright Publishing Corp.
Wesley, C. (1935). *Richard Allen, Apostle of Freedom.* Washington, D.C.: Associated Publishers.
Williams, E. (1966). *Capitalism and Slavery.* New York: Capricorn Books.
Willie, C.V. (1981). *Black Families.* Bayside, NY: General Hall.
Willis, J.T. (2006). *Why Black Americans Behave as They Do: The Conditioning Process from Generation to Generation.* West Conshohocken, PA: Infinity Publishing Company.
Wolfe, G. (1986, November 6). Colored Museum Is Author's Exorcism. *New York Times.*
Woodson, C.G. (1933). *The Miseducation of the Negro.* Washington, D.C.: The Associated Publishers, Inc.
Work Project Administration. (1972–9). *Slave Narratives: A Folk History of Slavery in the United States from Interviews with Former Slaves.* Westport, CT: Greenwood Press.
Wyman-McCarthy, M. (2018). Perceptions of French and Spanish Slave Law in Late Eighteenth-Century Britain. *Journal of British Studies,* 57(1), 29–52.

10

The Epigenetic Ramifications of the Trauma

Enslavement, Centuries of Chattel Slavery and Institutionalized Racism

Fatimah Jackson, Latifa Jackson and Zainab El Radi Jackson

The U.S. may be the most resistant to the fact that it practiced slavery and that this practice influenced the present. A greater shock is that a few "bad" people were not primarily responsible for this history and subsequent racism. Legislatures, courts, the federal and state governments have promoted racism since the Virginia beginnings of slavery in the U.S. Ironically, U.S. government-sponsored research has provided biological evidence of trauma, its after-effects in post-traumatic stress disorders and its intergenerational transference. In the following chapter, Fatimah Jackson, Latifa Jackson and Zainab El Radi Jackson review the possibility that such a biological marker could be left epigenetically. She and her team also provide a wide-ranging review of the physical evidence of slavery's brutality.

Epigenetics has emerged in recent years as one of the most important biological mechanisms linking exposures across the life course to long-term health (Haggarty, 2015). Epigenetic studies of both intragenerational and transgenerational epigenetic phenotypic modifications have proliferated. As a result, the multi-generational transmission of epigenetic changes and their phenotypic ramifications are well established. In this chapter, we propose that these changes have been transmitted in a dynamic, non-linear pattern over time (Burggren, 2015), retained intergenerationally, and are capable of modulating current health status.

In the study of epigenetics, the epigenome produces heritable changes in gene expression. It does so without alterations in DNA nucleotide sequences. This research tool offers a unique way to view the consequences of chattel slavery and institutionalized racism in North America. Studies of the epigenome are also a way to look at the protracted biological impacts of slavery on survivors and their descendants. We know that enslavement and its sequelae can have profound influences on the biology and psychology of its victims. Therefore, looking at enslavement and institutional racism from the perspective of epigenetics may offer new insights and unique perspectives on the pathological ramifications of multi-generational enslavement. Also, we can see the avenues of adaptive resilience that may have emerged in direct response to the challenge of enslavement (e.g., confinement, forced labor, inadequate nutrition, physical abuse, and psychological trauma) and state-sanctioned racism.

What Are Epigenetics and the Epigenome?

Epigenetics is the study of those non-genetic factors that influence gene expression and are transmitted from one generation to another. Changes in gene or trait expression can occur in two ways: (1) changes in the DNA sequence that leads to changes in DNA expression; and (2) changes in the associated protein structures that change the accessibility of DNA expression. The first type changes the DNA; the second changes how the DNA is used and is the focus of epigenetic research.[1] DNA modifications that do not change the DNA sequence can affect gene activity. Simply stated, chemical compounds that are added to single genes (non-genetic environmental exposures) can regulate the activity of those genes. Together these chemical modifiers are known as the epigenome. The epigenome is the multitude of chemical compounds that can influence how the genome expresses itself. Essentially, the epigenome tells the genome what to do—what specific protein to make. This is possible because each gene can make several different versions of a protein. These chemical tags, or markers, can influence which protein is made at a particular time and are responsive to environmental influences.

Our environment, the foods we eat, which medicines we are exposed to, the events we witness, and the experiences we are exposed to, can all influence the specific chemical tags that make up our epigenome. Furthermore, these chemical tags can be inherited from grandparents to parents, then their offspring, for at least four generations. Heijmans (2008) showed that six decades after the Dutch Hunger Winter of 1944–45, individuals who experienced it had significantly demethylated segments surrounding their IGF2 gene than their same-gendered siblings who did not experience the winter. In another study of Swedish famine victims, paternal grandfather's experience of famine conditions was correlated significantly to transgenerational effects in cancer expression in their grandchildren. Finally, there is also evidence that the offspring of Holocaust survivors experienced methylation of the FKBP5 gene (Yehuda & et al., 2016). These examples demonstrate some of the myriad ways that the environment can exert transgenerational impacts on humans. This means our great-grandparents' environmental exposures created chemical markers that we may still carry, and that may still influence the pattern of our gene expressions. The epigenome provides multi-generational effects on gene expression that can be of importance across the lifespan and between generations.

The importance of epigenetics cannot be understated for understanding the epigenomic consequences of chattel slavery and institutional racism. Like the European Holocaust, enslavement represents an extended period in which African Americans experienced elevated physical and emotional abuse, severe food restriction, and unrelenting physical exertion. These environmental factors lasted at least from 1619 to 1865, and then to a lest systematic extent until the present. Understanding the biological effects of these conditions on an individual and population contributes significantly to our understanding of the biological basis of health and disease in African Americans. This biology provides the key to the outcome of the most consistent themes of enslavement and extensive racial discrimination and trauma.

Definitions

Legacy African Americans: A term coined by Dr. Shomarka Keita (n.d.), refers to the descendants of mid-fifteenth through mid–nineteenth century Africans brought to the Americas during the transatlantic slave trade. These Africans (primarily from West, West Central, and Southeast Africa) were exposed to a unique set of historical circumstances in the Americas, (a "Legacy") that have influenced both their genomics and epigenomics. These individuals and their descendants can be contrasted in their historical and contemporary exposures to more recent African immigrants to the Americas. All are technically African Americans, but Legacy African Americans have the collective experience of past exposure to slavery, and long-term historical contact with institutional racism, discrimination, and oppression in North America.

Chattel Slavery: This term refers to the condition of legalized enslavement, whereby law, the enslaved person was the private property of another. A civil relationship exists in which one person has absolute power over the life, fortune, and liberty of another. Under chattel slavery, enslaved persons can be bought or sold as commodities. Besides, enslaved status was imposed on the children of the enslaved, at birth (Frost, 2011). Chattel slavery was practiced in the United States before the Civil War and has been prevalent historically as well in many other parts of the world (Gaspar & Hine, 1996). In chattel slavery, enslaved persons could only be free when they purchased their freedom, or when their owners allowed them to be free. Often, they remained enslaved for their entire lives, and their status of bondage was hereditary and hence multi-generational. This can be contrasted with indentured servitude, where a release from labor was possible after a previously stipulated period.

Institutionalized Racism: This is an intentional, unintentional, conscious, and unconscious reproduction of white supremacy in social institutions: government, education, business, finance (banking), policing, courts, and social services. Human groups are defined socially by biological descent and physical appearance as superior or inferior to other groups according to arbitrary physical, intellectual, cultural, or moral properties (van den Berghe et al., 2007). In the Euro-American context, institutionalized racism is the fulfillment of white expectations that people of color are inferior. Therefore, African Americans are expected to be at the bottom of the social hierarchy. The normal operation of this social system will produce racially unequal outcomes.

Trauma: This term refers to the deeply disturbing psychological and physical effects of an experience or injury (See Weathers & Keane, 2007). Trauma may produce tissue damage, altered biochemistries, as well as cause emotional wounds. Recent genetic analyses suggest that trauma may stimulate the deposition of chemical markers suggestive of distress, globally, or in proximity to specific genes that alter the production of specific proteins from these genes. This can then influence the affected individual's phenotype and subsequent health status.

An Overview of the Biology of Extended Trauma

From 1619 to 1865 (246 years), approximately one half million enslaved Africans were brought to North America. Their descendants numbered close to four million by 1860. As chattel slaves, for 10 to 12 generations, enslaved Africans were threatened with violence, tortured, beaten, overworked, poorly clothed, exposed to diseases, and undernourished. All of these events exerted tremendous stress on their biology and severely taxed their abilities to remediate effectively. The likely epigenetic effects were so dramatic that the stress modified the directionality of ancestral trajectories in survivors. In other words, enslavement in the Americas, and its sequelae produced a wide assortment of new and powerful selective pressures on African slaves. Under these conditions, old responses that had been effective in Africa were less advantageous, and even disadvantageous, in the American context.

The biological effects of these traumatic events can be grouped into three broad categories. First, there were changes in the epigenome, which arose from the forced movement of Africans to a novel environment in the Americas. Second, there were biological effects due to the trauma associated with enslavement and its maintenance. Finally, there were biological consequences due to the violence and racial discrimination of a new century of Jim Crow and apartheid after the emancipation from slavery.

One example of the relocation effects on biology is evident in the salt sensitivity of West Central Africans in the North American southeast (F.L. Jackson, 1991). West Central Africa is a region with little sodium in the soil, and thus low sodium in local plants. Genetic adaptations in West Central Africa to a salt-deficient environment increased biological fitness. West Central Africans were better able to retain salt and were at a survival advantage. The natural selective advantage of salt sensitivity was amplified under the high ambient temperature, humidity, and disease conditions of the transatlantic Middle Passage. In this setting, salt-sensitive phenotypes would have had an advantage in electrolyte conservation (F.L. Jackson, 1991, 2004; 2008). However, once in the U.S. southeastern, the descendants of survivors were forced to consume a high-salt diet. This consumption made them more susceptible to salt-sensitive hypertension, cardiovascular injury, end-stage renal disease, and stroke. The forced movement of West Central Africans to places like South Carolina created a "mismatch" between the environment of the enslaved and their background genetics. The interaction between genetic variations inherent in peoples of West Central African ancestry to the new environmental realities of the Americas has important implications for understanding the biological roots of current racial health disparities in stroke and heart disease.

Developmental Effects

No age group of enslaved African Americans was exempt from the stress of bondage. Besides day-to-day deprivation and overwork, punishments were meted out to all slaves in response to any disobedience or perceived infractions. Slave owners and overseers also abused slaves arbitrarily to assert their dominance and maintain control (Foster, 2011; Genovese,

1976; Jones, 1985). Additional stressors such as shackling, mutilation, branding, amputations, sexual exploitation, and imprisonment left their marks as well. Specific epigenetic effects also varied by life phase.

Prenatal Effects

Empirical research from Holocaust survivors supports the view that parental trauma or stress exposure can have a direct biological impact on offspring (Bowers & Yehuda, 2015). Parental trauma also provided a context for intergenerational transmission of insult via epigenetic modification of gametes and modification of the gestational uterine environment. Exposure to stress early in life has been reported to alter permanently the activity of the hypothalamic-pituitary-adrenocortical (HPA) axis, and the brain in general (Kertes et al., 2016).[2] Such exposure was risked by enslaved pregnant women carrying their pregnancies and knowing their slave-owners could separate them capriciously from their newborn at any time. Pregnant women were expected to fulfill work quotas right up to the week, or even the day, of delivery. Even pregnancy was not a barrier to punishment. Methods were devised to administer beatings to expectant mothers without ostensibly harming the fetus. Some mothers were forced as well to provide their breastmilk for the slave owner's family. Rapes by slave owners and overseers were the cause of many pregnancies, while other pregnancies were the product of forced copulations with other slaves.

Most infants were weaned early, within three or four months of birth. Then, they were fed gruel or porridge made of protein-poor cornmeal. This increased the child's potential to develop kwashiorkor, rickets, and pellagra. The enslaved had high rates of infant mortality. Historian Steven Mintz (2009) reports that infant and child mortality rates were twice as high among enslaved children as they were among southern European-American children. Chronic undernourishment was a significant contributor to this increased mortality. Even when it was to their economic benefit, slave-owners showed little concern for enslaved mothers' health or diet during pregnancy. Pregnant women were not provided any extra rations. This deprivation during slavery may still affect contemporary infant mortality rates among Legacy African Americans (Jasienska & Jasienski, 2008). Not surprisingly, enslaved mothers suffered high rates of spontaneous abortions, stillbirths, and deaths shortly after birth. Half of all enslaved infants weighed less than 5.5 pounds (2.49476 kilograms) at birth. Today, this is considered severely underweight.

The mother's condition has a direct bearing on their newborn's health. Glucocorticoids pass through the placenta to the fetus. This means that some postnatal impacts may have included altered brain development, reduced birth weight, and diminished endocrine function through alterations in the hypothalamic-pituitary-adrenocortical axis (HPA) (Smart et al. 2015). For example, in the Democratic Republic of the Congo, a study was done on newborns. It looked at the effects of prenatal maternal stress on methylation of genes regulating the HPA axis (Kertes et al. 2016). It was observed that chronic stress produced broad effects on the various components of the HPA axis. In this study, mothers, exposed to chronic stress and war trauma, had statistically significant methylation effects at transcription factor binding sites. This means that the stress-induced changes in the HPA axis led to specific epigenomic effects at important active genetic sites.[3]

Another possible route of interaction between environmental exposures and changes in the epigenome may be through the serotonin transporter *(SERT)* gene. This gene has been implicated as a link between life stress and depression, although the precise molecular mechanisms modulating this link are not defined (Wankerl et al., 2014). Epigenetic modification of SERT appears to play an essential role in the etiology of depression of pregnant mothers and young children. In a recent study of 133 healthy, young adults (Wankerl et al., 2014), researchers in Germany observed that maternal prenatal stress, and child maltreatment, were both associated with a depressed SERT mRNA expression profile in an additive manner. In addition to the link between prenatal stress and depression, and the impact of prenatal stress on early postnatal care (Bowers and Yehuda, 2016), there are additional findings. A potential association between prenatal insult stress and changes in gene expression has been demonstrated. This finding is implicated in the developmental programming of various chronic diseases later in life (Wintour-Coghlan & Owens, 2007).

Early Life Experiences

In the North American South, in the decades before the Civil War, half of all enslaved African Americans were under the age of sixteen (Mintz, 2009). Young children were not exempt from torture. The mistreatment of children, both physically (through beatings and other forms of torture), and psychologically (through slave-owner-initiated reward systems that encouraged them to betray their parents and other enslaved persons), is well documented in the literature. Early postnatal life is a critical period of brain development. Frequent exposures to malnutrition, and childhood trauma affected health outcomes over their lifespan, and into future generations. Within the last decade, researchers have published increasingly on the epigenetic mechanisms capable of explaining the impacts of new insults

(Galler & Rabinowitz, 2014). Sustained childhood trauma is associated with dysregulation of the hypothalamic-pituitary-adrenal (HPA) axis. Both HPA factors, *CRHBP* and *FKBP5*, increase the risk for suicidal behavior in children (Roy, Hodgkinson, DeLuca, Goldman, & Enoch, 2012). Indeed, suicides of enslaved African American children may have been masked in the historical literature as "accidents" (Anonymous, 2017). Other researchers (Kneeland, 2006) suggest that actual suicide rates were low among enslaved African Americans and were consistent with suicide rates for continental Africans and African-ancestry peoples living in other parts of the world. Kneeland (2006) proposed that low rates of suicide likely reflect cultural inhibitions to a practice that would have occurred only under the extremely oppressive conditions.

Late Childhood and Adolescence Effects

Adolescence is a time when physical and cognitive abilities are optimized as frontal cortical functions mature to adult levels (Crews, Mdzinarishvili, Kim, He, & Nixon, 2006). North American enslavement added two new profound conditions to which adolescents had to adapt. The potential for being sold and permanently separated from family and friends much intensified, particularly for adolescent males. For teenage girls, the harsh reality of sexual exploitation, forced cohabitation, and pregnancy became much more likely. Adolescence is also the time that there was the full realization of the permanency of life-long bondage. Enslaved parents and extended families could not protect them from punishment at the hands of their masters and other European-Americans. As the reality of their powerlessness became apparent, this realization for teens must have been a source of profound psychological dismay. At the same time, we would expect to see alterations in the stress response, as well as the beginnings of changes in physical health risk (Ramo-Fernández, Schneider, Wilker, & Kolassa, 2015). This stress response would be expected to result in depression and other psychopathologies (Stroud et al., 2009).

Maltreatment in late childhood and early adolescence has been studied and shown to produce characteristic changes in DNA methylation patterns (Mehta, Thompson, Morton, Dhanantwari, & Shefer, 2013). Mehta's team, working in Germany, studied the impact of differences in sub-adult environments on adult disease-related, genome-wide gene expression, and DNA methylation patterns in peripheral blood cells. Each of the study patients had post-traumatic stress disorder (PTSD). They were divided into two groups. The first was an adult childhood-abuse group with PTSD. The second was a PTSD group WITHOUT a history of childhood abuse. They subsequently observed significant, distinct biological networks for the childhood-abuse group that suggested differences in PTSD pathophysiology. Maltreatment, in this stage of the life cycle, can become a salient independent factor influencing specific biological modifications, ultimately producing a unique pathology of PTSD in adulthood (Mehta et al. 2013).

Furthermore, epigenetic effects observed in traumatized adolescents, starting their reproductive lives, may also be subject to intergenerational transmission. As a result, the epigenetic legacy of abuse could be expressed in the offspring of these adolescents, as well. Epigenetically, these modifications would be expressed in altered networks of neurotransmitters and neuromodulators. These changes include amines, amino acids, nitric oxide, and neuropeptides. An inflammatory response could be induced by the activation of these neuroimmune pathways (Mariotti, 2015).

Adult Effects

Depression disorders are the most common clinical outcome following trauma (Bao & Swaab, 2014). This was as much the case during slavery as it is today. Stress and childhood abuse were the most critical environmental triggers for adult-onset of PTSD among enslaved individuals, as they would be today (Voisey, Young, Lawford, & Morris, 2014). Enhanced glucocorticoid receptor sensitivity is present in adults with PTSD, although the molecular mechanisms are still under investigation (Yehuda et al. 2014). In a study of combat veterans, Yehuda and colleagues found that individuals with PTSD had lower levels of cytosine methylation in the promoter region in peripheral blood mononuclear cells (lymphocytes [T cells, B cells, NK cells] and monocytes). There were no such findings among combat veterans without PTSD. This research concluded that the observed alterations might reflect enduring epigenetic modifications. If this is correct, then we would also expect that these epigenetic changes would be transmitted to the descendants of Legacy African Americans.

Effects on Specific Organs and Organ Systems

Brain Injury

One of the expected physical consequences of enslavement, and the oppressive force required to maintain it is brain injuries due to accidents and beatings. Sudden acceleration-deceleration and rotational forces acting on the brain can induce traumatic brain injuries. Diffuse axonal injury has been identified as one of the chief underlying causes of morbidity and mortality in head trauma incidents. This type of injury appears in microscopic white matter because of shearing forces that induce pathological and anatomical changes within the brain. These changes can potentially contribute to significant impairments later in life (Sundman, Hall, & Chen, 2014). Today in the U.S., traumatic brain injury contributes to over 30 percent of all injury-related deaths (Wong & Langley, 2016). In the absence of contemporary safety precautions, we can speculate that slaves were exposed to this risk factor and suffered the consequences. Survivors of traumatic brain injury had increased vulnerability to devastating neurological disabilities that could adversely affect cognition, movement, sensation, and emotional function.[4]

In traumatic brain injury, when the peripheral nervous system is injured more than the central nervous system, some regenerative capacity is evident. In other words, some healing is possible when the injuries involve the less critical systems of the brain. Again, epigenetic changes seem to be at the core of such healing.[5] Slaves with increased exposure to blast waves, such as those working in mines, were subjected very likely to occupational setting-induced traumatic brain injury and abnormal gene expression. Blast-induced neuro-trauma (Bailey, Grinter, & VandeVord, 2016) is a prevalent injury within both military and civilian populations. Persistent inflammation characterizes the injury at the cellular level, which manifests as a wide range of cognitive and functional impairments. Epigenetic regulation of transcription is an important control mechanism for gene expression and cellular function, which may underlie chronic inflammation and result in neurodegeneration.

Simon (2016) also suggests that individuals exposed to mild stress to the brain from ischemia, hypothermia, or infection, can produce a transient neuroprotective state in the brain. Such a state reprograms gene expression via epigenetic changes in DNA methylation and histone modification. In the neuro-protected state, the brain responds differently to severe stress and sustains less injury. At the genomic level, the response of the neuro-protected brain to severe stress is characterized by widespread differential regulation (e.g., reprogramming) of diverse genes. This reprogramming of gene expression is consistent with an epigenetic model of regulation. With DNA methylation and histone modification, two epigenomic changes appear to mediate the changes in gene expression. These changes would then be responsible for a shift in the proteins produced. These changes are likely to produce significant physiological alterations and have potential behavioral outcomes. Increased risk for both hypothermia and infection among enslaved African Americans were frequently reported in *Born in Slavery: Slave Narratives from the Federal Writers' Project*,

1936–1938. This collection contains more than 2,300 first-person accounts of the experience of enslavement.

Damage to Bone and Muscle

There was frequent skeletal damage among enslaved African Americans, due to beatings and excessive work. While epigenetic effects on stress and disease outcomes can be visible, they are mostly invisible in skeletal tissue. New bone can be formed under conditions of biological stress, particularly in bone microenvironments that involve inflammatory changes (Klaus, 2014). Epigenetics studies and gene expression profiles suggest that hypomethylation and hydroxymethylation help control the expression of genes in the heart, brain, myoblasts, myotubes, and within skeletal muscle myofibers. Such regulation could promote cell renewal, cell maintenance, homeostasis, and a poised state for repair of tissue damage (Terragni et al., 2014). The ability to recuperate from fractured bones and damaged muscles occurs in three phases: inflammation, reparative, and remodeling. The rates at which individuals recover are a function of the prior health status, age, and current nutritional status. The nutritional demands of healing are high, particularly during the second and third phases of recuperation. Most important are energy, dietary proteins, an adequate blood supply, sufficient anti-inflammatory and anti-oxidant nutrients, and adequate vitamin and mineral intakes. Undoubtedly, the condition of enslavement affected each stage of recuperation. Of course, empirical data on slaves starting condition, average intake, and recovery aftermath were never collected.

Nutritional Inadequacies and Deficiencies

The diets of slaves and their descendants were inadequate due to insufficient food and lack of choices. In the southeastern U.S., the usual diet for slaves was corn and pig-derived products. Booker T. Washington, born a slave on the Burroughs plantation, in Franklin County, Virginia, on April 5, 1856, wrote, "Not much religion can exist in a one-room log-cabin or on an empty stomach" (Washington, 1901). Historical archaeologists have recovered artifacts of living conditions during slavery. Data and artifacts provide information on housing, use of space, food-ways, household equipment, personal possessions, and sometimes information on health care and hygiene. Some plantation owners kept records of food, clothing, and other allotments to slaves that supplement archaeological discoveries. Faunal remains in excavations have confirmed that pigs and cows were the principal meat in slaves' diets.

Other archeological sites show remnants of wild species such as opossum, raccoon, snapping turtle, deer, squirrel, duck, and rabbit. This evidence suggests that slaves supplemented rations given to them by their owners. Other sites contain lead shot, gunflints, and gun parts, showing that some slaves had access to firearms. Other excavations include oyster shells, lead fishing weights, fishhooks, and fish bones and scales. Traces of walnuts, grapes, blackberries, and hickory nuts were found, as well. While there was regional variability in diets, any dietary deficiency that increased mutation rates would be associated with increased risk of cancers, as would be the case for choline deficiency (Zeisel, 2012).

Distress from Confinement, Trauma and Restraint

In addition to beatings, confinement in cages, jails, and holes was a regular feature of enslavement. Confinement can induce distinct sympathoadrenergic activation and immunological changes. One of the earliest and most frequently cited related "anomalies" associated with slavery in the Western literature, was Drapetomania. This is a contrived "mental illness." In 1851, American physician, Samuel A. Cartwright, asserted that Drapetomania was the cause of slaves fleeing captivity (Findlay & Beard, 2000). Of course, this is nonsense. Slavery, and everything about it, was the bases for flight.

To be sure, traumatic stress induces persistent and functional effects on the epigenome (Vinkers et al., 2015). Trauma is associated with changes in DNA methylation throughout the lifespan, as discussed previously. We know, for example, that traumatic stress in early life can lead to permanent molecular changes in the form of epigenetic modifications. These changes can redirect the typical trajectory of the affected individual (Klengel & Binder, 2015), predisposing them to specific psychiatric disorders. We do not know how sustained (i.e., chronic) traumatic stress throughout life affects the human epigenome. Sustained trauma best approximates the experience of American chattel slavery. The pathogenesis of post-traumatic stress disorder's (PTSD) effects on the epigenome may take us closest to recognizing the repercussions of enslavement on the human psyche. Epigenetic regulation lies at the heart of PTSD (Zannas, Provençal, & Binder, 2015), and it appears that multiple tissue types and diverse channels of expression are affected. Post-traumatic slave syndrome (PTSS) is recognized as the enslavement equivalent of PTSD (DeGruy, 2017). PTSS has been described as a social condition that exists because of the multi-generational oppression of Africans and their descendants, resulting from centuries of chattel slavery. PTSS is recognized as contributing both to the pathology, and to specific aspects of group resilience, in response to extended enslavement.

Chattel slavery is associated strongly with chronic restraint stress, i.e., a method of chronic movement restriction. In animal models, chronic restraint stress has been associated with increases in brain-derived neurotrophic factor mRNA and protein in some areas of the brain (e.g., the basal lateral amygdala). However, the same neurotrophic factor mRNA and protein are decreased in other areas of the brain, such as the CA3 region of the hippocampus. Such a decrease can influence dendritic spine density (Bennett & Lagopoulos, 2014). This is significant because reductions in dendritic spine density are associated with increased susceptibility to schizophrenia and depression (Glantz & Lewis, 2001). Recent evidence implicates spiny synapses as essential substrates of pathogenesis in such disorders as autism spectrum disorders (ASD), schizophrenia, and Alzheimer's disease (Penzes, Cahill, Jones, VanLeeuwen, & Woolfrey, 2011).

Substance Abuse and Pharmacogenomic Vulnerabilities

In the United States, trauma and stress have been significant contributing factors to the use and misuse of pharmaceuticals, including alcohol. The effects of enslavement and institutionalized racial discrimination have influenced both alcohol and non-prescription drug use. In bioinformatics analyses of the human Haplotype Map populations, African-derived populations showed substantial allele frequency differences when compared to non–African populations. Legacy African Americans are African-derived and therefore demonstrate genetic patterns like other African-derived peoples. The differences seen in non–Africans occur at loci associated with both immune health and the alcohol dehydrogenase family of genes that are tasked with alcohol detoxification. For example, in studies of variants in the alcohol dehydrogenase 1B gene (rs1229984, and rs2066702), these genes are associated with susceptible alcohol phenotypes in Legacy African American women. However, gene-gene interactions are very important in regulating gene expression patterns. Alcohol susceptibility phenotype studies have, to date, lacked a neighbor gene context because we know so little about the genomics of African descended peoples. When neighboring genes are considered, it becomes very likely that adjacent immune function genes have been the primary cause for increases in the observed frequency of alcohol susceptibility variants in African ancestry populations. This means it is difficult to separate the genes influencing susceptibility to alcoholism from other genes influencing immune functioning, because of their close proximities on the same or nearby chromosomes. The complexity of the genomics of African-descended peoples for genes that enhance use and misuse of pharmaceuticals has yet to be fully explored.

Trauma and stress have been identified as two of the most important causative agents for substance abuse in the United States. Two variants in the cortisol gene have been identified as significant variants (rs1614972 and rs2298753), contributing to alcohol dependence in individuals. The African-ancestry population's strong allele frequency differences contribute to significant additional dependence vulnerability to illicit substances such as dopamine, opiate, and alcohol substances. A large number of studies, including genome-wide association investigations, have uncovered potentially relevant allelic contributors to the genetic and molecular basis of addiction phenotypes. Genetic studies, such as those conducted on the alcohol dehydrogenase (ADH) family, have been necessary for advancing our understanding of the genetic basis of addiction phenotypes.

A recent assessment of cocaine, heroin, morphine, crystal methamphetamine, and alcohol addiction genes identified, for the first time, the presence of seven addiction hotspots located across the genome. Although these drugs were not largely available to enslaved African Americans, the genes for addiction susceptibilities were already present in their genomes because these genes appear linked to genes influencing immune status. All but two of these hotspots share functional annotation between genes. They were observed, as well, to participate in addiction phenotypes and their co-located gene neighbors. Furthermore, when all genes within a hotspot window were mapped onto metabolic pathways, researchers identified both canonical pathways, such as acute alcohol intoxication, as well as more alternative pathways, such as those involved in systemic lupus (an autoimmune disease). Because addiction phenotypes show ethnic population specificity, publicly available polymorphisms from 11 populations were assessed at each hotspot location. Three striking ethnicity-based signatures arose, at chromosome four and chromosome six hotspots among the Yoruba, a tropical West African group. These Africans were distinguishable from all other ethnic populations studied. When significant genomic polymorphisms were compared to other genome-wide association studies, they differed from their neighbors in genomic frequencies, and also in where the histone family genes were located. These latter genes are critical to epigenomic processes and represent an additional layer of ethnic diversity in human populations.

This increased complexity observed in African-descended individuals and groups means that the standard Eurocentric measures of genetic susceptibility to drug abuse, in response to chronic stress, are of limited utility in assessing those of African ancestry. The genetic diversity among Africans is so great that you cannot even use one group of African peoples to substitute for another geographically distant group of African peoples! Furthermore, while the stress and trauma of enslavement and institutionalized racism can be expected to increase the disposition toward drug abuse, we are only in the early stages of research into the specific genomic and epigenomic profiles that may signal increased susceptibilities. In many respects, African-descended individuals and groups are a blank canvas for understanding the interactions of the epigenome and genome.

From an evolutionary perspective, African-descended individuals and groups are expected to display more genetic variation overall than non–Africans, due to our species origins and long residence in continental Africa, the initial larger population sizes in Africa (compared to outside Africa), and the elevated rates of evolutionary change observed in tropical environments. Besides, all non–African genetic diversity is a subset of African diversity. Therefore, it is not surprising that other genome-wide association studies (GWAS) comparing cross-ethnic variability in pharmacogenomics are also finding significant polymorphisms. High polymorphic variability has been identified in a slew of long-range trans-chromosomal linkages to well-characterized addiction genes such as Monoamine Oxidase A (MAOA), an enzyme that catalyzes dopamine, norepinephrine, and serotonin. Diversity in each of these physiologically important compounds can have important biomedical and behavioral ramifications.

Resilience to the Stress and Trauma of Slavery and Racism

Resilience is the process of recovering from adversity due to a stressful or trauma-causing event (Seery, Holman, & Silver, 2010). A resilient individual thrives when faced with adversity, and continues to function socially and interpersonally in a healthy manner (Connor & Davidson, 2003). High levels of resiliency are associated with lower psychopathology, and low levels of resiliency are associated with higher psychopathology (Connor & Davidson, 2003). Seery and colleagues (2010) explored a link between adversity and resilience. Exposure to an adverse event can negatively affect an individual's or a family's life, but it can also help develop resilience. Conversely, a lack of resilience may result in ongoing psychological distress, and eventually, the development of mental illness. Gilbert and colleagues (1998) discussed a cognitive mechanism referred to as the psychological immune system, which encourages recovery and healing after exposure to an adverse event. The immediate expectation after a catastrophic event is a negative response: psychological (e.g., depression) and physical (e.g., morbidity). However, the psychological immune system may activate a "toughening" effect to cope with past negative situations that individuals may not perceive (R. A Dienstbier, 1989; 1992). Toughness is described as the individual's ability to perceive situations positively (i.e., they are more manageable). Individuals who maintain high resiliency are better equipped when responding to difficulties.

Resilience and Immune Function

Cortisol levels elevate in response to environmental stress. Cortisol can help control blood sugar levels, regulate metabolism, help reduce inflammation, and assist with memory formulation. It has a controlling effect on salt and water balance and helps control blood pressure. However, chronic psychological stress alters cortisol levels and leads to the loss of the body's ability to regulate its inflammatory immune response. This ultimately makes populations under chronic stress susceptible to contracting diseases and accelerating disease progression. Normal cortisol levels decrease the release of a host of immune products that cause inflammation and signal healing. Long-term exposure to chronic stress makes cortisol tissues that should be cortisol-sensitive turn into cortisol-resistant tissues, leading to uncontrolled inflammation responses in individuals (Morris & Rao, 2014). This uncontrolled chronic inflammation degrades the body's ability to mount acute immune responses where inflammation is needed to attract immune system players. A series of studies were done among rural, southern, young-adult Legacy African Americans, with behaviors consistent with resilience to social adversity and environmental stress. Their cortisol levels paint a sober picture (Aiyer, Heinze, Miller, Stoddard, & Zimmerman, 2014; Ruttle et al., 2014). Results from these and other studies posit that resilience in these young people may be very shallow (Brody et al., 2013).

Biological evidence of stress is also seen in relative telomere length assessments in contemporary Legacy African Americans who experience day-to-day institutionalized racism: as measured by the use of racist language from Google searches. Telomeres are repetitive sequences at the terminal ends of chromosomes. Each time a chromosome is copied, slight errors in the replication process truncate these telomeres. The cumulative shortening of telomeres is associated with cellular aging in humans. Chae et al. (2014) found that relative telomere length, a measure of the molecular age of an individual, was shortened in individuals exposed to chronic racial trauma and animus. Racial animus is considered highest in the South, where Internet searches of racial epithets were most frequently done (Chae et al., 2016). This finding suggests that not only are the descendants of enslaved African Americans exposed to chronic racial and social adversity; they are also more likely to develop chronic inflammation consequently. Their bodies may be prematurely aging, in comparison to individuals who are not exposed to these same systemic environmental stressors. Furthermore, women who live in troubled neighborhoods have shorter telomeres, drawing a direct connection between environment and cellular age (Chae et al., 2016; Gebreab et al., 2016).

Epigenetics is at the heart of a series of feedback loops linking the environment to the human genome in a way that allows crosstalk between the genome and the environment. It offers the potential for modification of adverse epigenetic states resulting from events/exposures at earlier life stages (Haggarty, 2015). Research on the descendants of enslaved African Americans has demonstrated that they have considerable coping mechanisms or resilience for maintaining mental well-being. However, this coping has not been perfect. There are areas where coping has not been successful. Post Traumatic Slave Syndrome (DeGruy 2005) covers these areas (Sule et al., 2017).

Resilience to Psychological Stress via Adaptive Coping Mechanisms

Environmental exposure and internal experience provide the individual with the opportunity to develop resilience as a coping mechanism (Rutter, 1993). Resilience protects against the challenging demands of life, as well as protects against societal prejudice and racism (Neville, Tynes, & Utsey, 2008). Higher levels of resiliency and the ability to overcome adversity are associated with positive social, environmental support from family, community, and church (Boyd-Franklin, 2003). Walsh (2015) focused on exploring three factors in the familial support system: they are belief, organization, and communication systems within a family. These three factors are essential to building resilience. Henderson and colleagues (2015) researched coping methods after violent and non-violent deaths. They found religious beliefs and participation were essential factors in dealing with non-violent deaths for African American participants. In another study among urban youth, a relationship was observed between the specific indices of victimization, including peer violence, and the symptomatology and coping mechanisms utilized by the youth (McGee et al. 2019). In yet another study, Walker and colleagues (1997) collected daily diaries from participants, spanning three months to one year. When the participants were asked to recall memories from the diaries, they recalled positive and negative events that occurred. However, the emotions attached to the negative events faded almost wholly, compared to the positive event memories (Walker, Vogl, & Thompson, 1997). The outcome showed that, through autobiographical recollection, one could focus on the positive memories and overcome most of the emotions attached to negative ones (Walker et al., 1997).

Studies of suicide among Legacy African American females show that they are more likely to contemplate and attempt suicide than are their male counterparts and other groups (Flowers, Walker, & Thompson, 2014). However, the outcomes also suggest that, in general, for this particular group, death from suicide is low. Social and cultural support, optimism, and spirituality appear to be the reasons for this resilience, preventing successful suicide among African American women (Flowers et al., 2014). Also, resiliency was shown to be a protective factor for a group of 290 African American women in a community-based primary health care center who suffered from symptoms of depression (Holden, Bradford, Hall, & Belton, 2013). High resilience levels implicated less severe depressive symptoms, while low resilience levels indicated higher depressive symptoms from significant life stressors, such as unemployment. Women who scored high on resilience were better able to cope with depressive symptoms. Resilience was assessed using The Connor-Davidson Resilience Scale (CD-RISC), assessing spirituality, relationships, trust, acceptance, competence, and other factors in a 35-item, self-administered measurement tool (Connor & Davidson, 2003; Holden et al., 2013).

In another study focusing on high-risk environments, Legacy African American mothers with lower SES, spirituality, and existential well-being were crucial factors that reduced parental stress (Lamis, Wilson, Tarantino, Lansford, & Kaslow, 2014). Religious, spiritual, and family support were also everyday stress-reducing factors that increased resiliency for African American men (Chung et al., 2014). In a sample of 295 African American men, 92 percent of them reported that spirituality and family support promoted their resilience and shaped their responses to stress-related sources such as unemployment, poverty, discrimination, and racism (Chung et al., 2014). Another project focused on older African American women who experienced depression. Ironically, their resilience and spirituality response to adversity became a barrier when seeking professional mental health care (Ward, Mengesha, & Issa, 2014). Some of their depressive symptoms began in childhood or adolescence and continued throughout adulthood. However, the women normalized depression and were not aware of the symptoms. They believed the only coping strategy for the symptoms was to express optimism and engage in their religious practices (Ward, Mangesha, & Issa, 2014). Resilience for this group was a lifelong coping challenge. Poverty, adversity, feelings of worthlessness, and other psychological struggles the women experienced throughout their lives led them to believe that chronic depression was a normal response to their hardship. Therefore, they felt that it was unnecessary to use professional mental health services.

Miller and colleagues (2016) discussed the concept of "deep-skin" resilience. The concept is illustrated when a group of African American youths from disadvantaged backgrounds, who displayed high levels of conscientiousness, was found more vulnerable to infections than was their white American peers. For African American disadvantaged youths, achieving upward mobility is extremely challenging, and may lead to biological (i.e., cardiometabolic risk) effects (Miller et al., 2016). The reason for this difference in resilience is that achieving upward mobility requires disadvantaged youths to tackle social issues, such as racial stereotyping and discrimination, as personal challenges. Furthermore, Miller and colleagues (2016) found that deep-skin resilience is evident across the northern United States and is not limited to Legacy African Americans in the southern region of the country. This would suggest that these resilience-promoting behaviors are more broadly distributed among regionally diverse Legacy African Americans and thus may have their roots in their shared enslaved past.

Conclusions on Resilience in Legacy African Americans

The forced trauma and subordination of enslaved persons for two centuries strengthened the development of a collective cultural identity for Legacy African Americans today. Eyerman (2001) noted that this identity continued to develop post-slavery, and the traumas along the way were recollected through stories, books, art, and politics. To repair the social fabric of a traumatized group, a collective sense of identity was necessary, which is a form of resilience. This sense of identity provided a liberation roadmap for African American communities (Alim et al., 2008). However, where resilience failed, there is the Post Traumatic Slave Syndrome (PTSS). The syndrome is based on traumatic memories (long forgotten) and once successful coping behaviors practiced over generations. These practices are now dysfunctional. The psychological disorders related to PTSS are evident in the African American experience today: black-on-black violence, colorism, racist socialization (internalized racism), and ever-present anger (see chapter by DeGruy). For example, higher incidences of depression anxiety, and other mental disorders occur in African communities, compared with other groups in America, including African immigrants, who have not experienced slavery and institutionalized racism.

Summary

The large-scale capture, forcible kidnapping, and subsequent forced labor exerted tremendous stress on the biology of enslaved Africans. This stress provided the substrate for natural selection in New World African populations. The environmental and social conditions of enslavement, post–Civil War Reconstruction, and Jim Crow racism in the United States have had an enduring impact on African Americans and their descendants. Chronic stress associated with enslavement is manifested partially in elevated stress levels and, in turn, have served as catalysts for other adverse health outcomes. Elevations in circulating cortisol levels have been indicated as a significant influencing factor in psychological stress disorders such as depression and post-traumatic stress disorder. Stress responses were reinforced no doubt by the long-term food insecurity associated with enslavement. Chronic food deprivation and food instability are thought to have further exacerbated the trauma associated with other adversarial environmental influencers.

The picture we paint suggests long-term negative implications of slavery and institutionalized racism for enslaved African Americans and their descendants. However, the picture also must include significant evidence of resilience and adaptive survival mechanisms. Many of the disadvantageous consequences of a sub-optimal environment are ameliorated by resilience and adaptive mechanisms. Dynamic epigenetic phenomena may be evident in Legacy African Americans in graded, time-related changes. These changes may dilute certain epigenetically influenced phenotypes both within and across generations (see Burggren 2015). Conceivably, an epigenetic effect might also be amplified over multiple generations (as discussed by DeGruy [2005] in PTSS). There may be unexplored additive effects resulting from the pressures of environmental stressors, such as institutionalized racism. These stressors may that wax, wane and then wax again across multiple generations (see Burggren 2015). Epigenetic changes associated with significant trends in African American biological history provide a context for understanding the implications of this history on contemporary health disparities. Studies of transgenerational and intragenerational epigenetic effects should search for persistence of epigenomic modifications in the Legacy African Americans using highly sensitive, precise, interdisciplinary quantitative methods.

Improvements in technology and more extensive sampling of African-derived peoples will undoubtedly result in improved understandings of the dynamic interaction of the epigenome and the genome within the specific environmental setting of chattel enslavement and discriminatory, institutionalized racism. The biological trauma of abusive social, political, and economic systems on generations of African Americans has left an indelible mark on gene expression patterns that, like the disenfranchising systems, has multi-generational ramifications. Our current understanding of this trans-generational impact is tentative but highly suggestive. Further research will elaborate on these initial findings and provide additional validation of the significance of gene-environment interactions on population well-being.

Notes

1. There is a growing body of research that shows that histone protein alterations, relative levels of methylation and acetylation on DNA strands, and the presence of chaperone proteins are all significant contributors to genomic storage and expression profiles. The epigenome is the sum of these events for the entire genome.

2. While chronic stress fosters disease, presumably by activating the hypothalamic-pituitary-adrenocortical (HPA) axis, the research linking chronic stress and HPA function are contradictory. Some studies report increased activation, and others report the opposite. However, a recent meta-analysis showed that much of the variability is attributable to the nature of the stressor, and to idiosyncratic features. The timing of the stressor appears to be an especially critical element, as the hormonal activity is elevated at stressor onset, but reduces as time passes (Miller, Chen, & Zhou, 2007). Stressors that threaten physical integrity involving trauma and which are uncontrollable, elicit a high, flat diurnal profile of cortisol secretion (Miller et al. 2007). Ultimately, however, HPA activity is shaped by an individual's response to the situation.

3. The most important effects were in the following genes, corticotropin releasing hormone *(CRH)*, corticotropin releasing hormone binding protein *(CRHBP)*, nuclear receptor subfamily 3 group C member 1 *(NR3C1)*, and FK506 Binding Protein 5 *(FKBP5)*. Each of these genes is linked intimately to the hypothalamic-pituitary-adrenocortical (HPA) axis, and influences its functioning. This includes influencing infant birth weight.

4. Recent research suggests that epigenetic mechanisms such as DNA methylation, post-translational chromatin modification, and miRNA regulation of gene expression at the site of injury, can contribute to the downstream ramifications of traumatic brain injury.

5. Through systemic epigenetic activation of the histone acetyltransferase p300/CBP-associated factor (PCAF), acetylation of histone 3 Lys 9 promotes established key regenerative-associated genes (Puttagunta et al., 2014), ameliorating, in part the impairment initially associated with traumatic brain injury. PCAF is also involved in axonal regeneration following spinal cord injury, again through epigenetic mechanisms.

References

Aiyer, S.M., Heinze, J.E., Miller, A.L., Stoddard, S.A., & Zimmerman, M.A. (2014). Exposure to Violence Predicting Cortisol Response During Adolescence and Early Adulthood: Understanding Moderating Factors. *Journal of Youth and Adolescence, 43*(7), 1066–1079. doi:10.1007/s10964-014-0097-8.

Alim, T.N., Feder, A., Graves, R.E., Wang, Y., Weaver, J., Westphal, M., ... Charney, D.S. (2008). Trauma, Resilience, and Recovery in a High-Risk African-American Population. *American Journal of Psychiatry, 165*(12), 1566–1575. doi:10.1176/appi.ajp.2008.07121939.

Anonymous. (2017). The Making of African American Identity. National Humanities Center Resource Toolbox, 1, 1500–1865. Retrieved from http://nationalhumanitiescenter.org/pds/maai/community/text3/religionslaveswpa.pdf.

Bailey, Z.S., Grinter, M.B., & VandeVord, P.J. (2016). Astrocyte Reactivity Following Blast Exposure Involves Aberrant Histone Acetylation. *Frontiers in Molecular Neuroscience, 9*, 64. doi:10.3389/fnmol.2016.00064.

Bao, A.-M., & Swaab, D.F. (2014). The Stress Systems in Depression: A Postmortem Study. *European Journal of Psychotraumatology, 5*(1), 26521. doi:10.3402/ejpt.v5.26521.

Bennett, M.R., & Lagopoulos, J. (2014). Stress and Trauma: BDNF Control of Dendritic-Spine Formation and Regression. *Progress in Neurobiology, 112*(Supplement C), 80–99. doi:10.1016/j.pneurobio.2013.10.005.

Bowers, M.E., & Yehuda, R. (2015). Intergenerational Transmission of Stress in Humans. *Neuropsychopharmacology, 41*, 232.
Boyd-Franklin, N. (2003). Race, Class, and Poverty. In F. Walsh (Ed.), *Normal Family Processes: Growing Diversity and Complexity* (First ed., pp. 260–279). London: Taylor and Francis.
Brody, G.H., Yu, T., Chen, E., Miller, G.E., Kogan, S.M., & Beach, S.R. (2013). Is Resilience Only Skin Deep? Rural African Americans' Socioeconomic Status–Related Risk and Competence in Preadolescence and Psychological Adjustment and Allostatic Load at Age 19. *Psychological Science, 24*(7), 1285–1293.
Burggren, W. (2015). Dynamics of Epigenetic Phenomena: Intergenerational and Intragenerational Phenotype 'Washout.' *J. Exp. Biol., 218*, 80–87.
Chae, D.H., Epel, E.S., Nuru-Jeter, A.M., Lincoln, K.D., Taylor, R.J., Lin, J., ... Thomas, S.B. (2016). Discrimination, Mental Health, and Leukocyte Telomere Length Among African American Men. *Psychoneuroendocrinology, 63*(Supplement C), 10–16. doi:https://doi.org/10.1016/j.psyneuen.2015.09.001.
Chung, B., Meldrum, M., Jones, F., Brown, A., Daaood, R., & Jones, L. (2014). Perceived Sources of Stress and Resilience in Men in an African-American Community. *Progress in Community Health Partnerships: Research, Education, and Action, 8*(4), 441–451. doi:10.1353/cpr.2014.0053.
Connor, K.M., & Davidson, J.R.T. (2003). Development of a New Resilience Scale: The Connor-Davidson Resilience Scale (CD-RISC). *Depression and Anxiety, 18*(2), 76–82. doi:10.1002/da.10113.
Crews, F.T., Mdzinarishvili, A., Kim, D., He, J., & Nixon, K. (2006). Neurogenesis in Adolescent Brain Is Potently Inhibited by Ethanol. *Neuroscience, 137*(2), 437–445. doi:https://doi.org/10.1016/j.neuroscience.2005.08.090.
DeGruy, J. (2017). *Post Traumatic Slave Syndrome: America's Legacy of Enduring Injury and Healing*: HarperCollins.
Dienstbier, R.A. (1989). Arousal and Physiological Toughness: Implications for Mental and Physical Health. *Psychological Review, 96*(1), 84.
Dienstbier, R.A. (1992). *Mutual Impacts of Toughening on Crises and Losses.: Life Crises and Experiences of Loss in Adulthood.*
Eyerman, R. (2001). *Cultural Trauma: Slavery and the Formation of African American Identity*. Cambridge University Press.
Findlay, J.B., & Beard, D.J. (2000). *Drapetomania—A Disease Called Freedom: An Exhibition of 18th, 19th, & Early 20th-Century*: Bienes Center for the Literary arts.
Flowers, K.C., Walker, R.L., & Thompson, M.P. (2014). Associations Between Reasons for Living and Diminished Suicide Intent Among African-American Female Suicide Attempters. *The Journal of Nervous and Mental Disease, 202*(8), 569–575.
Foster, T. (2011). The Sexual Abuse of Black Men Under American Slavery. *Journal of the History of Sexuality, 20*(3), 445–464.
Frost, D. (2011). *Chattel Slavery: Rodriguez, Junius P. Slavery in the Modern World* (Vol. 1).
Galler, J., & Rabinowitz, D.G. (2014). *The Intergenerational Effects of Early Adversity* (Vol. 128): *Prog Mol Biol Transl Sci*.
Gaspar, D.B., & Hine, D.C. (1996). *More Than Chattel: Black Women Slavery in the Americas.* Indiana University Press.
Gebreab, S.Y., Riestra, P., Gaye, A., Khan, R.J., Xu, R., Davis, A.R., ... Gibbons, G.H. (2016). Perceived Neighborhood Problems Are Associated with Shorter Telomere Length in African American Women. *Psychoneuroendocrinology, 69*(Supplement C), 90–97. doi:https://doi.org/10.1016/j.psyneuen.2016.03.018.
Genovese, E.D. (1976). *Roll, Jordan, Roll: The World the slaves Made* (Vol. 652): Vintage.
Gilbert, D.T., Pinel, E.C., Wilson, T.D., Blumberg, S.J., & Wheatley, T.P. (1998). Immune Neglect: A Source of Durability Bias in Affective Forecasting. *Journal of Personality and Social Psychology, 75*(3), 617.
Glantz, L.A., & Lewis, D.A. (2001). Dendritic Spine Density in Schizophrenia and Depression. *Archives of General Psychiatry, 58*(2), 203–203.
Haggarty, P. (2015). Genetic and Metabolic Determinants of Human Epigenetic Variation. *Current Opinion in Clinical Nutrition & Metabolic Care, 18*(4).

Heijmans, B.T., Tobi, E.W., Stein, A.D., Putter, H., Blauw, G.J., Susser, E.S., & Lumey, L.H. (2008). Persistent Epigenetic Differences Associated with Prenatal Exposure to Famine in Humans. *Proceedings of the National Academy of Sciences of the United States of America, 105*(44), 17046–17049. doi:10.1073/pnas.0806560105.

Henderson, D., Bond, G., Alderson, C., & Walker, W. (2015). This Too Shall Pass: Evidence of Coping and Fading Emotion in African Americans' Memories of Violent and Nonviolent Death. *Omega (Westport), 71*(4), 291–311.

Holden, K.B., Bradford, L.D., Hall, S.P., & Belton, A.S. (2013). Prevalence and Correlates of Depressive Symptoms and Resiliency Among African American Women in a Community-Based Primary Health Care Center. *Journal of health care for the poor and underserved, 24*(4 0), 79–93. doi:10.1353/hpu.2014.0012.

Jackson, F.L. (1991). An Evolutionary Perspective on Salt, Hypertension, and Human Genetic Variability. *Hypertension, 17*(1 Suppl), I129.

Jackson, F.L. (2004). Human Genetic Variation and Health: New Assessment Approaches Based on Ethnogenetic Layering. *British Medical Bulletin, 69*, 215–235. doi:10.1093/bmb/ldh012.

Jackson, F.L.C. (2008). Ancestral Links of Chesapeake Bay Region African Americans to Specific Bight of Bonny (West Africa) Microethnic Groups and Increased Frequency of Aggressive Breast Cancer in Both Regions. *American Journal of Human Biology, 20*(2), 165–173. doi:10.1002/ajhb.20709.

Jasienska, G., & Jasienski, M. (2008). Interpopulation, Interindividual, Intercycle, and Intracycle Natural Variation in Progesterone Levels: A Quantitative Assessment and Implications for Population Studies. *American Journal of Human Biology, 20*(1), 35–42. doi:10.1002/ajhb.20686.

Jones, J. (1985). *Labor of Love, Labor of Sorrow: Black Women, Work, and the Family from Slavery to the Present*: New York: Basic.

Kertes, D.A., Kamin, H.S., Hughes, D.A., Rodney, N.C., Bhatt, S., & Mulligan, C.J. (2016). Prenatal Maternal Stress Predicts Methylation of Genes Regulating the Hypothalamic–Pituitary–Adrenocortical System in Mothers and Newborns in the Democratic Republic of Congo. *Child Development, 87*(1), 61–72. doi:10.1111/cdev.12487.

Klaus, H.D. (2014). Frontiers in the Bioarchaeology of Stress and Disease: Cross-Disciplinary Perspectives from Pathophysiology, Human Biology, and Epidemiology. *American Journal of Physical Anthropology, 155*(2), 294–308. doi:10.1002/ajpa.22574.

Klengel, T., & Binder, Elisabeth B. (2015). Epigenetics of Stress-Related Psychiatric Disorders and Gene X Environment Interactions. *Neuron, 86*(6), 1343–1357. doi:https://doi.org/10.1016/j.neuron.2015.05.036.

Kneeland, L.K. (2006). *African American Suffering and Suicide Under Slavery*. (Ph.D.), Montana State University, Bozeman.

Lamis, D.A., Wilson, C.K., Tarantino, N., Lansford, J.E., & Kaslow, N.J. (2014). Neighborhood Disorder, Spiritual Well-Being, and Parenting Stress in African American Women. *Journal of Family Psychology, 28*(6), 769.

Mariotti, A. (2015). The Effects of Chronic Stress on Health: New Insights Into the Molecular Mechanisms of Brain-Body Communication. In: Future Sci OA.

McGee Z, Alexander C, Cunningham K, Hamilton C, James C. (2019). Assessing the Linkage Between Exposure to Violence and Victimization, Coping, and Adjustment among Urban Youth: Findings from a Research Study on Adolescents. Children (Basel). 2019 Feb 27;6(3). pii: E36. doi: 10.3390/children6030036.

Mehta, D., Thompson, R., Morton, T., Dhanantwari, A., & Shefer, E. (2013). Terative Model Reconstruction: Simultaneously Lowered Computed Tomography Radiation Dose and Improved Image Quality. *Med Phys Int J, 2*(1), 147–155.

Miller, G.E., Chen, E., & Zhou, E.S. (2007). If It Goes Up, Must It Come Down? Chronic Stress and the Hypothalamic-Pituitary-Adrenocortical Axis in Humans. *Psychological Bulletin, 133*(1), 25–45.

Miller, G.E., Cohen, S., Janicki-Deverts, D., Brody, G.H., & Chen, E. (2016). Viral Challenge Reveals Further Evidence of Skin-Deep Resilience in African Americans from Disadvantaged Backgrounds. *Health Psychology, 35*(11), 1225–1234.

Mintz, S. (2009). *African American Voices: A Documentary Reader* (Vol. 5): John Wiley & Sons.
Morris, M.C., & Rao, U. (2014). Cortisol Response to Psychosocial Stress During a Depressive Episode and Remission. *Stress, 17*(1), 51–58. doi:10.3109/10253890.2013.857398.
Neville, H.A., Tynes, B.M., & Utsey, S.O. (2008). *Handbook of African American Psychology*: Sage Publications.
Penzes, P., Cahill, M.E., Jones, K.A., VanLeeuwen, J.-E., & Woolfrey, K.M. (2011). Dendritic Spine Pathology in Neuropsychiatric Disorders. *Nature Neuroscience, 14*, 285.
Puttagunta, R., Tedeschi, A., Sória, M.G., Hervera, A., Lindner, R., Rathore, K.I., ... Di Giovanni, S. (2014). PCAF-Dependent Epigenetic Changes Promote Axonal Regeneration in the Central Nervous System. *Nature Communications, 5*, 3527.
Ramo-Fernández, L., Schneider, A., Wilker, S., & Kolassa, I.-T. (2015). Epigenetic Alterations Associated with War Trauma and Childhood Maltreatment. *Behavioral Sciences & the Law, 33*(5), 701–721. doi:10.1002/bsl.2200.
Roy, A., Hodgkinson, C.A., DeLuca, V., Goldman, D., & Enoch, M.-A. (2012). Two HPA Axis Genes, CRHBP and FKBP5, Interact with Childhood Trauma to Increase the Risk for Suicidal Behavior. *Journal of Psychiatric Research, 46*(1), 72–79. doi:https://doi.org/10.1016/j.jpsychires.2011.09.009.
Rutter, M. (1993). Resilience: Some Conceptual Considerations. *Journal of Adolescent Health, 14*(8), 626–631. doi:https://doi.org/10.1016/1054-139X(93)90196-V.
Ruttle, P.L., Klein, M.H., Slattery, M.J., Kalin, N.H., Armstrong, J.M., & Essex, M.J. (2014). Adolescent Adrenocortical Activity and Adiposity: Differences by Sex and Exposure to Early Maternal Depression. *Psychoneuroendocrinology, 47*(Supplement C), 68–77. doi:https://doi.org/10.1016/j.psyneuen.2014.04.025.
Seery, M.D., Holman, E.A., & Silver, R.C. (2010). Whatever Does Not Kill Us: Cumulative Lifetime Adversity, Vulnerability, and Resilience. *Journal of Personality and Social Psychology, 99*(6), 1025–1041.
Simon, R.P. (2016). Epigenetic Modulation of Gene Expression Governs the Brain's Response To Injury. *Neuroscience Letters, 625*(Supplement C), 16–19. doi:https://doi.org/10.1016/j.neulet.2015.12.024.
Stroud, L.R., Foster, E., Papandonatos, G.D., Handwerger, K., Granger, D.A., Kivlighan, K.T., & Niaura, R. (2009). Stress Response and the Adolescent Transition: Performance Versus Peer Rejection Stressors. *Development and Psychopathology, 21*(1), 47–68. doi:10.1017/S0954579409000042.
Sule, E., Sutton, R.M., Jones, D., Moore, R., Igbo, I., & Jones, L.A. (2017). The Past Does Matter: A Nursing Perspective on Post Traumatic Slave Syndrome (PTSS). *Journal of Racial and Ethnic Health Disparities, 4*(5), 779–783. doi:10.1007/s40615-016-0328-7.
Sundman, M.H., Hall, E.E., & Chen, N.-k. (2014). Examining the Relationship Between Head Trauma and Neurodegenerative Disease: A Review of Epidemiology, Pathology and Neuroimaging Techniques. *Journal of Alzheimer's disease & Parkinsonism, 4*, 137. doi:10.4172/2161-0460.1000137.
Terragni, J., Zhang, G., Sun, Z., Pradhan, S., Song, L., Crawford, G.E., ... Ehrlich, M. (2014). Notch Signaling Genes. *Epigenetics, 9*(6), 842–850. doi:10.4161/epi.28597.
Thomas, C.L. (2012). Exploring Resiliency Factors of Older African American Katrina Survivors. *Journal of Evidence-Based Social Work, 9*(4), 351–368. doi:10.1080/15433714.2010.525411.
van den Berghe, Peter V.E., Folmer, Dineke E., Malingré, Helga E.M., van Beurden, E., Klomp, Adriana E.M., van de Sluis, B., ... Klomp, Leo W.J. (2007). Human Copper Transporter 2 Is Localized in Late Endosomes and Lysosomes and Facilitates Cellular Copper Uptake. *Biochemical Journal, 407*(1), 49.
Vinkers, C.H., Kalafateli, A.L., Rutten, B.P., Kas, M.J., Kaminsky, Z., Turner, J.D., & Boks, M.P. (2015). Traumatic Stress and Human DNA Methylation: A Critical Review. *Epigenomics 7*(4): 593–608.
Voisey, J., Young, R.M., Lawford, B.R., & Morris, C.P. (2014). Progress Towards Understanding the Genetics of Post-Traumatic Stress Disorder. *Journal of Anxiety Disorders, 28*(8), 873–883. doi:https://doi.org/10.1016/j.janxdis.2014.09.014.

Walker, W.R., Vogl, R.J., & Thompson, C.P. (1997). Autobiographical Memory: Unpleasantness Fades Faster Than Pleasantness Over Time. *Applied Cognitive Psychology, 11*(5), 399–413.

Walsh, F. (2015). *Strengthening Family Resilience* (3rd ed.). Guilford Press.

Wankerl, M., Miller, R., Kirschbaum, C., Hennig, J., Stalder, T., & Alexander, N. (2014). Effects of Genetic and Early Environmental Risk Factors for Depression on Serotonin Transporter Expression and Methylation Profiles. *Translational Psychiatry, 4*, e402.

Ward, E.C., Mengesha, M., & Issa, F. (2014). Older African American Women's Lived Experiences with Depression and Coping Behaviours. *Journal of Psychiatric and Mental Health Nursing, 21*(1), 46–59. doi:10.1111/jpm.12046.

Washington, B.T. (1901). *Up from Slavery: An Autobiography*. Garden City, NY: Doubleday & Company, Inc.

Weathers, F.W., & Keane, T.M. (2007). The Criterion a Problem Revisited: Controversies and Challenges in Defining and Measuring Psychological Trauma. *Journal of Traumatic Stress, 20*(2), 107–121. doi:10.1002/jts.20210.

Wintour-Coghlan, E.M., & Owens, J. (2007). *Early Life Origins of Health and Disease* (Vol. 573): Springer Science and Business Media.

Wong, V.S., & Langley, B. (2016). Epigenetic Changes Following Traumatic Brain Injury and Their Implications for Outcome, Recovery and Therapy. *Neuroscience Letters, 625*(Supplement C), 26–33. doi:https://doi.org/10.1016/j.neulet.2016.04.009.

Yehuda, R., & et al. (2016). Holocaust Exposure Induced Intergenerational Effects on FKBP5 Methylation. *Biological Psychiatry, 80*(5), 372–380.

Zannas, A.S., Provençal, N., & Binder, E.B. (2015). Epigenetics of Posttraumatic Stress Disorder: Current Evidence, Challenges, and Future Directions. *Biological Psychiatry, 78*(5), 327–335. doi:https://doi.org/10.1016/j.biopsych.2015.04.003.

Zeisel, S.H. (2012). Dietary Choline Deficiency Causes DNA Strand Breaks and Alters Epigenetic Marks on DNA and Histones. *Mutation Research/Fundamental and Molecular Mechanisms of Mutagenesis, 733*(1), 34–38. doi:https://doi.org/10.1016/j.mrfmmm.2011.10.008

Part Three

Solutions

Part Three: Solutions is a review of what can be done to resolve the psychological legacies of slavery. Now that we have provided examples of psychological legacies in Part One and discussed them and the resistance to them, we need to address the essential question. How do we ameliorate the dysfunctional legacies and advance the protective ones? This is a question about individual and community treatments as well as doing surgery on cultures—being very selective of what is cut out and changed. In Chapter 11, Frederick W. Hickling provides an example of just how such cultural surgery might be done to benefit both individuals and communities. Chapter 12 from Benjamin P. Bowser explains how one can conduct a psychosocial history to explore and uncover trauma and experiences that have affected one's family history. Scherto Gill, in Chapter 13, describes what is required to move from the very depths of trauma from slavery and racism's dehumanization to healing.

11

Shattering Delusions of Slavery
Psychosocial Re-Engineering of Postcolonial Jamaica

FREDERICK W. HICKLING

> *How can psychological and cultural liberation from the legacies of slavery succeed without patients and doctors going through therapy together? If the patients are troubled, their society is troubled; both the patient and community need treatment. This chapter demonstrates how all three —the patient, society, and psychiatry—must contribute to one another's healing. Collective healing is being done in Jamaica. Frederick W. Hickling can demonstrate this evolving claim from the work of several generations of Jamaican psychiatrists.*

In exploring Europe's dark history in Africa, and the origins of genocide, Sven Lindquist's (1992) scorching examination in the *Heart of Darkness*, lays bare the stark civilizing mission of European white supremacy. It was a vision of superiority and ethnic cleansing of lesser races: "In practice, the whole of Europe acted according to the maxim 'Exterminate all the brutes. Officially, it was denied ... but man-to-man, everyone knew..." (Conrad, 1899, p. 171; Lindquist, 1992). There has been an attempt to deny genocidal racism and the connections between white supremacy, racism, and the enslavement of Africans by Europe (Bell, Delgado, & Stefancic, 2005; Cunneen, Fraser, & Tomsen, 1997; Wise, 2013). It is time to assess the damage, devise new strategies of resistance, and begin healing.

It is the objective of this chapter to outline the development of creative psychological analytic tools. They have been devised in Jamaica to address the psychological effects of slavery on the Jamaican people. Some unique psychosocial and clinical challenges are described. Also, it is the objective of this chapter to describe our response to these challenges through public policy, psychotherapeutic research, and practice emerging from post-independence, post-colonial Jamaica. The effects of this re-engineering process have helped to shatter the residual delusions of slavery imposed by Europe on Jamaicans.

Psycho-Historiography of Slavery

The group analytic technique called *Psycho-historiography* provides novel and qualitative evidence of the legacy of 400 years of African slave labor on European plantations in the West Indies (F. Hickling, 2009). Psycho-historiographic cultural therapy was developed in Bellevue Mental Hospital, Jamaica, in the late 1970s (F.W. Hickling, 1989). This technique was developed in response to significant changes taking place in that institution. There was intense political pressure to de-colonize triggered by Prime Minister Michael Manley and the People's National Party in that decade (F. Hickling, 2012). Large group meetings were held monthly at the Bellevue Mental Hospital, with two to three hundred persons, consisting of patients, nurses, and doctors seated in a circle. Ten to twelve of the eldest persons present served as historians. They would initiate large group discussions using anecdotal memories about life in the lunatic asylum and madness in Jamaican society. The meetings were recorded and videotaped. The anecdotal memories were subjected to visual analysis, in which events from the colonial period were contrasted with present-day experiences. These contrasts showed connections between the past and present as dialectic relationships.

Psycho-historiographic analysis (F.W. Hickling, 1989) begins with a visual inspection of the historical contrast by the analysts and participants. Around these contrasts, vertical theme lines were drawn, and horizontal trend lines were established, again by group consensus. The group using single words or single phrases then labeled the theme and trend lines. Each line expressed the group's perceptions or insights about the themes or the trends. The theme lines represented a cross-sectional analysis at a point in time. Labels, at both ends of the chart, showed a dialectic relationship. The labels at either the top or the bottom of the chart represented the class and racial perceptions of each historical theme. The labeled themes were listed on separate sheets of paper and then used to derive insight about the following conditions. These themes and trends represented the real-life and underlying experiences of participants, which were dynamic and phenomenological. This was when patients realized that their memories and anecdotes were shared and were intergenerational.

The *Psycho-historiographic* analytic technique was adapted from the concept of historiography, developed initially by Thomas Becker, in 1938, and by Elsa Goveia, in 1958. Historiography is a method of analyzing historical data to derive outlooks, ideologies, and beliefs about the transitions and social forces compelling change in society (Goveia, 1956). *Psycho-historiography* captures historical materials from a group's oral anecdotes (Brodber, 1983). Graphic dialectic analysis of the material is used to stimulate insights about themes and trends. This technique is useful in helping people from various socio-economic and educational backgrounds to comprehend under-developed political and psychological constructs, to debunk myths about colonization, and to establish a framework for more effective efforts to make a change.

Although most of the anecdotal material used in the visual analysis came from the group discussion, some of the materials were derived from publications on different historical periods. Psychiatrists must always acquire from their patients, thorough a social examination, knowledge of where patients come from, what life has had in store from them, and what influences them. The psychotherapist can get a complete insight into each case. For therapy to progress and change to take place, the patient, too, must internalize insights about themselves and their circumstances. They must deal with forces that block action, do problem-solving and reality testing. They must master their anxieties and accept personal limitations and handicaps while fulfilling their life potential (Wolberg, 1967).

The following was the first significant finding of the Psycho-historiographic process at the Jamaican Mental Hospital: the European conquest of the Caribbean was derived from a delusion, an essential element of madness. Delusion is defined as an idiosyncratic and fixed false belief that is held with firm conviction and is impervious to a rational argument (Jaspers, 1913, 1967). The delusion is that it was by divine right that European invaders owned all that was theirs. This European delusion was held with firm conviction, and any attempt by non–Europeans to oppose it by rational argument was met with genocidal extermination. Our analysis showed that this European delusion soon *metamorphosed* into a secondary delusion: the racist ideology of white supremacy, namely, the belief that white people are superior to people of other racial backgrounds. White supremacy was buttressed and reinforced by religious exhortations that Black people were sub-human and that White people should rule non–White people, politically, economically, and socially. The Atlantic Slave Trade, Jim Crow Laws in the United States, and apartheid in South Africa are evidence of this delusion (Wildman, 1996). The European delusion decreed that African slaves were three-fifths humans, and Europeans owned them by Divine Right, which allowed Whites full sexual and vocational exploitation of enslaved Africans. Coupled with greed, the delusion of racial supremacy justified the extermination of indigenous people and spawned a social and economic system built on the labor of enslaved Blacks in the New World.

The Jamaican historian, Douglas Hall (1989), has substantiated the European delusions of slavery and white supremacy. Ethnographic research of the life of White British planter and slave owner, Thomas Thistlewood, in Jamaica, 1750–1786, provides exhaustive evidence of the white supremacy that motivated slavery. This study describes the role of dependency and cruel repression that protected profits for the White plantocracy. The delusion of British colonialism's "civilizing mission" was exposed. In the Thistlewood diaries, there were morbid details of the sexual depravity and cruel vindictiveness of slave owners towards Black men and women. They described the repression and violence that underpinned the behavior modification and social engineering of slaves' lives. Jamaican sociologist Orlando Patterson (1967) did meticulous research documenting the brutal practices of British colonial slavery in Jamaica: "cruel punishments were greatly responsible for high mortality rates … some (Negro slaves) are whipt, or even hanged for going into the woods…" (Patterson, 1967, p. 103).

Violent flagellation of women in the presence of their menfolk and children was a standard method of reinforcing mental enslavement. The famous engraving by William Blake, of a female Samboe slave in Surinam, depicts a young Black woman with deep lacerations hanging from a tree (Stedman, 1796). In the background are two White men and two Black men, the latter with whips. Based upon a speech given in Virginia, 1712, Willie Lynch described the methods of exploiting differences between slaves as a method of social engineering. The period 1500 to 1800 represents the manifestation of madness, which gripped Europeans. A complex collective delusion deems all people in the world with white skins superior to all others with non-white skins. It justified systematic eradication and enslavement of millions of people across the globe, from North, Central, and South Americas and the Caribbean.

Our Psycho-historiographic analysis called this complex delusional process the *European Psychosis* (F. Hickling, 2009). It is a drive to possess and own the lush and fertile lands on which non–White people dwelt and to plunder whatever resources they found. These critical actions established a complex system of delusional thinking, which has been imposed on the world since the 1494 expeditions of Columbus. They are at the foundation of human life and civilization, as we know it today. The primary delusion of European psychosis is that *"all of this land and all that exists therein belong to me,"* and the subsequent genocidal eradication of the rightful owners drove unquenchable greed. European plunderers did so without the slightest exhibition of guilt for their atrocities, and with only a trace of critical examination of conscience or morality. The secondary delusion of *White Supremacy* led to the development of African slavery and racism. The desire for economic enrichment drove them through slavery and property theft by the rape of Africa and the New World. In turn, these delusions have resulted in genocide, brutality, and repeated trauma for native people and Africans alike until this very day.

Violence and Complex Trauma

Violence was at the core of colonialism and slavery. Violence was necessary to maintain European psychosis through slavery. Violence was also necessary for resistance. Psycho-historiography revealed that there was a cyclical, thirty-year pattern of revolutionary violence to overcome the European psychosis. This cycle did not stop with emancipation. It continues unabated to this day. There was a slave revolt in Jamaica, approximately every 31 years, between 1655 and 1999 (Hickling 2000). There was the Spanish Negro Slave Revolt of 1663; the First Maroon War, led by Cudjoe, in 1690; the Nanny Rebellion of 1730; Tacky's rebellion in 1760; the Second Maroon War of 1795, and the Sam Sharpe Rebellion of 1832. All these rebellions heralded emancipation. The next violent rebellion in the thirty-year cycle occurred in 1865: the Morant Bay Rebellion. By the 1890s, unrest surfaced again with the charismatic religious minister, Alexander Bedward as a leader. The sugar worker's rebellion of 1938 came next before political independence was attained from Britain in 1962.

Independent self-government did not quell the pattern of cyclical rebellion. The charismatic, University of the West Indies lecturer, Walter Rodney, was the focus for the next episode of rebellious violence in 1968. The last episode of rebellion occurred in 1999, with riots triggered by rising petrol prices.

What prompts occasional violence from the colonized is the everyday violence of colonization. What needs explaining is why there is not constant rebellion. What goes on in the approximately thirty years between outbreaks? The answer is the psychology of colonization, with trauma at its core holding the colonized in check.

It is necessary to deconstruct the *complex trauma* experienced in the colonial and post-colonial periods, which is an outcome of the violence. Complex trauma is suffering that repeatedly occurs over a long period and takes the form of physical abuse, long-standing sexual abuse, domestic violence, and war. Cook, Spinazzola, Ford, et al. (2005) explain how the exposure to complex trauma results in a loss of core-capacities for self-regulation and interpersonal relatedness. This, in turn, leads to psychiatric and addictive disorders, chronic medical illnesses, legal, vocational, and family problems, all extending from childhood through adolescence and into adulthood. The Psycho-historiographic analysis at the Jamaican mental hospital confirmed that Jamaica was born and suckled in such violence and war. Its people have been expected to accept trauma and violence against them as a way of life set by the British colonizers who dominated the island for more than three hundred years. Some other psychological fallout from the past to the present that must be addressed is a disturbed racial identity and a specific personality disorder.

Disturbed Racial Identification: The Roast Breadfruit Psychosis

Problems of racial identification in Western societies for people of African descent have arisen out of their experience in European slavery and colonization. In some, the internalization of feelings of inferiority has contributed to problems of identity formation. Using the analogy of *roast breadfruit*, Hickling and Hutchinson (1999) explain increased rates of psychoses among the African and Caribbean populations in Britain. The breadfruit (*Artocarpus altilis*) is a fruit[1] found throughout the Caribbean. The green skin of the breadfruit turns charcoal-black when roasted on an open fire, but the inside flesh turns white. They applied the concept of the roast breadfruit when reviewing the racial psychological contradiction of Black people who consider themselves White. This concept is reflected in the fiction of Toni Morrison (1985) and in the work of psychiatrist Frantz Fanon (1965), to illustrate an effect of past colonialism on the mental health of Black people. This formulation identifies a form of mental illness posited as a core problem for Blacks, formerly colonial people living in Britain (Hickling and Hutchinson 1999). They are confronted continuously with their racial identity in a racist environment that is psychosocially and culturally toxic. This produces internal ambivalence, triggering the emergence of a *roast breadfruit syndrome*, which can deteriorate and metamorphose into psychotic and affective symptoms. This condition defies precise nosological characterization.

Black colonials who become "white" by thoroughly integrating the colonizers' language and culture into their psyche have been described in North America as *"Oreo cookie,"* after the chocolate biscuit with a white marshmallow sandwich filling. This too could be described as a syndrome. In Asian and Polynesian cultures, the same problem has been given the name of *"the coconut syndrome."* Hickling and Hutchinson suggest that African-Caribbean people who initially display behavior of being "functionally white" (illustrative of the roast breadfruit syndrome) can develop psychosis around their identity conflicts. North America and Europe provide the setting for personal and social confrontations with their blackness. This mental pathology reflects their racial confusion as an outcome of abnormal personality identity formation and the stress of social racism. Fanon (1965) had first identified the phenomenon whereby Black colonials could become and believe themselves to be "White" by integrating the colonizer's language and culture into his own psyche. Such individuals are usually without insight into this process and reject their own indigenous culture as inferior or primitive.

Shakatani: Personality Disorder Due to Slavery and Colonialism

A central preoccupation of my nearly fifty-year experience as a psychiatrist has been researching into the presentation and treatment of personality disorder. Hickling and Paisley (2011) suggest that this poorly understood mental illness is manifested in three phenomenological clusters. First, issues in the *management of power*, especially about authority figures and organizations, manifest by repeated conflicts, duplicity, transgression, and wrongdoing. Second, there are issues with *physiological dependency*, such as addiction to licit and illicit drugs, food, and gambling, as well as psychological dependency. Third, there are *psychosexual issues* manifest in phenomena such as hypersexuality and abnormal sexual functioning. The phenomenological approach outlined in this study is suggested as a viable replacement of the current classification in the American Psychiatric Association DSM-V, with the clinical triad identified as an Axis I disorder. I suggest the name *shakatani*, derived from the Swahili words *shaka* (problem) and *tani* (power), should replace the name and concept of the current Axis II personality disorder.

Shakatani (personality disorder) can be mild, moderate, or severe. Our work at the University Hospital of the West Indies, Jamaica, has shown that this condition occurs in nearly 42 percent of Jamaicans in both genders. A significant finding is that this condition occurs in all racial groups. This is nearly three to seven times higher than the prevalence rates of this condition reported in other parts of the world. Jamaicans seem to have a proclivity for transgression, which we conclude is rooted in the historical psychopathology of a slave society. The murder rate in Jamaica 2000–2015 has ranged from 40–60/100,000 and seems to be steadily rising. Some of our best minds have turned to crime. In a recent study of condemned murderers in Jamaica, fifteen percent were reported to have I.Q. scores of *Superior/Very Superior,* in a range double that of the normal population (F. Hickling & Walcott, 2013).

People with these personality disorders can be treated with *psycho-*

historiographic brief psychotherapy. They can improve by gaining insight into their thoughts, attitudes, and behaviors through *insight* and continued *behavior modification.* These patients often tell outrageous lies, even in the presence of overwhelming evidence to the contrary. Getting these patients to have insight into their lying, and to admit their duplicity, is not enough to remedy the problem. The therapeutic experience indicates that the transgressive patient often must suffer the consequences of their behavior and undergo a life-long behavioral modification program. A constant review of potential and recurrent transgressive behavior must be part of the follow-up management in treating these people. The paradoxical tragedy of these persons, who have this mental illness, is that many have extremely high intelligence, often hold high leadership office, and are some of the most productive entrepreneurs. The public policy implications of these psychiatric contradictions are profound. There must be widespread community diagnostic and therapeutic facilities established for the management of these mentally ill persons in our communities. Also, there must be effective justice systems, established with progressive punitive components, to contain the most blatant and dangerous transgressors. Truth and reconciliation strategies are usually not enough to deal with the most severely transgressive individuals. Fundamental psychological decolonization is necessary to address this psychosis, and problems in racial identity formation.

Psychological Decolonization

Because of Jamaica's and the Caribbean's continued economic dependence, the process of mental decolonizing became a primary focus of the post-independence experience. Reggae singer Bob Marley immortalized this decolonizing objective in the lyrics to "Redemption Song."[2] Few have acknowledged the role that psychiatry and psychiatrists must play in the mental decolonization of people. Early Jamaican psychiatric pioneers, such as Drs. Roy Cooke and Ken Royes in the decade before independence had signaled their insight into this process by calling for the deinstitutionalization of Bellevue Mental Hospital. They recommended the development of a Community Mental Health service. Their call was to the Pan American Health Organization (PAHO).

British colonialists had built the Jamaican Lunatic Asylum in 1862, which was renamed Bellevue Hospital in 1947. Up until independence, one hundred years later, this asylum was the single repository on the island for persons with mental illness. The conditions for the mentally ill incarcerated in the lunatic asylum in Kingston were appalling. There were overcrowding and ill-treatment of patients, recorded by the warden at that time as "a chamber of horrors" (Rouse, 1860). The physical abuses commonly inflicted on patients were described by Henry Taylor, the head of the West Indian Department at the Colonial Office, in 1861, as "The most cruel and revolting crimes" (Jones, 2008). Similar evidence emerged from the psycho-historiographic group analysis at Bellevue Hospital in 1978. A significant function of the Jamaican lunatic asylum was to sequestrate and contain those in the population with opposing cultural beliefs and ideologies supportive of British colonialism, especially those who constituted a danger to the British state.

In a recent book on insanity and colonialism in the Caribbean, British medical historian Leonard Smith (2014) attempted to negate the findings of the Jamaican psycho-historiographic process of the 1970s. He suggested that measures to remove, sequestrate, and care for the insane were the central element in colonial Britain's "civilizing mission": "British colonial authorities' … conscious motivations for their gradual establishment [of the asylum] throughout the empire comprised both benevolent and controlling intentions…. The 'civilizing mission' was clearly an important element in the development of institutions for the insane…" (Smith, 2014, p. 3). This continued defense of the British civilizing mission is intended to show that Black post-colonial societies are pathological, while the British homeland is not. There have been several studies in recent decades that suggest the risk ratio for schizophrenia was six to eighteen times higher for African Caribbean's in the U.K. than for Whites. British psychiatrists have strongly suggested that the cause of high rates of schizophrenia in migrants to the U.K. is that they brought this condition with them from the Caribbean and that the etiology of this condition is genetic. A watershed incidence study was done on first-contact schizophrenia in Jamaica (F. Hickling & Rodgers-Johnson, 1995). This study was replicated in Barbados (Mahy, Mallett, Leff, & Bhugra, 1999). Then, the matter was settled by the third study in Trinidad (Bhugra et al., 1996). The incidence of schizophrenia in the Caribbean was significantly less than that reported for Whites in the U.K. Therefore, the reportedly high-risk ratios for schizophrenia in African Caribbeans in the U.K. were a product of the host environment in the U.K. Hickling (1996) demonstrated that White migrants to Jamaica had a much lower rate of schizophrenia in Jamaica, compared to Jamaican controls. Whites enjoy significant elevation in social class in the Black host country. This suggests that the social systems in Black post-colonial countries like Jamaica seem to protect White people from developing schizophrenia (F. Hickling, 2009).

Selten, Slaets, and Kahn (1997) provided evidence of a similar high risk-ratio of schizophrenia in the African-Caribbean immigrant populations from the Dutch Antilles in Holland, as had been reported for the U.K.

They began describing what they called "the effect of urbanicity" (Selten & Cantor-Graae, 2005). This line of epidemiological reasoning led Selten and Cantor-Graae (2005) to hypothesize that the etiologic and long-term experience of *"social defeat"* may increase the risk for schizophrenia in Black Caribbean migrants to Europe. The social defeat was defined as the response of a subordinate position or as "outsider status." They suggested that racial discrimination would undoubtedly contribute to the migrant's experience of social defeat. Hickling's psycho-historiographic analysis (F. Hickling, 2005) suggested an alternative hypothesis: namely that African-Caribbean "madness and badness" are defense mechanisms to cope with the challenges posed by the "European-American psychosis." They represent an experience of *social defiance,* not social defeat: what Fanon called the *"pathology of freedom"* (Fanon, 1959, pp. 717, 723). Similar findings have been reported by Whitley (2011).

For Europe, the "Civilizing Mission" was the primary rationale for colonizing Africa and the world. The European colonial powers felt it was their duty to bring Western civilization to whomever they perceived as backward and inferior. Central to this idea was the European delusion of White supremacy. The British actualized this delusion through all the institutions they left in Jamaica. Decolonization requires uprooting the colonizer's central delusions.

Jamaica

The first phase of the mental health transformation of Jamaica (1962–1974) started with the training of six young psychiatrists at the University of the West Indies. Drs. Michael Beaubrun, Frank Knight, and Charles Thesiger developed the training program in psychiatry for medical students and psychiatric residents. Drs. Trevor Lindsay, Fred Hickling, and Janet La Grenade spearheaded the deinstitutionalization of the Bellevue Mental Hospital, and the development of the island-wide community mental health program. The decade of the 1970s represented the renaissance period of decolonization of the mental health system. "Psychiatry, the ugly duckling of Medicine, has at last begun to show signs of abandoning its ungainly profile, and in true fairy-tale fashion seems about to blossom into the majestic swan of the medical profession…" (F. Hickling, 1973).

By 1974, Bellevue Hospital housed more than 3,000 patients, living in desperate and deplorable conditions. Case studies of political dissidents, such as Alexander Bedward in 1895, provide hard evidence that the Jamaican Colonial State used the lunatic asylum and the Lunatic Asylum Law to muzzle political dissent (F.W. Hickling & Gibson, 2005, p. 85). The Lunatic Asylum Law, in conjunction with the anti–Obeah law used by the colonial authorities, led to the suppression of traditional African communal healing and treatment systems. Tertiary mental health care in Jamaica, through the Lunatic Asylum Law and lunatic asylum, also led to locking up members of the Rastafari movement, from the 1930s through the 1960s (F. Hickling, 2016). Leonard Howell, generally regarded as the originator of the Rastafarian movement, who established the first Rastafarian commune at Pinnacle in St. Catherine, became a target of police raids in the 1930s and 1940s. An irritant to the colonial government, Howells was incarcerated in the Bellevue Mental Hospital, and a police raid in 1958 eventually destroyed his commune (Dagnini, 2009).

In my early years working in the Bellevue Mental Hospital, I witnessed how Rastafarians were viewed as mad people, forcibly detained in the lunatic asylum. Their dreadlocks were shaved, and they were medicated against their will for their beliefs (Hickling 2009). Rastafari was vilified as mad and bad. At an American Psychiatric Association meeting held in Ocho Rios, Jamaica in 1969, Dr. Raymond H. Prince (1969), Professor of Psychiatry, McGill University, Canada, suggested that "…Rastafari was the product of 'delusional cultism'.…" Professor Ari Kiev (1969) challenged this view at that meeting. He countered that Prince's opinion reflected the false idea that Rastafarian beliefs are more unusual or deviant than the concepts of other religious movements. Kiev insisted that diagnosis must be based on clinical examination, and not the clinician's idiosyncratic views. Hickling and Griffith (1994) concluded that the Rastafari movement provided an affirmation of Black identity, and a moral framework for Black people emerging from centuries of slavery, colonization, and oppression. The challenge for us was to affirm Black identity and use psychiatry to affirm rather than deny decolonization. Psycho-historiographic cultural therapy was our answer to this challenge.

Psycho-Historiographic Cultural Therapy

Psycho-historiographic cultural therapy (PCT), initially described at the beginning of this chapter, can be carried out in a wide variety of cultural settings. PCT involves blending large group psychotherapy with oral tradition, the use of the circle, folk traditions, story-telling, poetry, arts, crafts, music, dance, and theater. These activities are combined with current psychopharmacology, culturally sensitive counseling, and individual psychotherapy (F.W. Hickling, 1989). "Psychotherapy is the treatment, by psychological means, of problems of an emotional nature in which a trained person deliberately establishes a professional relationship with the objective of removing, modifying or retarding existing symptoms; of mediating disturbed patterns of behavior and of promoting positive personality growth and development..." (Wolberg, 1967 Part 1:3).

In the 1970s, Jamaican psychiatry was struggling with implementing community psychiatry and deinstitutionalization. Mental health practitioners were trying to find a therapeutic vehicle that would unite widely diverse outlooks and expectations of patients and workers who were at different professional, educational ideological, and class levels. PCT aimed to bring about therapeutic change and to facilitate decolonization. It also aimed to destigmatize patients and to promote mental health education in the country. Developing a cultural therapy process was the major element in easing the transition of the mental hospital from a custodial to a rehabilitative hospital. Founding a cultural therapy center was essential to maintaining this transition at the Bellevue Hospital.

Cultural Therapy Center

One of the first projects of the Cultural Therapy Unit at the Bellevue Garden Theater was a pageant, in August 1978. It was the "*Madnificent Irations*," depicting the history and struggles of the mental hospital in Jamaica. The performance told the history of mental illness in Jamaica and the colonial development of the lunatic asylum. The pageant closely followed the anecdotal material, themes, and trends identified by the Psycho-historiography. The following verse from the pageant reflects the history of the Morant Bay rebellion in 1865. The British Governor of the island unleashed his troops on protestors in Morant Bay, killing hundreds of Black Jamaicans who were protesting the abysmal social and economic conditions in colonial Jamaica at the time.

(Jamaican patois original verse)	*(English language translation)*
Now di governor man Eyre	The British Colonial Governor Eyre
him sey him did dreader dan dread	Who claimed to be the cruelest of all
him sen fe him troop dem	Sent his troops to quell the rebellion
Dem hang an shoot eighty-five	They shot and hanged eighty-five protestors
as dem come, without trial	On the spot, any kind of trial
Hickling (1978)	Hickling (2017)

The pageant dramatized the political connection between the protests of poverty-stricken, colonial descendants of Africans enslaved in Jamaica, and the cruelty of the British colonizer. "The themes that emerged from psycho-historiographic analysis of the discussions at the meetings were used as topics for scenes in writing the scripts of the pageants. The theme of the struggle against enslavement and racism was evident in each production" (F.W. Hickling, 1989, p. 404).

There was a clinical benefit from the cultural therapy for the individual patients who participated. Participants showed significant decreases in medication in their psychosocial disability scores. They also exhibited significantly higher rates of improvement and discharge than did patients in the non-participant control group (Hickling 1989). Participation in psycho-historiographic analysis and the pageant demonstrated to hospital patients and staff the close relationship between colonial politics, social conditions, and the abnormal behavior of the colonial authorities. There were clear mental health consequences of these behaviors for the Jamaican people. This dramatic convergence of history and psychology also produced exciting insights for Jamaicans who were not patients at the hospital. At a 1979 performance of the *Magnificent Irations*, at a massive sugar plantation, Bernard Lodge and I overheard a group of sugar workers in the audience of over 3000 people, commenting in astonishment at the performance skill of the mental hospital patients on the stage: "If those people acting and dancing on the stage are 'mad-men and mad-women,' then we have to wonder—'is who mad, dem or we?'"

The PCT pageant also dramatized the profound insight that pioneering Caribbean (Martinique) psychiatrist Frantz Fanon articulated in his early writings. He identified mental illness as a "pathology of freedom" (Fanon, 1959). From his clinical experience at Blida-Joinville Hospital in Algeria (1953–1956), he pioneered the idea of "the therapeutic institution." He helped to advance the idea of transforming culture as part of social therapy. Fanon advocated the extensive use of group and institutional therapies, as well as the construction of a microcosm of the "real" world in the mental hospital. The patient should assume an active role throughout the day, through work, and by helping to organize various activities. Psychological decolonization through cultural therapy cannot just happen at the hospital. It must be extended to communities outside its walls.

Community Mental Health Public Policy Decolonization

In the early 1970s, some of the first psychiatrists trained in Beaubrun's UWI psychiatric residency program, in conjunction with nurses from the Bellevue Mental Hospital, launched a revolutionary community mental health and deinstitutionalization program in Jamaica. The initiative has become known as the "community engagement" program (Walcott, 2012). Jamaica is acknowledged as the first English-speaking country to implement reform of its mental health policy (Caldas de Almeida & Horvitz-Lennon, 2010). This program was based upon novel mental health legislation passed in 1974. The 3000-patient mental hospital population was reduced to 795 persons in 2015 (Munroe-Ellis, 2016). This is a 73.5 percent reduction in the first two years (F.W. Hickling, 1976). A community mental health system was developed for the island, as well (F.W. Hickling, Gibson, & Hutchinson, 2013), and offered primary care, mental health services in the nearly 400 clinics island-wide. The program of treating patients with acute psychoses in open general medical wards (OGMW) of hospitals is a unique and innovative service in world psychiatry (F. Hickling, McCallum, Nooks, & Rodgers-Johnson, 2000).

The Cochrane Review recognizes the program as an innovative service not replicated anywhere else in the world (F.W. Hickling, Abel, & Garner, 2002; F.W. Hickling, Abel, Garner, & Rathbone, 2007). This program has been so successful that by 2010, 44 percent of the annual admission of all acute psychiatric patients was to these facilities, and 67 percent of all psychiatric admissions were to community hospital facilities (F.W. Hickling et al., 2013). U.K. psychology professor, Raymond Cochrane, gave his opinion of the treatment of acute psychosis in open general medical wards: "The big difference is the use of general medical beds in ordinary wards for even quite severely mentally ill patients, and this does avoid stigmatizing them. It puts them into a "normal" hospital environment, and although I've only seen a little of that, it does seem to work" (Moses, 2011, p. 1).

Research evidence also indicates the success of these community mental health practices. F.W. Hickling, M. McCallum, L. Nooks, and P. Rodgers-Johnson (2001) showed that the relapse rate for patients with first-contact schizophrenia in Jamaica (13.7 percent) was much lower than the relapse rate for first-contact patients with schizophrenia in other developing countries (39 percent). It is significantly lower than the relapse rate for first-contact schizophrenic patients in first world countries (65 percent) such as the U.K. (Jablenksy et al., 1992). Creating a novel cadre of community mental health officers (MHOs), and community psychiatrists, has been the key to the success of the Community Mental Health Service (Beaubrun, 1966; F. Hickling & Rodgers-Johnson, 1995). The pivotal role of MHOs is highlighted in Kwame McKenzie's (2008) contribution to a Pan American Health Organization review.

The MHO model offers a "cost-effective model for community care and home treatment in areas where there are few doctors." It is an alternative strategy in developing countries where the remoteness of mental health professionals is problematic. These MHOs live and work in the same communities as their patients. The evidence-based data indicate that this transformed Jamaica's mental health system meets many of the country's post-colonial needs. There is 24-hour response time to acute mental illness, island-wide. There have been 2,500 severely mentally ill admissions in general hospitals annually, with a mean length of stay of seven days. Three of every four psychiatric admissions are to general hospitals, but there are 55,000 severely mentally ill clinic patients seen annually across the island. General practitioners island-wide see 60 percent of patients with mild to moderate mental illness annually. The government-owned National Health Fund subsidizes 80 percent of psychotropic medication for all classes of patients. However, services for children and the mentally disabled are still in their infancy. Psychoeducational and psychotherapeutic services are needed still for burgeoning personality disorders.

Primary Prevention: Mental Health Transformation

The University of the West Indies (UWI) has pioneered the epidemiology of mental illness in the Anglophone Caribbean over the past 50 years. With the stabilization of a community network of treatment services for most categories of mental illness across the region, the attention of the UWI has shifted. Our focus is on the identification of at-risk components of mental illness as the therapeutic attention moves from curative and maintenance to primary prevention. At the turn of the millennium, in 2004, the UWI moved toward creating the *Caribbean Institute of Mental Health and Substance Abuse (CARIMENSA)*. CARIMENSA was established as a center within the faculty of medical sciences, in February 2007. It has engaged in a private/public partnership with Psychotherapy Associates Ltd, one of the leading private medical research organizations in Jamaica (Figueroa & Henry Lee 1998). The famous Caribbean cultural icon, UWI Vice-Chancellor Emeritus, Rex Nettleford (2007), emphasized that the heart of CARIMENSA's operation would be a program of cultural therapy:

> A child learns the meaning of process and is better able to relate outcome to effort if he is encouraged to create a poem or a song, act in a play, make up a dance, sing in a choir or play an instrument in an orchestra as a normal part of his education. The *stock of ontology* are: the discipline that underpins the mastery of the craft, the demands made on a continuous recreation of effort and application, the travels encountered on the journey to excellence, the habits of realistic self-evaluation, the capacity for dealing with diversity and dilemma of difference. These constitute excellent preparation for learning, whether in the performing arts or in crucial branches of sport—themselves belonging to the family of performing arts. For learning to know, the *substance of epistemology*, learning to live together, the *essence of the creative diversity* characterizes Caribbean existence. This is about to overtake the entire world. All of this must serve the individual throughout his or her individual life.... Nettleford [2002, p. 185]. [Italics added by this author]

Jamaica, with one of the highest murder rates worldwide, is facing an immediate crisis of crime and violence (Lemard & Hemenway, 2006; United Nations Office on Drugs and Crime, 2013). Youth are both victims and perpetrators of crime, engage in high-risk behaviors, and experience high rates of unemployment and teenage pregnancy. With the secondary school dropout rates at grade 12 near to 30 percent, low academic performance and social dysfunction are two common indicators of maladaptive behavior. Children not reading by age eight are most likely to become involved in high-risk behaviors, including bullying, attacks on teachers, threatening, oppositional defiant behaviors, and sexual acting out (Huesmann, Eron, & Yarmel, 1987). Extraordinarily high levels of conduct disorder, school dropouts, and crime, poverty, and lack of basic psychological needs are triggered by parental abandonment, neglect, domestic and community violence, verbal, physical, and sexual abuse. Children who have such experiences develop severe *attachment disorders*, the precursors of high-risk, and anti-social behaviors (Schaeffer, Ialongo, & Hubbard, 2006). If unattended, these young people will become aggressive adolescents and adults, further fuelling the rising crime countrywide.

The *Dream-A-World Cultural Therapy* program has been developed as a suitable intervention. An evidence-based control group was set up at a primary school in Kingston in 2006. The selection criteria for participation were poor academic performance and behavioral problems (Guzder, Paisley, Robertson-Hickling, & Hickling, 2013). The program combined group therapy with the creative arts (drama, dance, art, and music). Discussions with the children were facilitated in a large group circle, facilitating collective sharing and reflection. The objective was to build social skills, empathy, identity formation, self-esteem, negotiation skills, and understanding of their daily social and school realities. The children were asked to imagine a new world on another planet, name it, conceive its inhabitants, and decide what to take or eliminate from their known world to this new one. They decided how they would look and what role they would play in governing the new world. They were taught to play musical instruments, compose songs, poems, and dances about their new world, which were refined and performed over the project cycle (F. Hickling, 2007). Funded by a grant from Grand Challenges Canada, the project was replicated as a two-year, evidence-based, control *scale-up* project in July 2013, in four primary schools in inner-city Kingston.

The Jamaica Ministry of Education invited CARIMENSA to implement the Dream a World Cultural Therapy program in 68 primary schools in Eastern Jamaica. All stages of the cultural therapy program have reported significant improvement in behavior and academic performance of participating students. In 2013, the Dream-A-World Cultural Therapy won the

Turn the World Upside Down Mental Health Challenge Award (2013). The London School of Hygiene and Tropical Medicine sponsored the award, based on open worldwide competition. The award's purpose is to identify and celebrate projects, practices, and ideas from low- and middle-income countries, which could be applied effectively to significant health challenges faced by high-income countries. The program progressed from 30 children in one school, for the proof of concept, to 100 children in four schools, and scaled up to 1,300 children in 70 schools. The cost per child fell from $2,500 U.S., per child, for the proof of concept, to $128, U.S., in its scaled form.

Conclusion

Overcoming the psychological delusions of colonizing Europeans, now embedded in the social fabric of the New World, is the greatest challenge facing psychiatrists and psychotherapists worldwide. This case study of the post-colonial, Jamaican psychosocial re-engineering has been presented to illustrate a model of engagement of our homegrown professionals. In our experience, collective insight is the first step in this social psychotherapy process. It is the recognition that insight on its own is not enough for transformation and change. Smashing the social mirror by shifting the social space that provides the delusion must follow insight. Embedding the insight for change and acceptance of blackness in the *cultural language and art forms* of the people must be the final step that provides the ultimate behavioral transformation and modification. For this, we need to re-school society by taking psychiatry to school. Only then will we shatter the psychological delusions of slavery imposed on people of color by European colonialism over the past five hundred years.

Notes

1. Botanically the breadfruit is a fruit. Culinarily, it is a vegetable when mature but not ripe—like eggplant, tomatoes, cucumbers, squash, peppers, etc., but a culinary fruit when ripe. https://www.quora.com/Is-breadfruit-a-fruit-or-vegetable.
2. Bob Marley Songs of Freedom … "Emancipate Yourself from Mental Slavery" … Redemption Song—Uprising Album; Island Records (1980).

References

Beaubrun, M.H. (1966). Psychiatric Education for the Caribbean. *West Indian Medical Journal, 15,* 52–62.
Bell, D., Delgado, R., & Stefancic, J. (2005). *The Derrick Bell Reader.* New York: NYU Press.
Bhugra, D., Hilwig, M., Hossein, B., Marceau, H., Neehall, J., Leff, J., … Der, G. (1996).

First-Contact Incidence Rates of Schizophrenia in Trinidad and One-Year Follow-Up. *Br J. Psychiatry, 169,* 587–592.

Brodber, E. (1983). Oral Sources and the Creation of Social History in the Caribbean. *Jamaica Journal, 16,* 2–8.

Caldas de Almeida, J.M., & Horvitz-Lennon, M. (2010). Mental Health Care Reforms in Latin America: An Overview of Mental Health Care Reforms in Latin America and the Caribbean. *Psychiatric Services, 61,* 218–221.

Conrad, J. (1899). Heart of Darkness U.K. *Blackwood Magazine, 1000.*

Cook, A., Spinazzola, J., Ford, J., Lanktree, C., Blaustein, M., Cloitre, M., ... van der Kolk, B. (2005). Complex Trauma in Children and Adolescents. *Psychiatric Annals, 35*(5), 390–398.

Cunneen, C., Fraser, D., & Tomsen, S. (1997). *Faces of Hate: Hate Crimes in Australia.* Sydney: Hawkins Press.

Dagnini, J. (2009). Rastafari: Alternative Religion and Resistance Against "White" Christianity *Études Caribéennes, 12.*

Fanon, F. (1959). Hospitalisation de jour en psychiatrie: valeur et limites. *La Tunisie médicale, 37*(10), 689–732.

Fanon, F. (1965). *A Dying Colonialism* (H. Chevalier, Trans.). New York: Grove Press.

Goveia, E.V. (1956). *A Study on the Historiography of the British West Indies to the End of the Nineteen Century*: Instituto Panamericano De Geografia E Historia.

Guzder, J., Paisley, V., Robertson-Hickling, H., & Hickling, F. (2013). Promoting Resilience and Competencies in High Risk School Aged Children in Jamaica: A Pilot Study of a Cultural Therapy Multimodal Intervention. *Canadian Journal of Child and Adolescent Psychiatry, 22*(2), 125–130.

Hall, D. (1989). *In Miserable Slavery: Thomas Thistlewood in Jamaica 1750–1786.* UK: Warwick University Press.

Hickling, F. (1973, July 13). A Plan for Psychiatry in Jamaica. *The Sunday Gleaner.*

Hickling, F. (1996). Psychopathology of White Mentally Ill Immigrants to Jamaica. *Mol Chem. Neuropathol., 28,* 26–28.

Hickling, F. (2005). Catalyzing Creativity: Psycho-Historiography, Sociodrama and Cultural Therapy. In F. Hickling & E. Sorel (Eds.), *Images of Psychiatry: The Caribbean* (pp. 241–273). Kingston, Jamaica: Stephenson's Litho Press Ltd.

Hickling, F. (2007). *Dream-A-World CARIMENSA and the Development of Cultural Therapy in Jamaica.* Kingston: UWI Carimensa Press.

Hickling, F. (2009). The European American Psychosis: A Psycho-Historiographic Perspective of Contemporary Western Civilization. *The Journal of Psychohistory, 37*(1).

Hickling, F. (2012). *Psycho-Historiography. A Postcolonial Psychoanalytic and Psychotherapeutic Model.* London: Jessica Kingsley Publishers.

Hickling, F. (2016). *Owning Our Madness: Facing Reality in Postcolonial Jamaica.* Mona, Jamaica: University of the West Indies, CARIMENSA Press.

Hickling, F., & Hutchinson, G. (1999). Roast Breadfruit Psychosis: Disturbed Racial Identification in African-Caribbeans. *Psychiatric Bulletin, 23,* 132–134.

Hickling, F., McCallum, M., Nooks, L., & Rodgers-Johnson, P. (2000). Treatment of First Contact Schizophrenia in Open Medical Wards in Jamaica. *Psychiatric Services, 51*(5), 659–663.

Hickling, F., & Rodgers-Johnson, P. (1995). The Incidence of First Onset Schizophrenia in Jamaica. *Br J. Psychiatry, 167,* 193–196.

Hickling, F., & Walcott, G. (2013). Personality Disorder in Convicted Jamaican Murders. *West Indian Medical Journal.*

Hickling, F.W. (1976). The Effects of a Community Psychiatric Service on Mental Hospital Admissions in Jamaica. *West Indian Medical Journal, 25,* 101–107.

Hickling, F.W. (1989). Sociodrama in the Rehabilitation of Chronic Mental Illness. *Hospital and Community Psychiatry, 40,* 402–406.

Hickling, F.W., Abel, W., & Garner, P. (2002). Open Medical Wards Versus Specialist Psychiatric Units for Acute Psychoses. *Cochrane Database of Systematic Reviews, 1,* 1–10.

Hickling, F.W., Abel, W., Garner, P., & Rathbone, J. (2007). Open General Medical Wards Versus Specialist Psychiatric Units for Acute Psychoses. *Cochrane Database of Systematic Reviews, 4,* 1–13.

Hickling, F.W., & Gibson, R.C. (2005). Philosophy and Epistemology in Caribbean psychiatry. In F. Hickling & E. Sorel (Eds.), *Images of Psychiatry: The Caribbean* (pp. 75–108). Kingston, Jamaica: Stephenson's Litho Press Ltd.

Hickling, F.W., Gibson, R.C., & Hutchinson, G. (2013). Current Research on Transcultural Psychiatry in the Anglophone Caribbean Diaspora—Epistemological, Public Policy and Epidemiological Challenges. *Transcultural Psychiatry, 50*(6), 858–875.

Hickling, F.W., McCallum, M., Nooks, L., & Rodgers-Johnson, P. (2001). Outcome of First Contact Schizophrenia in Jamaica. *West Indian Medical Journal, 50*(3), 194–197.

Hickling, F.W., & Paisley, P. (2011). Redefining Personality Disorder in Jamaica. *Revista Panamericana de Salud Pública/Pan American Journal of Public Health, 30*(3), 255–261.

Huesmann, L.R., Eron, L.D., & Yarmel, P.W. (1987). Intellectual Functioning and Aggression. *Journal of Personality and Social Psychology, 52*(1), 232–240.

Jablenksy, A., Sartorius, N., Ernberg, G., Anker, M., Korten, A., Cooper, J., & Day, R. (1992). A Schizophrenia: Manifestations, Incidence and Course in Different Cultures. A World Health Organization Ten-Country Study. *Psychol Med: Monograph, Suppl 20*.

Jaspers, K. (1913, 1967). *Allgemeine Psychopathologie [General Psychopathology]: Ein Leitfaden für Studierende, Ärzte und Psychologen* (Translated from the German by J. Hoenig and MW. Hamilton, Trans.). Berlin: J. Springer.

Jones, M. (2008). The Most Cruel and Revolting Crimes: The Treatment of the Mentally Ill in Mid-Nineteenth-Century Jamaica. *J Caribb Hist., 42*(2), 290–309.

Kiev, A. (1969). *Response to the Rastafari of Jamaica by Prince R*. Paper presented at the American Psychiatric Association, Ocho Rios, Jamaica.

Lemard, G., & Hemenway, D. (2006). Violence in Jamaica: An Analysis of Homicides 1998–2002. *Inj.Prev., 12*(1), 15–18.

Lindquist, S. (1992). *Exterminate All the Brutes. One Man's Odyssey into the Heart of Darkness and the Origins of European Genocide*. New York: The New Press.

Mahy, G., Mallett, R., Leff, J., & Bhugra, D. (1999). First-Contact Incidence Rate of Schizophrenia on Barbados. *Br J Psychiatry., 175*, 28–33.

McKenzie, K. (2008). Jamaica: Community Mental Health Services. In J. Caldas de Almeida & A. Cohen (Eds.), *Innovative Mental Health Programs in Latin America and the Caribbean*. Washington, D.C.: Pan American Health Organization.

Moses, K. (2011). Raymond Cochrane Interview—Panmedia Archive. Retrieved from https://www.panmedia.com.jm/blog/201307/cochrane-interview.

Munroe-Ellis, P. (2016). *Ministry of Health (MOH)—Management of Mental Health Services*. Retrieved from http://auditorgeneral.gov.jm/wp-content/uploads/2016/09/anagement_of_Mental_Health_Services_May_2016.pdf.

Nettleford, R. (2002). Draw Wisdom and Listen: How to Eat and Remain Human. In E.K. Hall (Ed.), *The Caribbean Community Beyond Survival* (pp. 182–188). Kingston: Ian Randle Publishers.

Nettleford, R. (2007). Foreword. In E.F. Hickling (Ed.), *Dream-A-World CARIMENSA and the Development of Cultural Thrapy in Jamaica*. Kingston, UWI: Carimensa Press.

Patterson, O. (1967). *The Sociology of Slavery. An Analysis of the Origins, Development and Structure of Negro Slave Society in Jamaica*. London: Grenada Publishing.

Prince, R. (1969). *The Rastafari of Jamaica: A Study of Group Beliefs and Social Stress*. Paper presented at the American Psychiatric Association, Ocho Rios, Jamaica.

Rouse, R. (1860). *New Light on Dark Deeds; being Jottings from the Diary of Richard Rouse, Late Warden of the Lunatic Asylum of Kingston, Edited by his son*. Kingston: Hall and Myers.

Schaeffer, C., Ialongo, N., & Hubbard, H. (2006). A Comparison of Girls' and Boys' Aggressive-Disruptive Behavior Trajectories Across Elementary School: Prediction to Young Adult Antisocial Outcomes. *Journal of Consulting and Clinical Psychology, 74*(3), 500–510.

Selten, J., & Cantor-Graae, E. (2005). Social Defeat: Risk Factor for Schizophrenia? *Br J Psychiatry., 187*, 101–102.

Selten, J., Slaets, J., & Kahn, R. (1997). Schizophrenia in Surinamese and Dutch Antillean Immigrants to The Netherlands: Evidence of an Increased Incidence. *Psychol Med., 27*, 807–811.

Smith, L. (2014). *Insanity, Race and Colonialism. Managing Mental Disorder in the Post Emancipation British Caribbean*. Basingstoke Hampshire: Palgrave Macmillan.
Stedman, J. (1796). *Narrative, of a Five Years' Expedition, Against the Revolted Negroes of Surinam*. London: J. Johnson & J. Edwards.
United Nations Office on Drugs and Crime. (2013). Global Study on Homicide 2013: Trends, Contexts, Data. Retrieved from https://www.unodc.org/documents/data-and-analysis/statistics/GSH2013/2014_GLOBAL_HOMICIDE_BOOK_web.pdf.
Walcott, G. (2012). *Countering the Prevailing Ethos by Practice: The Implementation of a Community Engagement Model in Inner City Communities in Kingston, Jamaica*. Paper presented at the 18th Annual Summer Program in Social and Cultural Psychiatry, McGill University, Montreal, Canada. https://www.youtube.com/watch?v=LyrpTVsN_3IJul.
Whitley, R. (2011). Social Defeat or Social Resistance? Reaction to Fear of Crime and Violence Among People with Severe Mental Illness Living in Urban' Recovery Communities.' *Cult Med Psychiatry* doi:10.1007/s11013-011-9226-y.
Wildman, S. (1996). *Privilege Revealed: How Invisible Preference Undermines America*. New York: NYU Press.
Wise, T. (2013). *Between Barrack and a Hard Place*. San Francisco: San Francisco City Lights Books.
Wolberg, L. (1967). *The Technique of Psychotherapy*. New York: Grune & Stratton.

12

How to Conduct a Psycho-Social History

Benjamin P. Bowser

Frederick W. Hickling provided a model of how we might de-colonize a culture by treating an entire community or country. The use of psycho-historiographical analysis in individual and group therapy requires facilitators to retool to take their patients back across generations of history, pick out the traumas, trace their effects on their present, and eliminate their behavioral outcomes. Psychologists and psychiatrists must use history as a therapeutic tool. In the next chapter, Benjamin P. Bowser shows how anyone who wishes to can conduct a social history of their or another's intergenerational family culture. Instead of whole communities, as in the previous chapter, social histories focus on family histories and influences. The focus of such a history is to find potentially traumatic events and definitive experiences and trace them forward in time through a "psychological genealogy." Bringing potential trauma and their effects to light are therapeutic in themselves and allow one to consciously deal with what had been invisible and unconscious influences on one's life.

There is a way to bridge historical slavery with the present. The legacy of slavery is not a set of experiences that must be proven to exist today. The legacy of slavery exists in the conditions that make slavery and racial oppression possible. We can do precise analyses of these conditions in the past and present. There are two places to start. The first is to construct family histories of the descendants of enslaved Africans by asking and then working to find answers to the following questions: Where did they live, when were they there, what did they do, and what happened to them? Then, collect any oral memories from elders and from the friends, neighbors, and family members who knew one's elders. What happens if the people who can provide this information are all gone, or wish to keep what they know a secret? There is a way around this problem. Do or share a similar search for others with families who lived in the same place, time, and circumstances. Making a social history is not a mapping of unique family histories, nor is it a genealogy. This is a mapping of the conditions and circumstances of a community. Such reconstruction of family and community histories should be a standard part of any psychological therapy, counseling, or history of slave descendants. Virtually all individual problems, as well as the strengths of African descendants, have roots in family and community experiences.

How to Do a Legacy of Slavery Psycho-Social History

Most Europeans of every social class have detailed family knowledge going back for generations. Africans can relate details about their families well over one hundred years. In contrast, there is a curious feature about families in countries in the Western Hemisphere with legacies of slavery. Most know virtually nothing about their family histories back more than two generations. Most often, family stories go unexplored, even oral histories, across the generations. European Immigrants once in the West exercise very little interest in their pre-immigration backgrounds until the second or third generation is assimilated fully as Americans, Brazilians, etc. However, even then, what they want to know and are satisfied with is superficial. Almost none want to dig deep enough into their past to learn the real reasons their great-grand and grandparents permanently left, either willingly or unwillingly, their neighbors, friends, and extended families. What compelled their families to take a one-way trip and relocate to another part of the world, sight unseen? Even those who have done genealogies know little about the social and historical context of their prior generations. However, in-depth genealogies hold essential keys to understanding oneself—documents that allow one to find and interview living family members, as well as to identify the pathways to attitudes, beliefs, and values transmitted across generations.

To not know or care about the past does not mean one is not influenced by it, as illustrated in this book. To not know or care how the past has influenced you to make the hold of historical legacies all the more potent because then history fully defines one's present and future. The idea that slavery or any other historical institution might still influence one's life in genetic, medical, or psychological ways is unimaginable. Remarkably, there are research tools routinely used to assess the influences of family and community in the past on individual behaviors in the present. There are now no reasons to be left in the dark about historical influences on one's family and self.

Social histories are now made in forensic social work to find and understand the influences and potentially mitigating circumstances for criminal and health-related behaviors (Watson, 2011). Forensic psychologists and psychiatrists do the same by assessing whether or not there were traumatic, cognitive, and neurological influences in criminal behaviors. Psychologists and social workers, such as Joy A. DeGruy, uncover social histories with direct application to individual and group psychotherapy. The cases she described in her chapter were based on social histories. People who wish to understand their family social and psychological circumstances do genealogical research and social histories. To even understand the environmental influences on family DNA and susceptibility to diseases, one must make social histories focused on what family members did, where they did it, and what was done to them. How can one make social histories that can explore the psychological legacy of slavery?

Exploring One's Legacy of Slavery

The goal of making a social history is to understand the multiple influences under which the person or people of interest lived. All conscious life is lived within not only physical but social constraints and contexts as well. We want to know what choices they had and took within the constraints of their social identities. However, the question arises: how do we know that what we find are validity and reliability. The answer is that first, we have to work toward face-validity and the persuasiveness of the evidence. Face-valid evidence is superior to none at all and is acceptable until better evidence is derived. Fortunately, with even face-valid evidence, it is possible to have more or less reliable information. Stronger reliability is demonstrated when more than one source identifies the same thing.

One starts research with a goal and plan based upon one's curiosity about a family story, legend, or saying. There may be something about oneself or about family members that are repeated across generations about which you wonder. One need not be curious about just flaws or weaknesses; one might start as well with trying to understand strengths or resilience. Your question is, from where did these behaviors repeated across generations come? The next step is to develop a game plan. Are there any documents that might shed light on your point of curiosity? Are there relatives, friends of relatives, neighbors, classmates, people they worked with, even police records, medical records, or relevant work records one can gather?

List the documents first, and from these documents, identify individuals that may be able to shed light on them. The next step is to prepare to interview relevant persons, and then to find them. The sequence of these steps is very, very important. Preparation is the key to good interviewing. Even if you have difficulty finding them, preparing the interview may point to alternative people to interview. Once you find the person that you wish to interview, create an interview environment that is comfortable and minimizes distractions.

If one has no immediate family or related individuals to interview, is it still possible to get answers to your questions? The answer is yes. They had neighbors, friends, other family, storekeepers, teachers, and service providers, as well as the children of neighbors, friends, and other families. They may have some knowledge of their lives and circumstances. Immediate family members are not the only ones who lived in the environment, experienced the community, and remember what went on. Remember also that there are different people whom they knew and dealt with at each stage in their lives.

How to Prepare to Do Interviews: Do not start doing interviews without first doing your homework. Read as much as possible about the times, place, and circumstances. It does not matter whether it was in the distant past or last year. Learn about not only the person of interest but also the person you are going to interview. Understand the context of their relationship with whomever you have an interest. If they were teachers, what did they teach? How long did they teach? What was the educational climate during their time as educators?

If one's interview or study is focused on mental health issues, the importance of a biopsychosocial history cannot be overstated. Evidence of low birth weight, maternal infections during pregnancy, exposure to metals, chemicals or alcohol during pregnancy, and a host of birth and gestational complications are associated with later-life psychiatric illnesses. Of course, no one piece of evidence is deterministic. However, physical and mental evidence can provide clues to increased risk of physical and psychiatric illness (Barker, Thornburg, Osmond, Kajantie, & Eriksson, 2010; Brown, 2011; Ekblad, Gissler, Lehtonen, & Korkeila, 2010; Freedman et al., 2011). The following is a list of possible sources in the U.S. from which one can gain insights.

- Family Bibles and diaries;
- Historical U.S. census records from 1790 to 1950 are available online;
- Historical slave census from 1790 to 1860 lists both slaves and slave owners;

- The 30 volume Slave Narratives: These interviews were conducted in every Southern State and county within each state;
- Names and places of Blacks lynched in the South (Patterson, 1970);
- Plantation records have been saved as state historical records;
- State historical records have information about industries, occupations and physical environment by county;
- City and town newspapers exist online and on microfiche back to 1800;
- Immigration records from U.S. Immigration Authorities and ships manifest;
- Court and property records that survived the Civil War are available by state and county;
- Military discharge and benefits records;
- Genealogical and Social Security, birth, marriage, cemeteries, and death records;
- Schooling: There are school yearbooks in libraries and reunion documents.
- Employment: social security records, where and when they worked and what are their job classification;
- Neighborhood conditions: Where did they live and when; what were the poverty measures, crime statistics, vacancy rates, and degree of racial segregation?

This list is not an exhaustive list of potential records. However, the richness of your social history is heightened when multiple records inform your interviews and support your eventual narrative.

The Census records in the U.S. go back to 1790 or ten generations and are conveniently online. Newspaper records go back even further and are also online. These websites are increasingly user-friendly and are available at a minimal cost. The key to using all these sources is to know the state, county, and approximate years where individuals and families lived. These historical records are well known among genealogists and are gold mines of information. They are particularly relevant to the descendants of enslaved Africans whose presence in the U.S. predates the mass immigration of Europeans to the U.S. after 1880. These records are not only of individual and family interest; they are part of the psychological legacy of any American whose history predates 1940.

Doing Interviews: There are no special protocols for doing legacy-related interviews. It is essential that before you begin formally asking questions, to establish rapport with whomever, you are interviewing. Talk until you, and they are comfortable with one another and have a sense of one another. Conduct the interview where you both have reasonable privacy and comfort and can hear one another. Have enough time not to be rushed. For these reasons, it is best to make an appointment with whoever you interview. If they wish to meet in a less than the optimal setting, you must be prepared to deal with whatever happens. Prepare your questions carefully in advance. They should be clear and distinct. You should know your questions well enough to ask them with minimal glances to where they are written. The best practice is not to read your questions. Instead, be familiar enough with your information to move from question-to-question and topic-to-topic through conversation. Be prepared to answer questions about the goal and intent of each question, and, if necessary, to rephrase them. Always start with open-ended questions for which there are no right or wrong answers, even when you know the answer. Open-ended questions allow your respondents to answer in whatever way they think is best. Open-ended questions also allow responses with the broadest array of answers.

Once you have established rapport, always ask for permission to use a small tape recorder or the recorder function on a smartphone. Make sure that you know in advance how to use the device, have enough power, and know what volume level you need in advance. Once they give you permission, begin asking questions. The moment the interview begins, your task is to facilitate their best responses to your questions. Let them talk. You may have to rephrase questions they may have misunderstood. Probe them with short additional questions or comments, if something is said that you did not anticipate or is revealing. Ask them to say more about that point. While the interview is underway, it might be helpful to take notes of points you wish to return to, and probe in more detail or repeat. Do not let note taking be a distraction. If they say something that is shocking, disgusting, surprising, immoral, illegal, whatever, do not react. Minimize your body language. Your task is to get them to answer your questions as best they can. You are not to judge them, argue with them, or make them feel that you have anything but respect for them. Save your personal reactions for when the interview is over and when you have left them. A successful interview is one in which the interviewee talks freely, wants to give you the information you seek, and would not mind saying more after you have finished. There are excellent guides available for interviewing that you can consult (Fontana & Frey, 1998).

Culture and Cultural Competence

One must be culturally competent whether one interviews members of one's ethnic group and social class or of another group and class. Culturally competent interviews, both social and clinical, require that the investigator have cultural self-awareness. This includes knowledge of one's ethnic history and the historical and current relationship between the interviewers' and interviewees' cultural experiences. It is helpful to have knowledge of, and immersion in, the relevant culture and social class. When interviewing, one must also be receptive to new information. Evidence regarding how a person and his or her family and community understand and make sense of the world in which they live is a core function of developing a social history.

The following are examples of social histories that two of my students did on family cultural issues that interested them. These histories were derived from interviews with family elders, and historical newspaper accounts from their family's state and county of origin (Bowser & Goma-Gakissa, 2012).

Case One

One student found out why her family insisted on remaining in public housing even when they had the financial ability to purchase their own home. Four generations back in the 1890s, they owned a large tract of valuable property in Alabama; their great-great-grandparents and great-grandparents were prosperous farmers with a large extended family. White night-riders came to their homestead and burned all the buildings to the ground; the young women in the family were raped, and most male relatives were killed. Surviving family members had to flee in the middle of the night. They subsequently re-established themselves in the 1920s and managed to buy a new property in Texas, but were burned out there as well. More family members were raped and killed. Their next opportunity to buy a home was in California in the 1950s, which was met with threats of arson from local Whites. These threats were particularly traumatic for this family, given their prior experiences. They refused to close the deal. The children and now grandchildren in this family were taught that property ownership is risky and dangerous despite the advantage that can come from it. It is better to continue living in rentals and public housing. This family came out of slavery well-off but was traumatized twice in Jim Crow, which is evident in family socialization regarding property ownership to this day. The grandchildren in this family must break this specific trauma by successfully purchasing and owning property.

Case Two

Another student wondered why most of the men in her family enjoyed fighting and going to jail. She also wondered why so few women with children in the family ever married. It turns out their family had also been burned out, and the women raped in the South during the 1890s. The rapes left a particular lasting trauma. The eldest women across three generations never forgave the men in their family for what happened and would not trust any man to protect them again. This belief in Black male vulnerability was passed on to successive generations. Male family members' manhood was always in question; so, fighting other men was the most direct way to demonstrate one's manhood. Men, who might have entered the family as husbands, somehow could not be trusted either and seemed never to measure up. The women in the family made all significant decisions, trusted only one another, and led their households. The current generation had no idea of the origin of their particular family culture. They considered it normal and had no reason to question it. Now, based on the revelation of the original family secret, the children are working on coming to terms with their family culture.

In both cases, these students were able with minimal resources and time to undercover historical trauma, which were held by family elders as secrets. The trauma their families experienced were direct outgrowths of racist reactions to their freedom from slavery. These traumas have shaped and burdened the lives of each successive generation. Grandchildren and great-children were acting out the reactions to this trauma as their family norms, had no idea of where their behaviors came from, or that there were alternatives. In each case, once younger family members learned about the trauma and its influence on them, they were shocked. The self-limiting and dysfunctional behaviors ceased to be norms for them. If they were able to go back into their family's past in slavery, there would be additional unaddressed trauma to be found.

Social histories can be compelling, liberating tools. Even for readers in countries without extensive records, as in the U.S., social histories are still possible through interviews with family elders, extended family members, and networks of neighbors and friends.

REFERENCES

Allport, G. (1968). The Historical Background of Modern Social Psychology. In G. Lindzey & E. Aronson (Eds.), *The Handbook of Social Psychology*. Reading, Ma.: Addison-Wesley.

Barker, D.J.P., Thornburg, K.L., Osmond, C., Kajantie, E., & Eriksson, J.G. (2010). Beyond Birthweight: The Maternal and Placental Origins of Chronic Disease. *Journal of Developmental Origins of Health and Disease*, 1(6), 360–364. doi:10.1017/s2040174410000280.

Bowser, B., & Goma-Gakissa, G. (2012). Exploring Slavery's Influence on the Psychology of Slave Descendants in the United States. In P. Lovejoy & B.P. Bowser (Eds.), *The Transatlantic Slave Trade and Slavery: New Directions in Teaching and Learning* (pp. 181–200). Trenton, NJ: Africa World Press.

Brown, A.S. (2011). The Environment and Susceptibility to Schizophrenia. *Progress in Neurobiology*, 93(1), 23–58. doi:10.1016/j.pneurobio.2010.09.003.

Ekblad, M., Gissler, M., Lehtonen, L., & Korkeila, J. (2010). Prenatal Smoking Exposure and the Risk of Psychiatric Morbidity into Young Adulthood. *Archives of General Psychiatry*, 67(8), 841–849. doi:10.1001/archgSenpsychiatry.2010.92.

Fontana, A., & Frey, J. (1998). Interviewing: The Art of Science. In N. Denzin & Y. Lincoln (Eds.), *Collecting and Interpreting Qualitative Materials* (pp. 47–78). Thousand Oaks: Sage Publications.

Freedman, D., Deicken, R., Kegeles, L.S., Vinogradov, S., Bao, Y., & Brown, A.S. (2011). Maternal-Fetal Blood Incompatibility and Neuromorphologic Anomalies in Schizophrenia: Preliminary Findings. *Prog Neuropsychopharmacol Biol Psychiatry,* 35(6), 1525–1529. doi:10.1016/j.pnpbp.2011.04.012.

Goffman, I. (1956). *Presentation of Self in Everyday Life.* New York: Anchor Doubleday.

Patterson, W. (Ed.) (1970). *We Charge Genocide: The Historic Petition to the United Nations for Relief from a Crime of the United States Government Against the Negro People.* New York: International Publishers.

Sennett, R. (Ed.) (1977). *The Psychology of Self.* New York: Vintage Books.

Watson, K.D. (2011). *Forensic Medicine in Western Society: A History.* London: Routledge.

13

Healing the Wounds of Slavery

Potentials and Challenges[1]

SCHERTO GILL

In this third part of the book, the previous two contributors have outlined some possible interventions in the psycho-social processes to challenge psychological delusions and resist cultural colonization. In this chapter, Scherto Gill describes both the imperative of healing and some possibilities of healing the wounds of slavery. In unpacking the notion of healing wounds, she argues that the slave trade and slavery are more than violent atrocities on a large scale. Still, instead, they are simultaneously historical, social, economic, political, cultural, and discursive processes of dehumanization. Therefore, healing must also be conceived from these diverse perspectives.

The Imperative of Healing

Between the 16th and 19th centuries, approximately 28 million healthy African men and women were captured from their homes and forced to march across their homeland to the sea, where slave ships awaited to transport them across the Atlantic to the Western Hemisphere (Lovejoy, 2012). Shackled in pairs with metal chains around their ankles and ropes around their necks, and subjected to violence and abuse, approximately half of the men and women perished on these forced marches. Of the 14 million who made it to the shore, only two-thirds survived the 5000 miles one to three-month middle passage across the Atlantic in the inhumanely cramped and disease-ridden holds of a ship (Smallwood, 2007). Many died of starvation, dysentery, and suicide. The remaining 7.4 million Africans who arrived in the Americas and the Caribbean, were sold into slavery. Half died of disease, hunger, exposure, overwork, and brutality (Sweet, 2003).

This mass atrocity referred to by some Africans and African Americans as *the Maafa*, a Kiswahili term for great trauma, has been understood as the most prolonged and most extensive genocide in human history (Anderson, 2007; Witmann, 2016). In addition to the physical and psychological harms inflicted by the inhumane treatment, enslaved Africans also suffered cultural trauma; they were forcibly removed from their homelands and forbidden to continue their cultural rituals and practices (Akbar, 1996, Koh, 2019). This cultural trauma has visible legacies in today's African American communities. W.E.B. Du Bois (1903) claims that African Americans were prohibited from practicing their culture by the U.S. legal and educational systems, despite many attempts made to re-energize, re-interpret, and re-legitimize African traditions and practices.

This historical and cultural trauma left lasting legacies beyond what have been experienced by captured and enslaved Africans and their descendants. These legacies are most visible in contemporary Africa. European slave traders sought to capture African men and women who were especially physically fit and healthy. They left behind the elderly, the disabled, and the vulnerable. The consequence is a culture of fear and insecurity due to centuries of violent slave trade followed by colonization, imperialism, and socio-economic exploitation and deprivation. This history poses a heavy and continuing political and economic burden today in African countries (Deveau, 1997). Today, whether a person's family lineage was enslaved or otherwise remains a divisive factor in some African communities (*ibid*.). The history of the trans-Atlantic slave trade is a "tenacious poison ... [that has] paved the way for new forms of slavery that continue to affect millions" (UKRI, 2020). It is estimated that even today, over 6 million people are currently subjugated to some forms of "modern slavery" in sub-Saharan Africa.

Racism is the most widely spread and most damaging legacy of the slave trade and slavery with worldwide repercussions. There are three interrelated kinds of racism—institutionalized, cultural, and structural. Racism is the consequence of the "myth of race" that allowed atrocities to be committed all during the slave trade and slavery (Smedley et al., 2020). Nearly 170 years after the British Slavery Abolition Act (first introduced in 1833), people of African descent living outside of the African continent are still victims of racism, xenophobia, discrimination, and prejudice in many different guises. Racism has been so extensive that Du Bois suggested that the problem of the color-line or the relation between the darker to the lighter skin peoples of the world is *the* problem of our time (see Franklin, 1993).

As outlined in earlier chapters, the psychological and cultural legacies of the slave trade and slavery cannot be ignored. This chapter suggests a path to racial justice and reconciliation. It is necessary to understand what healing constitutes and explore existing approaches to healing the wounds of history relevant to the context of the slave trade and slavery. Equally, it is imperative to recognize the root causes of slavery and continued racial inequality. Any attempts to meet the contemporary needs for healing the wounds of slavery must also consider structural violence practiced by our national and global economic and political systems.

Wounding and Healing

How should we understand healing wounds in the context of the trans-Atlantic slave trade and slavery? What constitutes healing? *Healing* is very much dependent on the notions of *wounding* or being wounded. In our context, people are wounded when they are *dehumanized* or treated as less than human (Smith, 2012). As such, dehumanization is an element of ill-being, the opposite of dignity and well-being (Gill and Thomson, 2019a). While dehumanization commonly consists of material, physical, psycho-social, economic, and spiritual harm, it must be understood as something pernicious and independent of these specific kinds of harm (Gill and Thomson, 2019b). Dehumanization is essentially a violation of a person's intrinsic value (Kant, 1785/1993).

Being dehumanized is something that others do to a person. The others may be an individual, a group of people, or a community. The others may act through an institution, a set of cultural practices, or use a whole system. For instance, an economic system based on maximizing profit will instrumentalize people, their work, consumption. This is everything about them (Thomson and Gill, 2020). Here, instrumentalization and dehumanization are interchangeable. When people are treated solely as a means to an end, they are dehumanized. Enslaved Africans were instrumentalized as both "modes of production" and "modes of exploitation" (Lovejoy, 2012). Dehumanization is especially harmful to one's sense of self; it damages one's human dignity, sense of wholeness, and consciousness of self. Africans and other people of color who are dehumanized and treated as objects devalue themselves (Watts-Jones, 2002; Hughes and Demo, 1989; Gates, 1987). This devaluation has been well documented as the basis of adolescent African Americans' self-loathing and substance use (Sanders-Phillips, et al. 2009).

Our conception of wounding as dehumanization involves four core components. The first is that a dehumanizing act does not just happen; it is committed by one or more persons, who can be haunted by what they have done as well (Painter, 2006). Second, dehumanizing acts tend to have traumatic effects on the dehumanized. When unhealed, traumas and their results are transmitted inter-generationally (Volkan, 1999). Third, dehumanizing acts produce dehumanized relationships. Finally, there are structural and institutional conditions that permit dehumanizing acts to occur (Gill and Thomson, 2019b). This four-fold distinction will allow us to examine dehumanization, traumas, and traumatic effects related to the legacies of the slave trade and slavery (Alvarez, et al., 2016).

It is traumatic to be dehumanized; the effects are harrowing. To discuss the relevant traumas and their consequences, we need to make at least three assumptions. First, as we have seen, the trans-Atlantic slave trade and slavery have profoundly harmed and damaged millions of people, their descendants, and communities. These traumas and their effects are not individualistic. They are collective and cultural. Second, we can assume that racism—the presumption of white supremacy and the inferiority of people of color—continues to take its toll. This means that there is a set of causal relations linking the trans-Atlantic slave trade and slavery to contemporary racism. Third, we shall assume that these harms and injuries are not limited to the damage inflicted on the descendants of enslaved Africans. They include harmful effects on the beneficiaries of the slave trade, slavery, and their descendants. All three assumptions can help us examine the possibilities of healing.

Healing

It can be said that healing making someone *whole*. This idea comes from the etymology of the word "healing" which is the Old English word "haelan" meaning "whole." Indeed, dehumanizing acts that wound someone and their harmful effects can make a person feel fragmented or shattered as if broken. One's emotional self-relationship and self-awareness are shattered. Dehumanization is a spiritual harm where a person feels disconnected from themselves (Robinson, 2010). Consequently, healing does not make a person whole. Instead, it makes one feel reconnected to one's whole self (cf. Derek Hicks, 2009).

Healing is not necessarily the opposite of wounding as a form of dehumanization. Healing is not "humanizing" per se since there cannot be a process of *humanizing* a person. This is because we are all already have intrinsic value or worth, and we cannot be made more so (Gill and Thomson, 2019b). Instead, through healing, it is possible for a person to fully recognize their intrinsic value and feel and act in accordance with such a recognition. In other words, one cannot humanize the human; one cannot give back or restore a person's dignity because they are already human and already have dignity. Instead, healing helps people to reconnect to their intrinsic dignity and restores self-awareness (Donna Hicks, 2011).

To better understand the systemic nature of healing, we might distinguish between *wounds* that can be treated and a *disease* that must be cured. Psycho-social suffering is like wounds that need to be treated through therapy, reparation, or reconciliation. In contrast, systemic dehumanization is akin to a disease requiring a cure or interventions, as is the case with inherent structural injustice and ending violent cultural and institutional practices. Healing is focused primarily on addressing psycho-social harms, where one should not lose sight of the need for systemic transformation.

Any healing endeavors and processes must be directed simultaneously at acknowledging the acts of wounding, alleviating the traumatic and harmful effects, restoring the interrupted relationships caused by the harms, and addressing the root causes of dehumanization. In this sense, the processes of healing must address the four components of wounding. Also, one must prepare for each healing process beginning with an examination of specific events and the original atrocity's historical contexts. Such analysis is essential to acknowledge acts of dehumanization, and to understand the wounds and harms caused, the enduring legacies of traumas, and to identify the roots of structural violence.

Healing Wounds of Slavery: Potentials and Challenges

Stanford Cloud, in his famous speech titled "The Next Bold Step Toward Racial Healing and Reconciliation: Dealing with the Legacy of Slavery," highlights that "most Americans don't really know the history and its resulting legacy" (Cloud, 2001, 167). The same applies to most societies in the Western Hemisphere. Arguments remain wanting to connect the trans-Atlantic slave trade and slavery to contemporary racism. This deficiency poses profound questions to healing the wounds of slavery. By exploring existing arguments to support healing the scars of slavery, the conceptual and methodological challenges need to be reviewed as well.

Addressing Acts of Dehumanization

Acknowledging dehumanizing acts in history is key to stepping onto pathways to healing. This requires collective courage and political will because it implies accepting responsibility and taking action to begin healing. There are examples of European and American leaders who publicly acknowledged the moral wrongs of the slave trade, gave apologies and asked for forgiveness (Davis, 2014). Between 2007 and 2009, a flurry of resolutions was passed by eight U.S. States, as well as separately by the Federal Government and U.S. Senate (although no bill was passed jointly with the House of Representatives). These were expressions of "profound regret" for the dehumanizing actions and injustices during the slave trade. These regrets included acknowledgment of continuing the legacy of slavery in current times (Medish and Lucich, 2019). The State of Delaware followed suit in 2016 (Hinkley, 2016). These regrets called for reconciliation, remembrance, and recognition (Davis, 2012).

A significant example of public acknowledgment and apology is the "Reconciliation Triangle" linking Liverpool (U.K.), Benin (West Africa), and Richmond (U.S.), which opened the possibility of healing internationally. Following the 1998 apology by Richmond's mayor in 1999, the Liverpool City Council made a similar apology for their role in the slave trade. In 1999–2000, the President of Benin made an international "tour of apology." He also convened members of the African Diaspora and slave trading countries to make a formal apology for Benin's role in selling fellow Africans into slavery. Then, this apology was repeated in Richmond. Reconciliation statues were erected in all three locations to mark these acts. Such initiatives may facilitate new social and economic structures to deconstruct the ongoing economic, social, and cultural divides between Africa and the West.

Public atonements are essential starting points for healing, but they can be hollow when grounds for support are missing in the harmed communities. Georgetown University's apologies and atonement for their involvement in the slave trade have contributed genuinely to healing according to the participating slave descendants (Collins et al., 2016; Urtz and Steinberg, 2017). It is also widely debated how reparations can be structured to exemplify acceptance of responsibility for wrongdoings and as an active making of amends (Araujo, 2017; Gardner Feldman, 2012). What should reparations consist of beyond monetary or material gestures? This question is further complicated when the agents and organizations responsible for acts of dehumanization, as in the slave trade and colonization of indigenous peoples, are no longer alive (Brave Heart and DeBruyn, 1998).

These resolutions in the U.S. raised the profile of historic dehumanization because they were covered extensively in the press and by national news media. However, unlike their German, Australian or New Zealand counterparts, the U.S. Governments made few specific action commitments, and only expressed broad aspirations. Their resolutions evaded the possibility that these apologies might be used as grounds for reparations. Since the resolutions, pro-reparations groups have been resurgent, such as Coming to the Table (CTTT), Reparations Working Group, and the National Coalition of Blacks for Reparations in America (N'COBRA). These groups have called for reparations to be made at all levels of society (CTTT, 2019).

Other types of formal apologies in the U.S. include those made by church groups such as the Episcopal Church and The Southern Baptist Convention. They have used their authority and influence to provoke change in the ways their communities relate to the history of slavery and its impacts today. There have been public acknowledgments by corporations as well, such as Lehman Brothers, and from former slave trading families. However, most of "White America" seems paralyzed psychologically in its capacity to confront this history openly and honestly (Corcoran, 2010). While these apologies and related actions have significant effects within communities, the levels of racial inequality in North America cry out for a concerted national effort. This could begin with a joint bill of apology and a clear and comprehensive program of investment to close gaps in areas such as employment, health, and education.

Even when agents and institutions have the moral courage to confront the past, it is questionable to what extent they are willing to atone publicly for their part in past and present dehumanization. The public apology places past atrocities directly in an open conversation, acknowledges the wounding, and legitimizes this acknowledgment. However, public apologies can also be politically deceptive by giving the appearance of a commitment to reconciliation without committing to any concrete action to change the plight of those affected (Yamamoto et al., 2007). This critique emphasizes the need for public apologies to go hand in hand with reparations and social actions. Reparations signal an obligation to be responsible for ending wounding and expresses a commitment to address the root causes of specific acts of dehumanization. There are other forms of reparation apart from financial compensation, such as returning land and providing better access to education and health facilities. In other words, reparations go beyond the merely symbolic apology and constitute a practical step towards structural reform. Indeed, public apologies highlight the need for systemic transformation. Otherwise, structural violence will continue to perpetuate wounding. Few have recognized the systemic economic root of trans-Atlantic slavery, one of the earliest industrial treatments of people as commodities.

Scholars and practitioners do not always agree on when and how acknowledgment might count towards healing (Brooks, 2004). For instance, if official apologies are offered, does this require the acceptance by the harmed to be meaningful? Put another way, when perpetrators express repentance, does it need the forgiveness of those injured? What is the answer to this question?

Hannah Arendt (1958/1994) suggests that the Holocaust was unforgivable. While Jacques Derrida (2003) argues that forgiveness only applies to what is unforgivable and collectively owned guilt can be problematic. For instance, Arendt (1964) regarded Germany's collective guilt at the end of World War II as confused. Often, people who were personally responsible felt no remorse, while those who were not directly responsible and even the generations born after World War II suffer from guilt. Arendt argues that collective guilt obscures the direct accountability of the individuals who should be held answerable for the atrocity. Alternatively, focusing only on individual culpability ignores the institutional nature and structural causes of dehumanizing acts.

The connections between truth, justice, and healing are another area of contention. Are these separate processes, or are they integrated? When actors acknowledge their part in an atrocity, does this require truth-telling and some forms of compensation to count as contributing to justice and healing? (Asmal et al., 1994; Hamber and Kibble, 1999). Besides, there is a perceived tension between justice as punishment and justice as restoration (Shriver, 1995). These do not have to be treated as mutually exclusive. However, the need to find quick ways to reduce violence, as in instances of racial injustice, often means that the root causes of the wounding, or institutionalized racism, are not addressed and wounding continues.

Addressing the Effects of Dehumanization

Healing consists, in part, in liberating persons from harmful effects that accumulate over time and are transmitted across generations. Healing requires treating the wounds themselves rather than just symptoms. Healing may also involve transcending a broken sense of self and moving toward wholeness with an awareness of one's innate dignity. Importantly, healing includes transforming psychological and cultural habits where there is self-imposed oppression (Friere, 1970) and learned helplessness (DeGruy, 2017), which, if untreated, allows continued dehumanization.

Breaking the silence and remembering past dehumanizing acts are essential to addressing traumas and their effects. Suffering can be diminished, grief eased, and tormented emotions assuage (Berlin and Miller, 1998; Eze, 2009). Safe public spaces for remembrance can contribute to healing (UNESCO Slave Route Project, 2020). These include memorial sites, burial sites, and museums, history textbooks, and celebrations of Black History week, films, literature, and theatre. Spaces for remembrance allow shared collective experiences that de-silence pain (Araujo, 2010), and help people recognize that dehumanization can be experienced in different ways. Such diversity puts a human face on often unspeakable suffering. Then, remembering is the prelude to mourning (Casey, 2009), and can highlight the need for justice and reinforces collective responsibility. However, there are risks involved in remembering—re-traumatization (Brounéus, 2008). Care must be taken to keep commemorations from being used as glorifying occasions for political elites (Cameron, 2003). Thus, remembering must be carried out in safe spaces and, at times, when people can feel respected and cared for rather than further robbed of their dignity (Edkins, 2003).

Memorialization can create the opportunity and space for an individual and collective reassessment of self and one's place in history (Gould, 2011). For example, The National Museum of African American History and Culture (NMAAHC) is an American national museum devoted exclusively to documenting and commemorating the lives, histories, and cultures of African Americans. However, the museum serves a second psychological function. Traumas and the effects of harm are complex, multi-layered, and memories of such experiences do not always distinguish the causes of historic wounding, the symptoms of intergenerational trauma, and the current experiences of ongoing legacies and structural violence (Deveau, 2006). Instead, these dimensions are intermingled in an undiscernible bundle (Urrieta, 2019). It is not clear where emphasis should be placed. How much attention should be on the legacies of dehumanization and the wounding? Should there be more on the resilience of the wounded and their transcending of pains and grievances (Rice, 2004). In advocating de-silencing, Deveau (2006, 248) cautions that we "need to maintain a constant vigilance if we are to prevent history from turning into a court where resentment is perpetuated."

Actively applying therapeutic approaches to address socio-cultural and psychological pathologies may contribute to healing. A 12-week program entitled *From the Cotton Fields to the Concrete Jungle* has successfully worked with groups of African American young men who reside in urban areas, arguably a population most vulnerable to trauma (Mullan-Gonzalez, 2012). It helps participants to make sense of trauma and experiences of traumatic effects. Social pathology includes high rates of suicide, domestic violence, and other social problems. Psychological pathology includes anxiety, depression, anger, and other mental health problems (DeGruy, 2017). Cultural trauma includes a lingering sense of alienation from one's own humanity and spiritual suffering (Nobles, 2013). Some of these symptoms and effects of trauma were inter-generationally transmitted. How symptoms are defined really depends on what is emphasized—the biological, psychological, social or cultural (Beltrán and Begun, 2014). Contentions around definitions of trauma point to the challenge of identifying concerted effort towards healing. Equally, identifying persons as *traumatized* has become another area of dispute. For some sufferers, a diagnostic term such as PTSD means an acknowledgment of their perplexing symptoms and a way to healing. For example, Joy A. DeGruy coined the term "post traumatic slave syndrome" (PTSS), which characterizes and explains the lived realities of many African Americans (DeGruy, 2017). However, for others, such a term represents a form of *medical labeling* that reduces the socio-economic and political complexities of dehumanization to a single individualized *disease category* (Jones, 2017).

According to the UNESCO Slave Route Project (2020), to address the wounds inflicted by dehumanizing acts requires identifying and contextualizing trauma. That is to make sense of trauma, understanding its harmful effects, transcending fragmentation, and restoring awareness of one's wholeness and dignity. Although trauma among the beneficiaries of slavery is not widely recognized, it is important to acknowledge such traumas and their effects. This may help the descendants of the beneficiaries of slave trade and slavery overcome blindness to their white privilege and accompanied feelings of guilt and anxiety. People of European descent often defend themselves by thinking that "slavery happened a long time ago" and by denying its oppressive legacy. Even if there is such a recognition of white privilege, it is not easy to perceive the arrogance, closed-ness, indifference and social divisions that accompany such privilege as a dehumanizing effect of slavery and racism. Judith Katz (1978) has developed a handbook for anti-racist training for people of European descent, but more awareness is required of "white healing."

Addressing the Dehumanizing Relationships

The effects of dehumanization include hostile relationships, indifference, mutual ignorance, and alienation. Healing encompasses processes in which people develop better relationships that involve as a minimum a mutual recognition of each other as persons of equal worth (Gill and Thomson, 2019a). Addressing dehumanizing relationships involves transcending antagonistic identity categories such as white-versus-black, perpetrator-versus-victim, and us-versus-them. Indeed, people harmed by slavery, and its legacies may feel that their sense of themselves is defined by trauma as a victim of racism (DeGruy, 2017). Healing in this context may entail creating safe spaces for participants to experience each other as persons, and to become freer of the antagonisms embedded in the exclusionary ways they self-identify (Marcel, 1951). Such awareness paves the way to exploring ways to self-identify that are more inclusive and therefore have healing power (Healing the Wounds of History, 2019; Gill, 2015). Such processes must foster historical perceptions that do not propagate feelings of hostility or indifference, and this requires that people develop the capacity to become close to others. This means overcoming self-absorption and nurturing an awareness of oneself and others as "we."

To shift from self and other-identification, we must reflect on the origin of identifying people of African descent as lesser humans. Such identification arose from the transportation and enslavement of Africans on a commercial scale and systematically treating them as objects for economic gain during the birth of capitalism (see Williams and Palmer, 1994). The categorical racial division developed from this history legitimized the slave trade and slavery. As Frederick Douglass pointed out: "The whole argument in defense of slavery becomes utterly worthless the moment the African is proved to be equally a man with the Anglo-Saxon. The temptation, therefore, to read the Negro out of the human family is exceeding strong" (Douglass, 1854).

Racist ideology became part of a socio-economic system that ensured the political and economic domination of Europeans and the oppression of people of African descent. The doctrine of white superiority and black inferiority became normalized legally, and racism becomes integral to the social structure and many people's psyche (Butler, 1993; cf. Horsman, 1981). People of African descent often see those of European descent as the oppressors or perpetrators, and those of European descent perceive African peoples as lesser human or as victims. Over time, these classifications become ingrained in groups' collective memory. Dehumanized relationships became the norm and seemingly resistant to transformation.

Beyond the identity discourses of race lies an economic paradigm that makes inhumanity possible by treating human life as a small cost for the sake of financial gain (Drescher, 2008). Healing directed at relational transformation must highlight the profits-over-persons mentality and nurture an awareness of the intrinsic value of being human within relationships (Thomson and Gill, 2020).

Racial healing programs must go beyond race as the only identity of the people they serve (Fields, 2001; Carter, 2008). This is because, as a lens to approach healing, race is highly contested. On the one hand, some writers question whether race should be the primary concern for relational transformation (see Ossorio, 2011). They argue that, as an identity category, race accentuates divisions because of the many attached sentiments such as humiliation, anger, guilt, arrogance, fear, and mistrust. On the other hand, healing seems to require working through and transcending these feelings (Gill and Thomson, 2019a). Besides being an ideology, racism is a psychology, and the more racism is confronted as a psychology, the more it emphasizes people's individuality and obscures racism's structural expressions (Bonilla-Silva, 2010). Instead, it is more helpful to realize that racial discrimination and injustice are reproduced and perpetuated by a system of economic priorities, political objectives, laws and regulations. Emphasizing racism as an identity and psychology undermines racism as a deeply seated structural feature of a society (Essed, 1991). The W.K. Kellogg Foundation's Racial Healing Circles and Truth, Racial Healing and Transformation initiative are programs that recognize the structural influences on human relationships and problematize race and racial identity within these contexts (Kellogg, 2016).

In the safe spaces to explore their own and others' lives in the light of slavery and its legacies, the participants of Kellogg's programs engage in "what ifs" concerning wounding, reconciliation, and healing (Kellogg, 2016). In doing so, the programs seek to create "new authentic stories that honor the complexity of the past while forging a more equitable future" (Godsil and Goodale, 2013). Human narratives intersect at multiple levels—stories from one person; those of a group; and those that cross cultures (Baumeister et al., 1990; Fivush et al., 2011). A key for moving towards more human relationships is the sharing narratives that cross such intersections (Pasupathi et al., 2016). Stories highlight what people have in common and, that story-sharing undermines dehumanization. These programs remind us that dehumanizing relations are a part of African American people's everyday lived realities in schools, hospitals, courts, workplaces, and on the street. These experiences must not be conceived of as only relational problems between groups. Such thinking masks the structural features of society that perpetuate the power relations shaping such relationships. Healing directed to relationships is not merely a process of reconciliation between individuals as representatives of social groups; it also requires institutional reform.

Addressing dehumanizing relationships must tend to the needs of the wounded and stresses the responsibilities of beneficiaries of acts of dehumanization. Some practitioners include a community-based restorative justice element in their practices of forgiveness and reconciliation, such as the Healing the Wounds of History program (Asseily, 2007; Gill, 2015). Here, the focus is shifted away from legal punishment and towards truth-telling and relational restoration (Gailey, 2015). However, forgiveness as a concept, together with its role in reconciliation, has been understood differently. Forgiveness is conceptualized as a conscious act of releasing feelings of resentment towards a person or a group who has caused you harmed, whether they deserve that forgiveness or not (Gill, 2017). For some, this should be unmediated (Derrida, 2001); for others, forgiveness is relational. Some writers claim that forgiveness separates the agents of wrongdoing from the acts of dehumanization. It transcends the actors' guilt or remorse, thereby altering the ethical significance of the past (Arendt, 1958/1994), and even purifying it (Levinas, 1969). Forgiveness also raises many questions, such as: Does forgiveness condone structural violence? Is forgiveness compatible with justice (Radzik, 2008)? Processes of forgiveness may make those who have been hurt feel coerced or under social pressure to forgive, which renders the process unjust (Jankélévitch, 1996). This suggests that forgiveness cannot be a precondition or an expectation in the process of healing relationships.

Other healing programs focus on trust-building, which requires the goodwill to let go of suspicions and misgivings, and to show trust before one is trusted (Corcoran, 2015). Trust takes time because it is the fruit of relational processes. When applied as a healing approach, activities of trust-building include offering opportunities for participants to show humility and vulnerability, to listen and to be heard, and to have open and honest conversations about the things that are blocking human relationships. Participants must care about others with genuine curiosity and offer the other one's presence. This points to the interconnection between relationship and trust, which are bound together. Integral to healing relationships is a commitment from communities to support a proactive process of seeking structural justice and socio-economic and political systems that are humanizing. Trust and co-action are also mutually dependent, and both rely on analyzing and diagnosing systemic malaises. Trust and co-action even live out new narratives expressing shared aspirations of collective well-being. For example, some White southerners have come to see their history from new perspectives because African Americans recognized the humanity of those who symbolize their oppression (Corcoran, 2015).

Healing Requiring Systemic Transformation

Slavery contributed importantly to the wealth of the West. In 1860, 80 percent of the gross national product of the U.S. was tied to slavery (Anderson, 2016). In effect, the economic prosperity of Western Europe and North America is due to dehumanization through slavery, colonization, and genocide. These practices caused unimaginable bloodshed and suffering. Continuing racial exploitation and oppression (Baptist, 2014) have left many countries in Africa, the Caribbean, and South America materially impoverished, economically underdeveloped and politically vulnerable. Their peoples have been left socially divided and spiritually wounded.

Throughout this paper, I have indicated some conditions necessary for transforming the politico-economic system. It is essential to recognize that trans-Atlantic slavery has its roots in economic exploitation engendering structural racism that keeps people of African descent disadvantaged. It is an inherent tendency of our economic system to treat people as commodities. This also means those who are vulnerable and at society's margins are harmed by the system. This understanding is particularly meaningful in understanding depersonalizing exploitative relations built into the system.

Profit-making business is mainly interested in the labor input of employees and customers as a source of revenue. This means that the human richness of community life tends to get degraded to transactional relationships between *individuals* who are otherwise indifferent to each other. In such a socio-economic context, relations between persons from different social groups are likely to be antagonistic, mainly when neighborhoods are divided along the lines of wealth and race.

Finally, it is crucial to understand that we are part of social systems that breed racism, and this is not a matter of personal choice. With this recognition, community groups might move to political action and suggest reforms to political leaders. Condemning structural dehumanization will require global leaders to publicly disavow narratives that support continuous discrimination against people of African descent. Likewise, it is necessary to change policies and institutional practices that are unjust and discriminatory. We need to reimagine governance processes and institutional structures that make it impossible for human beings to be treated solely as a means to economic gain.

Abolishing racist capitalism means a fundamental re-examination of the values that our institutions are built on and towards respecting the intrinsic value of human well-being and the equal worth of all persons. It starts here.

Note

1. This chapter is developed from two pieces of my earlier work: one is on understanding healing wounds (Gill and Thomson, 2019b); and the other a report that summarizes a recent research aimed at mapping the approaches and practices of healing relevant to the wounds of slavery (UNESCO Slave Route Project, 2020).

References

Akbar, N. (1996). *Breaking the Chains of Psychological Slavery*. Tallahassee: Mind Productions.

Alvarez, A., Liang, C., and Neville, H. (eds). (2016). *The Cost of Racism for People of Color: Contextualizing Experiences of Discrimination*. Washington, D.C.: American Psychological Association.

Anderson, C. (2016). *White Rage: The Unspoken Truth of Our Racial Divide*. New York: Bloomsbury.

Anderson, S. (2007). *The Black Holocaust for Beginners*. Newburyport, MA: Red Wheel/Weiser.

Araujo, A.L. (2017). *Reparations for Slavery: A Transnational and Comparative History* London: Bloosmbury Academic.
Arendt, H. (1958/1994). *The Human Condition*. Chicago: University of Chicago Press.
_____. (1964). Lecture on German 'Collective Guilt' a Fallacy, given in 1964 at Ford Hall Forum.
Asmal, K., Asmal, L. & Roberts, R. (1994). *Reconciliation Through Truth: A Reckoning of Apartheid's Criminal Governance*. Cape Town: David Philip Publishers.
Asseily, A. (2007). *Breaking the Cycles of Violence in Lebanon-and Beyond*. Brighton: Guerrand-Hermès Foundation for Peace Publishing.
Baumeister, R., Stilman, A. & Wotman, S. (1990). Victim and Perpetrator Accounts of Interpersonal Conflict: Autobiographical Narratives About Anger. *Journal of Personality and Social Psychology*, 59, 994–1005.
Berlin, I. and Miller, S. (1998). *Remembering Slavery*. New York: The New Press.
Beltrán, R. and Begun, S. (2014). "It is medicine": Narratives of Healing from Aotearoa Digital Storytelling as Indigenous Media Project (ADSIMP). *Psychology and Developing Societies*, 26: 155–79.
Bonilla-Silva, E. (2010). *Racism Without Racists: Color-Blind Racism and Racial Inequality in Contemporary America*, 3rd ed. New York: Rowman & Littlefield.
Brave Heart, M., & DeBruyn, L. (1998). The American Indian Holocaust: Healing Historical Unresolved Grief. *American Indian and Alaska Native Mental Health Research*, 8, 56–76.
Brooks, R. (2004). *Atonement and Forgiveness: A New Model for Black Reparations*. Berkeley: University of California Press.
Brounéus, K. (2008). Gacaca Courts Truth-Telling as Talking Cure? Insecurity and Retraumatization in the Rwandan Gacaca Courts. *Security Dialogue* 39(1): 55–76.
Butler, J. (1993). *Bodies that Matter*. New York: Routledge.
Bynum, M.S., Burton, E., & Best, C. (2007). Racism Experiences and Psychological Functioning in African American College Freshmen: Is Racial Socialization a Moderator? *Cultural Diversity and Ethnic Minority Psychology*, 13, 64–71.
Cameron, C. (2003). The Second Betrayal? Commemorating the 10th Anniversary of the Rwandan Genocide, paper presented at the 26th Annual Conference: Africa on a Global Stage, Flinders University, 1–3 October.
Casey, E. (2009). *Remembering: A Phenomenological Study*. Bloomington, Indiana University Press.
Cloud, S. (2001). The Next Bold Step Toward Racial Healing and Reconciliation: Dealing with the Legacy of Slavery. *Howard Law Journal*, 45(1), 157–176.
Collins, D. et al. (2016). Report of the Working Group on Slavery, Memory, and Reconciliation to the President of Georgetown University, June 2016. Available at http://slavery.georgetown.edu/wp-content/uploads/2016/08/GU-WGSMR-Report-Web.pdf.
Corcoran, R. (2010). *Trustbuilding: An Honest Conversation on Race, Reconciliation, and Responsibility*. Charlottesville: University of Virginia Press.
CTTT (2019). *The Time Is Now!* Available at https://comingtothetable.org/wp-content/uploads/2019/07/CTTT-Reparations-Guide-August-2019.pdf..
Davis, A. (2014). Apologies, Reparations, and the Continuing Legacy of the European Slave Trade in the United States. *Journal of Black Studies*, 45(4), 271–286.
Davis, A.M. (2012). Racial Reconciliation or Retreat? How Legislative Resolutions Apologizing for Slavery Promulgate White Supremacy. *The Black Scholar*, 42:1, 37–48.
DeGruy, J. (2005/2017). *Post Traumatic Slave Syndrome: America's Legacy of Enduring Injury and Healing (PTSS)*. Milwaukie, OR: Uptone Press.
Derrida, J. (2001). *On Cosmopolitanism and Forgiveness*. London: Routledge.
Deveau, J-M. (1997). European Slave Trading in the Eighteenth Century. *Diogenes* Vol 45, Issue 179.
Deveau, J.-M. (2006). Silence and Reparations. *International Social Science Journal*, 58: 245–248.
Douglass, F. (1854). The Claims of the Negro Ethnologically Considered: An Address Before the Literary Societies of Western Reserve College, at Commencement, July 12, 1854 Rochester, NY: Lee, Mann & Co., pp. 8–9.

Drescher, S. (2008). Capitalism and Slavery After Fifty Years. *Slavery & Abolition*, 18:3, 212–227.
Du Bois, W.E.B. (1903). *The Souls of Black Folk: Essays and Sketches*. Chicago: A.C. McClurg & Company.
Edkins, J. (2003). *Trauma and the Memory of Politics*. Cambridge: Cambridge University Press.
Egnew T. (2005). The Meaning of Healing: Transcending Suffering. *Annals of family medicine*, 3(3), 255–262.
Essed, P. (1991). *Understanding Everyday Racism: An Interdisciplinary Theory*. Newbury Park: Sage Publications.
Eze, M. (2009, 10). Healing the Wounds of Slavery. *New African*, 22–23.
Fivush, R., Habermas, T., Waters, T.E.A., & Zaman, W. (2011). The Making of Autobiographical Memory: Intersections of Culture, Narratives and Identity. *International Journal of Psychology*, 46, 321–345.
Franklin, J.H. (1993). *The Color Line: Legacy for the Twenty-First Century*. Jackson: University of Mississippi Press.
Freire, P. (1970). *Pedagogy of the Oppressed*. London: Continuum.
Gailey, T.H. (2015). Healing Circles and Restorative Justice: Learning from Non-Anglo American Traditions. *Anthropology Now*, 7:2, 1–7.
Gates, H. (1987). *Figures in Black: Words, Signs, and the "Racial Self."* New York: Oxford.
Gill, S. (2015). Healing the Wounds of History: What Works, How and Why? A critical reflection on Four Pilot Workshops, paper presented at the 4th International Conference on Transgenerational Trauma, Amman, October 2015.
Gill, S. (2016). Healing Wounds of History, Addressing Roots of Violence—A Psycho- Social Approach. *Programme Evaluation Report*, Beirut: Centre for Lebanese Studies.
Gill, S. (2017). Understanding Forgiveness: A Conceptual Map. *Working Paper*, Peace Charter of Forgiveness and Reconciliation.
Gill, S., & Thomson, G. (2019a). *Understanding Peace Holistically*. New York: Peter Lang.
Gill, S., & Thomson, G. (2019b). Understanding Healing Wounds. *Research Report*, UNESCO Slave Route Project.
Godsil, R., & B. Goodale (2013). *Telling Our Own Story: The Role of Narrative in Racial Healing*. W.K. Kellogg Foundation / American Values Institute.
Gould, L. (2011). Collective Working Through: The Role and Function of Memorialisation. *Organisational and Social Dynamics*, 11(1). 79–92.
Hamber, B., & Kibble, S (1999). *From Truth to Transformation: The Truth and Reconciliation Commission in South Africa*. London: Catholic Institute for International Relations.
Healing the Wounds of History (2019). What Is the Healing the Wounds of History Approach? Accessed at https://www.healingthewoundsofhistory.org/what-we-do/ on 1st April 2020.
Hicks, D. (2011). *Dignity: The Essential Role It Plays in Resolving Conflict*. New: Yale University Press.
Hicks, D.S. (2009). *Making the Wounded Whole: An Investigation of Healing and Identity in African American Religious Life and Thought*. ProQuest Dissertations & Theses Global.
Horsman, R. (1981). *Race and Manifest Destiny: The Origins of American Racial Anglo-Saxonism*. Cambridge, MA: Harvard University Press.
Hughes, M., & Demo, D. (1989). Self-Perceptions of Black Americans: Self-Esteem and Personal Efficacy. *American Journal of Sociology*, 95(1), 132–159.
Jankélévitch, V. (1996). Should We Pardon Them? *Critical Inquiry*, 22,552–567.
Jones, L. (2017). *Outside the Asylum: A Memoir of War, Disaster and Humanitarian Psychiatry*, London: Weidenfeld & Nicolson.
Jonnalagadda, D. (2019). Students Endorse Reconciliation Fee in GU272 Referendum. *The Hoya*, April 12, 2019.
Kant, I. (1993/1785). *Grounding for the Metaphysics of Morals*. Trans: J. Ellington, Indianapolis: Hackett (3rd ed.).
Katz, J. (1978). *White Awareness: A Handbook for Anti-Racism Training*. Norman: OK, University of Oklahoma Press.

Kellogg (2016). *Truth, Racial Healing and Transformation Implementation Guidebook.* Kellogg Foundation.
Koh, E. (2019 Cultural Work in Addressing Conflicts and Violence in Traumatized Communities. *New England Journal of Public Policy*: 31(1), 3.
Leary, J. (2005). *Post Traumatic Slave Syndrome.* Milwaukee, OR: Uptone Press.
Lévinas, E. (1969). *Totality and Infinity: An Essay on Exteriority (Totalité et infini)*, Alphonso Lingus (trans.), Pittsburgh, PA: Duquesne University Press.
Lewis, T. (2020). Transatlantic Slave Trade. *Encyclopaedia Britannica.* Accessed at https://www.britannica.com/topic/transatlantic-slave-trade, on 26th March 2020.
Lovejoy, P. (2012). *Transformations in Slavery: A History of Slavery in Africa.* Cambridge: Cambridge University Press.
Marcel, G. (1951). *The Mystery of Being, Vol. I: Reflection and Mystery*, trans. by G.S. Fraser. London: The Harvill Press.
Medish, M., & D. Lucich (2019). Congress Must Officially Apologize for Slavery Before America Can Think About Reparations. *Think*, Aug. 30, 2019.
Mullan-Gonzalez, J. (2012). *Slavery and the Intergenerational Transmission of Trauma in Inner City African American Male Youth: A Model Program—From the Cotton Fields to the Concrete Jungle*, Unpublished Doctoral of Psychology Thesis. San Francisco: California Institute of Integral Studies.
Nobles, W. (2013). Shattered Consciousness, Fractured Identity: Black Psychology and the Restoration of the African Psyche. *Journal of Black Psychology*, 39(3), 232–242.
Nunn, N., & Wantchekon, L. (2011). The Slave Trade and the Origins of Mistrust in Africa. *American Economic Review* 101(7), 3221–52.
O'Connell, H. (2012). The Impact of Slavery on Racial Inequality in Poverty in the Contemporary U.S. South. *Social Forces*, 90(3), 713–34.
Ossorio, P. (2011). Myth and Mystification: The Science of Race and I.Q. in S. Krimsky (ed.) *Race and the Genetic Revolution*, New York: Columbia University Press.
Painter, N.R. (2006). *Creating Black Americans: African American History and Its Meanings, 1619 to the Present.* New York: Oxford University Press.
Pasupathi, M., Fivush, R., & Hernandez-Martinez, M. (2016). Talking About It: Stories as Paths to Healing After Violence. *Psychology of Violence*, 6(1): 49–56.
Radzik, L. (2008). *Making Amends: Atonement in Morality, Law, and Politics.* Oxford: Oxford University Press.
Reece, R.L., & O'Connell, H.A. (2016). How the Legacy of Slavery and Racial Composition Shape Public School Enrollment in the American South. *Sociology of Race and Ethnicity*, 2(1), 42–57.
Rice, A. (2004). Remembering Iconic, Marginalized and Forgotten Presences: Local, National and Transnational Memorial Sites in the Black Atlantic. *Current Writing*, 16, 71–92.
Robertson, C. (2018). A Lynching Memorial Is Opening. The Country Has Never Seen Anything Like It. *New York Times.* (25 Apr 2018). Accessed at https://www.nytimes.com/2018/04/25/us/lynching-memorial-alabama.html on 2nd April 2020.
Robinson, E. (2010). *Disintegration: The Splintering of Black America.* New York: Random House.
Sanders-Phillips, K., Settles-Reaves, B., Walker, D., and Brownlow, J. (2009). Social Inequality and Racial Discrimination: Risk Factors for Health Disparities in Children of Color. *Pediatrics*, 124, S176–S186.
Shriver, D (1995). *An Ethic for Enemies: Forgiveness in Politics.* New York: Oxford University Press.
Smallwood, S. (2007). *Saltwater Slavery: A Middle Passage from Africa to American Diaspora*, Cambridge, MA: Harvard University Press.
Sweet, J.H. (2003). *Recreating Africa: Culture, Kinship, and Religion in the African-Portuguese World, 1441–1770.* Chapel Hill: The University of North Carolina Press.
Thomson. G. and Gill, S. (2020). *Happiness, Flourishing and the Good Life: A Transformative Vision of Human Well-Being*, London: Routledge.
UKRI (2020). The Antislavery Knowledge Network: Community-Led Strategies for Creative and Heritage-Based Interventions in Sub-Saharan Africa. Accessed at https://gtr.ukri.org/projects?ref=AH%2FR005427%2F1 on 2nd April 2020.

UNESCO Slave Route Project (2020). *Healing the Wounds of Slavery: Approaches and Practices: A Desk Review*, Paris: UNESCO.
Urrieta, J. (2019). Indigenous Reflections on Identity, Trauma, and Healing: Navigating Belonging and Power. *Geneology*, 3, 26.
Urtz, H. and Steinberg, L. (2017). University Apologizes for Sale of 272. *The Hoya*, April 21, 2017, Accessed at https://www.thehoya.com/university-apologizes-for-sale-of-272 on 2nd April 2020.
Volkan, V.D. (1999). Psychoanalysis and Diplomacy Part II: Large-Group Rituals. *Journal of Applied Psychoanalytic Studies*, 1(3), 223–247.
Watts-Jones. (2002). Healing Internalized Racism: The Role of a Within-Group Sanctuary Among People of African Descent. *Family Processes*, 41, 591–601.
Williams, E., & Palmer, C. (1994). *Capitalism and Slavery*. Chapel Hill: University of North Carolina Press.
Yamamoto, E.K., Kim, S.H. and Holden, A.M. (2007). American Reparations Theory at the Crossroads. *California Western Law Review* 44, 1–85.

Conclusion

Recommendations and Healing, Releasing Trauma's Grip

AIMÉ CHARLES-NICOLAS
and BENJAMIN P. BOWSER

In Part One: Commonalities (Chapters 1–5), contributors lay out the evidence of the psychological legacy of slavery in the West with examples from Belize, Haiti, Colombia, and Brazil. The legacies found in these countries exist in common where slavery was practiced, and which now have descendants of enslaved Africans. The last chapter in part one provides an example, based upon the enslavement of Dahomeans, of the cultural resources enslaved Africans drew upon to survive their ordeal. In Part Two, Chapter 6 provide discussions of the psychiatric legacies of slavery, Chapter 7 outlines the post-traumatic slave syndrome, and Chapter 8 explores the psychological conditions that constituted slavery. Chapter 9 addresses the opposition to acknowledging the effects of slavery in the U.S., and Chapter 10 discusses the epigenetic ramifications of the physical and psychological treatment of slaves carried across generations into the present by unaddressed trauma. Part Three addresses solutions and healing. The most fully developed and evidence-based effort to psychologically decolonized descendants of slaves is in Jamaica. The components of the programs are presented in Chapter 11. Chapter 12 explains how one can conduct community and family psycho-social histories to identity and confront historical traumas that have been carried across generations into the present. Chapter 13 addresses the conditions necessary for healing to take place and to eliminate the negative legacies of slavery.

What follows are ways to unravel the grip of the past on the present to free future generations.

From Chapter 1—Colorism in Belize: The following is the list of recommendations made by Elma Whittaker-Augustine in Chapter 1 based upon her reflections on the psychological legacy of slavery in Belize. Each recommendation is applicable throughout the West:

    1. The first step to unravel the legacy is to have awareness and then acknowledge the problem/damage. Black playwright and director of theater and film, George C. Wolfe, once stated, "wounds heal better in open air."

    2. After acknowledging the impact of colorism and other damage, the second step is to get knowledge of our origins and ancestries, which are essential to psychological liberation. We need to know our origins and histories. Black people cannot achieve emancipation from mental slavery and achieve racial and self-pride without knowledge of their origins and ancestry.

Knowledge can provide identity, racial pride, purpose, and direction. Included are the teaching of Black history, and the teaching of the history of people of color in school curricula. Teaching Black history will not only foster information essential to positive self-esteem and identity, but it will also combat the harmful misinformation that Africans do not have a history when compared to Europeans.

    3. The third step is to assume an active role in our mental liberation, and in assuming responsibility for our lives. To promote psychological well-being, people of African ancestry need to stop seeking acceptance from Whites and to stop using Whites as a reference point for what is positive and beautiful.

    4. The fourth step is to be mindful of the integral role that language plays in color prejudice. "Black" must lose its negative meaning. We need to know we have been conditioned socially to associate negative attributes and meanings to the color black, and that this has damaged our self-worth, esteem, definition, and identity. Therefore, we need to monitor language for prejudicial and stereotypical remarks and recognize and embrace the beauty of blackness.

    5. All of us should monitor the messages given to our children about who they are. They need to be taught not to let others define them and not to live a script written by others. Black people also need to acknowledge the resulting damage of rejection and even hatred of one's group. Black people, unlike other ethnic groups, provide little support and help for each other, and continue to find it difficult to unite around common causes. Instead, the current social situation reflects a continued increase in black-on-black crime where Black males are violently annihilating each other.

6. An additional positive step forward in Belize is the celebration of Emancipation from Slavery Day, for the first time in 2015. Those of us in other countries need to do the same.

Ms. Augustine offers a series of essential principles, as well:

1. Addressing the trauma/damage of colorism, and internalized negative connotations regarding black identity, cannot be reversed solely on an individual level. It requires a change, not only in the individual/personality structures but also in the community and national social structures.

2. The social support for black acceptance and pride is an essential part of the healing process. Therefore, advocating racial and ethnic pride for Blacks, as well as *pride in other ethnic groups, is essential*.

3. Everyone should know that a person cannot be entirely secure and possess positive self-esteem if his or her self-worth depends on maintaining the belief that he or she is better than or inferior to others.

It should be evident that these recommendations are suitable not only for Belize but for the descendants of enslaved Africans in every country where slavery was practiced.

From Chapter 2—Slavery and Psychological Trauma in the Haitian Crisis: Judite Blanc suggests the following ways to unravel the legacy of slavery:

Nothing less than the decolonization of the Haitian mind and the physical-political liberation of the Haitian body is required. We can begin this process by creating a psycho-educational and therapeutic system that integrates elements of native and western knowledge. Our objectives should be to do the following:

- Reorient Haitian education to address the needs of the Haitian people and nation;
- Acknowledgment and study of the unresolved traumas of national independence, and two centuries of external exploitation of the Haitian people;
- Work toward Haiti's *economic independence* and full participation in world markets. This inclusion will require a democratic government that respects the Haitian people, is aware of their many needs, and works toward fulfilling those needs.

The following are recommendations from Haiti:

1. We need research to understand the effects of multiple traumas. The objective of such research is to tell us how persons who have had such experiences might be treated effectively.

2. We need to organize and train a nationwide mental health service with clinics systematically dispersed. These clinics will focus on community mental health with a focus on addressing intergenerational and historical trauma.

3. We need a nationwide educational and public health program to address family violence against children.

4. Informal child servitude should be outlawed. Child labor should be regulated by law specifying minimum age, minimum compensation to the child and their family, and a guarantee of education. All children at work are to be registered, periodically interviewed, and, if they live away from their families, their work conditions should be inspected.

5. Primary and secondary school curriculums need to be reformed to begin integrating into Haitian education the intense and critical study of Haitian history and culture, science, and technology in addition to the French language and culture.

6. The colon complex, colorism, rootlessness, depression, and suicide must be addressed individually as psychological issues through the Haitian educational system and community mental health campaigns. Such efforts need to be in conjunction with a nationwide radio, television, and widespread culture efforts to raise awareness and consciousness of trauma symptoms and their resolution.

7. Haitian NGOs, both it and outside of Haiti, should lobby OAS and EU to explore developing economic trade and investments in Haiti. Haitians must undertake reforms to provide the appropriate government. Alternate geopolitical partners to the U.S. need to be sought to help develop and stimulate the Haitian economy and supersede U.S. neglect.

From Chapter 3—Afro-Brazilian Youth: Andréa Máris Campos Guerra and Ana Carolina André-Cadar make the following suggestions:

A tradition of resistance to slavery historically predisposes opposition to the economy and social system. The psychology of slavery predisposes Afro-Brazilian youth toward crime, while the tradition of slave resistance justifies crime and extra-mural means of financial support. This merger of culture and history in present-day favelas influences Afro-Brazilian youth. It cuts them off from the economy and encourages their engagement in crime.

Recommendations from Brazil appropriate for other countries with urbanized Afro-descendants:

1. Nothing short of a conscious effort on the part of governments to integrate Afro-descendant youth into their national workforce and

economy will reduce their economic incentive to engage in crime and their historical justification to do so.

2. Government funding is needed for Afro-descendant communities to organize arts, music, and education festivals to encourage study and reflection on their survival and thriving after the transatlantic slave trade and slavery.

From Chapter 4—Slavery's Legacy in San Basilio Palenque, Colombia: Alexandra Escobar Puche found that the "lumbalú" funeral rite passed down for generations, serves as a script for dealing with intergenerational trauma. The funeral service acknowledges a close and continuous relationship between those who have passed and the living. Ritual performers take on the mourners' traumas, post-traumatic stress, depression, and other psychopathologies that have accumulated over time. Whatever they do in the community is therapeutic and effective in relieving individual members of their psychological burden. Today, church ministers and performing artists that tap deep emotions in their audiences play such a role among descendants of enslaved Africans. They have transformed rituals from Africa and slavery into modern cultural events showing resilience as a feature of the psychological legacies of slavery. Implied recommendations follow:

1. Afro-descendant communities need to encourage their *arts* in all forms and expressions and encourage the participation of youth in them.

2. Afro-descendant communities need to preserve and encourage *rituals* that evoke strong emotions—church, funerals, dance, musical concerts with empathic ministers, and performers.

3. Trauma victims should *experience and participate* in arts and historical rituals—church, theater, dance, music—as part of treatment and therapy.

From Chapter 5—Those Who Disappeared: Bernard Dossa tells us what we can be confident about is that enslaved Africans brought with them a culture that prepared them to deal with the traumas and oppression they encountered. Today, this culture can be found in parts of present-day Togo, Benin, and Western Nigeria. The Dahomey region is inhabited then and now by the Adja-Fon peoples, who practice the Vodoun tradition of worship. They believe that there is a divine principle living in all things and that everyone is subject to these principles. The Fâ is an anthropocentric conception of the universe in the service of man. Those who believe and understand in divine principles can know, through the Fâ, the will of the Vodoun. This will is manifest in nature, dreams, and people.

Dossa observes that enslaved descendants from Dahomey in the West were successful in embedding their African beliefs in their Baptist,

Methodist, and Catholic faiths and continuing to practice Vodoun elements. Their underlying faith was protective during slavery and continues to be so today. However, there is something about animist faiths not understood an appreciated in the West. If one's ancestries entered pacts with nature through the Fâ, those pacts are to be honored, even in subsequent generations. To reject, not honor or forget one's pacts—underlying spiritual missions—has dire consequences. Enslaved Africans have such ancestral pacts, and those responsible for slavery interfered with them.

All descendants of Africans in the West venerate the earth and evoke the spirits by pouring water or small liquor drops onto it. Perhaps, we do not understand just how well calls to the spirits and ancestors have been answered. The unforeseen supernatural interventions may have disrupted the slave trade, ended slavery, and brought misfortune to those engaged in the slave trade and slavery.

The recommended traditional treatment from the ancestors of those engaged in slavery acknowledges the actual and spiritual damage they did and offers restitution to the spirits. For African slave descendants, the therapy consists of initiating rituals for permanent reconciliation between themselves and their original African spirits.

From Chapter 6—A Psychiatric Look at the Legacy of Slavery: Aimé Charles-Nicolas offers a series of clinical and counseling suggestions:

It must be stressed that the development of children's self-esteem does not take place through imitation. Children learn the *value of the self from what other members of the community communicate to them.* Harsh child-rearing is no longer necessary and is destructive to children's self-esteem.

1. As communities, we must put emphasis on children's self-esteem. Parents and guardians must understand and act on this point.

Public humiliation, so prevalent during slavery, is now a weapon of mass destruction of the self-esteem of children and adolescents. It makes the child feel shame and lessens their self-esteem. Parents and social workers must realize that self-esteem is the most valuable asset an adolescent has!

2. Humiliation, especially regarding race, in front of others, should be avoided if not eliminated.

Regarding the development of racial identity during slavery, nighttime gatherings were essential. Such meetings are no less critical today. Children should overhear and be engaged in song and dance and conversation about family, race, and history.

3. We need to be intentional about the intergeneration transmission of culture. Television, video games, and electronic devices

are no substitute for direct engagement and communications with family, elders, and community members.

We understand that, after the abolition of slavery, ex-slaves tried to forget the shame associated with being a slave. They tried to *raise their children with explicit dignity*. Their children could not and did not want to hear about slavery. Silence was the price of dignity passed from generation to generation. Do not speak about it. Forget it. *Shame is a dominant attitude of post-slavery societies.*

    4. We must, in our families and communities, provide a narrative to young people that defines who they are, from where they come, and how they got here so that they are not ashamed of their past. This narrative cannot be left to television, schools, and popular culture.

The institution of slavery may have ended, but White supremacy, shaped by four centuries of transatlantic slavery, did not. Colonialism and now globalism are sequels to and the consequence of slavery. An outcome is that White and Black identities are based upon a racial hierarchy. To what extent does an Afro-descendant believe the conventional popular cultural scripts (white beauty, morality, intelligence) that presume white supremacy? The more they do, the more they have internalized racism and racial inferiority.

    5. White and Black parents must intentionally challenge the cultural script their children learn that Whites are superior, and Blacks are inferior. They must do this to keep them from internalizing racism and racial inferiority.

From Chapter 7—Explaining Post Traumatic Slave Syndrome: Joy A. DeGruy offers the following suggestions from her Tools for Healing PTSS:

Vacant self-esteem is viewed and measured based almost entirely on the individual's positive or negative evaluation of himself or herself. Explored feelings include self-efficacy, perceived capacity, and self-worth. However, vacant esteem also considers one's racial/cultural self-appraisal and how a person feels about their racial-ethnic group and perceptions of beauty, i.e., hair texture, facial features, and skin color.

Educational Interventions:

    1. Individuals need to be introduced to the adaptive survival behaviors that have been identified in the PTSS book and Study Guide. Other books, articles, and films should be included that address the residual beliefs and practices that have been passed along

over generations following American chattel slavery. These adaptive behaviors should be scrutinized to determine if they lead to a positive self-appraisal or a negative one. The appraisal should inform whether a practice or belief should be discarded or maintained.

2. African American individuals, families, and communities have been miseducated and uneducated about their history and have looked to traditional educational institutions that have failed to inform them about their history and culture. There needs to be formal and informal instruction within the community on African American culture and history utilizing scholarly books and articles that accurately represent the African American experience before, during, and after slavery. These materials must be age-appropriate and easily understood by laypersons and available for individuals, families, and the community.

3. African American educators, community advocates, and counselors should assist individuals and families in creating a family narrative that acknowledges and embraces the lived experiences of the family. The lived experiences should include the difficulties and tragedies as well as the successes that the family has encountered. This narrative will help to provide a cohesive story that tells of triumphs and failures, but most importantly, describing the family's strengths and determination to keep striving despite fears and doubts. This narrative can be written or spoken, but most importantly, it should be shared.

Response to Anger and Violence

Anger and violence are among the more evident and concerning aspects of self-destructive behaviors associated with PTSS. Anger is often the result of an individual or a group experiencing persistently blocked goals, and unresolved angst due to external stressors.

Education and Interventions

1. African Americans must learn the role that major systems in America play in causing anger and violence. Black families need to find and maintain stable housing, the lack of which has attributed to personal and structural violence.

2. Meditation, exercise, and spiritual practices have been shown to reduce stress and reduce anxiety and mood swings. African Americans should adopt one or more of these practices as part of their daily routine.

3. Black boys are often not seen as children or as innocent. Far too many are perceived as dangerous and are treated with less tenderness and affection than their white counterparts. Physical touch has been found to reduce aggression in African American boys; a handshake or an arm around the shoulder goes a long way. Engagement in sports, dance, and music are healthy ways for youth and adults to expend positive energy and build confidence, self-discipline, and cooperation.

Response to Racist Socialization

African Americans of all ages have all been bombarded with negative messages that promote beliefs that African Americans are unintelligent, unattractive, and inferior. The best way to combat racist socialization is by promoting positive racial socialization.

1. African American individuals, families, and the community should focus on the positive contributions of African Americans through education, viewing films, and participate in culture-specific activities at home and the broader community.
    a. Sponsor book clubs about culturally relevant topics
    b. Host community meetings and invite black speakers
    c. Develop children's classes about Black History
2. Homes, schools, and community spaces should display African American reading materials (i.e., art, magazines, and clothes).
3. Help build strong positive relationships within the family and community. Seek out individuals that consistently demonstrate positive racial regard.

From Chapter 8—An Exploration of the Psychological Legacy of Slavery: While slavery has been outlawed legally and is an economic anachronism, the mechanics for psychologically maintaining slavery still exist. Fear of violence, powerlessness, physical and mental deprivation, dependency, and lack of personal regard continue in how African Americans are treated and in how some treat themselves. The model in Chapter 8 illustrates how psychological oppression condition and compel both dysfunctional and resilient behaviors. In principle, healthy functioning among Afro-descendants is dependent on enough resilience to offset the five types of oppression. In which case, the following are actions that Benjamin Bowser suggests should be taken to strengthen resilience and reduce racism's psychological abuse implied in the model.

To Strengthen Resilience:

1. The more details and specifics of White racial oppression are known and shared, the less effective this oppression is. Racial oppression is most effective against isolated individuals. Sharing cellphone videos of police oppression is an excellent example of shedding light on individual racial oppression aimed at all Blacks. Social support for those who experience these acts strengthens their resilience.

2. Encourage and strengthen Black institutional membership in which Afro-descendant history, culture, religion, arts, folklore, and exchange are valued, propagated, and practiced. Resilience can be learned and encouraged at family gatherings, church services, and programs, book clubs, arts festivals, social clubs, in barbershops and hair dressers, and theater performances.

3. Resilience is strengthened in face-to-face family and community gatherings. Electronic media, television shows, including BET programs, have the potential to be helpful to black psychological resilience, but in general, are not. "Black programming" is more often harmful because it still perpetuates white racial stereotypes that reinforce white supremacy and black racial inferiority. Afro-descendants do not control this programming whose primary mission is to advance profits, not black culture.

Reduce Oppressive Conditions:

1. Enhance employment and job training programs that target the Afro-descendant poor. These efforts have been shown to be effective in increasing employment and reducing poverty. It is impoverished Afro-descendants, segregated in racial ghettos and favelas, who are the most psychologically oppressed and whose resilience must be the strongest and is most often tested.

2. Afro-descendants must be encouraged to take advantage of every educational and employment opportunity. The higher the level of education and employment, the fewer who are impoverished and the fewer who use slavery-related cultural scripts to raise children, and who engage in crime or violence.

3. Afro-descendant community advocacy is necessary to continue anti-racial discrimination efforts in employment and housing. The psychology of slavery is maintained and reinforced for European and Afro-descendants wherever they are segregated and isolated racially from one another.

4. The number of community-level working coalitions of European and Afro-descendants needs to be increased as well as the range of problems they work to solve. European and Afro-descendants working together as peers contradict and reduce beliefs in White racial superiority and the need for slave-legacy behaviors.

From Chapter 9—The Psychological Legacy of Slavery in the United States: Edwin J. Nichols notes the challenge the U.S. poses. Denial of the barbarity of slavery in the U.S. is stronger than the denial of slavery in other countries with colonial histories. Such an admission would question the fundamental character of the nation and its people. An innocent people who "sit on a hill" of freedom and democracy could not do such things. However, they did. His first recommendation is:

1. Afro-descendants and globalists in the U.S. should mount efforts to have the U.S. government rejoin UNESCO, participate in, and publicize its educational efforts. U.S. citizens are the least informed of Western nations on international affairs and of efforts to come to terms with the legacies of the transatlantic slave trade and slavery in the West.

There are White Americans who say "get over it" to any reference to African slavery and any past or present trauma, hurt, or humiliation experienced by African Americans. "Getting over it" is exactly what we want to do, but not in the way that they want. The way to get over unresolved trauma, accumulated in the past and present, is not to ignore and forget it, as they would like us to do.

2. Afro-descendant media outlets and public personalities need to talk about the psychological legacies of slavery. Colorism, child beating, black-on-black violence, self-hatred, etc., all need to be in the Afro-descendant public consciousness. To know the source and origins of these behaviors is then to have an opportunity to reflect on them and change behaviors.

We must break through our silence and denial, confront what happened to us, and understand how the past affects us in the present. The ways we coped were a function of the times, but to do the same now limits our lives, consciously or unconsciously. Updating our coping strategies is how we will get over historical trauma.

3. The psychological legacies of slavery should be a topic of discussion and reflection on Afro-descendant healthcare, church, civic, community, service organizations. Church leaders and service providers should be called upon to do outreach to their constituencies, membership, and parishioners to offer alternative behaviors and ways for families and individuals to address dysfunctional legacies.

Resolving past trauma and legacy is not work that we can do alone. It requires a collective effort and may take generations. "Getting over it" is also about serving as witnesses to acknowledge what we forgot and deny. Reconciliation and coming to terms with the past, and its effects are essential to "getting over it." A new compendium on the status of U.S. race relations appears every twenty-five years. Some have strategies and recommendations on how to reduce racism in the U.S. However, all efforts to mitigate racism have been ignored by both Democratic and Republican federal administrations alike (Hawley & Jackson, 1995; Jaynes & Williams Jr., 1989; Kerner & et al., 1968).

    4. Consideration should be given to existing compendiums on race relations in the U.S. These documents can be the basis for federal, state, local government, and NGO efforts to mitigate beliefs in white supremacy among Euro-descendants and to reduce racial discrimination against Afro-descendants.

From Chapter 10—The Epigenetic Ramifications of the Trauma: Fatimah Jackson and her team make the following recommendations. The need to integrate new technologies in molecular genetics are reflected in their recommendations. Also, more sophisticated bioinformatic conceptual models are needed in the study of the trans-Atlantic trade and its multigenerational aftermath.

    1. Routine testing of epigenomic status is needed in all civil rights cases. We must know how much trauma, how much resilience, how much residual impairment exists in the descendants of enslaved Africans. This knowledge will tell us the extent to which institutional racism has influenced current populations.

    2. Integration of genomic and epigenomic results are needed to detect unique sensitivities in individuals and groups. Just as the characteristics of enslavement and racial discrimination have not been uniform throughout the Americas, the epigenomic consequences vary as well.

    3. There is a need to identify the nuanced interactions between a people's background genomics and the epigenomic they acquire environmentally and inherit from previous generations. This knowledge will lead to significant advances in integrative human biology.

    4. There is a need to develop precision medicines to address the needs of Legacy African Americans. The push for personalized medicine must address people's past if it is to be useful in their present. The epigenome connects us with our history while influencing present and future generations.

    5. Epigenomic data on Legacy African Americans must be linked

with metabolomic, peoteomic, and transcriptomic data. This will allow the multidimensional analysis of many levels of physiological effect simultaneously and in real-time. Advances in biotechnology, post-next generation sequencing, now make such multiple assessments possible.

6. Artificial Intelligence (AI) and develop algorithms using advanced bioinformatic tools informed by the historical and life sciences need to be trained to predict the impact of the past on the present.

From Chapter 11—Shattering Delusions of Slavery: The most effective use of psychiatry to address the psychological legacy of slavery in the West is found in Jamaica, and it is replicable. Frederick W. Hickling describes the development and use of psycho-historiographic cultural therapy (PCT). PCT evolved out of large group discussions about life in a mental hospital and madness in Jamaican society. The meetings in the hospital were recorded and videotaped. Anecdotal memories were subjected to visual analysis, in which events from the colonial period were contrasted with present-day experiences. These contrasts showed connections between the past and present as dialectic relationships. These sessions were combined with group psychotherapy, oral tradition, the use of the circle, folk traditions, storytelling, poetry, arts, crafts, music, dance, and theater. Also, there is the use of psycho-pharmacology, culturally sensitive counseling, and individual psycho-therapy.

Each of the therapeutic techniques used in Jamaican psychiatry is found in all Western Hemisphere countries and are not unique to Jamaica. Therapeutic communities elsewhere can use these techniques in combination, which are useful in helping people from various socio-economic and educational backgrounds. They help to comprehend under-developed political and psychological constructs, to debunk myths about colonization (race), and to establish a framework for more effective efforts to make changes. Psychiatrists who deal with the legacy of slavery must always be aware of their patients throughout the process, know where patients come from, of what life has in store from them, and of what influences them. For therapy to progress and change to take place, the patient, too, must internalize insights about themselves and their circumstances. They must deal with forces that block action, do problem-solving and reality testing. They must master their anxieties and accept personal limitations and handicaps while fulfilling their life potential.

Findings: It was determined through psycho-historiographic analysis that Jamaican society, psychology, and subsequent rates of black-on-black murder, etc., have come about in response to two historical European delusions internalized by patients. First, colonists believed it was by divine right that European invaders owned all that was seen (including the people). Second, there are the religious exhortations that Black people were sub-human and that White people should rule non–White people, in every way. Therapeutic communities elsewhere may find other historical delusions at the core of their patients' unresolved issues. Whatever is the basis of their patients' delusions, the consequence is Axis II personality disorders. Hickling refers to these disorders as "shakatani" derived from the Swahili words *shaka* (problem) and *tani* (power). People with these personality disorders can be treated with *psycho-historiographic brief psychotherapy. They improve by gaining insight into their thoughts, attitudes, and behaviors* through *insight* and continued *behavior modification*.

Wherever there is the goal of facilitating psychological AND cultural treatment, it is necessary to create therapeutic institutions that can treat both patient's psychology and cultures. More often, for descendants of enslaved Africans, their psychological issues are derived from racism and their culture. Hospitals and clinics in Jamaica are also involved in decolonizing the culture through extensive use of group and individual therapies, as advocated by Frantz Fanon. Others can do the same.

Community Mental Health: Mental health services are offered in all 400 of Jamaica's community health clinics. In a unique and innovative service in world psychiatry, patients with acute psychoses are treated as well in the open general medical wards (OGMW) of hospitals. Here is another example to follow.

Primary Prevention: Finally, there is a primary prevention effort underway. *Dream-A-World Cultural Therapy* program combined group therapy with the creative arts (drama, dance, art, and music). Children were asked to imagine a new world on another planet, name it, conceive its inhabitants, and decide what to take or eliminate from their known world to this new one. They decided how they would look and what role they would play in governing the new world. They were taught to play musical instruments, compose songs, poems, and dances about their new world, which were refined and performed over the project cycle. In effect, the children benefit from a brief psycho-historiographic experience. This program can be replicated as well.

From Chapter 12—How to Conduct a Psycho-Social History: Benjamin P. Bowser provides a how-to guide on conducting psycho-social family and community histories. The descendants of enslaved Africans and slave masters have within their power to use tools and resources to explore their own family history and the communities in which they lived. Each year, new records are added to the already extraordinary number and variety of history, genealogical, county, census, newspapers, and court records conveniently available online. All one needs is three pieces of information to get started: the state, county, and period when one's family lived in a specific place. Online one can do in a few days, work which required weeks of library and archival work on site. It is now necessary to search on-site only after exhausting state and local electronically available records.

In the 1960s, interest in slavery, Black and African history, and related topics emerged beyond a few senior scholars' writing. Two or three books pre-year were published on issues related to slavery and its legacies. It was possible to keep up with the field. After fifty years, the number of scholars, researchers, disciplines, and inter-disciplines has multiplied. Older work has been re-evaluated, and concepts and theories have been critiqued and advanced. For example, instead of histories of slavery in the U.S. or a specific state, one will now find histories of slavery in cities and counties and aspects of slavery. More research specialists are studying every part of the past than at any other time in history. There are not just historians; one will find sociologists, anthropologists, Ethnic and Africana Studies, journalists, psychologists, and a host of other specialists at work. So, anyone exploring their family and community will often find a great deal of the work already done. One must just look for it.

In chapter 12, Bowser encourages family explorers to go beyond genealogies and seek to find out and understand the events and experiences that shaped one family culture, which are passed on from generation to generation. Traumatic experiences, separations, diseases, violence, war, natural disasters, political events, once in a lifetime opportunities, gaining a talent or skill, witnessing a historic event, being in the right place at the right time, or in the wrong place at the wrong time can all have lasting impacts and be evident from documentary sources. The point is that it is possible to explore in one's family history and community backgrounds every issue examined at in this book.

From Chapter 13—Healing the Wounds of Slavery: Scherto Gill's chapter is perhaps the most thorough exploration to date of two things. The first is the damage done by slavery that has been carried on by racism. Second, she outlines what would be required to genuinely heal the psychological damage done to the descendants of enslaved Africans and enslavers alike. A few essential points were made:

Slavery was a four-hundred year-long process of dehumanization and traumatization. It assaulted the self-worth, tore the fabric of communities, and institutionalized violence and insecurity for every generation since its inception. The humanity, quality of life, and psychological well-being of slaves, slavers, and their descendants have all been reduced. No one escaped undamaged.

While the institution of slavery ended over a century ago, its psychological and cultural trauma has continued unabated into the present. If racism is unaddressed, it will continue to compromise the lives of future generations until it is addressed. Slavery's legacy and repercussions, if unaddressed, will not go away or fade in time.

Slavery and racism are something that human beings did to others and continued to do consciously and unconsciously to this day. How can the damage be addressed; how can healing take place?

Healing is not the opposite of wounding, nor is it to humanize another. Healing occurs when an individual fully recognizes their intrinsic value and feel and act out of that recognition. They never stopped being human.

The first preconditions for healing are:

1. Healing begins with a thorough acknowledgment of the dehumanizing effects of the slave trade, slavery, and its subsequent racism.

2. Public atonement of dehumanizing effects are necessary in order for the harmed communities to accept the atonement.

The agent or institution that atones must have moral courage and the political will to fulfill the first two preconditions. A public apology places past atrocities directly in open conversations, acknowledges the wounding, and legitimizes the acknowledgment. Breaking the silence and remembering past dehumanizing acts are essential to addressing traumas and their effects. Suffering can be diminished, grief can be eased, and tormented emotions assuage. However, the following preconditions are the most difficult.

3. Those who have suffered the wounds have to treat themselves. Healing involves transcending a broken sense of self and moving toward wholeness with an awareness of one's innate dignity. Healing includes transforming psychological and cultural habits, such as deliberate oppression (Friere, 1970) and learned helplessness (DeGruy, 2017), which, if untreated, allows continued dehumanization.

4. Those who have perpetuated the wounds also have to treat themselves; this includes those who were not enslavers but who have defended racism and White supremacy. The inherited presumption that races exist and that you are a member of a superior race is delusional—insanity. All of the attitudes and behaviors that are a consequence of this delusion need to be examined by self-reflection.

5. More importantly, racist institutions—police, schools, housing, work—that insure racially unequal outcomes and maintain the subordination of slave descendants must be acknowledged and dismantled as well. People devise and maintain racist institutions that are outcomes of racist attitudes and beliefs passed on across generations since slavery.

Healing of people on both sides of the racial divide is necessary to end the cycles of violence as well as unconscious and conscious racism and discrimination. Again, the descendants of enslaved Africans are not the only ones in need of healing. Whites cannot just acknowledge and atone for slavery and racism and move on. They must recognize and then deal with the damage that slavery and ongoing racism have done to them as well. Each side of slavery's history, descendants of slaves and slavers, is not independent of the other. Healing from the wounds of slavery will never be complete or successful without mutual liberation from the delusions of race and its effects. Finally, the wounding will not stop until institutional dehumanization in the economy is stopped. A post-racist humanization must replace it.

Truth, Reconciliation and Reparations

Measures taken to acknowledge and resolve the deaths and suffering that were outcomes of genocide and racial oppression are truth and reconciliation commissions (Tutu, 2019). Pioneered in South Africa and then used effectively in Ruanda, a panel of citizens acting as arbitrators meets in various locations throughout the country. People who experienced traumatic losses and abuses may come forward to testify. Defendants are called to be present to hear the testimony against them and to speak on their behalf. They are given immunity from prosecution in exchange for their participation. The commission's objective is to find out what happened in detail (truth) and to provide the parties with an opportunity to reconcile (reconciliation). The injured parties can come to terms with what happened to them and have their injuries and losses acknowledged as a necessary precondition to healing. The accused can realize the harm they caused, accept it, and engage in reconciliation with their victims.

The use of truth and conciliation commissions recognizes that genuine and lasting peace between the injured and those who committed the abuses can happen only after reconciliation. More often, the families and communities that these parties represent must now live together and reconstruct normal relations with one another. The idea is to reduce hatred, mistrust, fear, and revenge-seeking that can explode into new conflicts based upon unresolved issues from the past.

Twelve countries in South and Central America plus Haiti in the Caribbean have truth and reconciliation commissions. They are Argentina, Bolivia, Brazil, Colombia, Chile, Ecuador, El Salvador, Guatemala, Honduras, Panama, Paraguay, and Peru. Every one of their commissions is devoted to addressing the abuses of past dictators, civil wars, and human rights violations in the past century. The most common commission issues are people who "disappeared" and efforts to account for them. They are presumed to have been executed by the military or rebel groups. Canada has a truth and conciliation commission to address the forced separation of Native children from their families and their placement in schools intent upon wiping out the children's Native cultures. Ironically, every single one of these countries had African slaves, and most have Afro-descendant populations who are at the bottom of their social hierarchy. None of these commissions addresses their country's history of slavery and subsequent racism.

There is a problem with recommending truth and reconciliation to address the legacy of slavery in these countries, including the U.S. There are preconditions for effective implementation of truth and reconciliation (TR). First, TR was applied successfully AFTER apartheid was ended in South Africa and AFTER the genocide in Ruanda. Second, both parties, victims, and perpetrators, must have a relatively neutral third party, such as a new government, to sponsor the commission, and that can prosecute perpetrators who refuse to engage in truth and reconciliation. Finally, both parties must be willing to engage one another in reconciliation. However, despite slavery ending in all these countries, its legacy continues through racism. The government could not be a neutral third party in reconciliation in none of these countries. Those who would deny their legacy of slavery and the existence of racism heavily influence if not dominate their governments. Racism continues the perpetuation of traumas and insults from slavery. Under the circumstance, neither descendants of slaves nor perpetrators of racism are willing to engage in reconciliation. In sum, none of the conditions for successful truth and reconciliation exists in the nations that practiced slavery in the West.

While reconciliation on a national level is premature, there is the possibility of case-by-case reconciliations at local levels in each country. In the U.S., the Greensboro (North Carolina) Truth and Reconciliation Commission was not affiliated with either the federal or state government. It investigated from 2004 to 2006 what was called the 1979 Greensboro Massacre. In Maine, the Wabanaki-State Truth and Reconciliation Commission investigated child welfare issues. It might be possible to organize a limited number of truth and reconciliations specifically between the descendants of slave owners and their slaves. These would be compelling examples of reconciliation among the people at the center of the abuses of slavery and would go a long way to both explain and contradict racism.

Reparations

The issue of reparations for slavery is certainly not new. People have always protested the institution of slavery, from Seneca (4 BCE–65 CE) to

Epiphane de Moirans (1644–1689) and Francisco José de Jaca (1645–1690) and up until today. In 1686, these Capuchin monks demanded expressly the recognition of, among other things, "the obligation to *compensate* them or their rightful beneficiaries, for endured suffering and mortal risk incurred from the day of their deportation from Africa or from their birth in slavery to the West Indies up to their emancipation."

W.E.B. Du Bois wrote his 1896 dissertation on the suppression of the African slave trade precisely to call attention to slavery's after-effects. Proposals for dealing with the thorny problem of reparations for slavery have periodically recurred in the U.S. from the 1865 Special Field Orders No. 15 ("Forty acres and a mule") to the 2020 Democratic Party presidential primaries.[1]

The question of reparations is not posed in the same way today in all post-slavery countries. Differences in justice, police, and education matter. The degree of intensity of the resentment, anger, and feelings of injustice is behind the request for reparations. Even in 1686, monks had put forward the argument of suffering in their demand for reparations. We have shown in the previous pages how psychological suffering was at the heart of the slavery system: humiliation was used to subject the enslaved people and to destroy their basic self-esteem.

The U.S. is the only country in the West to fight a war to end slavery, which suggests how strong emotions are regarding race to this day. In the United States, the period following the abolition of slavery was marked by Jim Crow laws, which confirmed that "you are no longer slaves, but you are inherently inferior." These laws legalized humiliation. They were binding on all and would remain in effect until the Civil Rights Act was passed in 1964. The Ku Klux Klan was founded in Tennessee on December 24, 1865, just six days after the announcement that the Thirteenth Amendment to the Constitution of the United States had been ratified and adopted!

In the French colonies, the same day that the abolition of slavery was declared, in 1848, the slaves were all declared "free and equal citizens." After 1848 they did not experience lynching, house fires, castrations, or hangings. Even if slavery has left deep scars in the current mentality in the former French colonies, it is unthinkable for White police to kill unarmed young Blacks and be acquitted, as is the case today in the U.S. There is no racialization inherent in the functioning of justice, police, or education, which is compulsory and free, even if there is a hypocritical racial hierarchy in the way of thinking of many people. France is the only country that has promulgated (2001) a law recognizing the slave trade and slavery as a crime against humanity. But this law does not imply any form of reparations.

In the former French colonies, the reparations debate is waged on a moral plane: many voices were raised, from Aimé Césaire to Frantz Fanon, to claim that slavery was irreparable. And today, Alfred Marie-Jeanne, the Head of the Community of Martinique, says he is morally against "reparations and compensation" and prefers "development aid." However, we may consider that one does not necessarily exclude the other. The moral plane does not preclude the strictly legal plane: the crime is recognized by law, the victim, therefore, has the right to reparation (especially since the slave owners were compensated for their economic losses). But how? Given that the standard of living in the former French colonies is much better than that of the other Caribbean countries.

In the U.S., the discussion of how to deal with the repair of the legacy of slavery has often focused on the question of financial compensation. This is because of the problem of poverty and schooling. In fact, the history of African Americans is a long story of theft that persists from the time of slavery when their labor was exploited until today. Opponents to reparations allege practical difficulties:

Who will pay?

Millions of non–Black Americans are descendants of people who did not own slaves or who arrived in the country after the end of slavery; some blacks, and some Native Americans, owned slaves.

Who will be paid?

What about the one-drop rule? Will they have to sort out the descendants of slaves for compensation in proportion to the percentage of their African blood? Should reparations be paid only to poor Blacks? On a practical level, we suggest that it is possible to tie real reparations to specific abuses and local crimes.

However, repairing the psychological wounds of slavery must have a collective and individual dimension. The collective dimension can be community, and it must also be official. *It must include Blacks and Whites as equals.* It can take the form of regular commemorations, speeches, tributes, statues, museums, monuments, etc. "The official imprimatur of the state" would help. The state must also play a role, one that is primarily moral. This point is crucial because there is a perfect *continuity* between the humiliation of slavery, the humiliation of lynching, and that of the murders of young Blacks today. The judicial institution (the state) is implicated again and again. The state must promote restorative justice, reform the laws, monitor their application and profoundly transform mentalities within the judicial system. Many laws on the books are problematic, especially neighborhood-watch, stand-your-grounds laws, and citizen's arrest laws that allow private citizens to play amateur detective with guns in their hands.

Mentalities in the judiciary institution and the school system are linked to those of the population in general. These attitudes are based on the concept of the inherent "inferiority" of Blacks. Speeches and official statements can imply that "inferiority" is an inferiorization, a psychological construction that has been instilled in all psyches of Blacks and Whites, day after day, for centuries. The state must commit itself to the healing of the long-term psychological abnormalities created by enslavement: white supremacy and black internalized racism. Their consequences are conflicting: one causes pride and prejudice, the other shame and suffering. It will be more difficult to abandon the position where you feel superior than to rise from the position where you feel inferior.

Sometimes people who have been abused adopt the psychological configuration of victims. They have a negative perception of themselves; they consider themselves weak and helpless, which is a reality for many Blacks in the United States.

The position of victim has secondary benefits. We feel sorry for them; we consider them, and we help them. But the problem is that victims are afraid of losing support. So, they tend to remain in the status of victim. The individual who identifies as a victim suffers that victimization passively. Still, it can also be the result of an adaptation strategy, a strategy that puts them under the protection of the other.

Victimization and self-repair are opposed diametrically. Victimization can only lead to a false reparation since it establishes a relationship of hierarchical submission. Self-repair puts an end to hatred, which, without it, could continue indefinitely. It is critically important for descendants of the enslaved to avoid the crutch of victimization. At the same time, it is essential for the crime to be recognized by the state—to receive "the official imprimatur." This is the beginning of reparations and helps in the process of self-repair.

Does the victim of the psychological ravages of slavery have to wait for reparations to get better? This is precisely the question that Bob Marley answered with an emphatic "No."

To wait for our repair from the other is to presuppose that the other feels guilty about slavery. What should genuine reparations look like? We are nourished daily by everything that can benefit our psyche, our self-esteem, which gives meaning to our life. You have to ask yourselves what you really want, regardless of the other. We must match our actions to our desires and not to those of others. Dare to occupy my place, and only my place, and consider the long-term consequences of acts before taking action.

So, reparations are based on the premise that the original abuse ended, and the damage can now be assessed. Slavery in the West ended only as a legal and economic practice. Its psychology and cultural basis in racism continue to this day. How does one calculate damages for abuse that has not ended?

It would make sense if reparations to a group or individuals were understood as partial payment for ongoing oppression. Otherwise, what does one do after reparations are paid, but one's oppression continues? One is still economically marginalized and at the bottom of the social hierarchy. De-colonization is not complete. While one's oppression is ongoing, those who provided the financial compensation can claim that they have paid their debt to you. *You were compensated, and you agreed to the settlement.* How would one be judged in history for such strategic naivety?

Reparations must be part of a double enterprise of the liberation of thought, which involves a restructuring of both the inferiorized human being and the human being who has been denatured by the ideology of superiority and domination.

Note

1. P.R. Lockhart, "The 2020 Democratic Primary Debate Over Reparations, Explained," *Vox*, March 19, 2019.

References

Coates, T.-N. (2014). The Case for Reparations. *The Atlantic*. Retrieved from https://www.theatlantic.com/magazine/archive/2014/06/the-case-for-reparations/361631/

Hassan, A., & Healy, J. (2019). America Has Tried Reparations Before. Here Is How It Went. Retrieved from https://www.nytimes.com/2019/06/19/us/reparations-slavery.html.

Hawley, W.D., & Jackson, A.W. (Eds.). (1995). *Toward a Common Destiny*. San Francisco: Jossey-Bass.

Jaynes, G., & Williams Jr, R. (1989). *A Common Destiny: Blacks and American Society*. Washington, D.C.: National Academy Press.

Kerner, O., & et al. (1968). *Report of the National Advisory Commission on Civil Disorders*. New York: E.P. Dutton and Comp.

Tutu, D. (2019). Truth and Reconciliation Commission, South Africa. Retrieved from https://www.britannica.com/topic/Truth-and-Reconciliation-Commission-South-Africa.

Coda

Masters and Slaves No More

BENJAMIN P. BOWSER
and AIMÉ CHARLES-NICOLAS

Outcomes of histories much older than the transatlantic slave trade and slavery in the West are still with us. European Romance languages are legacies of Latin spoken over a thousand years ago. Present-day religious, legal, and academic traditions are even older than Latin. Tourists spend billions of dollars and Euros annually visiting historic sites where governments advanced, where people made sacrifices, nations were born, ideas took root, wars were won and lost, and the arts advanced. All this attention and money are acknowledgments that ideas, people, and events, which occurred hundreds and even thousands of years ago, that inspired our past, influence us today, and will shape our future.

In contrast, efforts are made to forget rather than remember the transatlantic slave trade and slavery in the West, which formally ended only 132 years ago. In Brazil, the U.S., and the rest of the Western Hemisphere, there are virtually no monuments, no days of commemoration, nor are there tourists seeking to know this history and its influence on us. Most of the written accounts of the transatlantic slave trade and slavery have only appeared in recent decades. Claims that slavery left no legacy or mark on the present are still firm. Such an urge to forget and deny indicates that entire nations are still unable to accept their past. Descendants of enslaved Africans, slave owners, and immigrants alike anxiously cling to historical amnesia that is laden with silence and charged with emotion. One hundred and thirty-two years is not a long time.

This book is about coming to terms with the consequences of capturing 24 million Africans and force-marching them to the sea (Curtain, 1969; Sweet, 2003). Half survived. Twelve million were put in the holes of ships; each captive had space smaller than in a coffin (71).[1] Two-thirds survived the months at sea in the Middle Passage. Most of the eight million Africans finally brought ashore as enslaved Africans perished from disease, exposure, brutality, and over-work (Sweet, 2003, p. 63). This history meets the U.N. Convention on Genocide's definition of genocide. The progeny of these enslaved Africans was treated as things; they were brought, sold, traded like cattle or furniture and worked as unpaid labor for their lifetime and their children's lifetime, and so on from 1444 to 1888–444 years. Marks have been left by the slave trade, slavery, and the denial of both on the psychologies of all descendants. Our purpose has been to lay bare this legacy so that it can be addressed finally and dispassionately.

Fortunately, the horror did not last forever. From the beginning, there were calls to end Western slavery. Abolitionists' efforts in Great Britain, attributed mainly to William Wilberforce, culminated in ending the British trade in 1808, and to ending slavery in the British Empire by 1834 (Carey, 2005). Slavery was a contradiction and an embarrassment to the French after the French Revolution. Victor Schœlcher, among others, drove this point home in the French Assembly, which led to abolishing France's involvement in slavery by 1848. Abolitionist efforts succeeded in the U.S. as well, but only after fighting a bloody and destructive civil war. The U.S. is the only country in the West to fight a war to end slavery. W.E.B. Du Bois wrote his 1896 dissertation on the suppression of the African slave trade and to call attention to slavery's after-effects. However, apart from easily ignored activists and Africanists such as Du Bois, the African slave trade and slavery in the West were treated as if they never happened for over a full century.

Potential for Holocaust and War

Unfortunately, the slaughter of Native Peoples and the African slave trade and slavery were not the last acts of mass genocide. The present-day chaos in the Congo is the outcome of its 132-year-old crisis that started after 1885. Five million Congolese were killed while enslaved in King Leopold of Belgium's private Congo Free State. In 1915, leaders of the Turkish government had 1.5 million Armenians massacred and expelled many more from Turkey. This 102-year-long conflict continues to generate unrest in the Middle East today. The German state sponsored the massacre of six million Jews in World War II. The holocaust had roots in the centuries-old persecution, pogroms, and segregation of Jews in Europe. The lasting effects on subsequent generations of Jews and non–Jews alike have yet to be calculated fully. In Kosovo in the 1990s, the ethnic Serbian minority, who are Christian, killed thousands of ethnic majority Albanians, who are Muslim.

They did so based upon a previous genocide that occurred in 1389. Both groups had coexisted peacefully and had even intermarried for generations, even through World War II. The original unresolved dispute is 600 years old. Then, there is the massacre of from 500,000 to one million Tutsi in Rwanda in 1994.

These more recent atrocities have led the world community to realize that modern ethnic and racial massacres come out of histories of unresolved conflicts and genocides. The after-effects of historical traumas simmer, even after centuries. Consciously and unconsciously, the original acts continue to haunt the lives of subsequent generations. More recent genocides tell us that if holocausts are not addressed and reconciled, they become the basis of future wars and international conflicts. Realizing that modern conflicts grow out of unresolved past conflicts has led to renewed attention worldwide to the long-ignored African slave trade and slavery in the West. In the introduction of this book, Aimé Charles-Nicolas reviewed the rising worldwide interest in this topic. Also, there have been continuous calls for attention to these histories by anti-racists, Africanists, and descendants of enslaved Africans in the West. For these reasons, The United Nations' Educational, Scientific, and Cultural Organization (UNESCO) recognize that it is critically important to understand the African slave trade and slavery in the West. There is a need to break the silence and educate the world community about it. As the single most prolonged act of dehumanization and destruction of human life in the West for this millennium, the African slave trade and slavery is also the most extensive, unresolved historical trauma today. It, more than any other, has the potential, if left unresolved, to generate crises in Africa, Europe, and the Americas for centuries to come.

De-Colonizing Slave Descendants

The need to act on the recommendations and solutions in the previous chapters is urgent. We cannot wait another hundred years. The descendants of enslaved Africans in the West are the most visible members of a worldwide movement of people of color undergoing decolonization. In the second half of the twentieth century, neo-colonialism (political independence without economic independence) made it very clear that national liberation was not enough to restore the dignity and integrity of formerly colonized and enslaved people. Controlling one's government is insufficient to throw off centuries of Western colonialism and insult. In decolonization, it is necessary to gain control as well over one's economic fate (Inikori, 2002; Tuhiwari Smith, 2012). However, it turns out that decolonization is as much cultural and psychological as it is economical. The necessity to throw off the psychology of colonization and slavery is even more important than throwing off economic colonialism. Where the mind and heart go, the body follows. This means having to address individually and collectively all the psychological barriers and legacies reviewed in this book—self-disdain and self-hatred, colorism, unwillingness to work together and support one another, ignorance and denial of one's history, anger and violence toward others like oneself, oppression of women, violence toward children, and white institutional racism.

One cannot be genuinely independent politically and economically and have a damaged and self-destructive personal and collective psychology (Ayittey, 2006). Notice that once colonized nations with leaders who have colonial mentalities regularly sell out their people for personal aggrandizement. Then, their people, equally damaged by colonialism and slavery, are unable to organize and stand up as a collective to discipline or overthrow their oppressive leaders. They will even replace one strongman dictator with another, both of whom maintained the nation's colonial condition and mentality. Colonialism and slavery produced psychological jails in the present; the inmates have been in jail so long that even when the door is finally unlocked, they do not know how to walk out and live free.

Fortunately, the old jail is crumbling. An unintended consequence of economic and social globalization is the use of the internet and social media to accelerate decolonization. More and more of the formerly colonized and enslaved are walking out of the psychological jails in which their history left them. To paraphrase Frederick W. Hickling (Chapter 11), they have "smashed the social mirror of illusions that oppressed them," that drove them mad, and with which they helped to oppress themselves. The newly liberated are hungry to know their history, to change their condition, and to challenge any former and current oppressors. They will stand up and do whatever it takes now to liberate their bodies, minds, and nations.

The Delusion of White Supremacy

Globalism is having other unintended consequences (Winant, 2004). Racism in the West, the delusion that one is superior to people of color, is maintained best in physical and social isolation. Economic growth now requires European (White) nations to collaborate, compete, and trade with non-Whites. This growth threatens the physical and social isolation racists need to maintain their belief in racism. Foreign people, things, and ideas contradict historical delusions about one's superiority and presumed higher place in society. People of color who are smarter, better off, and more privileged are seemingly everywhere, in public and on television. Besides, the intergenerational reproduction of white racial privilege and advantage over alleged lesser people requires complete white control over the economy and social order. Globalization takes away that control and replaces it with interdependencies. Consequently, Whites who racially monopolized jobs in well-paying industries and were solidly middle-class now find themselves increasingly unemployed and downwardly mobile. The COVID-19 depression has only accelerated this demise. In their mind, Chinese, Mexican, Vietnamese, immigrants, and Brazilian workers, who they believe are inferior to them, have taken their jobs. Ironically, in globalization, White people, rather than Blacks, have not just lost income; they have lost racial status and privilege as well. They are economically and socially downwardly mobile and on the threshold of having to work with Blacks, Latinos, and immigrants in lower-paying jobs. To make matters worse, they are asked to respect racial diversity in public, on the job, and in education. They cannot even escape their demise by watching television, which now shows a multi-ethnic and multi-racial world.

Millions of near and downwardly mobile Whites in the most developed countries in the Western Hemisphere and Europe are at the core of the West's increasing racism (Swain, 2002). They viscerally denial any legacy of the slave trade and slavery. They are angry, fearful, uncompromising, open to violence, and in no mood to be educated or open to the plight of others. There is no shortage of historical evidence that downwardly mobile people turn against their governments, embrace political demagogues and extremists, are open to fascist and nationalist appeals, persecute minorities, riot, and go to war and other extremes. The "patriots'" assault on the U.S. Capitol in 2021 is a prime example. Globally driven white downward mobility adds fuel to the fire because the formerly privileged also feel that they have been betrayed. White political and economic leaders abandoned them and allowed them to sink to the level of Blacks, Latinos, and immigrants.

Abandonment is what propels the enthusiastic and unquestioning support of the Trump Presidency in the U.S. and right-wing movements and political parties in Europe; some now even prefer aligning themselves with Russia (Acs, 2011). These Whites are ripe for demagogues who can say and do anything as long as they promise their base of supporters a return to economic primacy and their rightful racial supremacy. Such a political course of action invariably leads to fascism. Of course, no past demagogue has delivered for long on such promises without senseless wars and profoundly disappointing and injuring their nation and neighbors. The U.S. has already fought three questionable wars based upon delusions of supremacy over non-white people in Vietnam, Iraq, and Afghanistan.

Furthermore, whether one is downwardly mobile or not, a belief in white supremacy and the necessity to actualize it undermine and distort personal and organizational authenticity (Terry, 1981). For Whites in positions of authority, one may believe that everyone is equal before the law, but behind the law out of sight, they will do whatever they have to to maintain their privilege and advantage. The consequence of these two conflicting beliefs is that one must violate the principle of equality as in the case of criminalizing Blacks. That is, one must disproportionately arrest Blacks, convict them whether they committed a crime or not, and to fill prisons with them to show that they are criminal by nature. Likewise, in meritocracies with competitive jobs and university admissions, the most qualified should be hired or admitted (Halleck, 2019). However, to maintain White advantage and privilege, it is necessary to find some covert way to get around the prescribed qualifications. One has to claim to follow the ideal, but then covertly undercut the ideal. Otherwise, it would be impossible for Whites to maintain decade-after-decade near-monopolies of the better paying and more prestigious jobs and placements in colleges and universities. Such behavior distorts one's authenticity because one has to say one thing and do another, consciously and intentionally, knowing that it is unfair (and illegal). However, at the same time, those who use white privilege in this way believe that they are acting reasonably and principally. The bottom line is that the delusion of white supremacy not only undermines democracy and leads to wars; it also undermines personal and organizational authenticity as well.

We Must Act

The progeny of enslaved Africans have to work to free themselves psychologically from the legacies of slavery, as outlined in this book. The previous chapter reviews all of the suggestions and recommendations that chapter authors offered for resolving the psychological legacies of slavery. They focused on the need for descendants of enslaved Africans to liberate themselves mentally. Their suggestions have several points in common: acknowledgment and openness about family histories and experiences, education about the slave trade and slavery, and working collectively to learn one's Afro-descendant history and cultures. Also, there is a need for one-on-one sharing of family experiences with young people, self-reflection, and a review of taken-for-granted learned behaviors that might be dysfunctional. Other ethnic groups need to be encouraged to do the same reflection.

In the past century, there is a history of exhortations and even pleas to Whites of goodwill and influence to address racial injustice against Black people (Baldwin, 1962; Du Bois, 1903; Wright, 1957). All of these calls were ignored. It was thought that in time relief would come. Our call is different. It is time for people of European descendant, who recognize that the delusion of white supremacy can be sustained no longer, to work to change Whites who cling to this delusion. Racism, as was slavery, is fundamentally a white need and problem. The descendants of enslaved Africans do not cause or maintain racism. Nothing Black people can do or become will stop it. Whites need to act not to bring relief to people of color. They need to work in all of our best self-interests and to allow a liberated future to unfold. Furthermore, for Whites to act would mean a decisive rejection of racism. They will have to redefine whiteness without racism. The essential question is: Can people of European descent have a social identity without racism? Of course, they can. If there was no racism before slavery (Drake, 1987), people of European descent do not need racism after slavery. However, for this to happen, the new slavery (racism) would have to end psychologically and finally. Such an effort will be hard work. It is not easy to critique and then edit one's culture, beliefs, attitudes, and values.

Other Reasons to Act

Bernard Dossa (Chapter 5) suggests that much more is at work and at stake than we realize. The implications of his points are worth exploring. Africans captured and transported in chains to the West, believed they were part of an unseen spiritual world where there is a continuity between the present, the past, and the future (Sweet, 2003, p. 107). As living beings, they were connected to those who came before and who will come afterward. They had sacred bonds to this spirit world through ancestral pacts. These pacts are to be honored across time with dire consequences for those who violate them. Violations can happen in two ways. First, Africans and their descendants can forget who they are. They can forget their ancestors and their connection to the spirit world. Second, others by their actions can cause, knowingly or unknowingly, a break in the pacts between African believers and their ancestors and spirits.

Vindication, as Dossa explains, is that enslaved Africans and their descendants kept the faith and survived the slavery holocaust. They may have forgotten the original rituals they brought with them to the West, and their African languages and prayers were transformed over generations into new languages and Christian prayers. However, they did not lose their spiritual fundamentals, which helped them to cope, maintain hope, and survive across time. By the 1865 emancipation of slaves in the U.S., there were four million descendants of 400,000 slaves. The vast majority of survivors could function, were skilled, looked forward to marriage, formed families, had ambitions for their children, were not psychologically dysfunctional, paid taxes, and built schools, homes, communities, and churches. They were not a broken people, despite all that had happened to them. Perhaps, their gods did answer their prayers.

The elders in *The Slave Narratives* repeatedly testified that spiritual faith was essential to the morale and psychological survival of slaves. Black religiosity has indeed been demonstrated to be protective today for Black elders in health maintenance and Black adolescence against drug abuse and other self-destructive behaviors (Halgunseth, Jensen, Sakuma, & McHale, 2017). Alternatively, there were slaves and their descendants who lost their way, who, according to Dossa, forgot and violated their pact. There are no historical accounts of how many slaves poisoned themselves, killed their children and themselves, or who attacked their master and overseers, knowing that they would be killed. Slaves and their descendants had an infinite number of ways to commit suicide, and have others kill them. Undoubtedly, some felt that the gods and ancestors had indeed abandoned them. How could God and the ancestors allow slavery and its brutality to go on for so long? People who felt this way would have little reason for hope; perhaps they had fewer ties to the community and less protection from abuse and harm than those who believed. One can imagine that fewer non-believers survived.

The descendants of slave catchers, masters and overseers are not forgotten in the fate Dossa outlined. They inherited their ancestors' responsibility for violating the spiritual missions, pacts, and obligations to the spirits of all the Africans taken and held in slavery. European immigrants who did not participate in bondage and who were not responsible for slavery became implicated when they embraced whiteness and racism. They unwittingly joined the perpetuation and defense of the continuing injustice of slavery: Jim Crow in the U.S., whitening in Brazil, and institutional racism in both countries. Each generation of Whites that fails to acknowledge and reconcile violations of the spirit has been the object of millions of prayers for their demise over four centuries. According to Dossa, those responsible for slavery and their progeny live in violation of the spirits.

There may seem no immediate consequences to White violators of African pacts. However, in the African cosmology, those who violate the spirit lose their spirituality and end up engaging one way or another, in self-destructive behavior. Dossa suggests that, perhaps, the First and Second World Wars, fought over colonies, were not coincidences. Millions of Europeans were killed and traumatized; Europeans physically laid waste to Europe. It is no coincidence that the great European empires are great no longer. Perhaps, Whites' unwillingness to address racism (akin to making amends to the spirits) may have something to do with the mounting crisis in Western society and politics. Ironically, the key to the future for entire nations is through resolving the legacy of slavery in the present—racism.

Some readers might dismiss Dossa's counsel as nonsense. If it took four hundred years for the African gods and spirits to act, perhaps one needs a change in gods. Alternatively, if Dossa's counsel is nonsense, then so is counsel from Protestantism, Catholicism, Judaism, Islam, and Buddhism. The Roman Catholic Church did not declare enslaving another human being a sin until 1965, seventy-seven years after the last Western government outlawed slavery (Maxwell, 1975). For centuries, the Church blessed slave ships, their crews, and genocidal expeditions to Africa and the New World. So much for the African spirits and the Church's exercise of moral leadership. So much for the African spirits, and Western Churches' moral leadership. We might see Dossa's comments in the broader context in which the slave trade and slavery unfolded and wonder.

Humanism and Pragmatism

Whether or not one believes in a spirit world that we are accountable to, there are also humanistic reasons to acknowledge and work toward reconciling the legacy of slavery. Aimé Charles-Nicolas drove this point home in the introduction. Perspectives disciplined by science can make factual and objective contributions to advance humanity in troubled times. At the same time, we take note of the interrelation between individual mental and social suffering, and between psychology and people's material living conditions. Psychiatric symptoms such as the delusion of white supremacy, self and other disdain, skin bleaching, anger and violence, child beating, trauma, depression, and high anxiety cannot be viewed separately from the political and economic circumstances that produce them.

The bottom line is that oppression of any sort dehumanizes more people than the victim. This is regardless of whether the basis of inequality is race, gender, national origin, sexual orientation, or religion. Oppression eats away at the humanity of those who perpetrate it. Slavery may have ended formally more than a century ago, but its legacy, on so many fronts, is still with us. Not to talk about it, to do nothing about it, to ignore it, and to suppress knowledge of it, is to become, as Charles-Nicolas quotes Cyrulnik and Fanon, "victims of slavery and slaves of slavery." The silence must be broken in all the nations that practiced slavery and have slave descendants, who are, not coincidentally, at the bottom of their national social hierarchy. To quote Elie Wiesel again, "The executioner always kills twice, the second time through silence."

In addition to spiritual and humanistic reasons, there are the pragmatic ones for addressing slavery's legacies. If racism is unaddressed and goes unreconciled, even the most resilient and well-adjusted descendants of enslaved Africans will eat, sleep, laugh, work, and live every day on a tightrope. One way or another, they can fall into a psychological abyss at any time. Institutional and individual racism are waiting to give a push, to take their toll, extract a price, and diminish one in some way, despite one's best efforts. Even if one escapes destruction, one's children and grandchildren may not. They, too, will have to run the gauntlet and pay the price: some will not make it. Ending racism is good for everyone's mental health, the overall quality of life, and that of generations to come. One has a practical reason to address racism as an extension of the legacy of slavery.

Again, the descendants of slave masters and those who defend slavery and racism cannot escape the moral, spiritual, and financial bill their fore parents left for them. The bill is now due for payment. The costliest way to repay is to continue diminishing ones' self by doing nothing. That is to live the lie that one has no responsibility, that slavery never happened, or that it was "not as bad as they say." This is to be a slave of slavery, beaten without a whip, and to live a lifetime in utter fear. Alternatively, the pragmatic thing to do is to get ahead of inevitable insanity. Acknowledge the intergenerational crime, and work to reconcile the damage. In doing so, one could reclaim the humanity one's fore parents took from their descendants by their past actions.

Charles-Nicolas goes on from the French, "We intend to transform denial into a determination to take responsibility for the past and to make of it a point of departure to move forward." We will do this by ending denial and by transforming misfortune into an opportunity to rebound. We will reject denial as a refuge and accept the fact that the psychological legacy of slavery affects all of us in the West—the descendants of slaves, slave masters, and of European immigrants who never owned slaves. Blacks from the Americas were humiliated; Brazilians, West Indians, Guineans, and other inhabitants of the Caribbean, Panamanians, Americans, Colombians, Ecuadorians, and Belizeans have all felt the same anger and shame. After the forgetting and denial, we are discovering what had been done to our ancestors affects our emotions and affectivity. They find that the various transatlantic centers of slavery are all psychologically linked. The sins of the past continue to live with us and to burden the present. Again, these sins must be acknowledged. Whatever psychological damage was done must be acknowledged and resolved. Reconciliation within each culture and in the lives of its citizens is essential to come to terms with slavery's legacies. It is our fervent hope that this volume will contribute to ending the silence, will begin dialogues, and will reconcile the bondage of the past with the present.

NOTE

1. Aimé Césaire.

References

Acs, G. (2011). *Downward Mobility from the Middle Class: Waking Up from the American Dream*. Washington, D.C.: The Pew Charitable Trusts.
Ayittey, G. (2006). *Indigenous African Institutions*. Ardsley, NY: Transnational Publishers.
Baldwin, J. (1962). *The Fire Next Time*. New York: Dial Press.
Carey, B. (2005). *British Abolitionism and the Rhetoric of Sensibility: Writing, Sentiment, and Slavery, 1760–1807*. Basingstoke: Palgrave Macmillan.
Curtain, P. (1969). *The Atlantic Slave Trade: A Census*. Madison: University of Wisconsin Press.
Drake, S.C. (1987). *Black Folk Here and There* (Vol. 1–2). Los Angeles: Center for Afro-Americans Studies, University of California Los Angeles.
Du Bois, W.E.B. (1903). *The Souls of Black Folk*. Chicago: A.C. McClurg and Comp.
Halgunseth, L.C., Jensen, A.C., Sakuma, K.-L., & McHale, S.M. (2017). The Role of Mothers' and Fathers' Religiosity in African American Adolescents' Religious Beliefs and Practices. *Cultur Divers Ethnic Minor Psychol., 22*(3).
Halleck, R. (2019, March 12). Who's Been Charged in the College Admissions Cheating Scandal? Here's the Full List. *New York Times*.
Inikori, J. (2002). *Africans and the Industrial Revolution: A Study in Trade and Economic Development*. Cambridge: Cambridge University Press.
Maxwell, J.F. (1975). *Slavery and the Catholic Church*. London: Barry Rose Publishing.
Swain, C.M. (2002). *The New White Nationalism in America: its Challenge to Integration*. New York: Cambridge University Press.
Sweet, J.H. (2003). *Recreating Africa: Culture, Kinship, and Religion in the African-Portuguese World, 1441–1770*. Chapel Hill: The University of North Carolina Press.
Terry, R. (1981). The Negative Impact on White Values. In B. Bowser & R. Hunt (Eds.), *Impacts of Racism on White Americans* (pp. 119–152). Beverly Hills: Sage Publications.
Tuhiwari Smith, L. (2012). *Decolonization Methodogy*. Chicago: University of Chicago Press.
Winant, H. (2004). *The New Politics of Race: Globalism, Difference, Justice*. Minneapolis: University of Minnesota Press.
Wright, R. (1957). *White Man, Listen!* New York: Harper Books.

About the Contributors

Ana Carolina **André-Cadar**, Psy.D., Ph.D., practices psychology and psychoanalysis in Brazil and France. She holds an appointments as a clinical psychologist and psychoanalyst at the Ville-Evrard Psychiatric Hospital in Paris. Her work focuses on child and adolescent psychopathology, the effects of war on children in war, and the subjectivity of youngsters engaged in violent criminality. Her research also includes sectarianism in modern Syria and clinical issues of the new form of radicalism.

Judite **Blanc**, Ph.D., serves as a mental health therapist in South Florida. She holds an appointment as a professor at the State University of Haiti in Port-au-Prince. Her research focuses on epigenetic studies that explore prenatal exposure and traumatic transmission from mother to offspring. She is a coauthor of "Pensée afro-caribéenne et (psycho)traumatismes de l'esclavage et de la colonization" [Afro-Caribbean thought and (psycho)trauma of slavery and colonization].

Benjamin P. **Bowser**, Ph.D., is an emeritus professor of sociology and social services at California State University East Bay. His research focuses on race relations, research methods and public health, including drug abuse and HIV/AIDS prevention in African American communities. He is a past president of the Association of Black Sociologists. He has 50 peer reviewed research articles, 15 books and is a co-recipient of the U.S. Centers for Disease Control and Prevention James H. Nakano Citation for Outstanding Scientific Paper (Edlin, et al.).

Andréa Máris **Campos Guerra**, Psy.D., Ph.D., is a professor and researcher in psychoanalysis at the Universidade Federal de Minas Gerais, a corresponding member of the Brazilian School of Psychoanalysis and other associations, and is a practicing psychoanalyst. Her research interests focus on psychoanalysis and the law, particularly with regard to adolescence. She has written and coedited 13 books, 47 chapters and 54 scientific journal articles.

Aimé **Charles-Nicolas**, M.D., Ph.D., is a professor emeritus of psychiatry at the Université des Antilles and University Hospital of Martinique. For his work in addiction, psychiatry and HIV and drug abuse prevention, he was honored as Chevalier de la Légion d'Honneur and Chevalier des Palmes Académiques. He is the president of the Medico-Psychological Society (2014) and editor-in-chief of the *Journal of Psychiatry, Annales Médico-Psychologiques*. He has written four books and published extensively in French medical journals.

About the Contributors

Joy A. **DeGruy** is a nationally and internationally renowned researcher, educator, author and presenter, the president of JDP, Inc., and has over 30 years of practical experience in social work. She is the author of *Post Traumatic Slave Syndrome*, which laid the groundwork for understanding how the past has influenced the present and opened the discussion of how we can eliminate non-productive historical attitudes, beliefs and adaptive behaviors.

Bernard **Dossa** is a graduate of the general education college of Dangbo. He is a singer of traditional music, called Massè-Gohoun, and began explaining local customs from an early age. He is trained as a cultural journalist and has reported on religious and cultural events in Benin and Niger. His mission is to safeguard the customs and traditions of Benin and to share them with researchers.

Alexandra **Escobar Puche**, Ph.D., is a clinical psychologist at the Ville-Evrard Psychiatric Hospital in Paris. She is also program coordinator in the department of mental health in Medellin, Columbia. She has served in a number of roles as a mental health practitioner and researcher in Columbia and France, working primarily with families and young people.

Scherto **Gill**, Ph.D., is the executive secretary and a senior fellow at the GHFP Research Institute, a visiting fellow at the University of Sussex, and a fellow of the Royal Society of the Arts. She actively explores ways to implement ideas such as deep dialogue, ethics of caring, holistic well-being, and harmony in social transformation and peace. Her books include *Relational Evaluation in Education*, *Ethical Education* and *Being Peace and Making Peace*.

Frederick W. **Hickling**, M.D., FRCPsych (UK), is a professor emeritus of psychiatry and the executive director of the Caribbean Institute of Mental Health and Substance Abuse, University of the West Indies, Mona. His research focuses on African Caribbean mental health, schizophrenia, personality disorder, community psychiatry, psychotherapy, political psychology and cultural therapy. He is the author and editor of six books and more than 100 articles and book chapters.

Fatimah **Jackson**, Ph.D., is a distinguished scholar teacher and professor emerita at the University of Maryland, College Park, and a professor of biology at Howard University. She has conducted research on human-plant coevolution, particularly the influence of phytochemicals on human metabolic effects and evolutionary processes and population substructure in peoples of African descent. In 2012 she was the first recipient of the Ernest E. Just Prize in Medical and Public Health Research.

Latifa **Jackson** holds a Ph.D. in biomedical science from Drexel University. Her research focuses on the effect of violence and discrimination as chronic environmental stressors in African American young adults and their impacts on immune and epigenomic health. In the past several years, she has developed bioinformatics approaches to understanding disease in African Americans with the goal of understanding the psychosocial impacts of environmental stressors and how they can be quantified to contextualize health outcomes.

Zainab El Radi **Jackson**, MA, received a master's degree in clinical mental health from Johns Hopkins University. She is a cofounder of Jackson Wellness Group, which aims to understand the psychological needs of underserved communities.

Her research has focused on the interplay of epigenetics, trauma, transgenerational resilience, and mental health. Her holistic approach to wellness focuses on improving overall mind, body, and spiritual health.

Edwin J. **Nichols**, Ph.D., is a clinical/industrial psychologist, working in organization development. He has done organizational counseling in several countries, including Venezuela, Japan and China. He retired from the National Institute of Mental Health, where he was the first African American to serve as a Center Chief—Child and Family Mental Health. He taught psychiatry at Meharry Medical College, Nashville, and is a founding member of the Association of Black Psychologists.

Elma **Whittaker-Augustine**, Ph.D., practices clinical psychology in Belize, South America. She was the regional coordinator of the Belize Mental Health Program, a consultant psychologist to Cayman Islands Health Services Authority and to the Chrissie Thompson Memorial Hospital and Behavior Health Associates Cayman. She was a consultant psychologist for the University of Illinois Comprehensive Assessment and Response Training Systems (CARTS Program), and the Illinois Department of Children and Family Services.

Index

abolition of slavery in the United States (1865) 167; *see also* slavery in the United States
ACTe Memorial Slavery Museum (Guadaloupe) 6
adaptive inferiority 40
Adolescent African American Respect Scale (AARS) 128–129; *see also* The Portland Study
adolescent trauma 191–192; biological changes 191–192; epigenetic effects 192; *see also* epigenetics
African Burial Ground Project 124; *see also* Blakey, Michael
African-Caribbean 215, 218; *see also* Jamaica
African descendants 2, 3
Amandala Newspaper (Belize) 38, 42, 43; *see also* Belize
Americas on Educational Attainment study 44
Arab-African slavery 11–12
Atlantic slave trade *see* transatlantic slave trade

Becker, Thomas 212; *see also* psycho-historiography
Belize 34, 36, 37, 42, 44, 257, 258; colonialism in 36; colorism in 34, 35, 37–38, 42; history of slavery in 36; self-concept 40; societal impact of color prejudice 38; *see also* colorism
Bellevue Mental Hospital (Jamaica) 211, 217, 219, 220, 222; history of 217–218; *see also* Jamaica; psycho-historiography
Benin 90, 101; animism 90, 91; Institute of Research and Culture 89; *see also* Dahomeans
biological damage to slaves 193, 194, 199. 203; bone and muscle damage 194; brain injury 192–193; chronic inflammation 199–200; dietary deficiencies 194–195; immune function 199
Black behaviors 141, 142; coping mechanisms 143, 144, 145, 151; harmful 141–142, 144; positive 141; resilience 151; *see also* child-rearing practices
The Black Codes 15, 167

Black history 42, 258; benefits of teaching 258
Black inferiority 155, 168; *see also* racial inferiority complex
black-on-black violence 141, 147, 151, 154, 155, 202, 269
Black Reconstruction 146, 167
Blakey, Michael 124; *see also* African Burial Ground Project
Bosket, Willie James, Jr. 130; "Willie Bosket Law" (New York) 130
Brazil 7, 9, 14, 66–67, 101, 165, 257, 286; Afro-Brazilians 66, 69–70, 71, 72, 73, 75, 76, 77, 80, 93, 165, 260; European immigrants in 68; favelas 69, 72; Fica Vivo! Program 72–73; history of slave trade in 67, 68–69, 165; mortality rates 69–71; *necropolitics* 71; Portugese approach to slavery 165; "quilombos" communities 68, 72; systemic genocide, defined 70
Britain 164, 280; end of slavery 280; racial hierarchy 164; role of colonies 164
British Slavery Abolition Act (1833) 240
Brown v. Board of Education 169
Bureau of Justice Statistics 170; Black incarceration statistics 170; *see also* criminal justice system
Burgesses, State of Virginia 166; *see also* racial classifications

The Caribbean 17, 212, 215, 217, 218, 224, 240
Caribbean Institute of Mental Health and Substance Abuse (CARIMENSA) *see* University of the West Indies
Catholicism 101; comingling of religious practices 102
Cesaire, Aimé 13, 113
chattel slavery 119, 154, 185, 186, 187, 196; childhood trauma 190–191; chronic restraint stress 196; impact on epigenetics 190; definition of 186–187; *see also* epigenetics
child-rearing practices 131–135, 262; curbing eye contact 132, 135; "whipping" children 131, 133, 134, 135, 136, 137; *see also* humiliation; racist socialization

295

Civil Rights Act of U.S. 109, 146, 169, 170, 171, 275
Clark, Kenneth and Mamie 145; doll study 145–146
Cloud, Stanford 243
Coates, Ta-Mehisi 121
Cobbs, Price (author, *Black Rage*) 173
Le Code Noir (France) 162; conduct of slavery in French America 162; *see also* France
colonialism 36, 37, 42, 44, 107, 158, 214, 218, 281–282
color prejudice *see* colorism
colorism 33, 34, 36, 37, 38, 40, 42, 44, 46, 73, 74, 80, 165, 202, 257–258; in Brazil 165; color ranking system 36, 37; damage to self-concept 40, definition of 34; in Haiti 58; impact in Belize 38–39; role of language in 43; *see also* Belize; Brazil; *see also* skin color
Columbia 80–88, 257, 261; Afro-Colombians 81; "lumbalú" funeral rite 81–83, 89, 261; "Palenque" 80, 81; Palenquero 80, 81; role of boxing in 86–87; San Basilio de Palenque 80–81
Coming to the Table (CTTT) reparations group 244; *see also* healing
complex trauma 214; definition of 214; results from 214–215; *see also* Jamaica
Creolization 17, 100
criminal justice system in the United States 169, 170; police racism 170; treatment of Blacks 169–170; *see also* Bureau of Prisoner Statistics
Cross, William E. 148, 150
cultural commonalities of slaves 23–24
cultural racism 171–172
cultural trauma 149, 150, 240, 247; legacies of 240; *see also* intergenerational trauma; transgenerational trauma
Cyrulnick, Boris 8, 10, 102; *A Marvelous Misfortune* 102

Dahomeans 89–94, 257, 261; Adja-Fan peoples 90; ancestor veneration 94–95; clan scars 92, dehumanization of 102, 119, 281; psychological impact of enslavement on 91, 92; spiritual pacts 92, 93, 94, 95; Vodoun cult 90; *see also* Benin; Vodoun
decolonization 281–281
DeGruy, Joy A. 13, 37, 174, 232, 248; *see also* Post Traumatic Slave Syndrome
dehumanization 102, 241, 242, 244, 245, 247, 248, 250, 251, 252, 271; concept of healing 242–243, 245, 246; concept of wounding 241–242, 243; definition of 241; economic exploitation 251–252; effects of 242, 248; four core components of 241–242; public atonements 243–244; reparations for 244–245; resistance to 102; traumas resulting from 242; *see also* healing the wounds of slavery; wounding by slavery
Douglas, Gabby (Olympic gymnast) 122

Dream-A-World Cultural Therapy program 225–226; program practices 225; *see also* Jamaica
Dred Scott v. Sanford (1857) 167
DuBois, W.E.B. 240, 280
Duvalier, Francois (Papa Doc) 48; dictatorship in Haiti 48, 52; *see also* Haiti
Duvalier, Jean-Claude (Baby Doc) 48; president of Haiti for life 48; *see also* Haiti

education system 170–171; indirect discrimination 170–171
ego compensation 41; *see also* racial inferiority complex
Ellison, Ralph (author, *Invisible Man*) 111
Emancipation from Slavery Day (Belize) 44, 259; *see also* Belize
epigenetics 43, 52, 53, 97, 104, 184–186, 195, 200, 203, 257, 268; definition of 185; effects on those enslaved 187–188, 192; *see also* epigenome
epigenome 185, 188, 195, 197, 203, 268; description of 185; impact from traumatic stress 195; *see also* epigenetics
Estimé, Dumarsais 58; president of Haiti (1946) 58; *see also* Haiti
"European Psychosis" 212–213, 214; "civilizing mission" of 219; delusion of European White superiority 212; European drive for total ownership 213–214; as justification for slavery 212–213; role of violence in 214; *see also* Jamaica
The Eusebio De Queirós Act (1850) 67; *see also* Brazil
ever-present anger 125; reasons for 125–126; *see also* Post Traumatic Slave syndrome
exceptionalism of slavery 162; *see also* slavery in the United States

Fanon, Frantz 103, 121, 158, 215, 216, 222; "mental colonization" 121; "the therapeutic institution" 222
favelas 66, 69; *see also* Brazil
Fordham, Maj. John Hammond 168
The Fourteenth Amendment to the U.S. Constitution (1868) 167; *see also* slavery in the United States
France 7, 162–163, 275–276, 280; abolition of 109, 280; assimilationists 162; outcomes of 109; *see also* *Le Code Noir*
The Free Womb Act (1871) 67; *see also* Brazil
freedom from slavery 99–100, 102; resistance to 100, 166–167; strength of character 102
The Fugitive Slave Act (United States) 166

General History of Africa program 3; *see also* UNESCO
Genovese, Eugene 123
Glissart, Edouard 17, 95
The Golden Act (1888) 68; *see also* Brazil

Goveia, Elsa 212; *see also* psycho-historiography
Grier, William (author, *Black Rage*) 173
group shame 123; *see also* Post Traumatic Slave Syndrome

hair characteristics 122, 147–148; "kinky" 122, 147; straight 147; straightening 147; *see also* physical appearance
Haiti 46–63, 101, 163–164, 257; child-rearing practices 55; cosmocentric epistomology 61; demographics 46–47; "driverans" 58–59; Duvalier family 48; history of traumatic events 51–52; "horizontal violence" 57; impact of 2010 earthquake 49; insurrection of Santo Domingo slaves 47; primacy of French language 55–57; role of U.S. in 48–49; transgenerational trauma 51–52; *see also* child-rearing practices; transgenerational trauma
Hall, Douglas (Jamaican historian) 213; *see also* Jamaica
Healing the Wounds of History Program 250
healing the wounds of slavery 241–250, 257, 272, 273; breaking the silence 246, 247; process of 243; pro-reparation groups 244–245; rebuilding trust 251; reparations for 244–245, 274–275, 277–278, 288; results from 242; role of forgiveness 250–251; role of public atonements 244–246
Howell, Leonard 220; *see also* Rastafarian movement
humiliation 10, 20, 102, 109, 112, 113, 249, 262, 275; public shaming 102, 105
Hyde, Evan X. 36–37, 38

indentured servitude 165–166, 187
institutionalized racism 124, 185, 186, 187, 202, 203, 287; definition of 187
intergenerational trauma 81, 105, 126, 147, 148, 150, 151, 247; "protective factors" 126–127, 128; *see also* transgenerational trauma
internalized racism 74, 109, 119, 121, 148, 202; *see also* Brazil; racist socialization
International Classification of Mental and Behavioural Disorders (ICMBD) 12
International Decade of People of African Descent (2015–2024) 3

Jamaica 210, 211, 215, 222, 223, 257, 269; British colonialists 217, 219, 221; brutality toward slaves 213; Cultural Therapy Center 221–222; Dream-A-World Cultural Therapy program 225–226, 270; European desire for economic enrichment 213–214; Jamaican Mental Hospital 212, 218; Lunatic Asylum Law 219–220; mental decolonization 217; open general medical wards (OGMW) 223; psychosis treatment in community mental health system 223–224, 270; rebellions against "European psychosis" 214; role of psychiatry in 219, 221; *see also* complex trauma; "roast breadfruit syndrome"; shakatani personality disorder
Jamestown, Virginia 165
Jim Crow system 8, 15, 109, 125, 135, 143, 144, 145, 146, 152, 168, 169, 172, 173, 174, 203, 212, 236, 286; behavioral expectations 144, 168; psychological effects of 143; similarities to slavery 143

Keita, Dr. Shomarka 186

La Belle, Micheline 58
"Legacy African Americans" 186, 189, 196, 199, 201, 202, 203, 268–269; origin of 186; resilience of 199, 201; role of social and cultural support 201
"lumbalú" funeral rite *see* Columbia

"The Maafa"—The Great Trauma 240
McIntosh, Peggy 124; myth of meritocracy 124–125
mental decolonization 217; *see also* Jamaica
The Middle Passage 6, 51, 53, 89, 188, 239, 280
minstrel show stereotypes 142
Morris, Thomas D. (author, *Southern Slavery and the Law, 1619–1860*) 119, 122
Morrison, Tony 103, 215; *Beloved* 103
"mulatto" 122; *see also* skin color
multi-generational trauma 150, 174, 184, 268; biological effects 188; effects of relocating slaves 188; *see also* epigenetics; intergenerational trauma; transgenerational trauma

do Nasamento, Abdias 70; *see also* Brazil
National Coalition of Blacks for Reparations in America (N'COBRA) 245; *see also* healing the wounds of slavery
The National Museum of African American History and Culture (NMAAHC) 247
N'Diaye, Tidiana 11; Pap N'diaye 18
"New Approaches to Teaching Trafficking, and Slavery" (workshop) 2

Obama, Barack 6–7

Patterson, Orland (Jamaican sociologist) 213; *see also* Jamaica
physical ailments 110, 150; high blood pressure 110, 150; salt retention 110
physical appearance 24, 39, 41, 121, 147, 148, 149, 154; hair 39, 121, 122, 147–148; skin color 39, 121, 122; *see also* Belize; racial inferiority complex; skin color
Plessy v. Ferguson (1896) 168
The Portland Study 128–129; primary components 129; research results 129–130; *see also* The Adolescent African American Respect Scale; Post Traumatic Slave Syndrome

Portuguese slavery *see* Brazil
"Post-Traumatic Slave Syndrome" (PTSS) 13, 117, 118, 137, 138, 147, 195, 200, 202, 248; definition of 117; "protective factors" 126–127, 128; racist socialization 120–121, 122, 123; three outcomes of 118; *see also* DeGruy, Joy A.; intergenerational trauma; transgenerational trauma
post-traumatic stress disorder (PTSD) 13, 14–15, 20, 51, 87, 103, 119, 150 172, 191–192, 195, 248; *see also* Post Traumatic Slave Syndrome
prenatal trauma 189–190; epigenetic effects 189; link to depression 190; treatment of pregnant slaves; *see also* epigenetics; transgenerational trauma
psycho-historiography 211, 214, 218–220, 257, 269; analytic technique 211; definition of 212; in Jamaica 219–220; origin of cultural therapy 211, 220, 269; products of 212; *see also* Jamaica
psycho-social histories 232, 234, 236, 237, 270; biopsychosocial evidence 233; conducting interviews 234–235; face-valid evidence 232; goals of 232; purpose for 232; resources 233–234; who and what to include 232–233
psychological legacies of slavery 2, 20, 81, 103, 110, 113, 173–175, 232, 234, 257, 267, 269; depression resulting from 150, 155, 175; impact on child rearing 111–112; inability to express emotions 110–111; multigenerational trauma 173, 174; *see also* child rearing; transgenerational trauma
psychological trauma 12, 20, 50–51; disorders resulting from 12; effects of 12, 13; peri-traumatic factors 53–54; post-traumatic factors 54; pre-traumatic factors 53; symptoms of 12; *see also* Haiti; intergenerational trauma; transgenerational trauma
psychology of slavery 146–157; outcomes 154, 156; prerequisite conditions 153–154

"quilombos" communities 68; Palmares Quilombo 68; *see also* Brazil

racial classifications 19, 166; "Black people" 19, 166; Blacks as slaves for life 166; "negroes" 19; regulating inequity 166; unequal "races" 166; "White people" 19, 166; *see also* slavery in the United States
racial identity 145–146, 148, 150; stages of 148, 150; *see also* Cross, William E.
racial inferiority complex 40, 119, 145–146, 147, 168, 263; *see also* adaptive inferiority; physical appearance; skin color
racial segregation 145–146; impact on social identity 145–146
racially structured hierarchies 33, 107–108
racism 240, 243, 246, 249, 267, 270, 285; legacy of slave trade 240; "myth of race" 240; psychology of 249; three kinds of 240; *see also* dehumanization
racist socialization 119, 120–121, 123, 128, 130, 131, 132, 136; *see also* child-rearing practices; internalized racism; Post Traumatic Slave Syndrome
Rastafarian movement 220; history of 220; Pinnacle, St. Catherine commune; *see also* Jamaica
Rawick, George 143; *The Slave Narratives* 143, 144; *see also The Slave Narratives*
"Reconciliation Triangle" 244; Benin, West Africa 244; Liverpool, England 244; public apologies for slave trade 244; Richmond, Virginia; *see also* healing the wounds of slavery
religious and spiritual commitment 151–152; *see also* Black behaviors
Reparations Working Group 244; *see also* healing the wounds of slavery
resilience 102, 103, 112, 151–152, 198–199, 200, 202, 265; biological effects of 198, 199; as coping mechanism 112, 200; "deep skin" type 201–202; definition of 198; role of positive support mechanisms 200; role of religion and spiritual beliefs 151–152; social life 152
"roast breadfruit syndrome" 215–216; definition of 215; manifestations of 215–216; *see also* Jamaica
Rothstein, Richard 125

San Basilio de Palenque 80; *Masterpiece of Oral and Intangible Heritage of Humanity* 80; *see also* Columbia
Sauvagnat, Francois 10, 102
"scientific" justification for slavery 5–6
self-esteem 98–99, 102, 109; Black pride 99; definition of 98; destruction of 98; importance for children 98–99
Sexagenarians Act (1885) *see* Brazil
shakatani personality disorder 216–217, 270; description of 216; manifestations of 216; occurrence rates in Jamaica 216; treatment of 216–217; *see also* Jamaica
skin color 34, 35–36, 40, 43, 44, 58, 73, 74, 77, 103, 121, 122, 147–148, 165; damage to self-concept 40, 41, 44; European beliefs about 35–36, 240; influence of language 35; stereotypes about 103; *see also* Belize; colorism
The Slave Narratives 143, 144, 146, 149, 151, 155, 193–194, 286; music and dance 152; social life 152; *see also* Rawick, George
The Slave Route Project 2, 246, 248; *see also* UNESCO
slavery in the United States 113, 155–156, 162, 165–166, 172; abolition of 167; indentured servitude 165–166; "separate but equal" 168; system behind 172; *see also* exceptionalism of slavery

Smithsonian National Museum of African American History and Culture 6–7
substance abuse 196–197; genetic influences on 197; role of trauma and stress in 197; *see also* epigenetics; epigenome

Taubira, Christiane 10
theories of race 5–6
The Thirteenth Amendment to the Constitution (1865) 167, 275; *see also* slavery in the United States
transatlantic slave trade 5, 6, 8, 10, 12, 21–23, 67, 98, 100, 104–107, 164, 165, 212, 240, 241, 242, 245, 251, 267, 279
transgenerational trauma 14, 51, 75–76, 104, 105, 150, 173; history of 118–119; intergenerational transmission of 52–53, 81, 105; role of shame and guilt 105, 106, 112, 113; *see also* Brazil; Columbia; intergenerational trauma
traumatic brain injury 193; changes in brain response 193; neurologic results 193; *see also* epigenetics
truth and reconciliation committees 273; twelve countries sponsoring them 273

UNESCO 2, 3, 80, 246, 267, 281
United Black Association for Development (UBAD) 43
U.N. Convention on Genocide 280
Universal Negro Improvement Association (UNIA) 43
University of the West Indies (UWI) 219, 224; Caribbean Institute of Mental Health and Substance Abuse (CARIMENSA) 224, 225; *see also* Jamaica

vacant esteem 119, 123; manifestations of 120, 123; origins of 119–120; *see also* Post Traumatic Slave Syndrome; self-esteem
Vodoun 90–91, 92, 101, 261; Fà concept 261; religious beliefs 90–91; social practices 91; spiritual pacts 92–94; *see also* Dahomeans
voodoo religion 101
Voting Rights Act (1965) 169

White downward mobility 282–283
White supremacy 34, 106, 155, 166, 168, 210, 212, 214, 263, 272, 282; delusion of 282, 284, 287; relationship to slavery 106; *see also* healing wounds of slavery; wounding by slavery
Wilberforce, William 280; British abolitionists 280
Wilkerson, Isabel 135; *The Warmth of Other Suns* 135–136
W.K. Kellogg Foundation 250; Racial Healing and Transformation program 250; Racial Healing Circles and Truth program 250
Wolfe, George C. 42, 258
Woodson, Carter G. 123
World Conference Against Racism (2001) 8, 11
wounding by slavery 242, 243, 246, 247, 250, 272; in relation to healing 242, 272; *see also* dehumanization; healing the wounds of slavery

www.ingramcontent.com/pod-product-compliance
Lightning Source LLC
Chambersburg PA
CBHW021347300426
44114CB00012B/1111